...ean is one of the few
...ft of our generation."

—ERIC McFADDEN, Parliament-Funkadelic, EMT

$30 MUSIC SCHOOL

Michael W. Dean

$30 Music School

Senior Vice President, Retail Strategic Market Group: Andy Shafran

Publisher: Stacy L. Hiquet

Credits: Senior Marketing Manager, Sarah O'Donnell; Marketing Manager, Heather Hurley; Manager of Editorial Services, Heather Talbot; Senior Acquisitions Editor, Kevin Harreld; Senior Editor, Mark Garvey; Associate Marketing Manager, Kristin Eisenzopf; Retail Market Coordinator, Sarah Dubois; Production and Copy Editor, Sandy Doell; Technical Editor, Michael Woody; Proofreader, Gene Redding; Cover Designer, Mike Tanamachi; Interior Design and Layout, Bill Hartman; Indexer, Katherine Stimson.

Library of Congress Catalog Number: 2003114317

ISBN: 1-59200-171-8

5 4 3 2 1

Muska & Lipman Publishing, a Division of Course Technology ■ 25 Thomson Place ■ Boston, MA 02210 ■ www.courseptr.com ■ publisher@muskalipman.com

To my daughter, Amelia Worth. You rock, Kitten.

Acknowledgments

Thanks to London May, Lydia Lam, Blaine Graboyes, Skip and Beauty's Confusion, Joe Folladori, P. Kimé Lê, Reuben Chandler, Miles Montalbano, Lee Jones in Manchester, John Abella, Mike Stan, Doug Hilsinger, Jay Crawford, Tony Fag, Paul Kirk, Pete Steele, Aaron Nemoyten, Richard Urbano, Tiffany Couser, Tobi in Nuremberg, Michael Woody, JP Kelly, Tracy Hatfield. And as always, I wish to thank and praise Todd McNeill, my genius Web provider.

Thanks to Mike G. Kelley.

Credits for bands featured in photos in this book and on the CD:

The Sick Lipstick: Lindsey Gillard–vocals. Mark McLean–keyboards. Allan Graham–guitar. Dennis Amos–drums (not in any pictures—he asked not to be photographed).

An Albatross: Edward B Gieda—vocals. Jay Hudak—bass. Jeremy Gewertz—drums. Kat Paffett—synth. Phillip Price—organ. Jake Lisowski—guitar.

Babyland: Dan Gatto—vocals, electronics. Smith—percussion, noise.

About the Author

Michael Wareham Dean is a musician, filmmaker, and author who lives in Los Angeles. A singer who plays guitar, bass, and keyboards, he has been in five bands including the influential San Francisco rock group, **Bomb**. Michael has put out 12 records, some on his own label, some on independent labels, and one on Warner Brothers. He does most of his own booking and has toured America six times and Europe twice. He's played alternative rock since before the term "alternative rock" existed.

He also directed and produced the critically acclaimed music and art documentary, *D.I.Y. or DIE: How to Survive as an Independent Artist*. It has distribution and has shown in many film festivals, and Michael personally took it on U.S. and European tours.

Michael wrote the book *$30 Film School* (Muska & Lipman) and the novel *Starving in the Company of Beautiful Women* (Kittyfeet Press). He is currently working on *$30 Writing School*.

He was one of the first adopters of sharing his own music over the Internet and is a relentless promoter of art, both his own and that of others.

Michael's work has been reviewed favorably in *Spin Magazine, Maximum Rock 'n' Roll, The Face, New Music Express, Film Threat Magazine*, and countless fanzines. He's been interviewed on National Public Radio and on the BBC and featured on the front page of the *San Francisco Examiner*. He has been invited to lecture at Cal Arts Valencia, San Francisco's Yerba Buena Museum, Houston's Leisure Learning Unlimited, and the Los Angeles Museum of Contemporary Art.

He has been interviewed on television (NBC and cable) and on dozens of radio shows. His music has received extensive radio play on both college and commercial stations.

Michael says his goal is to "Create sweet-sinister beauty, produce jobs for my very creative friends, and make a plumber's wage at art."

Michael dresses like a 14-year-old skater, and has since he was 14. He doesn't care what you think. He's lived on dirt floors in abandoned buildings and worked in executive support positions in some of the largest corporations in the world.

Wanna interview Michael Dean? Contact him directly at **interview@kittyfeet.com**.

Contents

Chapter 9   Singing and Playing 179

Chapter 10 Finding, Playing, and Putting On Gigs 203

Chapter 11 Hardware Recording. 237

Introduction

I made a documentary film called *D.I.Y. or DIE: How to Survive as an Independent Artist*. In the "Extras" section of the DVD, there is an interview with musician Steve Albini in which he gives advice to young hopefuls, telling them, "If you can learn the same lesson by horribly disfiguring yourself in a fire or watching somebody else be horribly disfigured, if you can understand someone else's mistake and not make it, you're ahead of the game."

I had a good time in my run as a professional musician, but at times I made asinine mistakes that amounted to me sticking various body parts into many different fires.

I've suffered for my art. You don't have to.

I've played over 700 gigs in 43 states and 9 countries. I play music because I love it. Somehow I also made some money at it.

I will teach you how to do all of this.

I'll also teach you what *not* to do. This is possibly more important than what *to* do. While little mistakes are part of the process, big mistakes can *kill* the process.

Making music is a full-time job that most people do on top of their full-time job. So, you really don't have time to screw around *or* screw up.

This is the book I wish I had when I was starting out.

Michael W. Dean
Los Angeles

e-mail: **RockBook@kittyfeet.com**

Book Web site: **www.30DollarMusicSchool.com**

Michael's Web site: **www.kittyfeet.com**

What You'll Find in This Book

Everything you need to know to make and promote your own music, from picking a guitar to stringing a guitar to playing a guitar. From writing a song to making and promoting your own CDs. From making a useful Web site to booking a world-wide tour. And a good bit on keeping focused, staying strong, and maintaining your integrity.

The book also includes inspiring interviews with influential musicians, from Joan Jett to Henry Rollins.

Who This Book Is For

Musicians with beginning-to-intermediate experience level, although seasoned pros will probably find something new they can use.

This is a battle plan for people who have music in their blood and want to share that passion with the world and avoid the pitfalls. People who want to make excellent, kick-ass art. But mainly for people who just want to *rock*.

$30 Music School

Chapter 1

Band Politics

Many people who say, "Music is my life," don't back it up. It's more looks and swagger than talent and showing up. This is a book for people who actually want to *be* musicians, not just *look like* musicians.

Rock and roll ain't rocket science, but it takes a little work. Most books on music promise unattainable goals. This one is different; it offers realistic goals and a map for reaching them, drawn by a man who has actually met and exceeded these goals.

$30 Music School is a true insider's manual. I learned by trial and error so that you won't have to make the same mistakes. (You can make different mistakes!)

This is a quick-start course on how to jump into making music, get it heard worldwide, make a living, and not compromise yourself to the whims of the entertainment industry.

$30 Music School has useful information for anyone trying to get noticed in any kind of popular music: Rock, Indie Rock, Alternative, Metal, Nu-Metal, Punk, Hardcore, Crust, Hip Hop, Electronica, Trip Hop, and DJ. Even Country, Jazz, Swing, and Salsa.

Playing in a band is the number-one career goal of most young people. Yet most are not aware of what it actually takes to "make it." The chance of "making it" on the superstar level most people dream of is next to impossible. You would be better off buying lottery tickets.

However, it is *very* possible to make compelling music and distribute it worldwide on a smaller level. And even make some money.

The author has done all this.

Digital *D.I.Y.* (Do It Yourself) recording, distribution, and promotion is leveling the playing field. The middleman has less and less place in today's music. Peer-to-peer file sharing networks are crumbling the walls that large corporations have created to keep the masses out. As a result, the major labels are going the way of the lumbering dinosaur in the tar pits of the marketplace.

I will show you how to thrive in this new business environment.

Be the Ninja: Be small, fast, and brilliant, and you can survive where the big, bloated dinosaurs fail.

This book is all about cutting through the star-system crap and getting to the heart of art, to make great music that can reach the world on no budget.

$30 Music School is your ticket into the show—to do it yourself, not compromise your vision, and be *heard*.

Meet the Players

A great band is more than the sum of its parts, for sure. But what are the parts?

Also, how does it work? Well, there are several ways to run a band. A band can have a leader, it can be a solo act with side mice[1], or it can be a democracy. We discuss the pros and cons of all. Oh, and by the way, you're only as good as your drummer. Here's why. There's also a bit on why bands break up. (Read that part backwards and maybe it'll keep your band together!)

Most rock bands consist of some variation of guitar, bass, drums, and a singer. Sometimes there's a keyboardist, second guitarist, and/or a DJ. Sometimes other stuff.

Let's meet some of these nice folks.

Singer

Also called lead singer or vocalist.

The voice of the band, literally. A human voice has more inflection in it than a guitar, to the point where a singer is usually the most identifiable member of the band. The singer is the face of the band and sometimes the leader. (Though there are sometimes two different leaders in a band, one onstage and another off.)

The singer often has the largest ego in the band, and the least amount of musical training. And they're usually also kinda moody.

Favorite line: "*I might have been lying when I said I was lying.*"

1. *Mike Watt calls it "Being a Sidemouse" when he's a sideman backing a solo artist or playing bass in another act rather than leading his own band. He does both. I love that in a man.*

Figure 1.1 *Singer Sarah Amstuz actually does* not *have an obnoxious ego. She's the exception to all the singer rules. And she sings* really, really *well!*

Guitar Player

Also called guitarist.

A lot of the sonic power of a rock band comes from the electric guitar. And despite what most people think, guitarists are a lot more interchangeable than vocals in most cases. There are not a lot of guitarists I could spot in a blind test as easily as I could spot singers.

Bands used to have a *rhythm* and a *lead* guitarist, but that's kind of passé. Nowadays, smart bands know that if you have two guitarists, it's usually best to have them both play a little of each. Wanky solos are a little dated anyway. The coolest guitarists, in my humble opinion, add with-it sonic structures in interesting places rather than just "taking a solo" after the third chorus.

There's a punk rock thing I heard once that I liked a lot, and somehow never heard again: "Why have a solo when you can just have another line of lyrics?" Dig it.

Guitar players often give the singer a run for her money in the ego department.

Favorite line: "I coulda played *that*."

or

"What city am I in?"

Bass Player

Also called the bassist, plays the bass (or as it is technically called, "the electric bass guitar"), that funny thing with four (or sometimes five, six, or eight) fat strings that provides the "bottom" of the band's sound. The bass is the room-shaking *pulse.*

There is a theory that bassists are just frustrated guitar players, demoted at some point from guitar because no one else would play bass. But smart musicians will often play the bass to be in demand. I started out on guitar and demoted myself to bass at age 18 because guitarists are a dime a dozen and bassists are about a dime each. It was easier to start a band for me as a singer/bassist than as a singer/guitarist.

Favorite line: "What will I be doing in ten years?"

Drummer

The beat and groove and life of the band. Often the least appreciated player, but the most in demand (at least they were until drum machines came along).

People say, "You're only as good as your drummer," and it's true. The drummer is usually the first person fired and replaced when a band gets signed to a major label. And even if you ain't shooting for that, you will never be great if your drummer isn't. Because you can overdub every other instrument in the studio, but the drums have to be solid and played all the way through correctly in one take. You can't bullshit the drums.

So don't settle with the first drummer you try unless everyone is completely starting from scratch; then you can learn together. The Who did this, and so did a lot of punk bands.

Drums without music are noise, but music without drums just kinda falls out of the speakers onto the floor.

The drummer often has a kinda explosive and aggressive personality, because what they do is so physical.

Drumming attracts the loons.

Favorite line: "I didn't speed up. You did."

Keyboard Player

Also called keyboardist.

Used to be that this member of the band had the most musical training, usually years and years of having their knuckles beaten with a ruler by some piano teacher. But today, now that the keyboard is cool again, and it's easy to use, there are a lot of people taking it up who don't have the advantage (or the burden) of classical training. Which gives them a lot of insight to be creative without getting bogged down in virtuosity.

The keyboardist's role is often divided these days, blurred with computer sound design and production, DJ roles, and/or playing samples and beats off a hard drive or even scratching with vinyl.

Favorite line: "You guys should tune to *me*."

DJ

Stands for disc jockey, but they're rarely called that.

These days, some bands have a DJ in their line up. This can be as basic as "just the guy adding the scratching sounds" to being the driving force who actually composes the whole tune in the studio. In this case, the DJ often creates backing tracks that are played back live from a DAT (digital audio tape) or CD or from a hard drive.

Sometimes his role in concert is much like a conductor in an orchestra: the conductor in an orchestra actually does most of his work in the rehearsal, and much of his role live is just for show, and to honor all the work he did beating the band into shape. Oh, a conductor does do some useful things at the musical performance, like cue the players to come in at certain points, but they are very professional musicians. By the time the piece is performed, they already *know* where to come in. The DJ, like a conductor, is there much of the time for ceremonial and decorative reasons. The real work gets done when the audience ain't around.

Favorite line: "I'm a musician. Really."

Figure 1.2 *Andrei Sterling rocks the wheels of steel.*

Horn Players

Saxophones, trumpets, clarinets, trombones, and whatever else. Some would say they have no place in a rock band[2] Ska[3] bands say otherwise. But basically they are just band nerds (what high school marching band kids call themselves—some spell it "nurd") no matter how you look at it.

One of my favorite people in the world is a horn player (my daughter Amelia is a bitching trumpet player), so I'll be nice. But basically, you can get most of the

2. *With the exception of the band Morphine, in my opinion, the last good band with a woodwind or brass instrument was Jethro Tull. Interestingly, their biggest hit, "Aqualung," was one of their only songs without their trademark flute.*

3. *My editor asked that I explain Ska. You probably know this already, but Ska is a very infectious, upbeat form of danceable rock music from Jamaica. It's what Reggae evolved out of. Musically, the accent is on the off beats, the one and the three, rather than the two and the four like in most rock. The rhythm guitar is the lead instrument, with the strumming all upstrokes as opposed to the up and down of most rock (and the all-down stroke formula in most punk rock).*

   Then there is Celtic Ska, a mixture of traditional Irish folk and Jamaican Ska music that originated in the Brixton neighborhood of London, England. Interestingly, I am actually sitting in a coffee shop in Brixton as I write this—at the tail end of my European film/music/book tour. I can say from personal experience that all Jamaican music is very popular here, and is constantly blasted at high volume out of shops and cars. It's as ubiquitous here as hip hop is in America.

same effect with a keyboard or even a guitar (like The Birthday Party did on "Big Jesus Trash Can").

Horns look classy, though.

Favorite line: "I help write our songs; they just don't credit me."

Backup Singers

Someone who adds vocals behind the main (lead) vocalist to augment the sound. Often the backup singers also play an instrument, though in my band, we have a woman, Sarah, who is a backup singer only.

I went through a few singers before settling on her. I had to weed out the people with attitude and the people who couldn't sing very well. Sarah is sweet and sings exceptionally well. It's hard to find both in the same person.

Backup singer's favorite line: "Someday, I'll be the singer."

All That Other Stuff

Fiddles, Sitars, Washtubs, Triangles, Theremins, all that other stuff people pluck, bow, blow, or bang on to make noise.

They say, "If you're gonna play in Texas, you gotta have a fiddle in the band." Well, I've played in Texas without a fiddle in the band, and wowed the crowd. But to be fair, it was in Emos, a very bizarre and very weird rock club that was partially owned by the Butthole Surfers at the time.

It's all good. Anything can be cool in a band or on a recording, and you are only limited by your imagination. It used to be your imagination and your budget, but as we will see later, anything can be emulated with keyboards, computers, and virtual instruments. Or you can always have someone come in and play (usually for free) on one song on your record without having to commit to having an extra person in the band. It isn't a bad idea to emulate the film industry model of personal commitment in rock bands: You can do intense short-term collaborations with people, for as little as a day, and not have to be married to them. Just treat everyone nice, feed them, credit them, get the terms in writing, and move on.

Roadie

Short for road crew or sometimes road manager.

Not really a member of the band, but keeps the band rolling on the road. Duties can be any or all of: carrying, setting up, breaking down and maintaining equipment, driving, collecting the money, and playing wet nurse to sick and depressed musicians.

Favorite line: "Sure, Babe. I can introduce you to the singer."

Manager

Not really a member of the band, but makes sure he's paid like one. There are two kinds of managers:

- ◆ Friends of the band who just want a title and don't really know what they're doing. Can be a curse, especially if it's a spouse of a band member. But can sometimes work well and occasionally progress (like Sharon Osbourne) into the second type of manager:
- ◆ Actual professional managers who get everything done behind the scenes. They take 15 percent (or even 20 percent!) of the band's *gross* (not net— and they usually manage *several* bands). Therefore, bands usually don't get one until they're packing 'em in to the clubs, at least in their hometown. Because pro agents aren't usually interested in you until then.

Managers coordinate all aspects of an artist's career, from helping get a record deal, to hiring an agent, to occasionally playing wet nurse to sick and depressed musicians.

Favorite line: "What's the bottom line?"

Manager is often confused with:

Booking Agent

The first class of managers mentioned above (the wannabe, the friend who doesn't know what she's doing[4]), often think that their job is to book shows for the

---

4. *And it usually is a she, for some reason. Usually a little less than conventionally attractive, too. The same is often true of bookers who work at clubs. I guess they like being in demand to young cute rock boys.*

band. This is not the manager's job; it's an agent's job. And in California, it's actually illegal for someone to be both (a conflict-of-interest point of law harkening back to the studio system of Hollywood movies). So at some point if you start really happening, you might want a booking agent. This is covered more later. Don't worry about it for the moment.

Favorite line: "Of *course* they'll draw a crowd in your city."

Road Manager

The Manager (with a capital *M*) usually stays home and runs the show, and collects a hefty split. The road manager (small *m*) gets less, but it's a (hopefully) steady salary. She goes on the road and deals with day-to-day logistics, such as collecting the money and making sure the band gets everything on their rider.[5]

In the movie *(This is) Spinal Tap*, the character Ian Faith was actually both the road manager and the Manager. This is sometimes the case, but usually not at the hugest level. My friend was the road manager for one of the top bands in the country, and graduated to being the actual Manager. It's a *lot* of work though. He is often literally talking on two cell phones at once while also e-mailing someone with a little portable e-mail thing. He does this about 20 hours a day, every day. Like that line Ian Faith has in *Spinal Tap*, "There's no sex and drugs for Ian. I sleep two or three hours a night...."

The booking agent, the Manager, and the road manager are often frustrated musicians.

Favorite line: "Of course I can introduce you to the guitarist."

Groupie

People who sleep with musicians, basically to feel closer to the music. There are boy and girl groupies, and I often wonder, without the lure of them, how many people would actually put up with all the shit it takes to even be in a band, let alone get popular or make a living.

---

5. *The rider is the last pages of the contract, where the artist demands all sorts of creature comforts. The complexity and length of this list is directly proportionate to the popularity of the band, though on the way down the arc of a career, sometimes people will forget and still demand things way above their worth in the marketplace.*

One of my groupies, (Grace—she asked to be mentioned by name) who is also a good friend, once suggested a novel angle: that groupies are *apprentices* of the musician, trying to learn what she or he has to offer about life. I like that.

Favorite line: "What do you want me to do?"

So, that's the breakdown of the people in and around the average rock band. We might also add the very important behind-the-scenes people:

Soundman

Or sound *person*, if you wanna be politically correct, but that's never used, even though a lot of the better ones are women. One of my favorites calls herself a sound *girl* even though she's almost 30.

The soundman is in charge of running the *P.A. (public address) system* (the speakers that pump all the music for the whole band out into the audience; you know, those huge stacks on either side of the stage). The soundman has a complex job and can make or break the night. Good sound men are always in demand. Sometimes they're employed by the venue, but often they're brought with the band, especially if the band is making a lot of money.

Figure 1.3 *Sound girl Sandra Sterling rocks mixing board.*

If the soundman works for the venue, he's called the "house soundman." If he works for the touring band, it's just "the soundman" or the "band's soundman" or "our soundman."

Soundmen are often frustrated producers.

Producers

Producers are the people who run a recording session. They often make more money than the band, and good ones are paid millions by record companies to guarantee delivery of a hit recording. The name *producer* is misleading; they are basically what would be the director in film.

Producers do everything from giving the band a pep talk (and, in rare cases, pep pills) to rearranging the songs and harmonies to firing a drummer who can't play to a click track and getting the producer's friend to play drums in the studio. Also in charge of figuring out the band's wishes and tarting them out to the engineer. This is an older definition of producer, stemming from days when bands were not as tech-savvy as they are now. The idea was that the musician was incapable of telling the engineer what she wants. Today's musicians are far more able to do this themselves. But they can sometimes still benefit from being "produced."

An extreme example of successful producing, in the extreme capacity of the word, is the band Garbage:

I've always thought that those cats are geniuses. Garbage is three old guys who are brilliant songwriters and producers in their own right. (Between them, they've produced or remixed Nirvana, Smashing Pumpkins, Nine Inch Nails, Depeche Mode, U2, House of Pain, Killdozer, and a zillion other cool bands.) They really know their shit.

They also know the music industry well enough to know that the record-buying public doesn't want to look at three guys in their 40s. So they got a hot young chick who could really sing to be the singer. They write, produce, and play everything on the records. Live, they lay back in the shadows, dress in all black, get to play their songs to millions, cash fat checks, and let the very capable Shirley Manson fill the center stage spotlight. Talk about knowing your game....

A producer can really be anything. And sometimes it's just a person that the record company has in the studio to "guarantee" that the band stays focused. Sort of an overpaid babysitter. The subjectivity of a producer's decision-making capacity is explained in this joke:

Q. How many producers does it take to change a light bulb?

A. I dunno, what do you think?

Many producers used to be in bands; some of them had hits.

Favorite line: "I almost used to be somebody."

Engineer

Twists the knobs and such in the recording studio. Is usually a producer in training.

Favorite line: "I'm producing a record next month."

Engineer is assisted by the assistant engineer.

Assistant Engineer

The assistant engineer does the busywork to help the engineer: setting up microphones, threading the tape, and sometimes getting coffee. Is often paid not in money, but rather in studio time.

Favorite line: "I'm engineering a record next month."

Lone Wolf Musicians

People don't really need a band any more to make great music. Anyone with a modicum of talent, a lot of patience, and a bitchin' computer basically owns a recording studio now.

Favorite line: "I'm too busy to talk to you."

But at a live show, people want a band. This is based on years of looking at bands. This is changing to an extent, especially with hip hop. But people still want to see guitars and drums, at least for now.

Kraftwerk did a tour many years ago where the four of them stood stark still on a bare stage and controlled all the music with interfaces built into pocket calculators.

I love that. But they were *way* ahead of their time and did influence a lot of industrial music, disco, electronica, and even dance music like Afrika Bambaataa.

Another thing about the lone wolf musician is that often, the person who excels at mastering the intricacies of the nuances of the minutia of a dozen software packages and a dozen processes is not often the most compelling front person. Which basically is leading to a new definition of the word *producer*. Nowadays (especially in hip-hop), the producer is often the person who writes, arranges, plays, and records the *complete* musical backing track. Then the star just adds singing (or yelling) over that and you've got a hit. Or something. (Like Kelly Osbourne.)

This division of labor allows anyone to be a star, because they no longer have to really be a musician to make music. They just have to have style, and even that can be copied from everyone else. Note how most second- and third-tier hip hoppers act exactly the same onstage. Same with most second- and third-tier rock musicians too. Basically, all you need is a lot of gusto, and you gotta look good (or at least interesting).

Hip hop performers often buy completed backing tracks on DAT or CD. The producers will often make the tracks and sell one copy only to the highest bidder. The flip side of this is that the star rapper will often all but rip off the hungry young producer and use his track almost free for exposure.

Anyway, I just wanna hip you to the fact that music is made this way now. Look on any hip hop record. Chances are, there's a different producer listed for some or all of the songs. Often, it's a different producer for every song.

This division of labor also works in dance music, with Divas[6] and people like Right Said Fred ("I'm Too Sexy For My Shirt"), but there's no reason it couldn't work in other kinds of music. And it's not a bad thing to be: the producer, if the cards are properly played, can make a mint, and not get mobbed on the street, and have more freedom, a longer career, (because they can make hits even when they're too old to look cute onstage or in videos) and fewer of the pitfalls of being a star.

---

6. *This is what Mike De Luna and I did on the song on the CD called* Rock Your Body. *Mike was the Producer, and I was the Diva (though I did take his master and cut and paste in a middle eight, complete with backwards vocals and sound effects of an adult film)—check out **www.kittyfeet.com/tanse.htm** for our mockup of this.*

Art by Committee

Playing in a rock band is art by committee. That can yield an incredibly potent result, but also comes with a lot of baggage. I hate making decisions by *Robert's Rules of Order*. And just the logistics of getting four or five people who all have jobs, spouses, and self-will in the same place at the same time can be a Sisyphean task.

This week, as I am writing this chapter, I am also booking a fall European tour to go over and present my movie all across the UK and the continent. And I'm gonna play a little music (solo guitar and vocal) at some of the shows. And it's literally easier for me to book a solo tour in Europe than to book a show or sometimes even a practice here in LA and get everyone to show up. And my band isn't even flaky by band standards. That's just the nature of art by committee.

Why Bands Break Up

Basically, bands break up when they get to the point where it's easier to do that than to stay together. Usually this means that people have unrealistic expectations that are not being met. I have a saying I made up: "Expectations are appointments with resentments."

Fighting Over the Publishing Split

Publishing, which will be dealt with later in detail in Chapter 13, "Business," is an amorphous, Old Testament-based agreement between people who administer music and the Universe. It's a synthetic construct to pull money out of the sky, on behalf of administrators, and occasionally, a little of it ends up in the hands of the musician. It's often where the bulk of a pro's paycheck comes from. It is payment for use of the *song*, not the playing on the song, so the singer who writes the lyrics and the guitarist who writes the chords and melody get a lot more, usually, than the drummer who "just" keeps the beat. It is often a huge source of resentment, when a band sells a couple million copies and the singer is buying a house and his third sports car, while the bass player and drummer are still driving their lemons and rooming with roaches sharing a one-bedroom.

This is what broke up Jane's Addiction, according to the manager who managed them and later my band. It also broke up a lot of other bands.

The Doors split it four ways. So it didn't break them up. (Jim's insanity did, or his death, depending who you talk to, but that's another story.) A lot of more recent bands make a compromise somewhere in between, giving non-writing members a taste of the gold, but not an even split. That makes sense to me.

Artistic Differences

Officially, most bands say they break up over artistic differences. That's sort of a catch-all phrase for everything from, "I don't like that guy and didn't like being in the same room with him" to "He was addicted to different drugs than me," to actual musical differences.

Basically, keep in mind that when you start a band, you are entering into a marriage. Be careful and picky and suss people out. "Date" a while before you get swept up into rock and roll dreams and say, "We're gonna be this band *forever*." Take it one day at a time. That's all you can ever really have of anything, and sometimes it's easier to make something last that way than by selfishly demanding that it last forever.

Conclusion

The bottom line is that we play music because we love music. It moves us harder than almost anything. Try to remember that when the bullshit gets in the way.

If you're all messed up over your band, download Jeff Buckley singing Leonard Cohen's song, "Hallelujah."

I don't care how fucking tough you are. If you've got a soul, it's gonna make you weep.

That's why we play music.

Chapter 2

Songwriting Basics

Strong songwriting is what makes music great. It is what all compelling music, whether it's performed by Johnny Cash or Slayer, has in common. From some doe-eyed waif plaintively singing her poems while strumming an acoustic guitar to grating industrial thrash, if it's got a following, it's probably got a melody, a hook, and a chorus.

Here's what makes a great song, and here's how to write them.

Song Structure

In my book on filmmaking, *$30 Film School*, I talk about the three-act format that is common in most movie screenwriting. The gist of that format is this: Most successful films (commercially successful, or even just successfully reaching an audience in a profound emotional way) have a story that is based on a very structured format. The format is basically three acts: one short, one long and one short. The hero and his problem are introduced in act one. He spends act two trying to solve the problem. He repeatedly fails. At the end of act two or the beginning of act three, he passes a life test that gives him strength and courage. This is *redemption*, which enables him to finally pass the test.

While there are spectacular exceptions, most movies follow a very close variation of this formula.

All Western pop songs, from Bach through Marilyn Manson and beyond, often have remarkably similar structures. It's a three-part structure and actually shares something in common with all storytelling. It seems that, either through conditioning or something innate (probably a little of both), we want to experience linear art in three parts, whether it's a pop song or a movie.

Three-part songwriting structure usually goes something like this:

> Verse
>
> Chorus
>
> Verse
>
> Chorus
>
> Bridge
>
> Chorus
>
> Chorus

This is also called "ABABC" song format (more accurately it would be called ABABCBB). The letters here do not represent the notes; they represent the sections. A stands for the *verse*, (the main body of the song—the part that usually tells the story); B is the *chorus (*also called the *refrain*—the repeated part that usually has the strongest melody); and C is the *bridge* (also sometimes called the *middle eight*—because it's usually eight *measures* and comes in the middle of the song). Sometimes the bridge is also called the *break*, probably because it breaks the monotony once you are used to the verse and chorus. The name of the song is often found in the lyrics of the chorus.

Basically, a well-written song in any genre strives for a good balance between setting up a welcome familiarity through repetition and simultaneously breaking it. This is done (often in the break/bridge/middle eight) by introducing an unfamiliar element.

WHAT IS A MEASURE?

A *measure*, or *bar*, is a short unit of music, the smallest amount of music that can really be perceived as a recognizable song segment. In rock and roll it's usually four *beats*. A beat is the shortest undivided unit of measurement of time in music. Listen to a rock song, and your foot will automatically want to tap along with the rhythm ("along with the *beat*"). When you've tapped your foot four times, that's a measure in 4/4 time, which is most rock music. There are other *time signatures*, like 3/4, or *waltz* time, and 2/4, or *march* time.

The first half of "Smile And Spank" (on the CD) is in waltz time.

Also, "Ice Cream" by Sarah McLachlan is a waltz. "Sky is Falling" by Queens of the Stone Age is in 6/8, which is sort of a double-time waltz.

ABABC(BB) Form

On the CD-ROM, listen to the song "Faded" by the band Beauty's Confusion[1]. It is ABABC(BB) structure (if you take the pre-chorus and the chorus as one. A few pages up we'll talk about what a pre-chorus is.).

It's: A B A B C D C C (where A is the verse, B the pre-chorus, C the chorus, and D the bridge).

On the CD-ROM, listen to my song, "Li'l 25." It is classic ABABC(BB) structure, except for two variations: First, the middle eight—from 3:04 (three minutes and four seconds) to 3:36 in the song—is instrumental rather than having vocals. (Actually it does have some singing, but it is not a melody, and is electronically altered to the point that it might as well be a sound effect.) A middle eight break can have lyrics or not. Either way, it's just a departure from the parts of the song already established.

An *outro* is exactly what it sounds like—the opposite of an *intro*. It's a part after the song proper is over. The (BB) part of the outro is the same chords and melody as the chorus, but the feel is very different. The drum machine has stopped at that point, the tempo is slower, the guitar chords are *arpeggiated* (plucked as individual cascading notes, an arpeggio) rather than strummed, and the overall feel is dreamy rather than driving—a good choice for a song for a dead friend.

Listen on the CD-ROM to the song "I Loved You; Then I Died," which I wrote with my old band, Bomb. This is a slightly less straight example of the ABABC(BB) structure.

First there's an intro—guitar and drum noise suggesting the chord progression of the verse.

Then the verse, the part with "I met you in the graveyard, by the light of the moon...."

Then another verse.

Then the chorus, which is simply the words "I loved you; then I died" twice.

1. Skip from Beauty's Confusion also helped me with a few of the song examples in this chapter and in Chapter 4, "Effects." Generally, if the song being referenced is over 10 years old, I added it. If it is less than 10 years old, Skip suggested it.

Then a *Post-Chorus*. This is the instrumental part after the chorus. It first occurs from 1:39 to 1:50.

The one verse, then a chorus, then the post-chorus, with a variation (rhythmic stops). This segues into the middle eight (actually a middle sixteen)—the instrumental section from 2:51 to 3:06.

The outro is actually the reprised verse (A) section with a different feel. It's the part including the lyrics "I'd kill a million in every city for you" [2] and the heavy instrumental part right before that. Then this part is topped off by a repeat of the post-chorus, and crashes on a harmonically unresolved note at the end, leaving the listener feeling intentionally unsettled.

My faux-disco song, "Rock Your Body," on the CD-ROM (yes, that is me singing, believe it or not—check out the Web site—www.kittyfeet.com/tanse.htm) is classic ABABC(BB) structure. The verse is:

> Rock your body
>
> To the rhythm of the night
>
> Move your body
>
> Rhythmic delight
>
> Rock your body
>
> Music is your master
>
> Everybody
>
> Move it faster

The chorus is basically Jason Hawks going "Oh yeah, uh huh, oooooh girl, shake it," etc. This is a minimal song chord-wise, because the verse and the chorus have the same music. The only difference is that the chorus has a sitar sample. The middle eight is the rhythmic breakdown with backwards singing from 2:08 to 2:23.

None of the instruments on this piece are real; they are all samples generated within a program called Fruity Loops (see Chapter 12, "Software Recording").

---

2. This is also an homage to the Beatles, referencing their song "Michelle" in the words and rhythm of the line "I want you I want you I want you." This is also a good example of Fair Use. It's only enough to refer to the song without infringing on it.

S.P.Q.A.: Songwriting as a Lyric Delivery System

By Michael Woody

How to Write Effective Songs

Cut the crap. Get to the point. Make it and get out of the way. Anything else is conceit, which is fine in small doses as long as "the messenger" isn't pretending to be "the message." We're not selling colas here.

In that spirit, I wrote the song "S.P.Q.A." which translates, roughly, as "(to the) Senate and Public of America."

In keeping with the meaning of the title, which is explained somewhere on the CD-ROM, "S.P.Q.A." was conceived as an ongoing public diatribe over a few simple chords with no significant changes in the hope that anyone who knew how to hold an instrument could master the song in five minutes and then sing or rant their own diatribes over it. You're welcome to give it a go. I'm collecting variations, so send links to your downloadable MP3s to spqa2k@yahoo.com.

The overall phrasing for "S.P.Q.A." was designed to fit a specific lyrical meter, and all variations of my lyrics tend to maintain the original meter, but other lyrics could just as easily inspire different phrasing or even time signatures as long as the music complements the words. The point here is (to beat a dead metaphor) that the music is the engine propelling the song and the lyrics are the direction it's going. Whether it's a bumpy ride or not is up to the performers. Whether it's a worthy destination or not is up to the lyricist. The music is only a vehicle for delivering the lyrics, so it hardly matters if it's not the latest model full of state-of-the-art gadgetry. If it starts strong and keeps going at a steady pace, then you're bound to make it to the end with everyone on board. Only the audience can decide if the journey was worth taking. So do the best you can, with what you've got, with a sense purpose.

End of tortured analogy.

The music has to be varied enough to be interesting alone, typically during an intro, a solo, or a break, and not monotonous under what may be pages of lyrics. "S.P.Q.A." uses seven chords over eight beats, subdivided into two related four-beat patterns; one ascending and one descending, in semitones, from A Major. This gives plenty of room to play with how to drop in the lyrics. Conveniently, all of those chords together use all

12 tones, which means just about any melody can be worked into the song if you hit it with a big enough hammer.

The bar-to-chord foundation sequence is:

1-A, 2-A#, 3-B, 4-C, 5-A, 6-G#, 7-G, 8-F#

with all chords being major. Acceptable sequence variations between verses are limited to:

1-A, 2-A#, 3-B, 4-C, 5-A, 6-G#, 7-G, 8-G#

1-A, 2-A#, 3-B, 4-A#, 5-A, 6-G#, 7-G, 8-F#

1-A, 2-A#, 3-B, 4-A#, 5-A, 6-G#, 7-G, 8-G#

Anything else and the pattern changes beyond tolerance into a different pattern and becomes a different song entirely. That would be a musical vanity here since this song exists as a lyric delivery system. Besides stirring up the chords occasionally to keep the performers interested in playing the music, there is only enough musical variation to keep the listeners' attention focused on the words but not enough to redirect it to the music behind the words. There are good reasons why this distinction is of concern, not the least of which is to purposefully maintain listener interest in the point of the song: the words.

If your song isn't about anything, then feel free to indulge in gimmickry, just like the pros do.

A sure way to kill a song you're writing is to be the only one who can play it. This is not as certain a way as being the only one who hears it. That's an entirely different problem requiring unique solutions for us all.

Repetitive music can be given interest by adding some or all of these suggestions:

> Use variations in instrumental density. Unless you're a Flipper clone, don't play everything at the same volume at the same time all the time. Even Flipper didn't do it all the time. Musical statements come in phrases so make sure they have sufficient time and space for a complete breath. Lyrics have to sink in. In "S.P.Q.A.," the music drops out at the end of verse four for an a capella (without instruments) break (…"No chemical dumps next door to the White House") into the bridge

giving such a breath before it launches into a full band sound that recedes for the fifth verse.

Use variations of instrumental dynamics. The patented Soft/Loud/Soft = Verse/Chorus/Verse system popularized by Kurt Cobain is but one elegant illustration. As long as it serves the lyrics, then anything goes, right? Add periodic rhythmic embellishments and fills. Or, have nothing but embellishments and fills. At least make the decision to use them or not. In "S.P.Q.A.," the snare, the toms, most of the guitars, and the bass all add simple fills over their basic rhythms in various combinations at various times to compensate for the repetitive vocal meter.

If you must go this far, try variations in rhythmic density but not in the basic rhythm itself. More than new chords, a different rhythm signals a significant change in a song. The a capella break in "S.P.Q.A." also demonstrates this idea when the band drops out.

Resist repeating lyrics over repeating beats unless you're making a point. The "to the White House" Bridge and the "There's more important things than peace, you know" Chorus in "S.P.Q.A." are examples of this idea.

Provide potent lyrics in the first place, so it matters less how polished their performance is. If punk proved one thing, it proved that, no matter how raw, the right words over a great hook with sustained energy could change the world.

Include sonic novelties: harmonies, clever rhymes, affected vocal styles, odd mouth sounds, recorded sound effects, and so forth. Use sparingly and pointedly or risk becoming a one-joke novelty act like Spike Jones or Bobby McFerrin.

Create the densest possible sound that works and then, as a temporal sculptor, take away certain parts at certain times to provide dynamic/dramatic ebb and flow.

This is all just snack food for thought—to whet your appetite. I'm not offering suggestions regarding which musical seeds you should sow as much as I'm offering compositional scraps to your compositional compost heap.

—Michael Woody

See the SPQA folder on the CD.

ABABCC Form

On the CD-ROM, listen to my song, "Roach Gurl." This is (intro) ABABCC form. That breaks down as:

> Intro
>
> Verse
>
> Chorus
>
> Verse
>
> Chorus
>
> Bridge as outro

The intro is the rhythmic guitar and drum noise that begins the song. The verse is the "Every single cockroach…" part—the first singing you hear. The chorus is:

> "I don't want what you've got anymore
>
> You looked so good walking out my door
>
> I don't want what you've got anymore
>
> You shed a lot of sadness on my floor."

The bridge-as-outro is the ending part, with only the words, "You bled on my floor," repeated over and over. In ABABCC form, you go to the bridge but never return to the verse or chorus. I also did this on the Bomb song, "All My References Are Dead."

ABCABC Form

On the CD-ROM, listen to my song, "Golden Gate Bridge." This is (intro) ABCABC form. That breaks down as:

> Intro (guitar hook at the beginning)
>
> A part
>
> B part
>
> C part
>
> Intro hook
>
> A part
>
> B part
>
> C part

This is totally symmetrical, and there really isn't a verse or chorus. But it still works.

ABABAB Form

Another form I like a lot is ABABAB. Some would argue with me on this, but I don't really think every song needs a bridge. On the CD-ROM, listen to the song, "Promise," that I recorded with Bomb. This is (hook, intro) ABABAB form. That breaks down as:

Hook—vocal line "You're not my friend!" (Which is basically counting off the song—the rhythm is like the "one, two, three, four!" a lot of people use to start a song.)

Intro, which is "There's nothing in my heart today," sung four times over just drums.

The verse begins: "Well, Tony's in the tombs, with someone else's wife.

I'm just looking in the mirror, trying to get a life."

The chorus is the descending music with "and she cried" sung over it four times.

Then another verse, another chorus, and we're done.

AAAAAAAA Form

There are actually one-part songs that are compelling to listen to. Basically, they work on the premise of "Find a place that makes you feel good, and stay there." One of my favorite bands, Flipper, does this a lot. Check out their one-part masterpieces, "Sacrifice" and "Fucked Up Once Again."

Check out Michael Woody's sidebar, "S.P.Q.A.: Songwriting as a Lyric Delivery System," and the associated folder on the CD-ROM—Songs/SPQA. Here he offers several lyrics for the same song and the option to make your own song. Instant tune: Just add lyrics!

Hook Me

Hip Hop, Trip Hop, Nu-Metal, and Rap Metal often have very rudimentary melodies, but they usually do have them. And they can be great songs without much melody. And the melodies are sometimes even borrowed from the public domain, like in Korn's song, "Shoots and Ladders." This song has virtually no melody, almost no chord changes, and the lyrics are mostly borrowed from nursery rhymes. But it works as a strong song because the sing-song rhythm of these nursery rhymes are strong hooks, and are ingrained in us from a very early age.

TIP

> Some of the hooks in the song "Shoots and Ladders" (and a lot of other pop songs, including a lot of what Perry Farrell sings in Jane's Addiction) are even variations on what sociologists call "The Natural Children's Song." The Natural Children's Song is the "na na na na na na" melody/rhythm that children of all cultures seem to use to taunt each other. People who study this stuff suggest that since, even in isolated cultures with no contact with other cultures, children use this melody to play games and to make fun of each other, that we are born with this *song* in our heart. (This is old information. There really are no cultures with no contact with other cultures left. Everyone in the world drinks Pepsi these days.)

I've mentioned *hooks* several times now. Even in music where there is often not a lot of melody (and in most music with strong melodies), there will be a hook. A hook is an identifiable part of a song that is catchy or memorable. It's a part to "hook" you—like a fish or a junkie. You get hooked on it and can't get away. You want to hear it again. In some songs, the only hook is the chorus. In other songs (and usually stronger songs with killer songwriting), there is a chorus *and* a hook. It doesn't even have to have much or any melody. It can be a sound effect, like the motorcycle revving at the beginning of Motley Crue's "Girls Girls Girls," the bottle breaking at the start of Minor Threat's 53-second opus, "Bottled Violence"; or a vocal hook like the "You gotta keep 'em separated" line in "Come Out and Play" by The Offspring. That's not the chorus…the chorus is the part that begins "Hey, man you talking back to me" and ends "Hey, come out and play." While the chorus *includes* the "You gotta keep 'em separated" part, that part is really an extra thing to wrap your memory around: It's the hook.

An argument could even be made for the conversation at the beginning of (and throughout) Black Flag's "Slip It In."

Mac Davis even wrote the hit song, "Baby, Baby, Don't Get Hooked on Me," in response to his label pressuring him to write a song with a hook.

> **TIP**
>
> In life, like in songwriting, people are attracted to two things: The familiar and the new. Give them a bit of both.

The hook is sometimes the first thing in the song. When it is, it's the thing that makes your ear instantly go "Oh. It's *that* song." Like the cash register loop at the beginning of Pink Floyd's "Money."[3] (Also, this loop sets up the rhythm, which is in 7/8. It's a pretty complicated loop actually. The song also switches to a sort of syncopated 4/4 for the guitar solo.)

But not always. In my song mentioned earlier, "Li'l 25," I would say that the hook is the answering machine sample of that friend, Eddy (Sky) Caranza, at 4:48 in the song. He was terminally ill with AIDS. (A result of living too much of a rock and roll lifestyle. See Chapter 17, "Closing Arguments.") It was him leaving me a message to drive to San Jose and "Come see me before I die." I did. We watched *Batman* on TV, hung out, talked, ate dinner, and had a blast.

Syncopation

Syncopation is the rhythmic device of varying the placement of the beat off the standard of where you feel it would be. It is often used in funk. And often the accent is on the one. The singing in the first four lines of my song "My God Is a Woman" on the CD is sung in a syncopated manner.

You can also syncopate the instruments. This is done in a lot of funk. It is also done in an odd and not really funky (but very disturbingly cool) way on my band Baby Opaque's song "How Now Brown Mao" (How Now Brown Mao is on the CD).

Also check out The Blood Brothers' "Kiss of the Octopus."

The Recipe for Music

Basically, music is made up of Melody, Rhythm, Harmony, Dynamics, Tempo and Mood. We've covered the basics of melody above, as well as rhythm. Harmony is covered in Chapter 9, "Singing and Playing." Here's a bit on the rest:

3. Pink Floyd was one of the first bands to use loops. And they used them in the 60s, when you had to do them by splicing tape. Back then, only huge corporations owned computers, and they cost millions of dollars and weren't nearly powerful enough to edit music on.

Dynamics

The volume of music determines, in a large way, how it is perceived. Rising and falling volume and intensity within a song is called *dynamics*. Having good control of dynamics, individually and as a band, makes the music more interesting and gives you more control over the mood. You can actually practice this as a band, going from really loud to really soft in different parts of a song. A good exercise to get good at this is to play one part of the song very loud and one part very soft, and just roll two the parts back to back, going from very loud to very soft.

The classic grunge formula is to be really loud on the chorus and kind of quiet (but still powerful) on the verse. This is easy and works really well most of the time. It's a good place to start.

Songs that use this formula include Nirvana's "Smells Like Teen Spirit," "Heart Shaped Box," and "All Apologies"; The Pixies' "This Monkey's Gone to Heaven" and "Here Comes Your Man"; and Smashing Pumpkins' "Rat in a Cage."

The Pixies' "Where Is My Mind" actually does the opposite; it's loud on the verses and quiet on the choruses.

One thing I like to do is have the guitar cut out completely or almost completely on the beginning of the verses and build again as the verse goes on (with the drums and bass staying the same volume throughout). I do this on the second and third verses of "The Web" and the second verse of "Supergoose." Also, "Good Morning Captain" by Slint.

A good example overall of the use of a lot of dynamics in a song is Wheezer's "The World Has Turned and Left Me Here."

I like to start out with things quieter at the beginning of a song, and rise and fall in waves, but steadily build overall as the song goes forward. I use this "add as you go" formula also on length of parts. Notice that the instrumental part in "Promise" is twice as long before the second "And she cried" chorus as it is the first time around.

There are a million variations to all songwriting ideas, and you will find your own. You can start with some of these to get a feel for it and make your own formulas.

Tempo

Very slight variations in tempo, as little as two BPM (beats per minute), can strongly affect the overall mood of a song. I used to play with a drummer (Michael

Urbano, who now plays with Smashmouth) who had excellent *clock*—once he started a song, he kept it exactly the same speed through the end. He would often find the optimum tempo using an electronic metronome, write the BPM rate on the set list next to the song title, and use the metronome to listen to a little to start each song live. He would reset it to the correct number quickly between songs, hold it up to his ear, get the beat, set the metronome down, count off four or eight clicks on the hi-hat, and the band would join in. This worked great.

Michael was great also at serving the song. He was capable of playing amazingly complex parts, far more accurately than most drummers, but usually chose not to. He would only play exactly as much as the song required to make the singer sound great. I loved this. Not just because I was the singer—but because the singing is basically the song. He serves the song. He's never boring, but never overplays. I wish more people would consider this when playing music. It makes for much better music.

Timbre and Mood

I find it amusing that fans of different styles argue with each other, or even fight over musical taste, because the underlying song structure is often virtually identical in different styles. Often the only difference is the timbre (pronounced "tamber"). Timbre is the musical *sound* (what is different when an accordion plays a melody and when a distorted electric guitar plays the same melody).

Well, the clothing and hairstyles are also different sometimes. I guess that's why people fight.

Download www.kittyfeet.com/stuff/Cash.mp3.

It's my band, Baby Opaque (in Virginia, in 1984) doing the "traditional"[4] American folk song, "Long Black Veil," with Ian MacKaye singing backup.

Get yourself a copy of the older version by Johnny Cash. (One could use a file-sharing program for this, though I'd never recommend you do anything illegal.

4. *The copyright is generally attributed to Danny Dill and Marijohn Wilkin. Previous versions list it as "traditional American." There are several wild and crazy stories to explain this. One I have heard was that someone originally was supposed to record "an unrecorded traditional American folk song in the wild" for a university musicology class. And rather than going to that effort, they wrote this song but claimed it was traditional. After the song began to generate income, they changed their tune and admitted authorship.*

But you *could* get such a utility from Kazaalite.com.) There are several other country versions out there, including Nick Cave's 1986 version from *Kicking Against the Pricks*. They're absolutely the same song and melody. But the Baby Opaque version is straight-up Ramones-style punk rock. It is totally different from country versions in timbre, volume, tempo (speed), and attitude.

"Long Black Veil" (along with most country songs) is a great example of strong *storytelling* in a song. In fact, the story in this song *absolutely* follows the three-act format favored in most films. "Long Black Veil" has three verses, and even splits the acts absolutely at each verse. The first verse ("Ten years ago…") introduces the hero ("I"), and sets up the problem (someone was killed and the killer looked like me). The second verse ("Now the judge said, son, what is your alibi?") gives a problem to be solved ("If you were somewhere else, then you won't have to die") and the hero fails at trying. ("I spoke not a word, though it meant my life, for I'd been in the arms of my best friend's wife.") This has the hero passing a test, achieving *redemption*. And even though the hero dies, his soul and conscience are now pure, enabling him in death to be with the still-living woman.

Even though she's still, we presume, his best friend's wife. *Redemption* in country music is twisted. I love it. It always made me wonder why Tipper Gore only went after rock music with the PMRC. Probably because her husband, Al Gore, was a Tennessee senator at the time. And Tennessee is the world economic capitol of country music production.

To recap:

> This song's story is actually like a little movie:
>
> The first verse introduces the characters and explains the problem.
>
> The second verse offers tension, and a choice to be made.
>
> The last verse explains the redemption as a result of making the right choice.

> (first verse):
>> Ten years ago, on a cold, dark night
>> Someone was killed beneath the town hall light
>> There were few at the scene
>> But they all agreed
>> That the slayer who ran
>> Looked a lot like me

(pre-chorus and chorus):

> She walks these hills in a Long Black Veil
> She visits my grave when the night winds wail
> Nobody knows, nobody sees, nobody knows but me

(second verse):

> The judge said, "Son, what is your alibi?
> If you were somewhere else,
> Then you won't have to die."
> Well, I said not a word
> Though it meant my life
> For I'd been in the arms
> Of my best friend's wife

(pre-chorus and chorus):

> She walks these hills in a Long Black Veil
> She visits my grave when the night winds wail
> Nobody knows, nobody sees, nobody knows but me

(third verse):

> Oh now, the scaffold was high
> Eternity is near
> She stood in the crowd
> And shed not a tear
> Oh, sometimes at night
> When the cold winds blow
> In a Long Black Veil
> She stands over my bones

(pre-chorus and chorus):

> She walks these hills in a Long Black Veil
> She visits my grave when the night winds wail
> Nobody knows, nobody sees, nobody knows but me

I've done it in even less:

The shortest song I've ever written:

www.kittyfeet.com/ivy.mp3

It tells a complete story in two lines:

Ivy's getting married and I don't care.

Ivy's getting married and I won't be there.

TIP

I've done it in even less. Check out "Ode to a Cat" on the CD. The whole song is only three lines:

"You are a cat. And I am a man.

I'm so much bigger than you.

You'd better not bite me again."

The first line introduces the characters.

The second line explains their relationship and defines the problem.

The third tells a story, or at least implies a scenario of consequence. No cats were harmed in the making of this song, and I assure you that the crappy quality is a result of using a cheap microphone and a poor soundcard and nothing more. So take *that* as a cautionary example and avoid *that* scenario of consequence.

"Long Black Veil," by the way, also uses a songwriting device called a *pre-chorus*, a part that comes up every time before the chorus. It's the line "She walks these hills, in a long black veil…." This leads into the chorus proper, "Nobody knows, nobody sees, nobody knows but me." (Another song that uses one is "Friends of P" by the Rentals.)

My version of "Long Black Veil" begins with a pre-chorus rather than a verse. This can be a useful songwriting device. Some songs start with a chorus. It's all up to you. You'll get better and better at all this with practice. You will intuitively know where things should go the more you write songs and work with music and other musicians.

My version has a *breakdown*, actually a verse functioning as a middle sixteen. ("Now the scaffold is high, and eternity's near….") The chords are the same, but the music is brought down low. This breaks the monotony and makes it all that much more special when you bring the volume and power back up for the final pre-chorus and chorus.

Songs with breakdowns include, "Welcome to Paradise" by Green Day, Rancid's "Junkie Man" (the breakdown is a spoken word thing with Jim Carroll), and "'Til My Head Falls Off" by They Might Be Giants.

Like most of the techniques here, this trick works in any genre of music.

Here's a series of cartoons by Joe explaining how he works:

I think of little melodies and things, usually while falling asleep or bored at school.

1. INSPIRATION

I don't always work like this, but sometimes once I have a melody or something I'll sit down with a guitar or piano and organize things until I have a song.

2. ARRANGING

Lyrics are hard. I have a notebook I write things down in when it strikes me, but I generally come up with disjointed crap that I end up having to cut and paste together at the last minute to make into actual song lyrics. I'm kind of like a broke-ass William Burroughs. I think? Eh.

3. Lyrics

This part is fun. Once I have the song figured out, I get to sit down in my bedroom and play all the instruments into my computer. I have to be quiet about it at night, for my family's sake.

4. RECORDING

This is where I take the computer software I get for free (kind of illegally, I guess... whatever) and assemble all of the different tracks I've recorded into a song that sounds halfway decent. I'm not very good at this part, so most of my songs sound fuzzy and rough. Oh, well.

5. MIXING

Arts and crafts! After I repeat steps 1-5 a few times, I have enough songs for an album. At this point I start the physical production part - burning CDs, printing up covers, making artwork, etc. etc. This part is either a lot of fun or really boring. I forget.

6. MAKING THE CDs

I hate this part. Once I have an album finished, I have to convince people that they want to listen to it, and maybe even give me some money for it. I suck at promoting my stuff, mostly due to laziness. If anyone wants to be my manager and do this for me, I'll make you a pie.

7. Promotion

That's pretty much it, aside from the actual mailing out of the CDs if and when people order something. I hope this intimate, uncensored portrait of an artist at work has captured your imagination enough that you're willing to spend a few bucks on my music, or even just listen to an mp3 or two. Thanks for reading, and don't let the bad men get you down.   -JOE

8. END

Cartoon by Joe Folladori.

TIP

I, V, IV (pronounced "one, five, four," a.k.a. "a one-five-four chord progression) is the basis of a lot of rock 'n' roll (in the general "all rock" sense, and more specifically in the 1950s Elvis/rockabilly/blues/country/folk and all its stepchildren sense).

The roman numerals term I, V, IV refers to the relation of the chords in the key you're working in. If the key is C, then C is the one chord, F is the four (there are four whole tones from C to F) and G is the five chord (there are five whole tones from C to G). So, in the key of C, a one-five-four song will generally have some close variation of going from C to G to F and back to C. There are a million variations, but this is the basis of a lot of rock music. When you say "three-chord rock," you usually mean a one-five-four progression.

Examples include "I Fought the Law" (recorded by a lot of people, including the Clash and Dead Kennedys) and "Blitzkrieg Bop" by the Ramones. In fact, most Ramones songs used this formula.

A great example is on the CD, the Mathletes' song, "Tamalalia," which is actually about a real person, Tamarie Cooper, who does a yearly very popular musical play/dance/story revue thing in Houston called "Tamalalia." My sweetie, Tiffany, is in it most years. This song is I, V, IV in the key of C, so the chords are C, G, and F.

Nineteen-year-old genius Joe Folladori, who wrote the song and played everything on it (Joe *is* the Mathletes), may have exaggerated a little bit in the lyrics. I'm not sure.

You can *transpose* this progression to any key. In the key of G, the I-V-IV chords would be G-D-C.)

Joe's Web site is www.allstarpowerup.com.

Throw this book against the wall right now and go look at his site. I command thee....

The Writing Process

There are different ways to write a song, and different people use different methods. Some people use more than one method for different songs.

You can write the music first, and then write lyrics to the music. You can write the words first, and then write the music. You can write both at the same time. Sometimes (this is rare, and I usually consider it a blessing), they both come at the same time. This can almost feel like it's falling out of the sky into your hands—

like something or someone is writing through you. It's pretty cool. I did this on "I'm So Tired." Other times, I've labored over the music and lyrics for weeks, like I did for the Bomb song, "Spoked Feet." (The title of this song has nothing to do with the lyrics. Tony came up with the name because I was working as a bike messenger and was writing the song on my messenger clipboard in elevators between deliveries.)

You can write with a band all at once. With a band you can write by telling them what to do, or by everyone contributing parts and talking it out, or by just jamming (improvising). This can work well, and often the rhythm of the song will suggest singy-songy vocal patterns to sing over it. Some can evolve into lyrics. Often into silly lyrics that still work because rock lyrics aren't really poetry or literature. Some great rock songs have lyrics that look absurd when printed ("Whole Lotta Love" by Zeppelin comes to mind), and poetry set to music doesn't usually work.

Lyrics are just lyrics. I'd be willing to bet that the Nick Cave line "Zoo music girls" came phonetically out of the rhythm of the song. And Paul McCartney said that the first line for the song "Yesterday" was originally "Scrambled eggs. Ooh baby, I love your legs," which he used as a placeholder to sing and work on the melody and later came up with the words we know.

You and your band can also jam and tape it, and then later you listen to it alone and come up with lyrics and find which parts work.

Regardless, it's always a good idea to have a working tape recorder set up and ready to record. When inspiration strikes, you don't want to be looking for batteries or testing recording levels.

I don't read music. If I did, I would just write down melodies when they come to me. But since I don't, I have to record them before I forget them when they arrive. And believe me, they can arrive at any time.

If I come up with a melody and am not near a tape recorder, I call my home phone number and leave it on my message machine. Some cell phones also have the ability to record 30 seconds of music.

TIP

The dial tone on most phones is A 440 and can be used to tune a guitar if you don't have another reference around.

TIP

I sometimes carry a Dictaphone pocket tape recorder with me. And a pen at all times for lyrical ideas. If I have a melodic idea and no tape recorder nearby, I call my own answering machine and hum it to the recording.

Figure 2.1 *Dictaphone.*

You can also write with one other person, but I have some advice for that. Chuck Prophet told me this one: If you're writing a song with another guitarist, only use one guitar and pass it back and forth. Otherwise, if you each have a guitar in your hands, you just end up playing blues jams and don't get any work done.

I often write a complete song on the bass and bring the bare-bones completed song to the band. I will play the bass and sing all the way through, and they will write their parts around it and make it cool by creating an arrangement to flesh out the skeleton framework I present to the band. In this case, what I play and sing for them the first time is very close to what ends up on the record when we finally record it. I did this on "All My References Are Dead" with Bomb. (Although the vocal melodies tend to flesh out stronger with repeated singing.)

TIP

When a member of your band wants to show you a new song, let her play it and sing it all the way through without jamming along (unless you're the drummer and she asks you to give her a beat under it). Professionals always listen all the way through the first time. This is how you learn a song. You don't learn a song you've never heard before by noodling over it the first time you hear it. And it's actually insulting to the songwriter.

Regardless of how you write, listen to what you're playing. It's kind of a Zen thing. Let the song write you. The song will tell you, if you listen, which part wants to be verse and which wants to be chorus, what the next note or chord should be, and much more.

Writing a song is like having a baby or growing a seed. You can't yell at a flower and make it bloom. It comes in its own time. Sometimes it will just come. Sometimes you'll need to carry a song around for days and keep working on it, laboring over lines. You have to be patient with it, be ready to work, but if the Muse doesn't show, it ain't your fault. She might be busy elsewhere.

Lyrics and Singing

This is the easy part. They say, "If you can talk, you can sing." And it's true. The more you write your ideas down, the more they will make sense. Singing is easy, just practice it. Writing lyrics is just singing your thoughts over well constructed music. Let the melody find itself.

I find that when I first sing new lyrics over new music, the melody is not yet evolved and is only a few notes, usually off a blues scale. With time and repetition, the melody shows me where it want to go. I just have to listen.

Follow your heart, find your voice, don't try to sing like anyone else. Your voice is you. It's your speaking voice crafted around notes. It's natural.

Writing and Performing within Your Limitations

Limp Bizkit's Fred Durst can barely sing, but pulls off compelling performances. If he tried to sing complex melodies in a "singer" singing style, it would sound horrible. But he doesn't. And it works.

In fact, I recently saw a band open for my band, with a singer who could not sing but was attempting to. It was embarrassing. I was embarrassed for her. She was worse than the worst singer ever on *American Idol*. She was cute, and tried really hard, and her band was good, and in fact, the songwriting was pretty strong, but she was horrible.

And she was assless. My good friend, Tiffany, pointed out that this singer was really cute, but didn't have a butt. Neither did anyone in her band. Nor did most of their crowd. So this instantly became our name for bloodless, lifeless rock that sounds like the radio and offers none of the threat that made rock dangerous a long time ago. We call it *Assless Rock and Roll.* Or *No-Ass Rock and Roll.* Los Angeles is full of it, and all these no-ass rockers would probably literally kill to be on the radio.

I think a lot of people who do not have what it takes to make a living at music are convinced by the Music Support Industry that they can make it, if only given a chance. And a lot of them are insanely deluded. They shouldn't give up playing music, because anyone can make valid music. Music is valid if you enjoy playing it. But many of them should quit predicating their life on the belief that they can all "quit their day job." Being realistic about your abilities is important.

A lot of rappers and punk singers can barely sing, but work within their limitations well. This is one reason *producers* are so important in hip-hop. In most music, the producer is the person who is sort of the in-studio liaison between the band and the engineer, who works with both to get the best possible polished diamond out of the rough lump of coal that is the band. The producer basically takes the same role that a director takes in a film. In rock, a producer's role can sometimes involve helping with *arranging* (changing the order of parts in an existing song and/or directing the instrumentation of an existing song). Sometimes the producer also does a small bit of songwriting, but usually a rock group enters the studio with the songs already written. In hip-hop, the producer often writes the entire backing track, and the rapper just writes the lyrics and raps them over the track. Sometimes the rapper takes a more proactive role in the creation of these background *beds*. But often the producer is a *cut creator* who creates an entire song, melody and instrumental backing track. He then sells a single CD of it for exclusive use to the highest bidder. The rapper then just adds his own rhymes and performance over that to make the final song.

This is a reason many hip-hop albums have different producers listed for every song: The creation methodology is different from a band and doesn't entail being locked into the same person for every song. I like that. It's more like making films.

I did this with Mike DeLuna more or less on "Rock Your Body." He created the complete track in Fruity Loops and gave me the mixed-down track on a CD. I created and edited the middle eight in Sound Forge and then added the vocals in Vegas. I sang the lead in a *falsetto* (false high upper register men can use to sing like a woman), and my friend Jason Hawks sang the deep "Oh baby" prompting vocals.

Tiffany heard this and then asked, "Why is it that fake bands are so much fun?"

I answered, "Because you have no emotional investment in them. This often makes you free enough to rise above worrying about being cool and make something *truly* cool. Look at Spinal Tap—although part of what made them so cool is that their songwriting was better than most of the bands they were parodying."

Tiff also adds that making a fake song or band can be a fun way to get over writer's block. I would add, "Just be careful; it might end up more popular than your own band. Gwar started as a joke side project of a band called Death Piggy, and look at them now!"

Reduce your limitations by remaining open. Don't be afraid to ask questions of anyone. That's how smart people learn. People who are afraid to look stupid never learn. "The only stupid question is the one you don't ask."

Work within your limitations, but let your songwriting grow to match your growing abilities. If you keep an open mind, the music itself is the best teacher.

Inspiration

Spacing out is an important part of my personal timeline, and thus my artistic process.

My dad loves to tell the story about Henry Ford giving a tour of his factory to a group of investors. They passed one guy who was in his office staring out the window with his feet up on his desk. After they passed the door, one of the investors asked Ford why he would keep such a lazy man on the payroll. Ford remarked "That man came up with our last three big-money ideas, and he was in the exact same position when he came up with all of them."

Conclusion: Melody Good, Structure Good

Sometimes strong melodies are hidden under a scathing wall of noise, like with Jesus and Mary Chain or some Velvet Underground, but there's still melody. Sometimes the melody is very, very simple, but there's still melody. Sometimes the musical accompaniment is unusual, deconstructed, barely musical, but there's some structure.

Even seemingly unmusical compositions like the Beatles "Revolution Number 9" follow a structure, with repeating motifs and variations on a theme. Even noise bands like The Locust have structure. Our ears want to hear something set up, then a change, then a return to something we've already heard, usually with a variation.

If people like a band and want to tell other people about it and it makes them excited, there's probably melody in each part of each song. And these parts are probably in some form of three-part structure. Anyone who has any inkling of a desire to not only make great music, but especially to make a living at it, had better learn to write strong tunes. If I don't walk away from the first time I see you play with at least one chorus stuck in my head, I guarantee you'll never quit your day job with those songs.

Chapter 3

Guitars, Basses, and Amps

You need gear. What you don't need is to spend way too much time and money collecting high-end equipment and too little time learning to use it. In the next five chapters you will learn how to pick out quality guitars, basses, keyboards, drums, amps, effects, P.A. systems, DJ equipment, music computers, and microphones without going broke. Also, you'll learn how to protect them and how to fix them.

I highly recommend that everyone in the band read this whole chapter. The guitarist can learn a lot about music in general from the drum section and vice versa. Even if you think you're beyond it and know it all, I'm pretty sure you'll find *something* useful here. In my filmmaking book, I advised aspiring directors to do some work as actors to make them better directors. The $30 Way is to learn as much about everything as you can, to make you better at your little corner of expertise in the world of rock and roll.[1]

Figure 3.1 *Manny's Music in Hollywood.*

NOTE

Most of the equipment photos in this chapter were taken at Manny's Music in Hollywood (7360 Sunset Blvd.). Thanks to Judd for hooking us up. They rock and have big-store low prices with small-store good customer care.

They also have a store in New York City.

---

1. Keep in mind that when I say "rock and roll" or "rock 'n' roll," I am using the term generically, as in all rock music, not in the sense of the 1950s use of the term, like Elvis Presley and his contemporaries, although I would certainly include them, along with Black Sabbath, Minor Threat, Marilyn Manson, and everything in between.

Guitar As Girl

A lot of guys name their guitars. They personify their guitar and treat it like it's their woman. I don't. To me a guitar is a tool. nothing more. I don't sleep with my guitar, talk to it, or even usually pick it up unless I have a definite purpose: rehearsing with a band, writing a song, recording a song, or playing for a friend. I just almost never pick it up and "noodle."

I did when I was younger. A lot of how I learned to play was messing around on guitar in my room, but more often than not, when I picked it up, I played a song on it.

I actually learned to play guitar in public, playing when I was 14 and 15 in a park in Chautauqua, New York. It enabled me to easily talk to girls. I actually had groupies way before I could even really play.

This attitude is more process oriented than a lot of people's methodology for learning and playing an instrument. I find that a process-oriented, rather than goal-oriented, outlook works best for me. I play, I play a song, eventually I play the song with other people and make a record; then I go on tour. I don't set out saying "I'll buy an instrument and then try to be a rock star." I think a lot of people do this, but they are fooling themselves. Most bands I see are just putting on the clothing and playing the role.

Ian MacKaye says similar things in my flick *D.I.Y. or Die*. We have a similar mentality on some things. That's one reason I've always dug his deal.

Play to play music; play to create; hell, play to meet girls and guys, but don't put the cart before the horse. Get the basics down first.

Don't worry; that won't take long. It ain't rocket surgery. It's rock and roll.

And I like it.

Getting Your Gear

Guitars and drums and other equipment can be purchased new or used. There is a lot to be said for the value of older (vintage) equipment. Some guitarists feel that there's nothing like a pre-CBS Fender. (The CBS corporation bought the company from Leo Fender in 1965, and many say that the quality went downhill.) Some say that these attitudes are just appreciation of American workmanship from back when it was good. Others say it's simply snobbery. I'm not going to weigh in on that fray; I'll just point out that it exists.

Off-the-shelf new guitars are mass produced and may lack the charm of the older models, but improvements in technology have made them better in other ways. In the same way that new cars get better mileage than the bitchin' older models, newer guitars generally play well, sound good, and stay in tune, and some are quite reasonably priced.

I would just say that when you get an instrument, you should get the best damn stuff that money can buy, new or used. With simple equipment like guitars and basses and drums, a warranty doesn't mean as much as with a keyboard—something with a lot more electronics and parts that can fail. A guitar that is in good condition is likely to stay that way for a while.

> **NOTE**
>
> These guidelines are for acoustic as well as electric guitars, but the references to electrical aspects of the guitar will not apply unless the acoustic has a built-in pickup or microphone of some kind.

Figure 3.2 *Acoustic six-string guitar.*

Figure 3.3 *Acoustic twelve-string guitar.*

If you are a beginner, you should take someone more experienced with you when you buy an instrument. They will know what to look for and be better able to interpret the things I present here. Some of my advice requires an ability to play a bit already and the good ear that one develops from playing.

Just make sure that the guitar has a good sound, stays in tune, and isn't stolen. (Buying stolen equipment is bad Juju and will harm you more than help you.) With a guitar or bass (unless I specify otherwise, when I say *guitar* in this chapter, I am referring to both guitars and bass guitars), I usually tune it up, play a bit, and then apply the *Dean Tune Test* when the salesman isn't looking: Turn the volume down on the guitar and smack the back of the headstock with the heal of my hand very hard. Then I turn the guitar back up. If it's still in tune, then I'm still considering buying it. If not, I try another one.

Check to make sure the neck isn't warped. Eye down the neck from the pickup end, looking down with the headstock end away from you. Make sure that it isn't warped or bowed.

The guitar or bass should have a good tone and sound good through an *amp* (amplifier) at a low volume, a high volume, and with both clean and distorted settings.

TIP

Acoustic guitars are a lot more fragile (as well as sensitive to variations in heat and humidity) than electric guitars. *All* guitars should be treated as well as possible. Keep guitars out of direct sun, keep them dry, and don't let them get too cold. When you take your guitar out of the car on a cold day and bring it inside, opening the case abruptly, especially near a heater or fireplace, can crack the finish, or worse yet, the inside struts in the case of an electric guitar. You should open the case away from heat and fan the case lid for a moment to make the heat change more gradual. Then leave it in the case for about ten minutes to acclimate it to room temperature.

The guitar should have *sustain* when played with or without an amp. That is, the note should not die quickly after plucking it on both open (no finger on the neck) and fretted (finger on the neck) notes.

Check the *intonation*. Intonation is how in tune the guitar plays up and down the neck. Hit a harmonic on each string over the 12th fret. Then finger the note behind the 12th fret. They should be exactly the same.

Play some arpeggiated chords at both ends of the neck. They should sound in tune no matter where you play them up and down the neck.

Look for cracks in the finish. Small cracks in the finish of an electric guitar usually only make a cosmetic difference. On an acoustic guitar, cracks in the finish can make a difference in the sound, so consider buying a different one if they are present.

The electrical system of the guitar should be intact. There should be very little buzz in the sound of the amp. Electric guitars are grounded. There is a wire inside going from the pickup to the bridge, which actually deadens the annoying 60-cycle hum of the amp by dissipating it through the capacity of the player's body. Note that the hum will get a little louder when you take your fingers off the strings. But it should not get a *lot* louder.

Equipment should be UL listed. It should have the yellow Underwriters Laboratory sticker on the equipment or box somewhere.

You can use the headphone output that comes on some amps to practice without driving your neighbors or parents nuts. (Though I seem to recall that driving my parents nuts was part of the *reason* I took up the guitar.) You can also buy small amps that come with headphones, and clip onto your belt. These are good for learning or for warming up backstage. I always liked to take walks in the woods at night and play with my headphone amp, strolling about and playing to myself. Something about it felt very intimate…like I was playing to the Universe, and she was listening.

The jack where the cable plugs from the guitar out into the amp should be solid. Hold on to the jack sticking out to the guitar and wiggle it a little. There should be no crackling sound.

Some guitars have built-in pre-amps to improve the tone before sending it to the amplifier. These are called active guitars or guitars with active pickups or guitars with active electronics. (*Pickups* are the things under the strings that convert the impulse of the string to the tiny electrical signal

Figure 3.4 *Replacement jack.*

that can be boosted by the amplifier.) If the guitar you are considering has active electronics, check that too. Make sure that if your amp has inputs marked *Active* and *Passive*, you go into the Active one only if you are using a guitar with active electronics, or you may blow the amp.

TIP

Avoid guitars that try to go beyond simple active electronics and have actual electronic effects built into the guitar. Those things belong on a rack or on the floor. Putting them in the guitar itself is just asking for electronic or mechanical failure.

Whether the guitar has passive or active electronics, when you try it before you buy it, fiddle with the knobs on the guitar and try it on all its different settings and make sure it all works well. Try the top pickups, bottom pickups, and all the settings in between (the tone is different for each).

Active electronics usually entail having a battery in the back of the guitar. Make sure that the battery terminals are not corroded. Keep in mind that the battery should be removed if you ever plan to store one of these guitars, or any electronic equipment with a battery, unused for more than a month.

If you are trying out a guitar with passive electronics and the thing passes all these tests and is a bargain but has electrical crackles or a grounding buzz, you might consider buying it anyway, especially if it is at a greatly reduced price. And especially if you are handy with a soldering iron or have a friend who is. The electrical system on an electric guitar or bass is so simple that repairs are pretty much a no brainer. More on soldering later in this chapter.

Acoustic Pickups

If you're going to be playing acoustic guitar at all live, you *must* get one with a built-in pickup. It is extremely hard to mike an acoustic live, even solo, let alone with a band, and have it sound good. And even if you do, you'll be a slave to the microphone and be unable to move around. There are plenty of acoustics with built-in pickups or ones you can get at a store to adapt to an existing acoustic.

Whammy Bars

Whammy bars, or tremolo bars, are those things that some electric guitars have that bend all of the strings at once. They can be used very gently, as they are in some country and western music to add a little shimmer to picked chords, or violently like Jimi Hendrix and Eddie Van Halen did, to turn the guitar into an otherworldly growl. It's your call on how to use them, or whether to use them at all. Keep in mind that using a whammy bar makes it harder to keep a guitar in tune.

Locking Nuts

Some guitars have systems to lock the strings after tuning. You use a Hex Key (a.k.a an Allen wrench) to tighten them down after you stretch the strings and then tune them. They keep the guitar in tune (once the strings have been stretched and played for a day or so), but they also make it harder to replace a broken string quickly.

Hex Keys are also used to adjust the rod inside the neck, but this is only recommended for experts. While you can, in some cases, straighten a bent or warped guitar neck, you can really screw up a guitar this way.

Left-Handed Guitars

They exist. They have the nut and bridge and pickups reversed to allow the strings to be strung the opposite way. A few musicians, like Jimi Hendrix, just flip a right-handed guitar over (and just take a drill and a screwdriver and move the strap button) and play it left-handed.

Jimi Hendrix was from Mars, so if this doesn't work for you, don't worry.

My friend Mike Kelley adds:

"My two bits: …Jimi Hendrix would have a left-handed guitar strung for a right-hand play because he liked the control knobs up high rather than down low on the body. This could affect your playing style and sound because you would most likely go for a pickup change after a downstroke, possibly setting up a predictable rhythm. By having the controls up high you could flip or twiddle before the downstroke or come back after an upstroke to pick up switch or volume. Jimi actually played a lot of left-handed guitars, but they were strung normally.

"Also, Jay Stein, my left-handed playing friend, learned how to play right-handed guitars (with the strings upside down) simply because there are way more of them around."

Where to Look

New guitars can be purchased in any music store or online. Several big cities have a Guitar Center[2] store (nicknamed Guitar Safeway by some players because they are a huge overwhelming ordeal, much like a grocery store). You can also order from them online at www.guitarcenter.com, but I think a guitar is something you want to be able to try out in person. An exception might actually be some mass produced guitars. Jimi Hendrix is said to have liked the mass-produced CBS Fender Stratocasters because he could buy one anywhere and know exactly what he was getting.

2. *In big guitar stores, there are always a dozen egotistical and not very good young guitarists wanking away loudly at any given time, usually playing the current hit. Or "Stairway to Heaven." One review of my band Bomb (we actually had two very good and very innovative guitarists in the band) said "The guitars on this album are, at best, reminiscent of Tyranny and Mutation-era Blue Oyster Cult, and, at worst, Saturday morning at Guitar Center."*

My drummer swears by Nadine's Music here in Los Angeles. That's the big one a lot of "stars" go to. I've never been inside it myself.

You might want to go with a smaller neighborhood store (like Silver Lake Guitar Shop in Los Angeles, which is run by buddy Mike) for several reasons. One, you're supporting the little guy rather than a huge (possibly heartless) corporation, which is always a good thing in my book. All my books. Second, you will probably get better service over time. And finally, while you may end up paying a little more, you probably won't have a high-pressure salesman breathing down your neck.

A large store like Guitar Center will offer stuff at a bit of a discount because they buy in bulk, but the salespeople tend to hover over you and totally fluff your ego to make the sale. They will be like, "Dude, that guitar rocks. You're gonna get so many chicks with that!" Or, "Dude, that's the same guitar that _____ (whoever's on the cover of *Spin Magazine* this week) uses." Basically, they want you to buy big because they make minimum wage unless they make a lot of sales. And they don't make much. If you buy a guitar, they probably get enough extra to buy a burrito.

One advantage, though, is that they often can bargain with you and go below the sticker price. How far below depends on the store and the manager and how long the sales dude has been working there. If you are good at bargaining with people (a good skill to have if you're ever going to sell any kind of art, by the way), you can haggle with them. You can also dicker with the small store employee, but they will probably have less leeway than someone who works in a big Megalo-Mart type joint.

One way is to lowball them and literally show them the money. Before you talk to them, figure out how much you want to pay, and when they aren't looking, put only that amount in one pocket. When you go to talk turkey, pull out that wad and say, "This is all I have in the world, and I want to buy a guitar today." If they try to get you to make payments and want you to pay some now and some later, tell 'em you're leaving town today. Moving. Or going on tour. Whatever. It's okay to lie to these people, because they, while at work, are not humans. They are aggressive sales-bots that are basically just the pimply face on an unfeeling monolithic corporation. Tell 'em whatever you want.

A couple of other bargaining techniques are to get them to eat the tax, or to throw in extras, like a guitar stand, strap, strings, picks, a cable, or whatever. Get what you can.

eBay

eBay is a good resource also for used equipment. However, guitars and basses are usually, as I said, things that you probably want to try out in person. For this reason, you might want to limit your eBay search to auctions in your region; you can send the person an e-mail, and he might actually let you come over and try it out.

For less personal items, like microphones and effects boxes, and even for guitars, eBay can have some great deals.

I usually make it a point to deal only with people with a lot of positive feedback, which minimizes the risk of getting ripped off. (Feedback is the feature on eBay where people give references to people they've dealt with. Someone who does a lot of selling and buying on eBay will sometimes have feedback entries from hundreds of people. Usually, if they are honest, it will be like 300 positive feedbacks and one or two negative ones. This is normal. There are people who are unhappy with their own lives who will slam people even when they're honest. You can also check the people who gave the negative feedback and see if they have a history of this.

Another tip is to search misspellings. Some people might list a Telecaster guitar as a "Telicaster" or "Tele Caster," and then it won't show up in searches, and you might be the only person bidding on it. You can get total steals this way.

Another place to buy stuff is from your local classified ads or a local swap paper. Los Angeles has the *Recycler* (also online at Recycler.com), which has some cool deals.

The *Recycler* has free ads for private parties. As does Craigslist.com, one of my favorite resources.

You can buy from friends also. Anyway, like I said, get the best you can. Most musicians will own many instruments in their lives, and you aren't stuck with what you have. You can always sell it or trade up for something else, or have a few different guitars. Many guitarists have a few different ones that specialize for different tasks, live or in the studio. It's harder to switch guitars a lot during a set, so live you'll want one or two that cover all the bases.

TIP

If you can, you always want to have a spare guitar on stage on a stand, tuned and ready to go, so you don't have to kill time to change a broken string on stage. And it's good to have a friend who knows how to change and tune a string to restring the first one to use as a backup in case you break a string on the backup. In the studio, it's fine to have a number of axes (*ax* is a cheesy, outmoded word for your instrument). One might sound better for clean sounds, one might be better for crunchy loud parts, one better for slide guitar, and so forth.

What to Buy

The most common rock guitars are the Gibson Les Paul and the Fender Stratocaster. There are many, many other guitars out there, but you can't go wrong with one of these.

My favorite bass guitar is the Fender Precision bass. You can't go wrong with those either. Though the Fender Jazz bass is pretty sweet too. Currently I use an Epiphone. It's white. I don't know the model. It was cheap ($250 used), sounds good, and plays and stays in tune.

Figure 3.5 *Gibson Les Paul.*

Figure 3.6 *Fender Stratocaster.*

Figure 3.7 *Fender Telecaster.*

Figure 3.8 *My Epiphone bass.*

Figure 3.9 *My Epiphone bass close up.*

Figure 3.10 *Another close-up of my Epiphone bass.*

Figure 3.11 *Three bass guitars (Fender Jazz bass, a 5-string bass, and a Fender Precession bass).*

Shy away from the marketing hype, ask other, more experienced musicians their opinions, but basically just trust your instincts. The guitar you like will find you.

I remember in early 1984 when my band, The Day I Lost My Virginity, was playing a basement party to about six people in Arlington, Virginia. One of them was Ian MacKaye. He had just quit Minor Threat and was learning guitar to start a new band. After our set, he asked if he could play my Gibson SG for a minute. He picked it up, strummed a chord on it and said, "I'm looking for a guitar; I like this one. What kind is it?"

I told him.

He still uses a Gibson SG today.

Pawn Shops

You can use the "figure out how much you want to pay, and when they aren't looking, put only that amount in one pocket" technique in pawn shops even better than in big chain guitar stores. The rule is that you can get anything in a pawn shop for between 1/3 and 2/3 of the price on the ticket. Just lay that amount on the counter, say "This is all I have," and if they say no, pick your money up and walk out. They will follow you out and make a deal.

Guitar Cases

Get a good hard shell case for your guitar. It will protect it against bumps. Those soft cloth shoulder cases are lighter, but they give only the illusion of safety. They offer no protection.

Figure 3.12 *Hard shell acoustic guitar case closed.*

Figure 3.13 *Hard shell acoustic guitar case open.*

Figure 3.14 *Soft shell electric guitar case.*

Security

Once you have your instrument, make sure you don't lose it. Write down the make and the model and serial numbers and keep them in a safe place. (On guitars, the number is usually on the back of the headstock or inside the truss rod neck adjustment space, under the plastic cover. You may have to remove the screws to find it.)

Take at least two good photos of each instrument and piece of equipment, one of the whole thing, and one closer up, especially of any identifying unique flaws or alterations.

See if your homeowner or renters insurance covers instruments, and if so, add them to your policy. If not, consider purchasing separate insurance for your instrument. Keep the receipts somewhere safe. Not in the case with the guitar! A safe deposit box in a bank is your best bet.

Regardless, don't hand it over to thieves by being careless. Never leave an instrument in plain view in your car. Any junkie worth his fix will bust any window for any guitar. Put the guitar in the trunk (but not on a hot day; the heat can warp the neck) or better yet, bring it with you. If you're walking in a seedy neighborhood, bring a friend. And always walk with it between you and your friend, not on the outside, where it's easier to snatch and run.

Also, and especially if the latches on your case do not close securely, make sure that you walk with the latches facing in so if it opens, it falls against your leg, not on the ground.

When playing gigs, always have one person stay at each point while moving the gear; i.e. one person stays with the car, one on the other end. A guitar or any equipment in public is an open invitation to theft. After sound check, it's a good idea for one person to stay with the band gear while the rest of you go to dinner. This can be a band member, a roadie, or someone you trust who just wants to hang out with a band. Rotate band members so no one person gets stuck with this every time. And make sure you bring food back for them!

I sometimes go one step further: I intentionally make my possessions look like they're worth less than they are. My car is painted flat black with primer only. Same for my mountain bike. I've taken knives and spray paint to guitars.

If something already looks stolen, it's actually less likely to get stolen.

This is a big step and will reduce the resale value, but will make them less likely to get nicked. And will make you less likely to pawn them in times of difficulty, as you won't get as much for them.

Figure 3.15 *My ghetto-fabulous mountain bike.*

Tuners

Guitar tuners are inexpensive and easy to use. You just plug your guitar or bass into the input, turn it on, and turn the tuning heads (a.k.a. tuning pegs, a.k.a. tuning keys, a.k.a, machine heads) until the note is correct. The strings on a guitar are, in order from the fattest string to the skinniest, E, A, D, G, B, E. On a bass, they are E, A, D, G, an octave lower than a guitar. (See the tutorial on the CD-ROM for more on tuning.)

Figure 3.16 *Digital guitar tuner.*

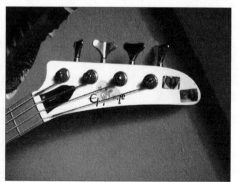

Figure 3.17 *Digital floor-model guitar tuner.*

Figure 3.18 *Tuning pegs on the head stock of my bass.*

Keep in mind that some basses now have five strings. There is an extra low string tuned a fourth (four whole tones; eight semitones) lower than the low E. It's low B. A lot of "nu-metal" bands use them: Korn, Limp Bizkit, Sev, and others. I don't love that stuff. It's like my friend says, "Skateboarding ruined music," but what do I know? I'm old. All I know is they all have four guys with shaved heads and one guy with Dreadlocks, a DJ, and usually two singers.

I've heard that "the goatee is the mullet of the millennium."

Strings

Guitars and basses need to have their strings changed regularly. At least once a month for guitars, and at least every two months for basses. Touring bands with money and guitar techs (roadies who only look after the guitars) usually get their strings changed every day.

Guitar strings cost about 5 to 10 bucks a set. Bass strings are thicker and break less but cost 20 to 40 bucks a set. I remember the bass player in New Order once said in an interview, "To me, success is being able to buy two packs of bass strings at once."

Figure 3.19 *Bass strings.*

Strings sound bright and powerful for only a few days, and the sound fades in brightness with playing, due to stretching and finger oils.

Most people at least try to get the money up to change their strings before going into the recording studio. One trick is that you can take the strings off your bass (or guitar, if you're *that* poor. I have been before) and boil them in a gallon of water (with an optional ounce of vinegar), dry them, and put them back on. They will sound new for exactly one day and then die and sound flatter than ever.

You can also take broken strings and tie them in a knot and use them again—the knot has to be above the nut.

Don't throw used guitar strings on the floor. I have heard of them accidentally getting caught in plugs in the wall, starting fires, and burning down a studio.

Strings are available in different *gauges*, or thicknesses. The thicker they are, the better and heavier the tone, but also the harder they are to play. I go for a medium-gauge guitar string, an .011 set (sets are gauged by the diameter in fractions of an inch of the small E string). A .009 set is light, a .013 set is heavy. Sometimes just listed as 9 and 13 or 09 and 13.

Figure 3.20 *Individual guitar strings out of pack. Note gauge listed on each paper pouch.*

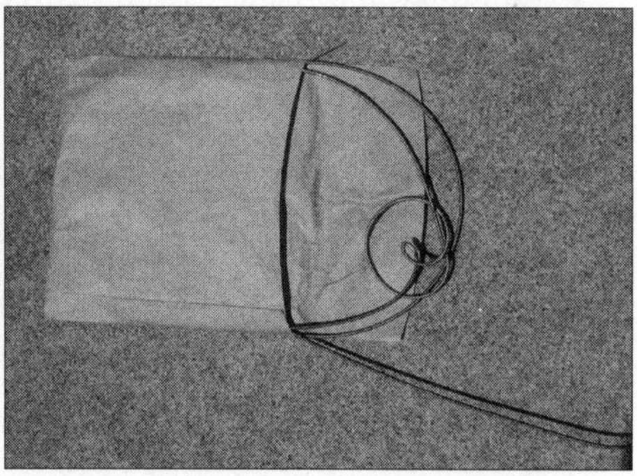

Figure 3.21 *Single guitar string in the pack.*

Changing Guitar Strings

Basically, you should change one at a time. Don't take them all off and then put all the new ones back on. This is bad for the truss rod inside the neck and can even harm a guitar, especially an acoustic guitar.

Take off one string and find the corresponding string in the pack of new strings. There is usually some kind of legend on the pack to tell you which is which. String the new one through the hole in the bridge. It's a little different on each model. On most acoustic guitars, you'll be gently pulling pegs out. On most electrics, you'll be pulling them through a metal bridge. If the guitar has a whammy bar, you'll probably be pulling them through the back of the body of the instrument.

If you're especially poor, save the old strings as spares. They'll sound dead compared to the new ones, but if you break a string, especially during a gig, you'll appreciate it—a dead string is better than no string. And at least dead strings won't need to be stretched to stay in tune. Wind the old string up and put it in the correct envelope that the corresponding new string came in so you'll know which string is which. Then when you're done, put the packs in the plastic pack that housed the entire new sting collection.

Pull the new string through the bridge, across the nut, and to the tuning head. Wrap it a few times around the tuning head before putting it through the hole. Then put it through the hole *above* the wrapped strings; this will keep the string from slipping out.

Next, pull the end of the string with one hand and turn the tuning peg with the other. Get it near to where it should be by touching the string being tuned on the fifth fret and turning it until it matches the next one or by using a tuner. Go down to the fourth fret for the G and B strings, and back to the fifth fret for the B and E. (See the *tuning* segment on the CD-ROM). Then pull a bit on the string at various places on the neck to stretch it a bit and tune it again.

Figure 3.22 *String winder is helpful with restringing a guitar quickly.*

Repeat five more times (three more for bass).

TIP

On guitar, I often buy an extra high E and B string when I buy a new set and keep them in my case. Those are the strings that break most often on most guitars, though on some guitars and with some playing styles, sometimes the G will break most. You'll figure it out with time and be able to prepare accordingly.

Amps

Amplifiers (amps) are the things that power your sound to drive your speakers. The term *amp* (not be confused with amperage, an electrical measurement, which you needn't really concern yourself with here) is often generic for not only the amplifier, but the amplifier and the speaker together. Often, they are in the same housing. This is called a combo amp. Combo amps are fine for small gigs, but for larger, louder, more professional situations, most people use a separate amp (called the head) and speaker. This is called a stack or sometimes a piggy back amp, because the amplifier sits atop the speaker cabinet.

Most speakers have wheels, sometimes removable. Wheels are important because amps are heavy, and you'll be carrying them a lot. If you don't have wheels, you can use a skateboard as a dolly. This seems like a no-brainer, but must not be, because I can't count the times I've seen some skate punk band put down their skateboards and huff and puff lifting and carrying their amps into a venue.

Guitar Amps

The most commonly used rock guitar amp is the Marshall Half-Stack, also just called a Marshall. It sounds great for loud, dirty, distorted playing, and is pretty much the guitar sound on most rock records. There are a million other guitar amps, but you can't go wrong with this one.

Examples: Fugazi's Ian MacKaye, Burning Airlines' Jay Robbins. Zebrahead and Jets To Brazil use them too.

A Marshall, however, does not have a good clean guitar sound. Some guitarists even have two amps on stage with a foot switch to go from one to the other. Dave Navarro uses one to go from a Marshall for crunch to a Roland Jazz Chorus amp for his clean sound. It's a cool contrast. The Roland is also used by Violet Indiana on "Busted," and LoveSpirals on "Our Nights."

Figure 3.23 *Marshall Half-Stack.*

Figure 3.24 *Roland Jazz Chorus.*

You can get an A-B foot switch cheap at any music store. Just tell them what you're going to do with it and go for the simplest one they have. It doesn't have to do much and needn't have active electronics. It is just binary—A B A B. It should be a passive box for a passive job. The switching box goes from the guitar (or effects) into a Y pattern into the two amps.

Some combo amps have two pre-amps built into the unit and come with a switch to go from one to the other. The switch jack plugs into the back, usually into a female jack marked Switch.

You can also get cool small amps, like the portable Pignose shown in Figure 3.25. This is the favored amp of street performers.

Figure 3.25 *Pignose Amp sitting on a bar stool.*

Don't ever plug a speaker output from an amplifier into another amplifier input. It will blow one or both amps. If you want to use one input with two or more amps, daisy chain them by plugging the guitar into one amp, and use the other input on the amp (many amps have two) to plug into the input of the next amp. The two inputs on most guitar amps are passively wired together without any circuitry between them to boost the signal.

You could also use a Y-cord to split the signal to send to two amplifiers.

Some effects (notably a stereo chorus) have one input and two outputs. They actually synthesize a stereo sound and are best sent to two amps on opposite sides of the stage. This will create a really cool swirling sound.

Bass Amps

The most used rock bass guitar amp is the Ampeg SVT. It sounds great for loud, solid, heavy, crunchy bass and is pretty much the guitar sound on most rock records. There are a million other bass amps, but you can't go wrong with this one.

They do weigh a ton, though (about 150 pounds actually, about 75 each for head and cabinet). I used an SVT on over 500 gigs in 6 countries and 35 states with Bomb, and my joke was that the SVT stood for Severe Vertebral Trauma.

Only get one if you have a roadie. And keep in mind, you'll probably spend at least 200 bucks a year replacing tubes, and at least that much re-coning the speakers that blow often. An SVT cabinet usually is an 8-10, which means eight ten-inch speakers, which allegedly is the equivalent of one 80-inch speaker. It sure sounds like it. There's nothing sounds like an old SVT in good condition. They ROCK.

With guitar and bass amps, the old ones are often cooler than the new ones. They are sought after as "vintage." But like a cool old car, they will often need more maintenance.

Figure 3.26 *My Carvin combo bass amp.*

My bass amp is a Carvin Cyclops RL6815 model (combo with a Carvin amp head R600). It's small and loud. Not as loud as an SVT, but way more portable.

The Carvin Cyclops is a transistor amp with a tube pre-amp built in. This is kind of the best of both worlds—the stability and relative lightness of a solid state (mostly transistor as opposed to all tubes) amp with the crunch of a tube amp, and with only one, not many, tubes to replace and burn out.

Figure 3.27 *Front of bass amp.*

Figure 3.28 *Close-up of front of bass amp.*

Figure 3.29 *Another close-up of front of bass amp.*

Figure 3.30 *Yet another close-up of front of bass amp.*

Figure 3.31 *One more close-up of front of bass amp.*

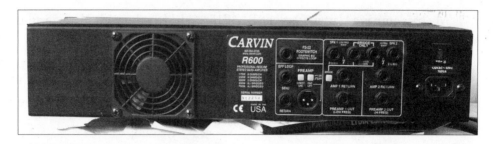

Figure 3.32 *Back of bass amp head.*

Figure 3.33 *Back of bass amp head detail.*

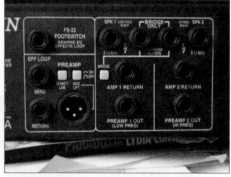

Figure 3.34 *Another close-up of back of bass amp head.*

Figure 3.35 *One more close-up of back of bass amp head.*

Another small bass amp I like is the SWR Bassic Black combo. My guitarist Mike Stan says, "The killer setup is to add a 2-10 (two ten-inch speakers) cab, which adds 40 watts and makes the amp sound amazing."

Make sure you read the owner's manual on any new equipment to know the ins and outs of its intricacies. Not everything is as intuitive as you'd think.

And don't throw the manual away. My dad always said, "If at first you don't succeed, take the directions out of the trash."

Sometimes if you don't have the manual, you can find it as a download or for sale in paper form on the Internet. Just search Google for the brand name, the model number, and the word "manual."

Power

Because the human ear is less sensitive to bass frequencies, your bass amp has to have more power than your guitar amp. A 300-watt bass amp is a good match to play with a guitarist using a 100-watt guitar amp. Both of these are loud as hell, by the way, and might be too much volume for a small club. You can always turn them down though.

Most amps have two volume controls: a regular volume and a master volume. The regular volume, usually on the left, controls the amount of distortion, and the master volume (usually on the right) doesn't add much distortion, only volume. Fiddle with the balance between the two and learn by experimentation what different settings sound like at the same volume. A good musician not only knows her guitar, but her amp too. She can get any sound she likes any time without a bunch of trying, because it's familiar territory. She's been there before.

If you can find one (they don't seem to make them anymore), the Tom Scholz Power Soak is a pretty cool tool. Invented by the guitarist from Boston, these are basically passive switchable arrays of power resisters that go between the amp head and the speaker. You can turn the amp up to 11 and then dial down the volume while keeping the awesome tone. Check pawn shops. Tom also made the Rockman, a portable battery-powered practice amp that clips on your belt. It can also be used to go directly into the board for recording without an amp, though you won't be able to get feedback, and the tone is distinctly 80s precious metal.

Speaker Impedance

Speakers all have an impedance rating, which is measured in ohms (sometimes shown by the Greek omega symbol: Ω). You don't need to know much about this except that the impedance of the amp and the impedance of the speaker should match. Some swear you can use a higher impedance speaker (like 8 ohms) with a lower impedance amp (like 4 ohms), but never the other way around, which might blow the speaker. Others swear anything but the same impedance is problematic and can damage both amp and speaker. Better safe than sorry.

Some amps have different jacks for different ohmage output or a switch to change it. If you buy a combo amp, they should already be matched.

Figure 3.36 *Speaker output on mixer. Note ohm minimum notice.*

Speakers also have a wattage rating (called watts or w). You can use a higher wattage speaker with a lower wattage amp, but never the other way around, which will blow the speaker.

Amp Cases

Get cases for your amps. Anvil makes the best cases. They are also referred to as Anvil road cases. They are solid wood covered with plastic, with metal corner reinforcements and foam inside to keep your amp safe. They have funny little latches which take some getting use to, but are very secure. These cases can protect an amp from being damaged when it falls off an eight-foot stage, which is probably going to happen eventually. Some amps can be used while in the case, with just the front and back panel removed. This will protect them during use, not just during transport.

Anvil road cases are great, especially if you ever ship your gear on a plane. Make sure you stencil your band name on the amps and cases too. This makes them easier to keep track of at the gig *and* the airport. Though I don't think Bomb would have gotten through today's security shipping our gear.

Guitar amps are actually quite fragile because they often contain tubes. There are entirely solid-state amps (transistor only), but they don't sound as good. You need older technology, tubes, to make a loud guitar sound good.

Figure 3.37 *Anvil case.*

Figure 3.38 *Anvil case again.*

> **TIP**
>
> When you ship your guitar on a plane in the cargo hatch, loosen the strings a bit. The changes in pressure at high altitudes can damage your guitar, especially an acoustic.
>
> Some guitarists actually buy a ticket for their guitar and strap it in to the seat next to them.

Cables

You need cables to connect amps, microphones, instruments, mixers, and speakers.

There are several different types of cable, and they are not interchangeable. They should be used for their own purpose specifically.

Guitar cables are made of insulated coaxial cable. This is basically a braided outer cable inside the rubber covering. The braided part has another rubber insulating layer inside, and in the middle is the other wire. The braiding protects the signal from radio interference and hum.

Some are curly and some are straight. I find that the curly ones actually get tangled more, though they do look cooler.

Both ends of a guitar cable terminated by ¼-inch male *plugs,* which go into ¼-inch female *jacks* on the guitar (or bass) and amp. (If I have to explain why they are called male and female, you probably aren't old enough to lift a guitar and might want to wait a few months before trying all this.)

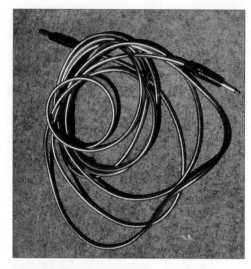

Figure 3.39 *Guitar cable.*

Guitar cables come in lengths like 6 feet, 10 feet, 15 feet, and 20 feet. Cost: $10 to $50. You probably want at least a 10-foot cable. Keep in mind that longer cables have a little more signal loss and more hum.

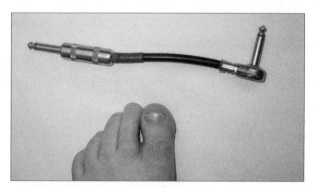

Figure 3.40 *Six-inch effects cable.*

There are also short cables for connecting one floor or rack mount effects peddle to the next one. They are usually six inches long. Cost: $5 to $10.

Speaker cables look much like guitar cables (1/4-inch male jack on each end) but are not shielded. Sometimes they are flat with both wires next to each other. Using a guitar cable as a speaker cable can damage the speaker or P.A. amp. Using a speaker cable as a guitar cable will add a lot of unwanted 60-cycle hum to your sound. Cost: $10 to $50.

Figure 3.41 *Speaker cable.*

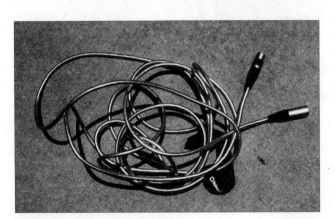

Microphone cables are a little thicker than guitar cables and have XLR plugs on one or both ends. Most P.A. systems have an input for XLR and for ¼-inch jacks on each channel. Cost $15 to $40.

Figure 3.42 *Microphone cable.*

Figure 3.43 *Male end of XLR microphone cable.*

Figure 3.44 *Female end of XLR microphone cable.*

If you try your microphone and it should be working but isn't or sounds bad or quiet, you may need an impedance-matching line transformer. It plugs between the end of the microphone cable and the female input.

XLR cables all have a little quick release push button switch on the side that you have to push before disengaging them.

Figure 3.46 *Quick release push button switch on side of XLR plug.*

Figure 3.45 *Line transformer.*

Cables all look quite alike and tend to get left behind at gigs or picked up by accident (hopefully) by another band. I print stickers with my name, band name, and phone number (or name and e-mail address) and stick them on my cables and basically on every piece of equipment I own. That won't stop a thief, but it will keep someone from accidentally taking it and make it easier to return if they do, or if you leave it.

Cables eventually stop working. They fray internally and the connection becomes intermittent. This also happens to the inside of the jack on the guitar, and to a lesser degree, on the amp. If you're rich, you can just replace the gear or pay someone to fix it. If you're not rich, you (or a roadie) can open them up and solder them yourself. See the "How to Solder" section in Chapter 5, "Microphones, P.A. Systems, and Troubleshooting."

Guitar Stands

Guitar stands are a lot better and safer for your instrument than just leaning them up against an amp. They are cheap and fold up easily. But make sure you put stickers with your name on them on all three parts because they tend to get lost a lot.

If there's a nightclub where you know people, you can usually get them (and other stuff) free. They usually have a closet full of cheap music parts, tuners, microphones, and so forth that bands drunk on booze and power forgot to pack up at the end of the night, especially when they were trying to get some ugly girl or boy to come home with them. Ask the soundman at the club.

Figure 3.47 *Guitar stand.*

Figure 3.48 *Acoustic guitar on guitar stand.*

Guitar Straps

You need a strap if you're going to play a guitar or bass standing up. They are all pretty similar, and you can go as basic or as complex as you like. I avoid ones made of chain; no matter how cool they look, they will start to hurt your shoulder, especially with a heavy guitar like a Les Paul. I use a basic cloth model, wide and made of a similar material to a car's seatbelt.

They attach at the top and bottom of the body of the guitar by putting the holes in them over the little strap buttons on the guitar.

There are also locking systems, but I don't use them.

Most guitarists string their cable through the bottom of the strap to keep the cable from accidentally getting pulled out of the guitar during a gig.

Conclusion

So now your band has a guitar and a bass and some quality amps. That's the basic bare bottom minimum to get started. Maybe now you'd like some effects to sweeten up (or ugly up) the sound? Read on....

Chapter 4

Effects

Effects boxes, or effects, are those groovy little things on the floor that the guitarist (and sometimes keyboardist, bassist, or even singer) is always stomping on. They are basically single-purpose or multipurpose circuits to alter the sound, housed in a (hopefully) rugged case.

Effects usually get plugged between the guitar (or keyboard, or bass, or singer) and the amp, connected by very short (three- or six-inch) guitar cables (also called "jumpers" or "1/4 jumpers").

TIP

All guitar cables, unlike speaker cables, are shielded to prevent radio interference. Shielded means that they have extra braided wires inside the rubber covering to keep jet plane transmissions and such out of your amp. Speaker cables do not need to be shielded, because they are at the end of the chain. The guitar cables are at the beginning, and everything that goes through them is amplified by the amplifier.

Usually only wah wah and volume pedals have actual *pedals*, resembling automotive accelerators, that rock back and forth to change the tone in some way. Otherwise, the "pedal" or effect box is a simple On/Off foot switch for the effect.

Some guitarists eschew them entirely, equating them with being false and impure, the musical equivalent of wearing a couple of condoms at once. Others overuse them, hiding a lack of talent behind them. Still others use them tastefully, or at least purposefully and with thought, to spice up an already compelling style. And still others, like Doug Hilsinger and Jay Crawford from my old band, Bomb, use an array of a dozen or so in a mind-bogglingly transcendent and totally controlled manner that is one of the most amazing things anyone can do to the inside of the human ear without licking it.

Sometimes effects are used to create a wall of sound that just sort of takes over. Melt Banana often uses almost all these effects at the same time. Check out "Lost Parts Stinging Me So Cold."

The list of available effects is long. Here is a list of commonly used ones, in approximate order from most common and least indispensable to least common and most dispensable:

◆ Distortion

◆ Fuzz Box

◆ Delay

◆ Wah Wah

◆ Compressor

◆ Reverb

◆ Chorus

◆ Volume Pedal

◆ Flanger

◆ Phase Shifter

◆ Pitch Shifter

◆ Vibrato

◆ Noise Gate

◆ Envelope Filter

◆ Octave Divider

◆ Guitar Synth

◆ Talk Box

Almost all pedals and boxes have a switch to turn them on and off. *Off* is bypassed; the signal still gets through but is unaffected. *On* is the effect being added to the signal. Some have a light to indicate this status; some don't. Try to get the ones that do. It will help you on stage. You won't have to guess or quietly play a note to know what's coming when you hit a chord. And also, all those little blinking lights sort of feel like little friends on stage with you.

Effects boxes usually cost between $100 and $400 new, and between $30 and $200 used. Check eBay and pawn shops, and remember, the old ones are often cooler than the new ones.

Figure 4.1 *Big Muff distortion pedal.*

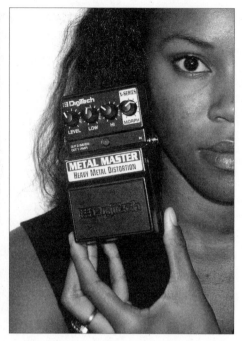

Figure 4.2 *Metal Master distortion pedal.*

Distortion

Distortion imitates the warm, hard, growling sound of an amp cranked up full, even at low amp volumes. Adds sustain. Pushes the amp towards feedback. When played at full volume, a guitar with a distortion box plugged before the amp sounds even more powerful. The word *distortion* sounds like it would be a bad thing, but in this capacity, it's a good thing.

A distortion box usually has two or three knobs: volume, distortion, and sometimes some kind of tone knob.

TIP

My editor, Sandy, didn't get this. She added: "Michael: I'm kind of lost now. You were talking about effects boxes and distortion pedals, but how can a pedal have a knob? I thought we were talking about distortion as an effect that you could create using an effects box, but now it sounds as if it's an actual physical thing that has knobs. Can you clear that up for me?"

My very smart tech editor (and good friend) Michael Woody, added: "The pedal on an effects box, other than wah wah and volume, is strictly the On/Off switch. The knobs attenuate the various effects associated with the pedal and are adjusted by hand. I've seen Jay and Doug (Bomb) do this during live shows mid-song, and it can be both compelling and befuddling to behold. The pedal on old wah wah and all volume pedals is the only attenuator, and the On/Off switch is typically at one end of the pedal arch."

Distortion and fuzz boxes (and, to a lesser degree, most effects boxes) add a bit of volume to the signal, so it is useful to have the volume knob on an effect, to roll this back if you want to. Otherwise, every time you hit the switch on an effect, it will make you WAY louder than the rest of the band. This is not good. Except maybe you would want to leave one of your distortion or fuzz boxes (many guitarists use more than one) set a little louder than the unaffected sound, to give you an edge to make a solo stand out.

Or you could just leave them all louder than everything else. Set at 11.

All rules demand to be broken.

Good examples of a distortion box at work: Linkin Park: "One Step Closer." Pennywise: "Unknown Road."

A distortion pedal is sometimes also called a fuzz box, though technically this is a particular kind of distortion. A true fuzz box has a little bit more of a tight, less overdriven, more 60s sound.

Michael Woody also added, " It might be worth mentioning here that the fuzz box is responsible for certain renowned 60s bass tones (Jack Bruce from Cream, for example), not just guitar sounds."

Fuzzbox examples: Portishead: Portishead, "Elysium." Hooverphonic: "Jacky Cane."

Figure 4.3 *Digital delay.*

Figure 4.4 *Another digital delay.*

Delay

Delay is also referred to as an echo. It adds an actual physical repeat to the sound. The amount of repeat is measured in milliseconds (a.k.a. ms—thousandths of a second). You can make the delay anything from about 100 milliseconds (100 ms—also called a *slapback echo*—imitating the tape echoes that they used on the vocals of old rock-a-billy records. Or East Bay Ray's lead guitar in Dead Kennedys) to about eight seconds. At anything above a second, you probably wouldn't play it in rhythm in a song, unless you played sparsely and the band played to you, because all the notes would get covered up. (Keep in mind this rule is *made* to be broken.) You can also play single-note parts and play to yourself, in a sort of round setting (*round* as in how some songs, like "Row, Row, Row Your Boat," are made to be harmonized simply by having second and third singers come in late with the same melody). Brian May did this really well in Queen on "Brighton Rock."

Advice from an Expert

I asked East Bay Ray about this and he said:

"I used a Maestro Echoplex for *all* the Dead Kennedys albums, and I still use them in the studio to record. It has a tape cartridge with a recording head that moves to adjust the delay time. The unit you describe is another way of doing it; the Watkins Copy Cat and the Roland Space Echo are examples. I've only been using digital live for the past few years. I mostly use a delay of somewhere under 300 ms with feedback, Holiday, Moon, etc., and did the rock-a-billy slapback, maybe 100 ms, on only a few songs. Moon is also an example of harmonizing with the previous notes played."

A good standard setting for a delay is something in between, like 20 to 400 milliseconds, depending on the speed of the song and the desired effect. At this rate, you can play leads and single note parts over the music, especially slower playing, with a beautiful otherworldly thickness. Think David Gilmore in Pink Floyd. And check out the Bomb song "Hate Fed Love" on the CD. Most of the single note guitar on that one has some delay. Also check out Tristeza's "Respira," and "Everything's Not Lost" by Coldplay. And "Explosions in the Sky" by Godspeed You Black Emperor, and "House of Jealous Lovers" by The Rapture.

There are analog delays and digital delays. Both have their pluses and minuses. They just have slightly different sounds. Try them both. Some guitarists feel that they have enough differences if they have one of each.

Delays usually have three or four knobs: Delay speed, Mix (ratio of Dry—unaffected signal to Wet—affected signal), feedback (or regeneration)—the number of distinct echoes for each note played. Also determines how closely the delay comes to going "over the top" in a wash of noise. This can be used as an effect in and of itself. It's cool to hit a note or chord and let it spill over into noise. Then you can reach down and manipulate the knobs manually while this is happening, to change the pitch in a bizarre "space ship" way. Flipper did this on "Ha Ha Ha" on the vocals.[1] Bomb did it a lot with the guitar. Then hit the Off button and go

---

1. *I mention a lot of songs that I couldn't get the rights to put on the CD. You could just download them with Kazaa (kazaalite.com). But I can't really recommend that because it might not be legal to do so, and as I have told you often, I would never recommend that you do anything illegal.*

back to playing normally. This can work great over a tight bass and drum groove, and it gets better the more you work at it.

The guys in Bomb were great at this.

Delays also sometimes have some kind of tone or volume knob.

Some delays also have a built-in chorus and built-in pitch shifter setting.

There are also actual tape delays—a larger box that has a loop of spinning magnetic tape. Under the tape is a record head and several play heads varying degrees of distance away. East Bay Ray used one on the first few Dead Kennedys albums before he went digital.

The tape adds noise and wears out with time. And you can't set speeds between the few presets based on the heads. But nothing else sounds like these. Look in pawn shops.

Wah Wah

This is an actual pedal, not just a box. It has a rocker pedal that is like the gas pedal on your car. Changing the angle with your foot changes the tone. Basically a wah wah is a tone knob controlled by your foot. There's also a switch to bypass the wah wah, usually under the end of the pedal in the front. So, to use it, you have to stomp the rocker pedal forward to turn the switch on, then move the pedal back and forth while you play. Some good use is in Portishead's "Roads," Morcheeba's instrumental "Who Can You Trust?," Dinasour Jr.'s "Little Fury Things," Red Hot Chili Peppers' "Sir Psycho Sexy," 31's "Freak Out."

Usually used four different ways:

1. For the clean, muted, "wacka wacka wacka" 70s funk sound—pedal being rocked in rhythm with the strumming. (Think "Theme from Shaft.")

2. Combined with distortion and pushed back and forth slower for a screaming rude rock sound (almost any Jimi Hendrix). Also check out the rhythm guitar in the Bomb song, "All My References are Dead" on the CD—though one guitar is a wah wah and the other is an envelope filter.

3. Set in one place as a tone control. (Think Brian May of Queen's lead sound.)

4. Used wrong. Just randomly used, not in rhythm or with reason. Used just because it's there. This is the most common use of the wah wah.

NOTE

I got help from my younger, hipper friends with song examples in this chapter. A lot of help. They also helped a bit with examples in Chapter 2, "Songwriting Basics," and all the equipment chapters. The younger, hipper friends are KTRU (Houston) radio DJ, Daniel Joseph Mee (www.thejonx.org) and Skip Frederiksen from the very cool Florida band Beauty's Confusion (www.beautysconfusion.net). Thanks, guys.

Compressor

A compressor (or compression) reduces the dynamics of a signal, raising (or *boosting*) the low volume and lowering (or *attenuating*, a.k.a. *cutting*, a.k.a. *rolling off*) the high volumes. This increases sustain and gives a better tone, especially for lead. Usually has two knobs: compression (amount of compression) and volume.

It is used on the drum beats in "Mysterons" by Portishead.

Reverb

Reverb imitates the sound of a large wide open room. It is similar to delay, but instead of distinct separate strong echoes, it is an infinite number of smaller echoes. Think of the sound of being in a metal room and yelling "Hello!"

It gives the sound of the instrument a little more depth, though too much of it tends to obscure the actual notes being played, especially when used in combination with distortion, delay, or other effects.

Reverb is usually produced by sending the signal through springs. This is usually done in the amp itself. That's why sometimes when you hit your amp or move it while it's plugged in you hear a horrible SPROING sound. (I have actually heard someone hit their amp as an effect in a song.) The Fender Twin Reverb and Fender Deluxe Reverb are good examples of amps with reverb springs.

On an amp with reverb springs, there is usually a knob on the front of the amp to control the amount of reverb, then there is usually a female jack on the back of the amp marked "reverb" or "reverb foot switch." Into this you plug a foot switch. This switch usually comes with the amp. It is a passive switch used to turn the reverb on or to bypass it.

Figure 4.5 *Fender Deluxe Reverb.*

Sometimes reverb units are freestanding and not built into the amp, although these are rare compared to in-amp units.

Examples: Radio 4: "How The Stars Got Crossed" and "No More Room For Communication." Moby: "Everloving." The Innocence Mission: The Innocence Mission album, heard in the vocals of all songs, especially "Notebook." Hum's "Isle of the Cheeta."

Chorus

A chorus box, in theory, adds the illusion of two instruments playing the same things at the same time. In reality, they just basically make the sound thicker and more shimmery. Kurt Cobain used one a lot.

Technically what they do is split the signal into two parts and let one pass through unaffected (the *dry* signal), and the other side of the signal is detuned very slightly and has a very tiny delay added to it. (This is the *wet* signal.)

I guess the idea is that two instruments playing together can never, by nature, be absolutely tuned identically or played in an absolutely identical rhythm. They are always off, due to the physics of making a string resonate and such, a matter of fractions of a semitone, and off in time by a millisecond or so, even when played by the most adept human players.

Chorus boxes usually have two or three knobs: chorus (amount of detuning), mix (dry-to-wet signal ratio) and sometimes some sort of tone or volume knob.

Examples: The Chase Theory: "FM Radio." Third Eye Blind: Third Eye Blind (album) (1:05 into the song "Motorcycle Drive-By" and throughout the album). Edwin McCain: "I'll Be." Smashing Pumpkins: "Sweet Sweet." Nirvana: "Come as You Are."

Volume Pedal

Like the wah wah, this is an actual pedal, not a box. It has a rocker pedal that is like the gas pedal on your car. It is the same idea as a wah wah, but instead of controlling a tone knob, it controls a volume knob. This can be used just to fine-tune your guitar volume, but better than this is to use it as an effect in its own right— to swell the volume, and make the guitar sound more like a violin by removing the attack (beginning) of each note. This sounds extra cool in combination with other effects, particularly delay and distortion.

Example: Sarah McLachlan: Fumbling Towards Ecstasy (album) heard all over in the guitars.

Flanger

A flanger is an electronic attempt to imitate the sound they used to put on records in the 60s using two tape recorders with the same signal, where you lean on one of the *flanges* or tape reels in the studio and get a sort of jet sound. The beginning of "And The Cradle Will Rock" by Van Halen is a good example of a flanger box on a guitar.

Flanging is even more noticeable on drums, and is often added with a rack-mount flanger in the studio.

Figure 4.6 *Flanger.*

Usually has three or four knobs: speed, flange, mix, and volume.

Jimmy Eat World, "If You Don't, Don't." Smashing Pumpkins, "Luna."

Gas Food Lodging Soundtrack (J Mascis) (most of his score is with a flanger).

Phase Shifter

A phase shifter (or phaser) is an electronic attempt to imitate the sound they used to put on records in the 60s that was obtained by running an instrument through a rotating speaker cabinet, like the *Leslie* speaker that came with Hammond B3 organs and weighed more than an SVT bass amp. Leslies are sometimes actually still used, like on the guitar on "Black Hole Sun" by Soundgarden, but are usually only used in the studio because they are so heavy and kinda fragile. A phaser sounds a little like a flanger but is distinctly different.

Usually has two or three knobs: speed, phase, and sometimes volume or tone.

Smashing Pumpkins: *Siamese Dream*, "Luna" (very subtle). Ivy, "Blame It On Yourself."

Jimmy Eat World, "Sweetness."

Pitch Shifter

Does exactly what it says: changes the pitch of a note. Is sometimes incorporated into other units, like a digital delay, and is sometimes freestanding. Can be set to a perfect interval, like a third or a fifth, to play parallel harmony with oneself. Set at a fifth, with some distortion, it would allow you to play a power cord with one note! This could yield some cool fast heavy results if you play up and down the neck with it on. Can also be set to some in-between ratios, like halfway between a third and a fourth, or set to a tritone, for some very sick and twisted sonic results.

Usually has two knobs: pitch and mix (ratio of wet to dry signal).

Extreme pitch shifting can be heard on Rage Against The Machine's music, especially on the solo to "Killing In The Name."

Vibrato (Also Called Tremolo)

An automatic pulsing interruption of the signal. Like reverb, this is usually a function built into the amp but is occasionally freestanding. Also, like reverb, is usually controlled by a foot switch plugged into the back of the amp and altered in amount with a knob (usually two) on the front of the amp. The two knobs are Depth (mix of dry to wet) and Speed (speed of interrupt or pulse in the signal).

Actually, vibrato in this case is a misnomer. This pulsing variation in volume is really tremolo. Sometimes this function is correctly identified on an amp as Tremolo, not Vibrato. But usually not.

Vibrato is a gentle (or sometimes extreme) oscillation in pitch, like that produced by pumping on the whammy bar on a guitar.

Ivy: "Disappointed" (subtle).

Hooverphonic: "2Wicky" (actually an Isaac Hayes sample, on the intro guitar line).

Figure 4.7 *Tremolo pedal.*

Noise Gate

Does exactly what the name implies. Reduces noise. It does this by completely cutting the signal off (to zero) when the volume falls below a certain level, which is set by the Threshold knob. The idea is that you set the threshold to just above the level of the noise produced by the guitar and amp when you are playing nothing.

Envelope Filter

Envelope Filter is a sort of automatic wah wah. It wahs the tone more depending on the attack (how hard you pluck the string). Sounds funky. Jerry Garcia used one a lot on guitar. Flea uses one on bass.

Sounds very similar to wah wah. Maybe "Narcolepsy" by Third Eye Blind.

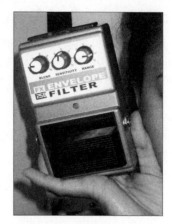

Figure 4.8 *Envelope filter.*

TIP

You can buy, or if so inclined, make, a purely mechanical pedal with a rocker that can control (with a break cable type attachment) any knob on any other pedal.

Multi-Effects

Multi-effects units are a combination of some or all of the above. They usually have a cover and fold up into a suitcase type thing and lay on the floor. They have a lot of different effects built into one unit, and you can program them in any way you like. For instance, you can give them numbers (shown on a digital readout) according to where they are used in the set, so you can just tap through.

The only problem with a multi-effect unit is that if it goes out, you're hosed. With separate units, if one dies, you just remove it from the chain of boxes and go on with your day.

Figure 4.9 *Multi-effects unit.*

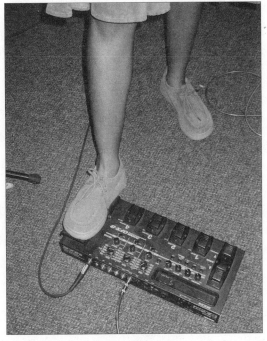

Figure 4.11 *Another guitarist using a multi-effects unit.*

Figure 4.10 *Guitarist using a multi-effects unit.*

Octave Divider

An octave divider adds a second tone one octave lower to any signal. With a guitar, it sounds like a bass playing along with the guitar. This actually can free up the bass guitar to go off on other stuff.

Usually has one knob, Mix, which controls the ratio of dry to affected tone.

This effect can be mimicked with a pitch shifter set to exactly one octave down also.

Lightning Bolt uses it on the bass in "13 Monsters."

Guitar Synth

Guitar synthesizers are a lot more complicated than most effects and not used that much any more. I do remember a minute in the early 80s, around the time that The Police album, "Zenyatta Mondatta," came out, when they were everywhere. But they ain't too common now. Which is a pity, because the better ones have an unbelievable array of options. But this also means you can probably pick one up in a pawn shop or on eBay easily.

> **TIP**
>
> Tech editor Michael Woody adds, "Not to editorialize outside my job description, but Adrian Belew still uses guitar synths extensively and put out a disk (they're not records anymore, of course) called *The Guitar As Orchestra* which is, to quote a Web site, 'A fascinating and original use of guitar synthesis where the role of the orchestra is replicated by solo guitarist. Even down to the opening applause!'"

There are ones that work as freestanding effects boxes, like the Electro-Harmonix model, and ones that work with a proprietary guitar or at least a proprietary pickup that must be retrofitted to your guitar. The latter sounds like more work, and it is, but it gives you a lot more options in audio capabilities. They can make your guitar sound like *anything*, from a violin to sounds that have never been heard before. Ever.

With a guitar synth, you can reconstruct all aspects of the sound, including the *envelope*. Envelope is a combination of attack, sustain, and decay. These are different for every acoustic instrument, and with a guitar synthesizer (or any synthesizer), you have complete control over all these parameters, usually with knobs labeled Attack, Sustain, and Decay.

Most older guitar synthesizers, especially the earlier models, have a little bit of latency. That is, when you pluck a note, there is a very small delay between the time you hit the string and the time the affected tone comes out the other end. This is because of the incredible amount of machine math that goes into controlling an electronic digital synthesizer with an analog input.

Garbage: "Queer." (Skip sez, "I don't know if these are guitar synths, Michael. It's hard to tell; they could just be synths.")

Ivy uses one on "Long Distance" and "One More Last Kiss." Strokes uses it a lot.

Talk Box

Odd little 70s thing used by Peter Frampton, Joe Walsh, Aerosmith, and Alice in Chains. Basically, a talk box is a powerful speaker in a box attached to a tube that you stick in your mouth. You play while mouthing words into a mike, shaping the guitar sound with your lips and tongue. Sounds like the guitar is talking.

Skip sez, "A lot of electro bands these days use a vocoder, though (for vocals), which I know you know is similar, like The Faint and their album *Danse Macabre* and bands like Soviet."

E-Bow

An E-Bow is not an effects box, but rather a little handheld thing that you use to hover over the strings near the pickups. It uses a battery-powered coil to produce a concentrated magnetic field that drives the string without your having to pluck or even touch it. It produces a bowed sound and can also provide infinite sustain on a single note. It can sound pretty good right out of the box and amazing with a little work. Great for textures and background noises and great when combined with other effects, especially distortion and delay.

They're about a hundred bucks new. Comes with a useful tutorial.

In General

Effects boxes have cool names made up by marketing drones. These names are often just reflecting whatever's happening in popular music this week. For instance, there was a fuzz pedal called the Heavy Metal Pedal. I think that it's pretty much the same circuit design they later retooled and sold as the Grunge Pedal. Ignore this crap and go with your ear and your heart and recommendations from smart musicians.

Each extra effect you add to the chain between your guitar and your amp adds a little bit more noise. When recording, only hook up the effect you want to use on that song (and maybe a noise gate at the end of the chain). When playing live, set up all your effects with the shortest cables possible to join them. Six-inch or even three-inch chords should do it.

Put the effects that add more volume to the signal first in the chain. I would put the fuzz or distortion first. That way you will be boosting the signal, not the noise.

Effects can be powered by a battery or an AC adapter. AC adapters can add noise, but batteries don't last long. Effects draw a lot of juice. Most effects draw a little power even when off as long as a cable is plugged into the input. If you're not playing for a while and you're using batteries, unplug the input side.

You can get a power supply in a music store that is made for delivering (hopefully) steady and (hopefully) noise-free power to multiple effects at the same time. Sometimes it is also mounted on a board or carrying case to make it easier to transport the effects as a single unit.

Makeup cases are useful for carrying extra junk to a gig. You can put an effect or two, your tuner, extra strings, a string winder, a slide, some batteries, and some CDs in one. And consumables and even makeup if you're into that sort of thing.

Effects are not a substitute for talent or quality songwriting. Work with your effects and get to know them as well as you know your instrument. They are basically another instrument, or at least an extension of your instrument. Learn to use all the controls on each one. Be able to get the exact sound you have in your head without having to fiddle around too much. Be able to jump to the right setting for every song instantly. Be able to jump to the right setting between songs, even between parts in a song. This is one advantage of multi-effects units: programmability.

Keep track of when the batteries are running down; the knobs will work differently and unpredictably (another reason to use an AC adapter). And learn to be able to use them in the dark, or near darkness, because sometimes it will be nearly dark on stage if the light man does a blackout between songs.

Some amps have an Effects Loop. This is an input and output on the amp where you can put your effects chain directly into the amplifier, rather than between the guitar and the amp. This gives a better sound with less added noise.

Rack Mount Effects

Some effects are not the floor box type. They are rack-mounted effects, a.k.a. a rack mount, which are higher quality, lower noise, more expensive effects, built to screw into a rack, which you buy separately. The rack usually has a power supply, a fan (to cool the electronics), and sometimes built-in light. Rack-mount effects cost more, are more complicated, do more, and sound better with less noise. Many professional players use these instead of the ones on the floor. But it's all up to you. There are advantages and disadvantages both ways.

Figure 4.12 *Detail of rack-mount screw holes.*

Figure 4.13 *Rack-mount equipment.*

Conclusion

Equipment is just the tools you use. Don't get hung up on it and fetishize it, as it will distract you from truly being creative.

I once asked Miles Montalbano if he could recommend any books for the "Recommended Reading" section of *$30 Film School*. He named a bunch of poets, novelists, and painters, and then added, "Anything besides books on filmmaking."

I loved that.

George Thoroughgood did an interview in *Guitar Player* magazine about 20 years ago. They kept bugging him to talk about his equipment specifications, and he just talked about baseball. It was my favorite interview ever in that magazine, even though I don't like baseball.

East Bay Ray told me that he considered *Guitar Player* magazine "guitar pornography." It does have centerfolds. It has little to do with art as far as I can see. It's about the image of being a guitarist.

Real artists inspire me regardless of the medium. I can learn more about music from some filmmakers than I can from many musicians. And we wouldn't even necessarily have to talk about music for me to learn.

What I'm getting at here is that people focus on the wrong aspects of an art. The technical is the least of it. Guitar playing, filmmaking, riding skateboards, and fine oil painting are more similar than they are different.

> The most beautiful thing we can experience is the mysterious. It is the source of all true art and all science. He to whom this emotion is a stranger, who can no longer pause to wonder and stand rapt in awe, is as good as dead: His eyes are closed.
>
> —Albert Einstein

$30 MUSIC SCHOOL

Chapter 5

Microphones, P.A. Systems, and Troubleshooting

Microphones, a.k.a. mikes, are devices used to turn an acoustic signal, like a voice or a drum, into an electronic signal that can be recorded or amplified. PA systems allow the microphone to be heard.

We'll also add in a little here on repairing stuff. Because part of being a D.I.Y. musician is taking care of your own gear.

Different microphones have different pickup patterns. This refers to how they pick up sound. A cardioid (a.k.a. unidirectional) pattern is heart shaped; it picks up most sensitively from the front and the sides, but not much from behind at all. They are good for live miking of vocals.

Figure 5.1 *Microphone on mike clip on mike stand.*

Two mikes are commonly used for rock: The Shure SM57 microphone is better for instruments, and the Shure SM58 is the standard for vocal. Both are reasonably priced ($120 to $170 new, way cheaper used). An even better vocal mike is the Sennheiser 835, which lists for $280.

All three of these are dynamic mikes, which require no external power supply. The Shure 16AM-CHN is an example of a condenser microphone. These require a battery in the mike or line transformer/adapter/power supply box or Phantom Power (power provided by the mixing board), are more sensitive, and better for miking from further away, for instance, miking a whole drum kit from above, or for recording a band from the audience or from above the audience.

If you are using a powered mike, remember to turn the battery off when not using it or the battery will wear down faster. There will probably be a switch on the power supply box.

Figure 5.2 *Generic Radio Shack mike with omnidirectional pattern drawn in.*

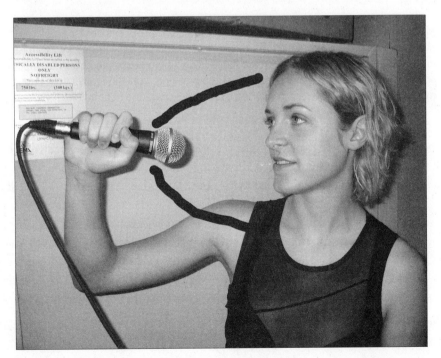

Figure 5.3 *SM58 with unidirectional pattern drawn in.*

Many mikes have a switch on the side to turn the power off and on. This is useful when the mike starts to feed back. Feedback is the squeal you get when a microphone is pointed at a speaker, and the signal forms a feedback loop, getting louder and louder. You can cut this by cutting the switch off and back on or by moving the microphone away from the speaker. If you know this, you will get better at cutting it without thinking. Eliminating feedback is also the soundman's job, but do what you can from the stage to help him or her.

P.A. Systems

The P.A. (a.k.a public address system. Pronounced *pee a*) is the amp the singer sings through in practice. It's what you plug the microphone into. At a gig in a club or stadium, it's a bigger system, and the whole band is put through it. The drums are miked, the guitar amps are miked, and the bass amp, keyboards, and DJ's turntables are usually input through a small unit called a direct box.

TIP

Michael Woody adds, "I understand the PA to be a complete system for amplifying acoustic sounds (vocals, pianos, percussion, etc.) and possibly for reinforcing already amplified instruments, including at least one vocal microphone, an amplifier, and the speakers. The various cables should go without saying, but who knows. A sound mixer is also typical and required when using more than one microphone."

The mikes and direct boxes on stage go through a snake, which is a box that routes all the cables to the soundboard, a.k.a mixing board, a.k.a. mixer, at the back of the room. This is where the soundman hangs out. The mixer has a number (usually 16 or 32) of inputs, a.k.a channels. Each one deals with a separate microphone or direct input, a.k.a line input. For instance, in a professional setting, the drum kit will have seven or more mikes on it: one each for bass drum, high hat, snare, both rack toms, and then two overhead to get the cymbals and overall sound of the kit. Each guitar amp will occupy one channel; same with each vocal. The soundman raises and lowers the volume and EQ of each channel to get a good mix.

Woody adds, "In my experience, a snake is a collection of several discrete cables within a single larger cable with a breakout box at one end (on stage) and loose connector at the other end that plugs directly into the sound mixer. It can send instrument signals from the stage to the mixer as well as send monitor signals back

Figure 5.4 *Rack-mount graphic EQ.*

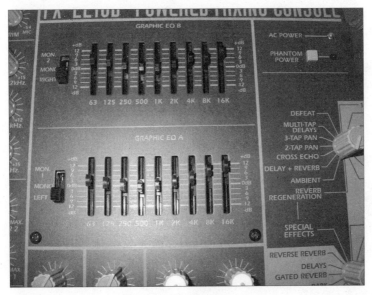

Figure 5.5 *Close-up of master graphic EQ on a mixer.*

to the performers, assuming they have monitor speakers with built-in amplification. There are variations, but this is what is generally considered to be a snake."

EQ is equalization. This is the amount of high frequency, middle frequency, and low frequency sound in each channel. This is built in to each channel of the mixing board.

A mixer usually has a master EQ for the whole mix, also.

The mixing board will usually have several monitor mixes available. A monitor mix is the amount of each instrument going to each monitor speaker.

Monitors, a.k.a. monitor wedges, are the speakers on stage that face the band, rather than the audience, so the band can hear themselves. Different mixes are useful because one band member might need to have a different mix than another band member. For instance, usually the singers will need to hear more of themselves and less of the guitars. The bass player will often want a lot of the snare drum to help him stay in the pocket.

The mixing board usually has an effects send to a rack-mount reverb, which the soundman usually adds to the snare drum and the vocals only. Sometimes they'll add a lot of it to a singer if he sucks. You can't really cover up a lack of talent, but they will try.

Figure 5.6 *Monitor.*

Figure 5.7 *Singer with monitor.*

The soundman (or woman) is in charge of running the P.A. He (hopefully) knows how to do a good sound check (the process of getting all the sounds good—done before the gig when the venue is empty).

Keep in mind that the sound of the room changes when full of people. The sound is absorbed and responds differently than it did in sound check. A good soundman knows this and compensates.

In stadium situations, the soundman who runs the system feeding sound to the audience (the house mix) will be a different person than the one mixing the monitors, using a different mixing board. In a club, it's usually the same person on the same board.

Very professional bands will bring their own P.A. and soundman. Bands that are on their way but can't afford that yet will often bring their own monitors and monitor mixer soundman, so that at least they sound good to themselves on a consistent basis. This makes for a better performance and gives the band a modicum of control in a world where they are otherwise often powerless.

Smaller bands will sometimes have their own smaller P.A. system, which can be the entire P.A. (mainly for vocals) in a small venue or anywhere that does not have a P.A., like a party (keep in mind that you'll need more power for the same volume outdoors).

A *powered mixer* is a good choice for this. It is a mixer that includes a power amp. You plug it directly into the speakers.

This system could also double as your monitor system in a bigger venue that has its own P.A. system.

Figure 5.8 *Small portable powered mixer.*

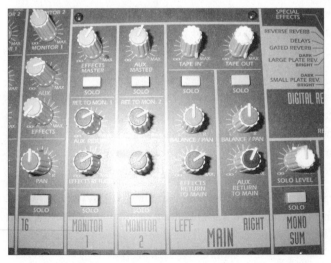

Figure 5.9 *Close-up of powered mixer.*

Figure 5.10 *Another powered mixer.*

Figure 5.11 *Speaker on small portable P.A. system.*

Figure 5.12 *Bass speaker on small portable P.A. system.*

Figure 5.13 *Cheap powered mixer.*

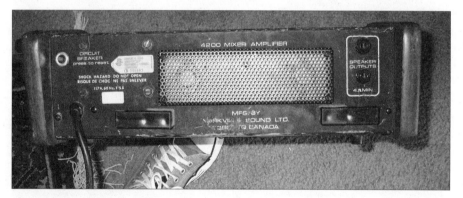

Figure 5.14 *Back of cheap powered mixer.*

Troubleshooting

New equipment is usually covered by the warranty. And repairing stuff yourself will often void this warranty. But a lot of the equipment I use is either used or old and not covered anymore. So I had to teach myself troubleshooting and basic repairs.

The basic methodology I use for finding out what's wrong is this: If there's no sound coming out of my amp when the guitar is plugged in, I figure it must be something in the chain: guitar, cable, effects pedal, cable, amp, speaker, or speaker cable. So I replace each one of the elements with a substitute that I know to be working until I isolate the problem.

Then I work within that unit to find the problem. For instance, if I find it is the amp, I try that amp with a different speaker. Or that speaker with a different amp. I unplug the unit so I won't get shocked and take it apart (carefully laying all the screws somewhere that I won't lose them and separating them into piles and labeling them if I think that it's going to be confusing when I go to put it back together) and look for visible problems: wires that have come undone, parts that have fallen down inside, jacks that are physically compromised. Then I fix that, plug the unit back in (being careful not to get shocked if the unit's still open), and see if that fixed it. If not, I look further.

A good thing to own is a VOM or volt/ohm meter (or sometimes voltometer or voltmeter). You can get them for about $30 and up at Radio Shack or a similar store. They are useful to see where the voltage is flowing. If you can read a circuit diagram, a.k.a. schematic (the schematic for an amp is often glued inside the amp or at least published in the owner's manual), you should be able to easily trace where the problem is. You can also use one to test to see if there's a short sending power between your guitar strings and the mike, so you won't get shocked.

Sometimes it's as simple as a blown fuse. Fuses exist for a reason. They melt and break the flow of current easily and are there to protect the circuitry of the amp. You can usually see if a fuse is blown by inspecting it visually. But sometimes the break is almost microscopic or hidden from view down in the metal housing on the end. The ohm function of a VOM is useful for testing fuses. Take them out and test their resistance. If it is low, they are good. If the needle doesn't move at all, they are blown.

Make sure you use the right fuse. Never use an automotive fuse for a guitar amp! And make sure the fuse you use has the recommended voltage and amperage rating for the piece it's protecting. A fuse that's rated too low will blow too often. Too high and it will not protect the amp. The amp will blow before the fuse.

Never bypass a fuse with a piece of foil or a wire. This is asking for trouble: ruined equipment or even a fire. If your fuse keeps blowing, there is probably a reason. If you can't figure it out, maybe it's time to take it in to a competent repairperson.

Sometimes the fuse is accessible from the rear of the amp; sometimes you have to take it apart. Sometimes the fuse, or even a second fuse, is inside the amp on the circuit board. This is bad planning as far as I'm concerned, because it makes it hard to get to quickly. You need a screwdriver and some time. If it's accessible from the back of the amp, it takes seconds.

I used to keep a small box of fuses duct taped to the side of my SVT amp head.

Some amps have circuit breakers, which are basically switches that function as reusable fuses. Just press the button to reset them. But first make sure you look for whatever it was (overload on one circuit? too many amps plugged into one outlet? need to put a fan on an overheated amp?) that made it trip.

It is good to develop a relationship with a good repairman in your town. Ask more experienced musicians in your scene who's good and won't rip you off.

Figure 5.15 *Circuit breaker button on the back of a mixer.*

CAUTION

Approach all equipment repairs with caution. You can die. The author and the publisher take no responsibility if you open your gear and start messing around. Just because I'm willing to die for my art doesn't mean you should.

Don't get shocked. Electrolytic capacitors (usually blue cylindrical-shaped things with two wires coming out of them) and cathode ray tubes (TV and computer monitor screens) can store charges and shock you even when the unit is unplugged. Experienced repairmen usually discharge them after unplugging the unit and before working on them by carefully shorting them out with the metal blade of a plastic-handled screwdriver.

Power strips (with surge protectors) are good for plugging several devices into one outlet. Often, gigs will not have one. Carry a power strip with you to gigs, and make sure it has a circuit protector (like a reusable flip-switch fuse). Make sure it's grounded and UL rated.

Figure 5.16 *Power strip with surge protector.*

Every piece of equipment you use that plugs into the wall should be UL rated. There will be a sticker somewhere on it to tell you this.

Write your name with a Sharpie on the power strip somewhere. They all look alike.

How to Solder

Soldering is the act of melting a low–melting point metal alloy (typically tin mixed with lead) onto two or more wires or connections to permanently bond them. For electrical work, you *must* use rosin-core solder, not acid-core. It will be marked. Acid core is for plumbing, and if you use it on electrical parts, they will actually dissolve and come undone with time.

A soldering iron costs about 10 bucks. (Radio Shack is a good bet. Just give a fake name there and tell them "I don't want to get the catalog" or they'll spam your mailbox with catalogues for the rest of your life.) A soldering gun is a bit more heavy duty and costs 40 or 50 bucks. If you're going to be doing a lot of this, I recommend the gun.

To use it, plug it in and let it warm up. Make sure you don't touch the tip, or you'll get burned. I usually see when it's hot enough by licking my thumb and quickly touching it and pulling away. This is dangerous, but I've never been burned by it. If the spit sizzles, it's hot enough. You can also wait until you see/smell a little smoke from it. There won't be any the first time you use it, but after the first use, there will be a little residual rosin from the solder to make some smoke.

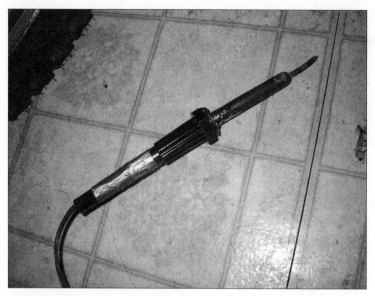

Figure 5.17 *Soldering iron.*

Figure 5.18 *Solder.*

First you have to *tin* the tip, which means touch a little bit of solder (solder looks like wire, but melts on contact with the tip of the iron) to the hot tip of the iron. If it's hot enough, solder will flow onto the tip and cover it with a thin shiny layer. If the tip has been used a lot, it may have too much oxidized material on it to get a good tin going. In that case, I would rub it on a piece of sandpaper, then rub it quickly on a piece of paper to rub the sand off. Then it should take a tin quite well.

Once you've tinned it, you just melt a little more solder onto whatever it is you're trying to join. If it's wires, you might want to twist the ends of the wire together first. You can also get a jig at Radio Shack that is basically a clamp with roach clips on the end to hold different parts. It essentially gives you extra hands, because it seems to take more than two to effectively solder: one for the iron, one for the solder, and one for whatever you are soldering.

To join two wires, first strip them with a wire stripper or a knife. Be careful not to cut yourself or cut too much wire. This gets easier with practice.

You just flow the solder on to the two parts to be soldered. A trick is to heat them both before applying the solder. If the parts are hot, the solder will flow better. Make sure the parts aren't attached to something heat sensitive, like an integrated circuit. If they are, you can first attach a heat sink (a roach clip, or "alligator clip" as they're called in electronics stores, with fins to dissipate the heat) behind the parts to be soldered.

Once the parts to be soldered have the molten solder flowed to them, let them cool for at least a minute. Then they should be electrically and mechanically bonded for life.

Try not to get molten solder on the floor or, God forbid, on yourself. It is very hot and will burn anything in its way. I usually solder over a workbench that is made of Formica and doesn't matter if it gets little burns on it.

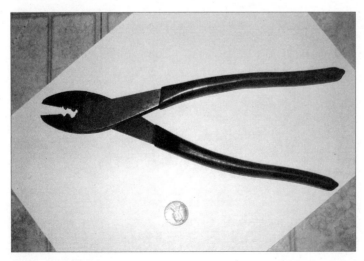

Figure 5.19 *Wire stripper.*

Also try not to breathe the fumes produced by soldering. Rosin-core solder does not produce fumes nearly as toxic as acid-core, but still it will bug your lungs. And the lead in solder is toxic. Open a window.

When you're done, unplug the soldering iron and let it cool. It takes several minutes to be cool enough to touch (longer than it took to get hot), so don't space out and forget it was on and burn yourself or start a fire.

Conclusion

Okay…we've got guitars, basses, amps, mikes, and something to plug those mikes into. The band is nearly outfitted. Only a little more to go on this gear stuff. But it's fun, because it's the loudest part. Here come the…drumroll please… DRUMS!

$30 MUSIC SCHOOL

Chapter 6

Drums

Drums are the backbone of rock. The beat, the life, the blood. People say, "You're only as good as your drummer," and it's true. Drums are the primal element in rock and roll. Basically, modern drums are imitating a hollowed out log with some animal skin stretched over it, and "hit with wooden clubs" (I forget who said that). Drums were, historically, probably the first instrument.

The rock drum kit, sometimes called a drum set (and even a trap set, though this term is used less and less) is basically a one-man band. It's a combination of several instruments that are played by several different people in a symphony or marching band: bass drum, snare drum, crash cymbals, and tom toms.

The most basic kit has at least this: a snare drum, a bass drum (also called a kick drum), high-hat cymbals, and a floor tom. That's called a three-piece kit. (You only count the drums, not the cymbals.)

Most companies don't sell a three-piece kit. If you want one and can't find one, you might pay less to special order the components than to buy a four-piece kit and not use it all. Do the math.

Figure 6.1 *Four-piece drum kit.*

Most kits also have at least a ride cymbal, one crash cymbal, and one or two tom toms (also called rack toms).

Some kits have all this and then add a bunch more rack toms, too many crash cymbals, a cowbell, timpani, timbales, and even a gong. This attitude was popular in the 70s, but most drummers today are more stripped down with their kit. I kinda like the stripped-down approach. Some of my favorite drummers use very little more than a three- or four-piece kit. I sometimes wonder about people with *huge* kits. They make me think of guys who spend a lot of money on their car. Like maybe they're making up for some elsewhere, perhaps something anatomical....

Drummers who use big kits: Neil Pert of Rush, Chad Sexton of 311, the guy from Dave Matthews Band, and Damon Che from Don Caballero. Primus, both Brain Mantia and Tim Alexander.

My ex-drummer, Reuben Chandler, says, "Half-assed drummers such as Keith Moon operated under the assumption that if there was a space...fill it. That way, in your undisciplined thrashing you'd at least sound really fast."

Some of my favorite drummers use tiny kits. Like Mick Harvey of

Figure 6.2 *Crash cymbal.*

Figure 6.3 *Chimes.*

Birthday Party and also of The Bad Seeds. Chad Smith of the Red Hot Chili Peppers, Meg White of the White Stripes, Tre Cool of Green Day. Dave Grohl in his Nirvana days. The guy from the Liars…and Tony Fag from Bomb. Tony developed his signature "boogadigga" beat out of adversity. He didn't have money for a double-bass kit, so he alternated a double-bass beat between his single bass drum and his floor tom. And he didn't have a high-hat clutch until the Warner Brother's record. He lost his clutch when he was a teenager and never had money to replace it. So he just used his high-hat to keep the beat with his foot. But you couldn't really hear it, which made the drumming he was playing sound more primal and stripped down and thus more powerful.

Drums, like guitars, have gotten cheaper for good new stuff, due to technological advances in the manufacturing process. (And due to globalization, and sending work to countries where labor is insanely cheap—but that's another book entirely.) As you would when purchasing a guitar, it's probably a good idea to take someone who knows what he's doing with you when buying your first drum set. You will find drums, like all musical instruments, at the same places you'll find guitars: music stores, eBay, want ads, pawn shops, mail order, and through the grapevine.

Avoid the cheapest of the cheap crappy rock drum kits—stuff that's made for little kids that will fall apart—you know, the kits that are like $199 retail new. You'll have to probably pay 500 bucks or more for a good solid four-piece kit that's going to last long enough to actually play some gigs with it. And cymbals and hardware are several hundred bucks extra.

Reuben sez "Tell kids not to pay more than 50 percent of retail for drum equipment." Reuben helped me out with this chapter, because I know less about drums than any other instrument—I sing and play bass very well, play guitar okay, am passable on keyboards, but when I get behind the drum kit, it sounds like a drunk guy falling down the stairs.

I asked Reuben how to not pay more than 50 percent of retail, and he said, "It's true for any musical purchase. Go in and look at the price and offer them 30 to 40 percent. You should be able to settle on 50. Go at the end of the day just before closing. They've either made money that day or want to. If they've made it, then with you they'll make a little extra. If not, then they've made some. If they don't want to deal, walk out."

Good advice. And I thought that only worked in pawn shops.

Drums involve a lot of hardware. It's a lot of work to set them up, it's a lot of work to play them, and it's a lot of work to break them down. Often the drummer doesn't get to be very involved in the writing process and, as a result, doesn't make as much money as the other guys in the band, and does more physical labor. And he's the brunt of most of the meanest jokes:

Q. "What do you call a guy who follows a bunch of musicians around and goes to all their gigs?

A. The drummer.

Q. What's the difference between a rock drummer and an extra large pizza with anchovies?

A. The pizza can feed a family of four.

Q. What's the last thing the drummer said before he got kicked out of the band?

A. "Hey guys! Let's do one of *my* songs!"

So fewer people want to play drums than any other instrument in the band. Everyone wants to be the singer or the guitarist. They get all the chicks (or all the guys). The bass player gets to be up front on the edge of the stage. Even the keyboard player usually has more input in the songwriting process.

So *great* drummers are hunted to extinction. If you find one, treat her with little baby kittyfeet and be extra nice to her because great drummers are so damn hard to find and hard to keep. If your drummer is great, after *every* gig there's gonna be a few people circling like chummy sharks to steal him from you. Good drummers who aren't insane and are easy to deal with are usually being paid like a grand a week (or a grand a night) to tour with someone else. (Drummers often *are* insane. Drumming attracts lunatics. After all, what kind of person wants to hit things all night?)

What to Get

Premier is the best bet for the money. Tama are good, too. Reuben sez, "Their Swingstar and Rock Star lines are both affordable. Stewart Copeland only used their Swingstar series when he played in The Police. They're the bottom of the line...so they are rugged and cheap."

Figure 6.4 *Tama bass drum.*

Figure 6.5 *Pearl bass drum.*

Figure 6.6 *DW bass drum.*

Sonar and DW are good brands but very expensive new. There are lesser known brands that might work, too. Try 'em all out. It's fun.

So, a good kit would be a 12" snare, 10" tom tom, 16" floor tom, 20 or 22" bass drum, an 18" ride cymbal, a 16" crash cymbal, and a 14" high-hat. There are variations on this, and a few inches either way is fine, but this is a good place to start.

A bass drum has a foot pedal, a.k.a the bass pedal, that controls it. It hits the bass drum head with a mallet. This and the snare are basically the heart of the rock beat.

Figure 6.7 *Bass drum pedals.*

Some drummers buy a rock pad, a hard plastic circle that sticks on the bass drum head. It makes the drum head last longer before it sounds dead or breaks. A rock pad changes the sound, though; it makes the bass drum less of a thud and more of a click. Think any record produced by Dave Jerden ("Nothing's Shocking" by Jane's Addiction). Many, many people prefer this sound, but I like the thud better.

The snare drum has wires called a *strainer* (sometimes called snares) stretched under it that give it the characteristic chattering, rattling sound associated with the snare sound. It usually has a release on the side of the snare drum to release the tension or "turn off" the snare. With the tension released, the strainer no longer chatters and basically becomes a tom tom.

The strainer rattles sympathetically from other music even when you aren't playing the drums. When your band is playing quietly on parts you don't play on, you might turn this off so it doesn't rattle. Then turn it on before you come in. Total pros do this instinctively. Make sure you turn it off when they're recording overdubs you don't play on.

My band doesn't have much money, so we share a studio with another band. I turn the strainer off on their drummer's drums every time we practice so it doesn't rattle to our music. I try to remember to turn it back on at the end of the session.

Figure 6.8 *Strainers on the bottom of a snare drum.*

Bottom Heads?

Some drummers put heads on the bottom of their drums to improve the sound. Technically, the snare is the only drum that *requires* a second head. But, especially for recording, many drummers like the sound of a second head. Sometimes they take it off for live because it's louder that way. (Reuben adds that you can just tune your first head higher in tone to make it cut through, too. But that will affect the tone, too. Experiment to find settings that work for you that, with experience, become *your* sound.

Remember that you have to tune the bottom heads as well as the top heads.

Most drummers put a pillow in the bass drum to dampen it a bit and give it a deeper sound. If they put a second head on the front, they usually cut a small round hole in the front head to allow it to be miked easier. See London May's comment on the CD-ROM.

Figure 6.9 *Bass drum head.*

Figure 6.10 *Floor tom head.*

Tuning Your Drums

Drum heads have to be *tuned*. This is basically tightening the bolts around the rim that holds the head tight. You do this with a drum key.

You want to tighten them all equally and spread the tension evenly across the head. You should tune them until they sound good. This takes practice, and you might want to get someone who has done it to show you.

Some drummers, when recording, even tune the bass drum to the key that the song is in.

Figure 6.11 *Drum key.*

NOTE

Back in the 70s, a lot of drummers would wear their drum key on a chain or string around their neck as a necklace. It's probably more convenient to keep it on your key chain.

Cymbals

Paiste, Sabian, and Zildjian are the top brands, and all are good. Making cymbals is a mixture of science and voodoo. The alloy and process are always carefully guarded trade secrets. (In fact, Zildjian, who keeps the formulae in the family, is the oldest family-run business in the world, starting in Turkey in 1623.) Two cymbals of the identical brand and model can have subtly different makeup in their harmonic overtones. Basically, try 'em all out and find the ones you like.

Drum Sticks

Use the heaviest sticks you can when you start playing. That'll build up your wrist strength.

TIP

Lifting small weights will help build strength for drumming or playing guitar. It's best to lift small amounts and do many repetitions rather than heavier amounts fewer times.

If you break a lot of sticks (and you probably will), you can go two different ways with buying them: You can either buy the expensive ones, which break less, or buy the cheaper ones in bulk. Six of one....

Vater brand sticks are very good and range from five to eight bucks a pair. You can buy no-name sticks for two bucks a pair. Or in bulk for as cheap as $12.99 a case (a case is 24 pairs). Lennon Rehearsal Studio in San Francisco used to sell used (but not broken) sticks left behind in the studios for a quarter each.

Figure 6.12 _Drum sticks._

You can roll sticks on a table to see if they're warped. Warped sticks play funny and break easier. You can look for lines in the stick where there is an imperfection in the wood of the tree it's made from. A stick will often break along these

Figure 6.13 *Rods.*

lines. Keep in mind that since sticks are made from wood, there are bound to be natural imperfections. But better sticks are hopefully made from better grades of wood. The manufacturer has someone sitting on an assembly line looking for crappy wood and taking it off the belt and tossing it (maybe to be made into the cheaper no-name sticks). Sticks marked Computer Matched are usually better than those not thusly marked.

You can also play with brushes or ProMark Rods to get a quieter sound. Either is good for acoustic sets or songs. (I refuse to call this "unplugged." MTV made that up, and I was playing acoustic shows before MTV existed.)

Drum Cases

You'll also need cases for your drums. Some drums come with cases that are basically thick pressed paper. They will fall apart eventually but are better than nothing. Most drummers who play any kind of regular gigs get hard molded plastic cases that hold up a lot more. Good cases can cost as much as the drums. Anvil road cases cost more, but are even better.

Figure 6.14 *Hard shell drum cases.*

Drum Machines

Drum machines are pretty damn cool. Drummers were threatened by them when they first came out a few decades ago, and with good reason. They never miss a beat, you don't have to pay them, and they never show up late or stoned. You don't have to muck about in the studio strategically miking them to get a good sound, and they never speed up or slow down unless you program them to.

There are a few things a real drummer can do that a drum machine can't, but with advances in technology this gap is becoming narrower and narrower. Drum machines can't improvise or vary from the set list as easily, but other than that, pretty much the only thing that drummers can do now that drum machines can't do on stage is look cool. Bands that don't have a drummer onstage look pretty lame. This is one reason that rap guys jump around a lot, throw up the standard off-the-shelf hand motions, and dance a lot: They are basically trying to cover up the fact that, in all but the most unique exceptions, most hip hop live is basically karaoke.

These days, what a lot of bands do is use a drum machine in the studio and a drummer live.

Drummers who were threatened by this and just said, "Damn machines; I hate them" often fell behind. Drummers who saw the future adapted. My friend Michael Urbano went out and bought one of the first drum machines that came out and got really good at programming it. He will even be called to bring his drums to play a session, have them all set up and ready to go, try a run through, and then suggest to the producer that he use his drum machine instead. Musicians should not be threatened by advances in technology; they should adapt to them. Record companies, however, *should* be threatened by technology. We will talk more about this in Chapter 14, "Business," and Chapter 15, "Starting Labels and Production Companies."

More and more, hit songs are being done with only a drum machine in the studio. *All* hip hop, any pop stuff like Britney Spears, and any R&B contemporary schlock like R. Kelley is all done with a drum machine. When they play it live, drummers sometimes play, sometimes not. If they do, they're playing like a drum machine. Except hip hop; they just rap to a recording of the backing tracks most of the time. Drummers who want to survive would do well to learn to play like a machine.

Some of my favorite music, Nine Inch Nails, is done with a drum machine *and* real drums. This can be an intensely powerful combination. Ivy and Gravity Kills do this also. Marilyn Manson does it a lot. Fugazi does it in "Closed Captioned."

When I was a kid, *real* musicians were so threatened by electronics that they issued statements against them. The first many albums by Queen all had a proud disclaimer on the back, always some variation of "Absolutely no synthesizers were used on this album." (When they finally used a synthesizer on an album, it totally sucked.) I remember people wanted their money back when word got out that Electric Light Orchestra was using backing tapes of string sections to augment their live sound. Lots of bands use tapes, samples, drum machines, synthesizers, and more today and make no attempt to hide it. Asking for your money back for this would be ludicrous today, but in the feathered hair cocaine haze of the 70s, it seemed justified.

Two of the most common synthesizers are the Roland 707 and the Roland 808. They have an older analog sound but are still coveted in hip hop and even rock.

One I like a lot is the Boss DR5. The Alesis SR-16 is great, too. You can find both cheap in a pawn shop or on eBay.

TIP

Something you could do that I don't see bands do much is program your drum parts and record them to a CD. Then you don't even have to mess with the buttons live. Bands usually use a DAT (digital audio tape machine), which is more expensive. But you do need a stable CD player. I would also bring duplicate CDs in case one gets scratched.

Drum machines kick ass. They sound good out of the box, are easy to program, and have gotten a lot cheaper. There are several software drum machine emulators available. You program them with your mouse. Hell, they're cheap or even *free* if you have a computer and don't mind using borrowed software. (Of course, I would never advise you to do anything illegal.)

Two very cool emulators are Reason and Rebirth from Propellerheads software.

Check their Web site at www.propellerheads.se.

One of the coolest sites for emulators is this absolutely free site: www.keyboard-museum.org/d_machines/vdrums.html.

The drum machine emulators all run in Flash and look and sound like the originals. While Reason and Rebirth can output directly to a sound file, for these you'll have to record out through your soundcard to get them on tape or on your machine, but they work, and the price is right.

Keep in mind that any audio generated by Flash will have the compression of an MP3 because that is the native audio file format in Flash. So sound produced by Fruity Loops and other software-based sequencers, or anything from a real drum machine, will sound better. But good music could be produced and recorded using these Flash-based emulators.

Actual drum machines are programmed using the knobs on them. They are all different, so you'll have to read the manual.

Songs on the CD with hardware drum machine for the drums (as opposed to real drums, software, or sequenced or played electronic drums) are: "SPQA" and "Smelly Piano."

Other examples include: "It Could Be Sweet" by Portishead, "Porcelain" by Moby, "Nellee Hooper Edit" by Sneaker Pimps, and "Different" by Sage Francis.

Electronic Drums

You can also get drum pads that trigger samples when hit; it's kind of the best of both worlds between the sound of a drum machine and the human touch of an acoustic drum kit. London May has an electronic kit set up in his home studio. It requires no tuning, miking, or anything. You can sit down anytime and play and get a great sound right away. He used it when we recorded the theme song for my film, *D.I.Y. or DIE*. Listen to "D.I.Y. Theme Song" on the CD. The song is me on vocals, bass, and guitar and London on drums. It took under three hours to record and mix, from walking into his house to walking out with a completed master CD. And that included a hard disc failure and having to start over at one point.

The sound he used is pretty straightforward: pretty much an imitation of a drum kit. But you can also use them for more electronic-sounding drum sounds. Depeche Mode and KMFDM do this. The band VHS or Beta uses them also.

Skip adds, "Akira Jimbo uses a mix of digital and acoustic drums in his setup."

Get Creative

These toy drums sound pretty cool. I could see using them in the studio on one song.

Figure 6.15 *Toy electronic drums at Circuit City.*

Coda

There's only one thing every top ten band ever has in common, regardless of whether it's rock, pop, blues, soul, punk, or whatever: The drums are really, really good. Drums on all hit recordings are totally locked in time in a groove that makes your foot move whether or not you want your foot to move. A weak drummer makes any band weak. A really groovin' drummer makes a good band very good. A really groovin' drummer makes a great band transcendent. So be good, or get a good drummer, with good gear. Or get a machine and learn to use it.

Chapter 7

Electronic Music and DJ Equipment

DJs who perform in clubs on their own are often deified and treated like rock stars, and they sometimes do a lot more than just spin records.

Lots of bands have DJs who perform in the studio and onstage and add depth, sort of like a keyboard player, but using turntables, samplers, and sequencers.

Some music is entirely based around the DJ and then performed live with a band.

I know even less about DJ music than I do about drums, so I just interviewed some folks. They explain it pretty well, so I'll just shut up and show you what they said.

Skip Frederiksen

Skip, a.k.a. Moxx, is the DJ for the Florida trip-hop band Beauty's Confusion. I interviewed Moxx on the subject of electronic music. You can learn more about Skip and the band at www.beautysconfusion.net and www.monochromevision.net.

Q. Describe the music creation/DJing you do.

A. I write all kinds of music from melodic punk to trip-hop, shoegaze to trance, hip-hop to new wave, and everything in between. I guess I spend most of my time writing trip-hop and abstract hip-hop because

Skip Frederiksen.

it's my favorite style of music to listen to as well as write. The only DJing I do would be of the scratch nature. I have no interest in beat mixing and DJing live. (I leave that stuff to people like BT/Oakenfold and whoever.) I just do a lot of scratching (a-la Portishead, DJ Qbert, that kind of stuff). Most of my music writing is assisted by my best friend and bandmate, Joel Legros. He completes 95 percent of the ideas I have, whether it's songs for Beauty's Confusion or just some random projects or movie score-type music we have going. I don't know what I'd do without him. He inspires me as a musician and as a friend and has helped me finish my song ideas by probably 1200 percent. He writes all the time, and I see that he gets shit done, so then I do the same. I write whenever I can, however I can. Most of the writing and recording takes place in my studio, but sometimes I'll bring my laptop and headphones to a bookstore or coffee shop and work on ideas with that.

Q. Do you use Macs or PCs?

A. PCs.

Q. What hardware and software do you use? How do you use it?

A. Software

Native Instruments plug-ins and VSTs (includes Battery, Absynth 1.3, Pro-53, FM7, Vokator, Traktor, Kontakt).

Joel and I swear by the Native Instruments plug-ins. We use Battery for programming drum parts, Absynth for creating lush pads and ambience (and anything related to the movie score-style stuff we write), Pro-53 for basically any type of sound we want from aggressive to laid-back, weird sound effects and more. It's modeled after the old Prophet 5 synthesizer by Sequential Circuits. FM7 for lots of clear, bell-like sounds (modeled after the super-powerful 80s synth the DX7 by Yamaha). FM7 is very versatile and can be programmed easily to edit and create new sounds. It can do everything from long drawn-out ambience to cool new wave-style leads and anything else. Vokator is a cool vocoder (for getting robot-like sounds), but it can also do a lot of crazy effects. We don't use that as much as the other stuff. Traktor is a cool program for DJs that allows you to beat match, beat mix, and do all sorts of cool stuff...definitely mainly geared toward DJs. Kontakt is a great sampler, though I don't use that much either.

> **NOTE**
>
> A pad is a long, drawn-out ambience or subtle drone. In synth talk, when you need something to "fill" out a part in the song—something that creates atmosphere or a dream-like quality, or sometimes tension, too. Just basically a sound that kind of fades in, and while a key is held (or a chord), the sound usually changes slightly and gives it a sense of movement. And when you let go of a key, the sound typically takes a few seconds to decay.

VSTs and DXis are virtual instruments, which you can control by connecting a keyboard via MIDI to your computer. They usually need a host, which is a sequencer application (such as Cubase or Cakewalk Sonar) that can host DXIs or VSTs. VST effects are like virtual instruments, but they are virtual effects units. Instead of having a hardware reverb unit, for example, you have the software version that looks exactly like the hardware (rack screws and all) and sounds the same, shown on your computer monitor.

With VST effects and Direct X (DX) effects, you can generally get a clearer sound with effects than with some hardware, which will probably hiss. Because virtual effects are totally electronic, they are clean and great sounding and can enhance production tenfold…no hiss, no cable noise, no nothing.

We have a Roland v-drum electronic kit and an AKG C2000B condenser mic for recording vocals.

Figure 7.1 _Roland TD6 digital drums._ All photos in this chapter by Skip unless otherwise noted.

Lounge Lizard Virtual Rhodes/Wurlitzer Electric Piano

We use this thing in practically all of our songs. It perfectly emulates the vintage Fender Rhodes electric piano and the Wurlitzer 200 electric piano. Bands like Ivy use the Wurlitzer in a lot of their songs and it sounds great. Portishead uses both the Wurly and the Rhodes. Their song "Roads" is actually a reference to the piano; the intro to the song is a Rhodes piano with a tremolo effect. Morcheeba uses the Wurly and Rhodes in practically all of their songs. They just have an amazing sound. Nothing beats the real thing, but the Lounge Lizard is definitely a powerful virtual instrument, and at a tenth of the cost (or less, nod, nod, wink, wink) of getting a real Rhodes and Wurlitzer.

Emagic EVP73 Virtual Rhodes Piano

I tend to favor this virtual Rhodes over the Lounge Lizard. I don't know why, I just think it sounds warmer and prettier. Seems to respond more like a real Rhodes than the Lounge Lizard, though the Lizard is far more programmable. You can make that sound like a Rhodes or a piece-of-shit toy piano from 1961. I have owned a real Rhodes Stage 73 Mark I piano, and I think the EVP73 sounds a lot more like the real thing.

Sampletank XL 1.3

Joel and I use this exclusively for the solo violin and grand piano. Sampletank has a lot of amazing sounding samples, very versatile, with tons of great effects. Any type of *real* sound you want (pianos, strings, bass guitars, and more) can be achieved with Sampletank. Highly recommended. Though a huge, huge resource hog. Bogs down your PC bigtime, and we have a fast system.

Novation V-Station

We use this in every single Beauty's Confusion song. We had a Novation K-Station (the hardware version) but sold it to buy the V-Station. This thing is great for trance, ambience, phat basses, noisy, aggressive leads, pretty leads, whatever. Has a built-in arpeggiator, which we sync to the song's tempo via our sequencer— very useful for ideas and stuff. This is worth every penny. Not to sound like we work for Novation (we don't), but their products are seriously kick-ass. No electronic music producer or electronic band should be without Novation gear or software.

Fruity Loops 3.56

I mainly use Fruity Loops to make (what else?) loops. It's great for creating song ideas from scratch. It's powerful, fun as hell to use, and has great sounds that can be tweaked beyond belief. I always use an external keyboard controller, though. There are many musicians out there who can make full songs by drawing notes with the mouse. Not me, I need to tap my ideas in on keys. The only way to go. Fruity Loops is very inexpensive and incredibly powerful. Another highly recommended piece of software. We used Fruity Loops for the drums on our song, "Windmills" on our first EP. We also used it on several other songs, coming up on our full-length.

Figure 7.2 *Controller keyboard.*

Reason 2.0

Reason is powerful as hell. You can create any type of music with it from hip-hop and R+B to straight up techno, trance, goa, breakbeat, whatever. I use Reason exclusively to create loop ideas for Beauty's Confusion. Our song "City" (on our upcoming full-length record) was made mostly with Reason. Ninety percent of the parts in "Faded" were programmed and played in Reason, except for Joel's guitars and Jenna's vocals, of course. We made the beat using ReDrum and the intro pads using the NN-XT sampler. The bass line was made using the SubTractor. Loops were made with the Dr:rex Loop Player. Reason is so cool because they offer a lot of things called refills, which are patches designed exclusively for each Reason virtual instrument. The refills are relatively cheap and much more editable than a basic sample loop CD. You can also find tons of free refills on the Web. The only thing that sucks about Reason is you cannot use VSTs or DXis (external plug-ins). They want you to use that program exclusively, which is why they call it Reason, I guess. But something that's really cool is that you can sync it to Cakewalk Sonar or any other sequencer that can *rewire* (running both Reason and the sequencer in sync). There, you get a lot more options. Reason sounds phenomenal and is so powerful. We love it.

Cakewalk SONAR XL 2.0

I make all of my solo music in Cakewalk Sonar, Joel makes all his solo stuff in Sonar, and we do all our band stuff with Sonar. The reason we love it is because it's three things in one—an extremely powerful MIDI sequencer, an extremely powerful digital audio workstation; it has looping capability just like Acid Pro and costs $100 less than Acid. It's very easy to get full songs alive and kicking in Sonar. We can drop a drum loop in for inspiration, play some live keyboard parts via MIDI, and add guitars and vocals on top, all in the same program. Very versatile.

Figure 7.3 *Midi mixer.*

Very easy to use. We swear by it. It's also pretty damn stable as far as programs go. It crashes from time to time as all programs do, but it's the most stable, and I've used them all, from Cubase to Logic to Pro Tools. Sonar is the way to go, plus it's the least expensive out there.

Edirol PCR-30 MIDI Keyboard Controller for Virtual Instruments

We use the Edirol 32-key PCR-30 MIDI controller to tweak our virtual instruments. It has eight knobs and eight sliders to control all aspects of synthesis and tweaking sounds. It has presets, which can be recalled for any of the soft synths (software synthesizers as opposed to hardware) you're controlling (or hardware, for that matter). The keys feel great (not cheap at all). It's small enough to connect to a laptop anywhere and write music. We use it to control our V-Station, Native instruments plug-ins, and Fruity Loops and Reason.

Figure 7.4 *Beauty's Confusion main studio.*

Hardware

Hardware here is sort of the bridge between the old school and the new. We're talking the fun stuff that controls or works in concert with all the fun software stuff we mention in this chapter.

Keyboards

Keyboards are cool. Organ, piano, synthesizers: All add a depth to music that is not possible with just guitar, bass, and drums.

Keyboards were out of style for a while but seem to be back in. Trends don't really affect us $30 Schoolers, but it's worth mentioning. They are used a little differently than they used to be. In the 70s, the operative word for keyboards was *virtuoso*, with many keyboardists like Keith Emerson and that guy from Yes having overtly classical training and a tendency towards showoffism. I quit loving that stuff when I quit smoking pot.

Today the keyboard is usually used to just add little bits here and there, as well as samples. I like the way the keyboards are used in Marilyn Manson—sparse, but as kick-ass as a rock guitar. Gwar has keyboards, believe it or not, but it's only sampled sound effects, and they aren't onstage. A keyboard onstage wouldn't fit the Neanderthal Gwar image; they're in the sound booth. There's a sound effect for each key (blood spurting, dinosaur yelling, nuns burning, people being tortured, and more), and each key is marked with a piece of tape and a Magic Marker, and the band's soundman is in charge of "playing" it.

> **TIP**
>
> Ironing boards make cool keyboard stands.

Most bands use the keyboard as well as guitars for the main crunch of the sound. Some use drums, bass, and keyboards *without* a guitar. My band Devil Kitty did this; so does Mike Watt's band, The Secondmen.

Check out my guitarless Devil Kitty tune, "Hey Louie," on the CD. It rocks and sounds good, even without a guitar. And the keyboards are far from virtuoso, but they totally work.

There are tons of cheap keyboards: Roland Juno-60 (no MIDI capability but can be retrofitted with a MIDI kit by www.kenton.co.uk). Going price used $300. Used by Satisfact, The Faint, Fountains of Wayne.

Roland Juno-106 or Roland HS-60 (Juno-106 with speakers, different color scheme)	Used by everyone. Going price for one that works $450.
Yamaha CS6x (decked-out synth)	Going rate $600.
Yamaha AN1x (awesome analog-modeling synth)	Going rate $450.
E-mu XK-6 Extreme Lead synth	Going rate $600.
Novation Nova or Supernova II	Going rate $1000.
Roland D-50 (used by Enya among many others—classic synth)	Going rate $350.
Yamaha DX7. THE 80s "movie score" synth	Going rate $400.

If a keyboard has MIDI capacity, you can also use it to trigger other MIDI-interfaced devices, including computers, with unlimited samples and actions. You can even get a stripped down controller keyboard (keyboard that must be used with an external MIDI system) cheap and use software that you might be able to get free if you try. The Casio VL-1 VL1 Tone Synth is a good one, as is the Edirol PCR-50. Good feeling keys, lots of knobs and buttons (all fully assignable). About $250.

Keytars

A keytar is a keyboard that is designed or retrofitted to be worn around the neck like a guitar. Very cheesy. Best used only in irony. This is done well in Marilyn Manson. I call people who play them without irony "ketards." A common one is the AX-7 MIDI.

Bela Fleck uses one.

Taurus Bass Pedal

No longer made, but cool as hell. Look on eBay or in pawn shops. The Taurus Bass Pedal sits on the floor, and you can play it with your feet, even while you play guitar. It's one octave of bass foot fun. Good for long bass notes rather than fast fancy playing.

Used by Rush in "Tom Sawyer," and The Police in "Spirits in the Material World."

Yamaha NS10m Monitors

I found a pair of these at a local thrift store for $10. One woofer didn't work, but I got it replaced for $90. These things go on eBay for $450 a pair. Can't believe I found them. Basically, the legend goes like this: If you can make a mix sound good on Yamaha NS10ms, it will sound good anywhere. And that's true, which is why these small speakers are in every recording studio in the U.S.A. Powerful, sound great, and the industry standard. We use them all the time in our music making.

Behringer Mixing Board

For any studio, no matter how small, you need a mixer for EQ and just to route everything into the computer. I have every input filled in the mixer. Behringers are cheap and sound great, and mine has mic pre-amps on each channel, which give you more gain and better sound for recording guitars and stuff like that.

Pioneer CDJ-1000 for Scratching

The best vinyl simulation out there. I got one of these because every time I scratched vinyl on my turntable the needle would skip. I hate vinyl because:

1. The needle skips, especially if you don't own the DJ-industry-standard Technics 1200 table.

2. You can't use your own copyright-free samples to scratch on. With the CDJ-1000, you get the feel of vinyl plus the response of scratching vinyl, and you can play CD-Rs of your own samples to scratch on and never have to worry about copyright or anything. It's seriously perfect; I don't know how Pioneer did it. You can scratch as hard as you want, as fast as you want, and nothing will skip. It's a great piece of music gear, especially for someone like me who worships DJ Qbert, DJ Shadow, and Geoff Barrow of Portishead. All of them use real tables, but for me, digital's the way to go.

Numark Matrix 3 Pro DJ Mixer

Best mixer for scratching, plus it has inputs and outputs for routing effects like reverb and delay. I love the Matrix 3 because when you scratch, there are three ways to make the sound:

1. The crossfader, which is the most versatile way to scratch.

2. The channel volume (up-down slider—good for doing scratch echo fade-outs and stuff).

3. The Transform buttons, which I use a lot because I can get good, fast scratching sounds. You simply press the button, and it cues in the sound. It's a lot faster than opening the crossfader. I learned this technique from Geoff Barrow when I saw the *Portishead: Live in NYC* video six years ago. He uses the Transform buttons a lot in his scratching. A lot of "pro" mixers don't have Transform buttons. In a way, it's like cheating because it's easier to press the button than to crossfade, but this Numark mixer rocks. Great price, solid mechanics, and the crossfader is optical (uses light instead of a variable potentiometer slider), so your crossfader lasts a lot longer than a cheap mixer.

Synths

Roland HS-60 (Juno-106 with Speakers)

The Roland Juno-106 is used by practically everyone in electronic music. There's a good reason for it. It sounds fucking amazing. Old school, warm, phat analogue sound. Insanely tweakable. No menus to dig through. All your sound editing is done from sliders above the keys. I love this synth, and I use it in all of my music. Beauty's Confusion songs would not be complete without it.

It's the old school Duran Duran/OMD/Thompson Twins synth.

I love the 80s new wave sound, and the Juno-60 is *it* when it comes to that. It's also great for weird-ass electronic noise and warbling. The 60 does not have MIDI like the Juno-106, which allows you to connect it to the computer or any other MIDI device, but a lot of people argue that it sounds better than the 106. I'd have to agree. You can get MIDI kits from www.kenton.co.uk for a few hundred bucks to allow you to connect the 60 to a computer, and that's very useful and a good upgrade idea. The Juno-60 has been used by everyone in the 80s, and one of my

Figure 7.5 *Roland HS-60.*

favorite now-defunct bands of the mid 90s: Satisfact. The synth has an unmistakable sound. Awesome.

Roland D2 Groovebox

I use the Roland D2 to add some variety in our live show. It's a great pattern sequencer, and you can drop parts in and out on the fly, using the buttons on it. Great for improv or just messing around. It has a four-inch "launch pad," which you can touch to change parts, edit sounds, tweak, whatever, which is really fun. I don't really use it too much for songwriting, just for beat-making and patterns to mess around with. Really powerful box, though. Need to connect a keyboard to it to make it really shine.

Yamaha CS1x Control Synth

My first synth, and one of the best synths for the money. This keyboard was created for techno/trance enthusiasts, and it has some great sounds; plus, it's fully programmable. One of the first synths in the mid-late 90s to have knobs again like the old school synths of the 70s and 80s. I've used this synth for all the keyboard parts on our song "Outcry."

Figure 7.6 *Yamaha CS1x and Roland-HS-60 and DJ gear.*

Casio CZ-1000 Phase Distortion Synth

I love anything that sounds 80s. This synth is used by Vince Clarke of Erasure and formerly Depeche Mode. I love this thing; it's awesome. You may think it sucks because of the name Casio, but I assure you, this is not some consumer piece of garbage. This synth kicks serious ass, and I've used it in several BC songs.

Various Sample Libraries/Loops

We use samples in our music, and I'm not ashamed to admit that, because all of us can play instruments anyway. I encourage sampling as long as it's legal and you're using royalty-free loops (otherwise you get in a shitload of trouble, especially if any of your music makes it commercially). I buy sample libraries from time to time, mostly hip-hop libraries. I love the grittiness of hip-hop samples. All great hip-hop groups use sample CDs and loops in their music. Tribe Called Quest did it; De La Soul did it; The Nextmen do it; Sage Francis, and more. Sampling is beginning to finally get some respect in the music world. Before, it was known as songwriting for people who couldn't play one note on an instrument. But now it's gained respect because of people like DJ Shadow who utilized their samplers in creative ways. I'm glad sampling is finally getting respect. It is a great way to get inspiration if you are completely stuck and cannot even think of one note to play in a new idea. Oftentimes, when I'm completely stuck with no ideas in my head, I'll drop a drum loop in my sequencer and just start writing some keyboard parts to it. And it will become a full song in two hours.

Samples and loops always spark my creativity. I will never stop using them. I just think a lot of the libraries out there are way too expensive ($50 to $90 per CD). Joel and I have started creating our own sample loop libraries and selling them through www.monochromevision.net. They're only 10 bucks each, with artwork and all, and feature over 600 MB of awesome loops per disc. We aren't putting shitty stuff out either; we're putting a lot of effort into creating great loops for people because it's great loops that inspired us in our songwriting. We figure that with all the gear in our studio and with years of music-making experience, we could put out some really good quality stuff. So I guess in a way, we're giving back to the sampling community. Hopefully, some people will check out our site and listen to some demos and stuff.

We've included a few free for you on the CD with this book. Look in the folder called monochrome. The ones with this book are in MP3 format to save space, and they sound pretty good, but on our commercial CDs, they are uncompressed and sound *great*.

Guitars

Guitars used by Beauty's Confusion:

> Gibson Les Paul studio (Joel)
>
> Ovation acoustic/electric (Joel)
>
> Takamine acoustic/electric (Jenna)
>
> Yamaha lefty acoustic/electric (me)
>
> Fender lefty Strat (Stratocaster) (me)

In Beauty's Confusion, we can't just make music that's entirely electronic based. Some of my favorite music blends electronics with live instruments. That's what we wanted to achieve with the band. Joel writes 98 percent of our guitar parts and uses his guitars to record them; Jenna writes 75 percent of our piano parts with her digital piano, which she records live into our sequencer; and I write 90 percent of our drum parts on my Roland digital drumkit, which I play with sticks and all. We're big on the organic/synthesized mix in music. Portishead does it; Hooverphonic does it; Archive; Morcheeba; Ivy; and more.

Q. Do you use existing creations to work from, create your own, or both?

A. As mentioned earlier, we sometimes start an idea with a sampled loop, but more often than not, we write everything from scratch. We wrote "Faded" from scratch, "Blue Deluge" from scratch, and "Innocence Destructing" from scratch. It just depends on the mood. I love samples and usually start my ideas with a drum loop or bass line and just build it from there. However the song gets done doesn't matter to me, as long as it gets done.

Q. How do you perform live? What's taped, sampled, triggered, and what's actually played and sung? Do you play to a click? With time code?

A. Our live show is hard to explain, and it changes every time we play. Joel is always on the guitar (either electric or acoustic), but sometimes he plays some keyboard parts. I'm on the acoustic drum kit 90 percent of the time. (The other time I'm scratching the CDJ-1000, while a beat is playing from a CD, which I'll explain in a few minutes. Sometimes a beat is playing throughout the song from a CD, and I'm doing live keyboards and scratching. Jenna is always singing her lead vocal parts live, but we have her harmonies being played from a CD. Jenna also sometimes plays guitar, too.

So let me explain about the CD....

Basically, we write our songs first in the computer and finish all vocals and production. Then we create a live file with the same song elements. I put a click track panned hard left in the mix, and most of the music is a mono mix panned hard right. I say "most of the music" because I leave out most drums because I play them live. The reason we do the whole click-track-left, mono-music-mix-right thing is because there is basically no other way to play a live show without everything being chaotic. By having the click track hard left, I can get only the click in my headphones, through my Numark mixer. By having the music hard right, the backing track CD can come through the house P.A. through both speakers because it's a mono signal. With the click-track on the left, the audience doesn't hear it, only I do...and I need it for obvious reasons.

The reason we use a CD instead of MIDI or time code, DAT machine, or laptop is because, quite simply, my laptop can't handle playing a sequence without crashing or having audio dropouts because it's four years old. DAT machines are a pain in the ass because you can't change the set on the fly. You have to fast-forward and rewind if you'd like to make changes in the set. CDs are easy because I can play CD-Rs and skip around by track number if we want to modify the set. We use a Numark CD player with good anti-shock because anything else, as the old 80s deodorant saying goes, "would be uncivilized." The CD has the backing tracks, which play most of the keyboard parts, any additional drum parts to fatten the drum sound live, Jenna's vocal harmonies, and anything else we are unable to do live such as base lines.

We're a three-piece, so we can only play so many instruments live. It's sometimes difficult to get a good mix. Sometimes Jenna's harmony vocals are too low, sometimes too loud. Sometimes the bass line is swampy, and so forth, but it comes with the territory. It takes a few tries to get it right, but usually it doesn't take too long. We don't want any other members in our band, so that's why we have to do it the only way we know how. Plus, I doubt that anyone would be into our music as much as we are. It's tough to find passionate, serious people who aren't drug-abusing idiots or prima donnas.

Something I wanted to point out to anyone out there who is reading this who might be thinking "Oh, all their shit is prerecorded; they don't do shit live." It's not like that at all. It's a hard process. People respect Nine Inch Nails, and 75 percent of their live show is a DAT machine. You do what you have to do, and anyone who thinks that our live show may be boring or "non-talented" because I press Play to start a song…they should research this stuff and maybe they wouldn't be so biased. I've heard some local people talk shit about us because we have the pre-recorded backing track, but whatever. I just laugh because we all do *some*thing live. I'm doing the drums, Joel's doing 96 percent of the guitars (sometimes we pre-record some lead guitars on the backing track CD), and Jenna does 96 percent of the vocals live, plus she plays guitar while singing. And we're not one of those bands who doesn't get into it live. We play like it's the last thing we're ever going to do. I hate unpassionate live performers. The stage is so fucking energetic. It's like, just because we play a mellower style of music doesn't mean we aren't rocking out or grooving with all we've got. When I get off my kit to scratch, during a breakdown or something, I freak out on that turntable. I jump around, groove, whatever. The other members of the band are equally energetic. So I dunno…. I just wanted to point out to anyone thinking that just because you use a backing track live, it doesn't mean you are a talentless idiot. As I said, it's tough, but we do what we have to do.

Q. Any closing comments?

A. Thank you for offering to include us in this book. You are a very influential person to my entire band (everyone should see Michael's documentary *D.I.Y. or DIE*), and it's been great corresponding with you via e-mail for the last few months. I hope we can continue to correspond. You are the type of person the struggling independent artist needs in his life, to give him the kick in the ass he needs to do his shit and do it right. Oh, and I'd like to say "Hi" to my wonderful girlfriend and best friend, Megan.

Hey, Michael, here are some great electronic music writing resources:

www.tweakheadz.com

Rich is an awesome electronic musician who knows his shit from front to back about MIDI and anything relating to synthesizers and tweaking electronic instruments.

www.computermusic.co.uk

UK-based magazine with tons of tutorials on how to write music with computers—heavily based on electronic music styles, but also offers a good deal on recording guitars and live drums and vocals. I've learned a lot about production from this magazine.

www.tripnotic.de

This site is the sole reason I started Beauty's Confusion. After hearing Portishead and the Sneaker Pimps and then Moby's album "Play," I found out there was a *huge* number of groups from around the world that do music known as trip-hop—which is basically mellow hip-hop/jazz/dark, moody stuff with somber vocals, usually female.

www.sonicstate.com

Great site with tons of synthesizer reviews and news. Very informative.

www.timespace.com and www.soundsonline.com

The standard companies in sample CD libraries—kind of high-priced, but they have everything, plus demos. If you've heard music, chances are you've heard tunes created from samples on sample CDs put out by these companies.

www.acidfanatic.com

Sells cheap self-produced loop CDs…nice guy, usable samples, cool site!

www.monochromevision.net

Joel's and my company. The company includes:

◆ An independent record label

◆ Sample loop CD company

◆ Poetry book publishing company

◆ Indie film/movie-score company

◆ That Web site I told you about a while back called http://femalevocals.com. We are still working on finishing it. A huge resource for female-vocal music, in all indie/alternative genres.

www.indiebible.com

The best book on self-promotion, ever.

www.rlabels.com

The most comprehensive list of mostly indie labels on the Web, and ever. *Great* site!

www.auralgasms.com

A cool resource featuring a lot of melodic, talented, and under-appreciated bands, both signed and unsigned.

www.reasonfreaks.com and www.reasonrefills.com

For Reason refills.

www.samplenet.co.uk

For free samples. Lots of good stuff.

Here are my recommendations for great electronic-mixed-with-real-instruments albums (90s to now):

> Archive: Londinium (Island Records, 1996)
>
> The Faint: Danse Macabre (Saddle Creek Records, 2001)
>
> Moby: Play (V2, 1999)
>
> Esthero: Breath from Another (Sony, 1998)
>
> Hooverphonic: The Magnificent Tree (Sony, 2000)
>
> Olive: Trickle (Maverick Records, 2000)
>
> Radiohead: Kid A (Capitol/EMI, 2000)
>
> Portishead: Dummy (Go! Beat, 1994)
>
> Satisfact: The Unwanted Sounds of Satisfact (Up Records, 1996)
>
> Garbage: Garbage (Almo, 1995)

Here's the complete process for how we created two of our songs, "Faded," and "Blue Deluge" (both are on the *$30 Music School* CD-ROM).

"Faded"

"Faded" started with Jenna and her acoustic guitar. She wrote the chord changes and main vocals, and then we went straight into the electronic production. Here's how that process began:

We opened up Propellerhead Software's Reason to write the intro pads, using a patch called LandPad in the SubTractor rack. Then I programmed an intro beat, which we wound up using throughout most of the song. We used the ReDrum rack, and the kit Dublab Brushkit1. So far, all these patches/kits are default instruments that come with Reason. Then we programmed a basic bassline using another SubTractor rack; this time we used a patch called HyperBottom, which is a great bass sound that we've used for a lot of our songs. It's full, clean, good bass sound for our style of music. So there we had the basic groove of the song.

As Jenna begins the second verse, we have this acoustic guitar patch, AcGuitarOctUp on the NN-19 rack. Immediately following that is the Novation K-Station, and a patch I don't remember; it's a grooving arpeggio throughout the second verse and the choruses. We added that later, after we took each instrument's track in Reason and bounced them separately as audio files to work in Cakewalk Sonar so we could add guitars and vocals.

As the bridge comes in, there are some Recycle drum loops we dumped into the Dr: rex rack mount. The drum loops add more balls during the choruses and stuff. I love combining drum loops (at least two) on choruses or parts that are building up within the song. Creates a nice blend, good mix, and my logic is, "Why use one drum loop when you can use two that sound twice as good?" After the bridge is over, it does this weird "sparkly" sound... as Jenna is singing, "...Here...." That's just a noise from one of my sample libraries. It seemed to fit the end of the bridge, right before the breakdown. When the last choruses come in, you can hear this synth swell thing. It kind of descends and creates a sad element right before Jenna sings "Enslave me" on the last choruses. That was done with a Novation Nova IIx, which I used to own but sold to buy a three-chip DV camcorder for indie film-making (see Michael's other book, *$30 Film School*!). I forget what the patch was called, but it was so pretty, so I used it.

Another Nova IIx patch plays throughout the last choruses. It sounds like a distorted Roland TB-303 or something. Again, I forget what that patch was called, but it worked really well as an outro.

So that basically sums up how we arranged the song electronically. Then, of course, the guitars were added (all written/played by Joel), and then Jenna records her lead vocal and then the harmony; we use an AKG C2000B condenser mic ($200 and one of the clearest mics we've come across). We've tried a bunch and we like it the best. So basically, most of the song was written with Reason 1.1 with some Novation K-Station and Novation Nova II. (We've since upgraded to Reason 2.0.)

"Blue Deluge"

The verses for this song were written by Jenna on her digital piano. She showed the basic idea to me, and I wrote the bridge and chorus parts. The song came together relatively quickly, and as many times as we've played this song live, I still love it as much as when I first heard it. It's so damn sad, and it is a very personal and honest summary of a bad relationship Jenna went through a few years ago. So anyway, here's how we arranged it:

We were looking for a good beat in our sample collection and found one that was depressing as hell and went with it, removing it in places where we wanted to have just Jenna and the keyboards. Initially, we were going to make the song strongly piano-based but realized that a piano wouldn't be good for the held-out chords, and that a vintage Fender Rhodes piano would be a lot more somber. Jenna recorded the held-out chords using the Rhodes. We threw a relatively slow tremolo plug-in (Syntrillium Software's free Tremolo DirectX instrument, which is a *great* tremolo effect for digital recording) on the held-out Rhodes chords. You hear a piano come in on the third line of the song; that's me and my E-Mu Proformance rack mount (same thing used by Moby throughout his "Play" and "18" albums). Then I come in with some scratching. I did about half of the song's scratching live, and the other half was just some scratch samples that I arranged in Cakewalk Sonar in a certain pattern that I thought would work pretty cool in a non-subtle way. The song is very down-tempo, but the scratching that comes in before the second verse is intense. I like the dynamic. All the other scratching (the kick drum fast scratches immediately following the second verse) I did live with my Pioneer CDJ-1000 digital turntable. The male voice heard before the chorus comes in and before the last verse ("ah-wa-ah-wa-ahwa-ah…ahwa on") is also done live with my CDJ-1000. You hear some dreamy synth sounds before the last verse also. Those were done with my sorely missed Novation Nova IIx, with the patch called "Lush." That's basically it. Joel was listening to a lot of Coldplay the week when we were recording this, and his parts are kinda Coldplay-ish (kind of like what their lead guitarist would do), which I don't think is a bad thing at all because we all love that band. Then Jenna recorded her lead vocals, then harmony vocals, and there it is.

One thing I wanted to point out when I mentioned all of those patches we used in Reason and the Novation synths: A lot of electronic-based bands have this mentality of "We can't use the factory presets because that's not being creative." We hate that mentality because, honestly, as much fun as it is programming your own sound from scratch or heavily editing a factory preset so it doesn't sound like the original at all, it's a big time-waster to do that. I think if you have an idea, and a factory preset fits what you hear in your head, then it's all good. Some synth programmers take two hours tweaking a factory preset to maintain their "originality," and I think the songwriting or creativity may suffer because of that. In my opinion, there are two mindsets when making electronic music: trying to get the idea in your head out and into a sequencer as fast as you can, and spending hours and hours tweaking presets so you have "original" sounds the next time inspiration strikes. I'd rather not waste time creating sounds, especially if a song needs to get out. I just wanted to mention that because I've read interviews with bands who despise factory presets and go out of their way making something noisy or weird.

It's cool and all, but being creative with riffs is a lot more stereophonically/aurally stimulating than a creative sound with no soul behind it. I guess you can use the whole jazz analogy—less is more. Miles, Coltrane, Charlie Parker—all their recordings are stripped down to the bare essentials in their rhythm sections: four-string upright bass, four-piece drum kit, grand piano. And all of it is gorgeous, dynamic, and diverse. Ha, I just realized I'm kind of contradicting myself because in my band, the more variety of sounds, the more inspired I am. My point is, I'd rather be writing the songs than programming sounds for future songs.

Interview with DJ Kafka

Q. How do you want to be credited?

A. Howard Anderson d.b.a. DJ Kafka, a.k.a. Maui Haui, Joe Schmoe, Mr. Wrong.

Q. What is your Web site?

A. www.djkafka.com and www.mp3.com/djkafka

Q. Describe the DJing you do.

A. I try to hit all the bases. I try to make every show a memorable experience for everyone. I call myself DJ Kafka because I do a lot of weird music and stuff that you wouldn't necessarily expect (in line with the writer Franz Kafka). I like to play a lot of remakes, remixes, and parodies. I like to make people laugh and have a good time. The most important thing is to keep people dancing.

Q. Do you use turntables, samplers, sequencers, keyboards, and other devices and programs?

A. I use two turntables, mixer, dual CD deck, and sometimes my laptop when playing live. I practice using samplers and keyboards as well as programs on my laptop but haven't felt a need to try it live. I expect to use the sampler as soon as I feel that I have it flawlessly mastered. DJing is something that I am totally into, and I don't want to do a bad show when I'm not quite prepared.

Q. Which of each do you use?

A. I use a Vestax PMC-15 mixer, a BBE Sonic Maximizer, a cheap Numark dual CD deck, and two Gemini XL-500 turntables. My P.A. is a Fender PD-250. My sampler is a Boss Dr. Sample. I practice using a digital delay (I have forgotten the brand, and the decal is rubbed off) that is an *awesome* effect but is kinda broken and I don't feel confident bringing it to shows.

Q. How do you use them?

A. I have always brought mix tapes to parties and have made tapes and CDs for friends. I had thought of going into DJing for a long time. A friend was having a low-budget wedding and was sad that she didn't have a DJ or band. That clinched the deal. I went out that afternoon to the local used band gear place and spent my rent money on the mixer and turntables. After I did the wedding, I realized that I needed to get some money back to pay off the gear and bullshitted my way into a paying gig at a local bar. I told the owner that I would play the first time for free and if I packed the place he would pay me $300 a night thereafter. I packed the place and he screwed me. He told me he could only afford $200 a night and I took it. Now that I had a paying gig I had to try to look professional. I cut up some scrap lumber and built a rack for all my gear. I put stickers all over it so I looked seasoned. I use the equipment in the traditional DJ fashion. Mixer in the middle and the turntables on either side. I keep a box that fits about 30 CDs close to the mixer at all times. I keep my "desert island" discs in this box so in case of emergency I can just grab any disc and throw it in without even thinking and push Play and it will most likely be something cool. Most of the discs in this box are discs that I burned myself and are filled with stuff that I play the most.

Q. Do you use existing creations to work from, create your own, or both?

A. I do both. I actually started 10 years ago remixing your stuff! (Bomb). This was long before I thought I would ever be DJing. I did it for my own enjoyment. I found one of the tapes a couple of months ago but don't have my four-tracker anymore. (Rule #1: Don't lend out your equipment to people you don't know.) Now I use Sonic Foundry Acid and Sound Forge for creating songs. I have a bunch of instruments that I don't know how to play, but I use them to make cool noises that I eventually use. I have a drummer right across the street if I need some special beats. I use an old friend of yours for guitar or bass—Skip Lunch[1] (of the Treebirds) is an incredible guitarist and is a great inspiration to keep me motivated to make my own music. He has a huge collection of vintage instruments and effects that we will toss into recordings. I plan on making an album with him this fall.

---

1. *Skip turned me on to punk rock. And taught Natalie Merchant how to be in a band.*

Q. Describe your typical work day.

A. Usually I start by cleaning out my studio that doubles as my office. I often have something that I have had burning in my head that I have to record. I will clean everything off my hard drive that isn't necessary, to make it run faster. Then I fire up Sound Forge and open samples of stuff that I had been collecting until I find the one that is right. I snip the samples or loops out and put them into a new folder that I will *name X-song - drum or guitar*, where X is the name of the song I am working on. I do this until I have all the loops or samples together and then run Acid. I arrange and rearrange until it sounds cool or I run out of time. I have 50+ songs stored on CDs and hard drives that I need to finish or be happy enough with them to call them done. I have a hard time with calling something done as I always feel that I could do it differently or add something else to it. Mix, remix, repeat, and so on. I helped produce an album for a group called Bells Of (Teenbeat Records) that we listened to some songs over 100 times before we called them good enough. We mixed it until within two or three hours of the deadline. I need to learn when to stop. I *have* learned to back stuff up. I had a hard drive crash where I lost 10 gigs of samples. Hours of Skip playing guitar and stuff that I had been working on for years. I was so bummed.

Q. Any closing comments?

A. Don't do it for the money or you will be sorely disappointed. I play 10 free gigs to one paying gig. I do it for the love of music and making people happy. I play a lot of Burning Man[2] parties. These people are really into dancing, and it is great to see them spinning fire to the groove I am laying down. I play for free just about every time I am asked (outside of clubs). When the club gigs come along, I get paid well. When I get paid, 99 percent goes into getting more music, better equipment, or something else that I need to make it a more enjoyable experience for everyone. I have thousands of CDs and records. I imagine that I will need 1,000 more paying gigs to pay off my addiction, but I'll give up my mixer when they pry it from my cold dead hands!

2. My editor asked me to define this. In case you live in a cave in the desert of Nevada and don't know, Burning Man is an annual ritual/festival/party/orgy where about 20,000 freaks descend on the Nevada desert, make art, noise, love, and a mess and roll around in radioactive mud. Then they burn a big wooden man on a bonfire and go home. It costs 120 bucks. I stay home and watch cats for people who go.

The parties he speaks of here are not the event proper, but parties for Burning Man addicts that simulate the environment in Los Angeles. It's to hold them over until they can go back out and get skin cancer at the real thing.

Interview with DJ Satan

Q. What is your Web site?

A. www.dj-satan.com. I have an e-mail list for anyone who wants to sign up. Contact me from the site.

Q. Describe the DJing you do.

A. I mostly just spin at local parties, thrown in and around LA by a group of my Burning Man friends called Gigsville. I started out as a DJ among them, and they're the ones who know me best (and who originally gave me my name). I haven't really expanded my reach, although I get nibbles here and there to spin at remoter places for different crowds.

Figure 7.7 *Photo of DJ Satan by chase@chaseandkelly.com.*

I like breakbeats the best, always have. Ever since the early rave tunes, when they used to mix up the styles inside each track. Now the dance genres are a lot more ghettoized, but that does make it easier to describe and select the types of music I'm after. I also enjoy trance, especially what I call "desert trance." You know what I mean, tracks that sound best in the great outdoors. But I have a newfound taste for house, and I can be heard spinning it at any given time. It almost always goes over real well. When it's specifically a Gigsville gathering where I know pretty much everyone, according to their more freeform ethic I make it known that people are welcome to bring their CDs to the console and request me to play their favorite songs. It could be anything, really, and for them I'm always happy to.

My spinning style is pretty straightforward—just beat matching and mixing for the dance tracks I spin, and then just standard radio-style segueing when it's normal rock/funk/disco or old school tracks. I've *just* started to become comfortable at turntable scratching, so I've been doing some of that lately.

Q. Do you use turntables, samplers, sequencers, keyboards, and other devices and programs? Which of each do you use? How do you use them?

A. I have a variety of equipment, which I use in different musical situations. I have the typical Technics 1200 turntables, which I bought used, plus a dual CD deck (a

Denon 1800) for my actual DJ gigs. I've been spinning for 4 1/2 years, and as I said I'm starting to do more freeform things like scratch. I have a very run-of-the-mill mixer, however, the Stanton RM 100, which has a noticeable level dip when you move the crossfader. Therefore, I don't feel comfortable scratching on that mixer. It has no way to adjust the crossfader level setting, either. (Folks, save up and get a Pioneer or a Rane instead!) Being a DJ turns out to be a very, very expensive hobby when you're not getting paid up front.

I have a Mac PowerBook laptop that can run either OS9 or OSX, and an older Akai 2800 sampler that I use for my electro-industrial act, Fifth Column Fetish. I will have that going again, I think, as soon as I get MOTU Digital Performer and the new MOTU 828 Mk. II interface, because that thing has eight digital audio channels, MIDI, *and* a couple of different remote sync functions. Then I can start making more DJ mix CDs; I only have one out now, done with the help of some friends. I also have a couple of vintage drum machines, a Roland TB-303 and a TR-606, which I will be able to sync via the 828.

Q. Do you use existing creations to work from, create your own, or both? Describe what you do with each.

A. My drummer friend Matty Nash plays in a nine- or ten-piece percussion ensemble called The Mutaytor, which he and I basically founded. If you live in LA, you've likely already seen them; they've played everywhere Burning Man-type events have taken place—acoustic and electronic percussion, very colorful, lots of fire spinning and hoop spinning, costumes and such. When we started out sometime in 1999 it was just me programming my own patterns on the 303 and 606 and playing them over Matty's drumming, manually matching his tempo. He would hear me through a monitor turned way up and sync up with me as well. I later borrowed and used a newer Roland 505, which has more diverse drum and synth sounds on it, but then I quit Mutaytor in 2001, about two years ago. They've expanded since then and gotten more elaborate, but I'm just not really into playing extended drum jams; I'm now looking to get back into electronica and rock 'n' roll, actually, do FCF again and other things.

Whenever I played with Matty, though, it was as DJ Satan, although I wasn't strictly playing records. I beatmatched using my own rhythms. When I DJ normally, most of the time people expect to hear others' records anyway. During the years that I did Mutaytor, occasionally there was a gig or two where I was scheduled to do Mutaytor *and* open or close with my DJ set. So, I had to set up my turntables and the P.A. and my Mutaytor setup. That got to be way too strenuous and nerve-racking to do all at once, and horror stories would happen: I would forget to bring crucial pieces of sound gear before driving 100 miles to the gig, because I was struggling to get through my workweek while preparing for basically two acts at once. From then on, I vowed it would be just one thing at a time.

I didn't start out with a very big record collection. All I had was pretty much the weird alternative and industrial stuff I listened to and collected during college. So when I started, I knew I had to accumulate enough techno 12s for at least an hour and a half set that I would want to spin in the first place. It took a while; shit's expensive, even when used! And most of the time I'm collecting new 12s anyway, since I want to have some leading edge and keep my dance vinyl set from going completely stale.

Over the years, as soon as some event came up, I'd learn that they'd want me to play a downtempo set, so I'd go out and shop for downtempo vinyl; then at some later party, they're wanting to hear disco and funk, so I'd need to go and pick up those pure funk and pure disco compilations. And meanwhile I wanted to keep my eye open for as many of what might be considered old school "classics" as I could—just in case I had a chance to earn a little respect from those who'd been around and heard it all. The good news is, I now have the tracks in hand, and at each gig down the line I have a little more flexibility and latitude to deal with what a crowd may expect. But to me the ultimate lesson in collecting music to spin is that every gig is potentially different, and you have to be ready to play *anything*.

Q. Any closing comments?

A. In wanting to DJ in the first place, I saw the opportunity to fill a niche that no one else occupied—entertaining friends and others by both playing them things they wanted to hear and introducing to them my favorite things I think they *should* hear. But after a while, people's expectations can get the better of your own expectations. I can't tell you how many times I'm somewhere spinning, playing my funkiest track, and I'm approached by some chick telling me, "Can you play something we can *dance* to?" Then I have to decide whether that person's just being an asshole or whether I'm actually killing the vibe. The point is, as the DJ, you end up being responsible for the entire party. Not the guys who put it on, not the bartender, not whose house or space it takes place in, it's you. So if you've never DJed before and start spinning for others, your responsibility for everyone's vibe can catch you off guard.

But it can be a ton of fun. It's a real rush when I've done a perfect beat match, and I hear a cheer or two rise from the floor. I've emptied out whole rooms, but I've filled rooms back up, too. As long as you have a vision in mind of where you want to transport people throughout the evening, you can't really go wrong.

Whew, I've said a mouthful…. Thanks for the interview!

In Summation

Electronic music production, the hardware in conjunction with the software, is a basically unlimited field. There is no limit to the amount you can know. This makes it a great field for people with a thirst for knowledge. But don't get too caught up in the technical aspect of it to the point of neglecting the music. The music and the craft should always always *always* come first.

Chapter 8

Operations: Practice Space and Human Resources

Rock and roll can be created in the sleaziest of sub-basements. It often fructates out of slimmering conditions that only a fungus could love. But there's nothing wrong with at least making sure that your equipment won't be harmed or stolen or rust. And you don't want to get electrocuted or have the cops close you down for noise.

Some of the people who make the greatest rock and roll have personalities that only a mother could love, and then only with great effort. But this needn't be the case—you can find somewhat sane people to work with. After all, you're going to have to live with them; why get stuck with a psychopathic cretin?

A Place to Play and Some Friends to Play With

You need a secure place to play music, where you won't bother other people and they won't bother you. There are several options available.

You also need good people to play with. We will explore both a place to play and people to play with in this chapter.

Lockout or Hourly?

The best-case scenario for a place to practice would be a huge air-conditioned room with a stage and lights and a P.A. system and even chairs for an audience. You would have 24-hour access, you would be the only band using the space, and you could leave your equipment set up and ready to go. There would be recording equipment and microphones set up permanently to record any great ideas you come up with, and there would be a fully stocked kitchen.

Bands that sell millions of records have this. You probably won't.

The other end of this spectrum is the hourly studio. These are available in most large cities. Basically, you bring your gear (or rent theirs) and buy blocks of time, usually in three-hour packages. This can add up, but it's usually reasonably priced, and it certainly does motivate you not to screw off and waste time.

Hourly studios are usually between $30 and $60 for a three-hour block, with a P.A. You'll pay probably 20 bucks more each for a drum kit, guitar amp, and bass amp.

Many bands practice quietly in a member's living room when they are writing new songs, or before they get a drummer, or between gigs, and just rent hourly when they need to play loud.

In between is what my band has: 24-hour lockout in a small, secure room that we share with another band. This is a good option if the other band is respectful of you and your stuff. It's a nightmare if they're not.

You can usually find a place to practice by asking other bands or by looking in the Yellow Pages under "musician services." You can also look in the local entertainment weekly. Every town seems to have one. (LA and New York have about 10.) They will have listings every month for hourly and lockout studios. You can also check the classifieds in these papers for bands looking for a place to share. The actual studio buildings usually have a bulletin board in the lobby or hall. You can get in and look at it or post your own ad looking for a space to share.

You might have to follow another band in. If it's a big place, you won't wait long. People go in and out all day. Just look like you're supposed to be there. Carrying a guitar or drum sticks might help. Or if it's a small place without a lot of foot traffic, wait outside and nicely ask someone going in if you can come in for a second and check the bulletin board. They might say no, as people in these places usually worry about suspicious people (you). In that case, just wait and ask the next person.

If you're sharing with one other band, you'll probably pay about $200 to $350 a month. Lockout studios are generally 400 to 700 bucks per month per room, depending on how big they are, how secure, and whether or not they come with a P.A. system. How dangerous a part of town they are in is also a factor. These places are often in industrial districts or other scary 'hoods where many businesses would be afraid to operate.

The place my band rehearses is called Downtown Rehearsal. It is one of two buildings in Los Angeles owned by the same company. (The company used to own a studio in San Francisco by the same name, but some dot com bought the building for eight million dollars, kicked all the bands out, and promptly went bankrupt. It's still empty.) Each of these buildings in Los Angeles is 100 rooms each, and about three bands use each room. There are several such places owned by different businesses in Los Angeles. Doing the math here gives you a realistic idea of the amount of competition for gigs in Los Angeles. And believe me, most of these bands look at it as competition—people don't move to LA to just play music; they move here to try to get famous.

TIP

Got a stuck window (or door)? Rub a dry bar of soap on the track where the parts are rubbing. Do this before summer if you can. (My editor will probably ask me to delete this, saying it has nothing to do with music, but my editor has probably never been stuck in a practice space with windows that won't open in August in Los Angeles.)

Both buildings owned by this company are in questionable 'hoods, at least as far as a place you want to keep tens of thousands of dollars worth of gear. Both are surrounded by homeless encampments. We *always* take precautions when loading out and in before and after a gig. One person stays with the gear at all points, at all times. And the homeless junkies always offer to help. I politely decline.

Unlike when you rent an apartment, there is no rent control for band spaces, and the landlord can kick you out or raise the rent any time she feels like it. Rent control covers only places where people live, not band practice places.

Our place is actually a pretty good deal, the room is $480 a month, we share it with two other bands who are rarely in there, and our share is $160 a month.

You will usually have to put down some kind of security deposit.

I would recommend changing the locks when you move in if the building manager will let you. Most likely he will if you pay for the locksmith and give him a copy of the keys. I would do this because you have no idea how many previous tenants still have keys. Put in a deadbolt (or two). Also, be wary of other ways people could get in. The only time I ever had a studio ripped off was a place in San Francisco where the thieves went through the wall. All it took was a knife or a box cutter to go through the three layers of plaster board that comprised the walls.

> **TIP**
>
> You usually aren't allowed to live in your studio, but some bands actually sneak around and live in them in these tough economic times. It's tough and you have to find somewhere else to shower. If you do, a YMCA or other gym membership is a good investment.

> **TIP**
>
> A lot of these studios have mirrors on one or more walls, so if you're vain, you can rock out to yourself and work on your sassy dance moves.

You had better be a good judge of character if you're going to share a space with another band. The average rock band has between $5,000 and $20,000 worth of gear, and you'll be handing key copies over to someone else. Obviously, if you can afford it, don't share with another band. But if you have to, here are some tips:

◆ Be respectful. Don't use their stuff. Again, don't use their stuff. Have the cell phone numbers of all people who share the studio posted on the wall, and if you must use something of theirs (for instance, if you're recording and you break a snare drum head and don't have a spare head and need to borrow theirs), call first.

◆ If you *do* use their stuff, for whatever reason, and you break something, you are responsible for replacing it. I don't care if it's a very old amp with tubes that were about to blow. If they blow while you're playing through it, you have to pay. None of this, "I'll only pay half because they were going to blow anyway." You owe it *all*, dude. And if something you used needs repairing, you not only have to pay for it, you need to take it to the repair shop, and pick it up, and bring it back. But never just take something out of the studio without telling the person first. If you find you must, leave a note. And offer to get them a replacement until their stuff is fixed, even if you have to rent it.

◆ If you blow the other guy's amp, 'fess up. Don't lie and pretend the mice did it.

◆ If you do use their amp with permission, write down the settings for all the knobs before you change anything, and return it to their pet settings when you're done.

◆ Does it seem like the other band is using your gear without permission over and over and then denying it? There are ways to bust them. Write down your settings, and see if they change. (Though they could be one step ahead of you, writing down and returning it to your settings when finished.) You can always take the tubes or your fuse with you, but then they might fry it by bypassing the fuse with foil or a wire, or it might be one of those amps that will be damaged by turning it on without the tubes in.

◆ You can spy on them. Start dropping in unexpectedly, or set up a little spy camera, or cheaper yet, a tape recorder. Some Dictaphones have a voice-activated mode, where you can leave them and they will only start recording when someone starts talking. (You'll want to cover the little red light with a piece of duct tape.) I busted someone using my gear this way once. (You can also catch your lover cheating on you and lots of other stuff this way.) Note: Check local laws. Spying on people, even with good reason, might not be legal, moral, or ethical in your jurisdiction. And I would never recommend that you do anything illegal, immoral, or unethical.

◆ Also, get good at recognizing drug habits. If someone in your band or the other band starts to develop one, it might be a good time to change the locks again.

Make Your Own Studio

Another option is to make your own space in your garage or basement. This can be an excellent, cheap, secure solution, but you'll have to soundproof a bit if you have neighbors. I find that the usual egg cartons lining the wall that most cheap recording studios use to deaden the echo won't really keep much of the sound _in_, and your neighbors will hate you. Concrete is good, as are sandbags or poured sand. Layers help too: Sand, then air, then wood, then sand, then concrete will deaden almost any sound, but it's gonna cost a little money and take some time to do it right.

Make sure your building and outlets are grounded, and make the place comfortable. An

FIGURE 8.1 _Ground termination pipe outside my studio. This pipe goes 10 feet into the earth._

old couch is nice. And most bands hang up some posters and art to inspire them. (Most young males hang up pornography, but that's an absolute cliché at this point.) Don't put a TV in your studio; it will kill your creativity.

TIP

A lot of studios are rather damp, especially if they're in basements. Moisture in the air will eventually kill guitars and keyboards and make drums and guitars go out of tune quicker in the meantime.

You can buy a dehumidifier from Sears or a hardware store for under a hundred bucks. It will pull water out of the air and into a square bucket. Make sure you empty the bucket regularly. They're kind of noisy, so turn it off before you record.

Staying Clean

Clean your practice space regularly. A lot of great music has come from filth, but I find that there's nothing wrong and everything right with a clean environment in which to rock. At least make sure there's no food or soda or beer bottles lying around, because this will attract ants and roaches.

Conclusion

Get a place to play, a place where you'll feel comfortable and where your equipment will be safe.

Finding, Keeping, and Firing Musicians

Running a band of any type basically makes you a small business owner. And part of any small business is the Human Resources Department. Because you will be wearing many of the hats in your rock and roll small business, you will be running this department yourself. Here's what it entails.

There are basically three phases of Human Resources that you'll have to perform:

- ◆ Finding musicians
- ◆ Keeping musicians
  and if need be
- ◆ Firing musicians

Finding Musicians

Placing ads and word of mouth are the most common ways to get a band together. I try to shy away from ads because you end up weeding your way through a lot of idiots, and not many great bands started from people placing ads. Most start from word of mouth. But a few did start through the classified section, including Dead Kennedys, so it's worth a try. Dead Kennedy's guitarist East Bay Ray got his "East Bay" nickname from the ad that started the band—he lived in the East Bay (Oakland) and the bass player, Klaus, wrote down what Ray had in his ad next to his phone number, "East Bay. Ray." without the periods.

Writing an Ad

The classic way this is done is something like this:

> (Type of music) band seeks (instrument) player. We sound like (popular current group) meets (popular older group) in a dark alley and they fight. We have rehearsal space, gigs, a coffee machine, groupies, and major label interest.
>
> You: cool hair, pro gear, transpo, ready to commit and rock to the top. No poseurs!

The band is usually lying about the "major label interest" part. It usually actually means "We are interested in being on a major label," not "A major label has expressed interest in us." This is because to have a major label interested in you these days, you basically have to already have a following. Any band with a following probably fills vacancies through word of mouth and never has to deal with placing ads.

I hate the part of the musician-finding process where you are asked, "Who do you sound like?" I find this constricting—very in the box-type thinking—and it ignores the fact that the most original bands are founded by people with very different tastes, not very similar tastes. People with the same tastes tend to get together and sound like whatever's on the radio that week. I usually respond "Pink Floyd and Minor Threat," and if the person is still talking to me, there might be a reason to pursue further discussion.

I used to say, "Who are my influences? How about who I've influenced? People in Soundgarden, Jane's Addiction, Red Hot Chili Peppers, and the Flaming Lips all have my records. I don't know if I've influenced them, but they like my music.[1] And I've recorded with people from Cracker, Smashmouth, Wallflowers, Parliament Funkadelic, Samhain, Dead Kennedys, and the 10,000 Maniacs," I stopped saying this because it sounded too cocky and made people think I was lying, even though I wasn't.

I dunno, I guess what I'm saying is that all of this "Who do you sound like" doesn't ring very true in my heart. And it's often unintentionally misleading—that ad that East Bay Ray placed to start Dead Kennedys said he was looking to start a new wave band, and the DKs were about as far from that as you could imagine.

But still. It does give people a handle to see if you're playing ball in nearby ballparks. But I find a better way is to cut a demo on a four-track or your computer (see Chapter 11, "Hardware Recording," and Chapter 12, "Software Recording") and upload an MP3 (see Chapter 13, "Make and Promote Your Own CDs") and put the URL in your ad. This is very important—the person will instantly be able to hear if you are of a comparable style and level of competency to even bother with. And it doesn't hurt to see a photo of someone you're considering working with. You might send them one of you, too. Hearing each other via MP3s can save you both the time and expense of setting a meeting, driving across town, lifting amps, and more.

Also, if an applicant overuses terms such as "My equipment, my amp, my, my, my," he probably isn't very professional. Pros take it for granted that they have good gear. Amateurs are all about the gear, because that's all they have. People with talent don't need to brag about possessions. They have talent.

Pretty much everyone has access to the Internet these days and can at least download a short song on dial-up and check you out. If they aren't set up to do this or can't figure it out, they are probably not technically advanced or smart enough for you to want to deal with anyway, to be quite blunt.

I also tend to write ads that offer some of my outlook on life and art and commerce—this kind of sorts out people who are coming from a completely different take and will feel like they're wasting their time with me. This does take the risk

---

1. *My editor asked me to clarify how I know this. It's different in each case. Some because I've seen them at our shows and talked to them, some because they told me, and some because someone who knows both of us told me.*

of blowing off someone who might potentially be good, but probably won't. Especially if you live in a major city, there are so many people to choose from that I think it's okay to do this.

Here's the ad I wrote and placed on Craigslist.com (an amazing free resource I highly recommend—for finding anything, not just musicians) that got me part of my current band:

Fuck Getting Signed

Guitar and keyboard wanted. YOU: post-punk spooky cool brilliant shimmery psychedelic hard rocking & competent. We also need two female backup singers.

US: Excellent singer/bassist and drummer. Looking for stellar musicians with no alcohol/drug/spouse problems for amazing band.

We are looking for strikingly original players to play NOW.

WE AIN'T LOOKING TO GET SIGNED. We've both been signed and we didn't like it. Big labels treat musicians poorly. We have no desire to help those fat old pimps make any more money. They have enough. They don't need us and we don't need them. We would like to see them fall. They contribute nothing to the world.

KAZAA KAZAA HEY!

We don't mind being popular and that is quite possible without a big label. And we love to play. LOVE IT!

Many people say, "Music is my life" but don't back it up—It's more looks and swagger than talent and showing up. We are looking for reliable people to learn songs quickly, write their own parts, bring their own sound to this quickly & efficiently and PLAY.

Singer is professional filmmaker/writer who doesn't have a lot of time to write new stuff, so.... We have 25 or more totally complete, kick-ass songs ready to go. They are all better than most of what is on the radio. That is not hyperbole, nor is it bullshit bravado. It's the truth.

I will pay for rehearsal studio. We will split all gig money equally.

We want very good, confident-yet-humble people who can learn a tape, show up on time, be in tune, play well, and remember the stuff. Rehearse three times a week for a month and then start playing gigs. A lot. You should be able to travel regionally a little bit.

I'm not gonna bother with the "We sound like, we listen to...." Yuck.

Don't need it.

We don't have a vision, we have actual music.

IF THIS RINGS TRUE, Download these songs I wrote, sang and played:

"All My References Are Dead": http://www.kittyfeet.com/hatefed.htm

and

"Too Many Babies": http://www.kittyfeet.com/too_many_babies.mp3

and

"The Web": http://www.kittyfeet.com/the_web.MP3

and

"Roach Gurl": http://www.kittyfeet.com/roach_gurl.mp3

(these are four of the songs we'll be doing)

Please learn them and call me.

Michael Dean
213-555-zzzz
Los Angeles

This was quite effective at chasing off the people I didn't want to deal with. I found my two backup singers, Andrea and Traci, with this ad.

But when our guitarist left and I decided to replace him with two guitarists, I needed to be less demanding, so I pared the ad down to this, and I must say I got a lot more responses:

Have Gigs. Need Second Guitar.

"Kittyfeet" is a really good band with songs and gigs. We played one gig. Drew 49 people on a Wednesday night. Played great, and then our excellent guitarist moved out of town.

I've turned down four gigs this week. We need another guitar player. You?

YOU: spooky cool psychedelic hard rocking & competent. Can learn a set in one night from the CD. We're looking for stellar musicians with no alcohol/drug/spouse problems for amazing band.

US: I pay for rehearsal studio (downtown).

Excellent singer/bassist, drummer guitarist and two female backup musicians.

Photos here: http://www.kittyfeet.com/newband.htm

Songs here:
http://www.kittyfeet.com/hatefed.htm
http://www.kittyfeet.com/too_many_babies.mp3
http://www.kittyfeet.com/the_web.MP3
http://www.kittyfeet.com/roach_gurl.mp3

These are four of the songs we'll be doing. If you want to gig NOW, learn these and e-mail me please.

Many people say, "Music is my life" but don't back it up—It's more looks and swagger than talent and showing up. We are looking for reliable people to learn songs quickly, write their own parts, bring their own sound to it quickly & efficiently and PLAY.

Singer is professional filmmaker/writer who doesn't have a lot of time to write new stuff, so.... He has 25 or more totally complete, kick-ass songs ready to go. They are all better than most of what is on the radio. That is not hyperbole, nor is it bullshit bravado. It's the truth.

Michael Dean
Los Angeles

By the way, our excellent guitarist hadn't moved out of town. He was still in town, but he was a flaky bitter drunk (even though he has a really good heart). I saved his face by making up a fib. He reads Craigslist, and people would know who I was talking about.

That was long ago, and no one will know who I was talking about, so I am telling you the truth right now.

I had already found my drummer, Reuben, without an ad. He was an old friend from San Francisco. He hadn't played in years, but, although rusty, he was still a really good drummer. It's like falling off a bicycle.

Once people answer the ad, I usually ask them to play or sing for me over the phone. If they won't, they probably aren't good enough or confident enough to play in a kick-ass rock band. Like Reuben says, "A real lead singer will drop trou any place, any time." While I wasn't actually asking them to take off their trousers, he's right—anyone who isn't willing to sing probably isn't a singer. Same with guitar players.

I am always polite when talking to people—musicians have fragile egos and are often nice people. When it's obvious that they wouldn't work out or be happy in my band, I am kind. I never slam them to the ground, even if it seems they didn't really read the ad and they start telling me how much they want to get signed or whatever.

I had a friend who tried out on guitar in a band with a drummer I used to play with—the guitarist was cool and had a unique style but wasn't as technically good as the drummer. The drummer stopped him after about a minute and said, "You're a fucking fool. Why did you even bother to reply to my ad? It asked for good musicians. You aren't even good enough to call yourself a musician and you are wasting my time." The guitarist was crushed and gave up music for a spell, which is a pity, because he makes some pretty cool stuff on his four-track, stuff I found quite listenable. This drummer should be hanged for that, in my opinion. I'm just glad I ain't playing with people like that anymore. I won't do it, no matter how good they are. It's emotional suicide.

While jamming, here are some things to look for. These indicate that the person might be a good member of a band. They:

- Show up on time (or call if they are going to be late).
- Do what they say they'll do, like if they talked to you Tuesday and said they'd call back Wednesday night, did they? Or did you have to call them?
- Tune up their instrument, know their equipment, and have a good tone.
- Are respectful of you.
- Learned at least the chords and changes to the song(s) you gave them to learn.
- Came up with good parts of their own to bring something cool to complement your changes.
- Play well, or at least at a similar level to you.
- Listen to what you are playing and react to it. That is, they are playing *with* you rather than just playing in the same room with you.
- Have good musical ideas.
- Don't play way louder than you (some of the best guitarists I've played with were people I actually had to ask to turn *up* the first time we played).
- Are enjoyable to be around.

If, after jamming for a bit, it's apparent they aren't the right person for you, you can just say something like, "I don't think we're a good match," and if they have any emotional maturity (probably unlikely; we're talking *musicians* here...) they will be cool with it. Also, you can ask them, "If someone more your style answers my ad, can I give them your number?" Then you are honestly trying to help, and the news that you don't want to be musically married to them will come easier.

Most professional bands do not find people with open casting. Sometimes they pretend to (like Korn holding nationwide open call guitarist auditions), but it's usually a publicity stunt. At that level, it's almost always done by professional referral. Major labels sometimes even have a "Mister Rolodex" guy whose full-time job is putting together bands.

But when you're starting out, word of mouth can be useful, too. Your friends will usually know what you're all about and know people to point you to. Asking at music stores, record stores, or college radio stations can work, too. I find that asking around and telling people that you're looking, in conjunction with an ad, is a good way to fish for players. It has worked for me; I've found people both ways.

Don't be afraid to knock on doors. Literally. I met one of my oldest friends and sometime musicial collaborator, Beau Brashares, when we were teenagers because I heard him playing loud guitar and knocked on his door. His dad let me in. I walked up into his room and didn't introduce myself. I just said, "Play something *really* fast." He did, and we've been friends since.

Once you find someone who is competent and like-minded, set up a session with her. Bring her to your studio if you have one, or get together at one of your houses. When auditioning guitar players, bass players, singers, or keyboardists, it's always a lot better to jam with a drummer keeping a beat. Or a drum machine or computer looping program.

Start out by playing one of your original songs that you uploaded as an MP3—a song they've heard before. If you haven't written any songs yet, you can play a song by someone else, but keep in mind the point is to make it your own, not to sound just like the record. Also try playing unscripted together a little, jamming, improvising, and see how you interact. Sometimes the muse is shy and the magic doesn't show up on the first session. Keep your mind open to the possibility that you can try again later for that.

Remember: *You don't have to commit to the person on the first "date."* You can often use the first time you jam with someone as "round one," winnow out the people you don't want to play with, and then use the resulting short list for your callbacks. I even try to avoid the terms "callback" and "audition." We're all peers here.

Just treat everyone well. Don't act like a Hollywood casting agent where you have all the power and you're doing the lowly applicant a huge favor. You aren't and you ain't. (And if you are ever in a position where you are popular and auditioning unknowns, you have an even bigger responsibility, in my view, to be humble and nice and not an asshole.) You probably aren't going to be paying these people until you've been playing out a while, so you can't treat them like employees. And even paid employees have to be treated with dignity.

Also remember the golden rule of showbiz: *"Be fair to everyone. You meet the same people on the way up that you meet on the way down."*[2]

---

2. *Also remember the golden rule of hiring anyone: Be careful who you employ; you may have to fire them at some point. Or worse yet, live with them.*

Keeping Musicians

Robert Fripp[3] once said that there are three things that keep people in a band, and that two out of these three criteria have to be satisfied for each person to stay in the band:

- The love of the music
- The friendship with the musicians
- The admiration from the audience

I would probably add "The money you make" to that list, and say, "Everyone has to be satisfied by any three out of four."

When you start a band, there will be no money and no audience yet, so you'd better like the people and the music. At least you'd better be able to be in the same room with the people without wanting to kill them. If you can't stand them from the start, keep in mind that it ain't gonna get better with time. It's like an abusive marriage: It will only get worse. Better to end it now rather than later when the people have a lot of time and effort involved in it and will hate you for firing them. (And if there's money involved, they will probably sue you, too.)

You're gonna have to live with the people you pick for a long time (and in very close quarters if you go on tour). So find people you like. Or at least people you don't dislike.

It's hard to get good players who are reliable to be in a band. It's kind of like that old saying, "You can have it fast, cheap, or good. Any two out of the three. Take your pick." It's nearly impossible to find people who will learn songs quickly, do it for free, be cool to hang out with, *and* not be late all the time. People like that stand out, and someone else usually has them in another band already. But there are good people; you just have to find them and then use your people skills to keep them.

It's important for everyone in the band to be assertive with communication and logistics. If someone calls and leaves the message, "I got called for some last-minute

---

3. *Robert Fripp is a genius. He's also a cranky old man and has been one since he was a young man. A long time ago I saw him do a free lunchtime concert in the lobby of one of the World Trade Center towers. There were about 200 people listening raptly and a bunch of others milling past behind them. Remember that this was lunchtime in one of the busiest places of business in the world. Some of the people in the back were chatting and Fripp actually stopped the show to* yell *at them for talking.*

    That's like going into a restaurant in New Orleans and complaining that the fish is burnt.

work tomorrow and I can't afford to turn it down. I'm gonna have to cancel practice," it's frustrating, because then there's several more phone calls that you have to make to pin down a make-up practice. But if they say, "I got called for some last-minute work tomorrow and I can't afford to turn it down. I'm gonna have to cancel practice, but I'm available Wednesday night, Thursday night, or Sunday afternoon, and I have my cell phone with me today," it's a little less stressful for you.

And never forget to compliment people! Regularly and sincerely. There's nothing wrong with being regularly supportive of your fellow musicians if you're being truthful. "I like your new song a lot," "You're singing is getting a lot better," even "It's good to see you" or "I like playing with you." Mark Twain said, "I could live a week on just one kind word." Most musicians have such delicate egos that they can usually only live a few hours on a kind word. Be supportive of each other. Because at first, no one else will be.

Firing Musicians

Iggy Pop said, "I love firing people!" I don't love to fire them, but I am much more attuned now than I used to be at telling when things ain't working. When I was younger, I would often stay in a situation (musical or otherwise) that was bad for me—either the people were creepy, flaky, or just not competent. I feared not having a band and would stay in a bad one rather than leave. I would never do this now.

It's a tough call sometimes. If the music is great, and you're making money and getting adulation from lots of people (i.e. if three out of the four criteria are met), it is easy to stay in what basically amounts to a dysfunctional relationship.

You should fire people in a way that doesn't lead to you having a disgruntled employee on your hands. Especially an employee that you never paid and who probably *spent* money (at least gas money) to work for you.

If you have a problem with people, it usually makes sense to give them a chance to fix whatever they are doing wrong. This has two positive results. First, if you actually have a valid point, maybe they will realize it and correct it, once you respectfully point it out. Though probably not. This leads to the second point: If you give them a warning and they don't correct it, it's more on them and less on you when you finally *do* fire them.

When you do have to 86 someone, it's best done with thought and a little planning and a lot of consideration. This beats just getting pissed at someone and screaming, "Fuck you, get out!" in the middle of a practice. That will create an enemy, and enemies are a big waste of time and energy—energy you should be putting into creating and spreading your music.

When you have to fire someone, you first have to consider whether to do it in person or on the phone. Doing it by e-mail is *really* tacky, though writing it down does help you think out your logic better. One thing you can do is write it out as a letter to get it clear, and then *don't* send it to them. Use this as your notes when you finally fire them in person or on the phone. (Also, anything you put in writing can be used against you if they decide to sue.)

I recently fired someone in my band for being flaky and bitchy. I would have done it in person, but my car was out of commission, and he didn't have a car and was taking a two-hour bus trip each way to rehearsal. I figured, and rightly, that it would piss him off less to be fired over the phone than to make him spend four hours total on the bus just so I could fire him. I explained this to him on the phone, and he actually appreciated it. I also had asked him to be less flaky a few weeks earlier, several times, so he was not surprised and not very mad at me.

This is a best-case scenario. It doesn't always work that well.

We're all heard tales of disgruntled employees returning with guns after being fired and shooting up the place. This is not likely, but does happen to the point where corporations have very strategic plans in place for firing people with dignity. You should be no different and keep in mind that rock musicians tend to have even fewer life skills and coping mechanisms than the average person. This is for two reasons: One is that, as Frank Zappa said, a guy who spends 12 hours a day of his formative years in his room mastering an instrument tends to be deficient in some other area, like hygiene or ability to relate with others. The second reason is that rock and roll tends to attract, by definition, people with low self-esteem and large egos. Look at me…I spent all of my 20s caught up in a façade of "I'm a rebel man; I don't have to play by your rules." This has evolved into a happy crank in his late 30s who rarely leaves his house unless it's to go 3,000 miles away to be paid to lecture somewhere, which happens often. The rebel-rebel "rock and roll lie" is the basis of much of what drives the rock support industry (people who make their living catering to the hopefuls: guitar manufacturers, independent publicists, do-nothing managers who charge money up front, and so forth). I would exclude the book in your hands from that list, because I feel this book actually offers realistic advice on "making it" on a small level rather than simply offering dreams of a probably unattainable huge rock star level of success.

So, basically, when you fire someone, remember that you are probably dealing with someone in his 20s or 30s with the coping skills of a small child. I have heard this called the King Baby model of psychotherapy—picture a toddler on a throne, pooping and screeching and demanding things, and being catered to by his subjects (fans) and Queen (girlfriend/mother). Keep this in the back of your head when dealing with musicians and you'll do fine. Just remember that there is no "later" for toddlers (or musicians), only "now." They all want what they want when they want it. The things that make someone want to jump up on stage and say "Look at me, World!" are usually deficiencies. We all have them. All musicians. Especially lead singers. Especially short lead singers. Trust me. I know.

TIP

Dean's Rule of Singers: "(Usually) the more compelling a singer is on stage, the more personal problems he has off stage."

If you have to fire someone, treat them the way you'd want to be treated. Put aside the passion and keep to the logic. Don't blame them; just state the facts. And since a band is a marriage, you could take a tip from marriage counselors. This applies while trying to work things out instead of firing someone, as well as ending it with them when they don't work out: Talk about how you feel rather than what they did wrong. "It frustrates me when you solo over my singing all the time," rather than, "You don't care about me and don't respect me, and I know it because you play too loud." "When you're constantly late to practice, it makes us feel angry," rather than, "You're an asshole and you're always late."

Another good angle is to talk about doing it for the music rather than taking it personally. And isn't the music what it's all about, anyway? At least in theory? "It would serve the song better if you simplified your drum fills during that chorus," rather than "You suck and you hate me and you're playing too much!"

Ya feel me?

This wording can work in a firing, too. "We feel that your incessant drinking and aggressive behavior is no longer serving the band. We got into this for fun, and it's not fun. Maybe you'd be happier in another band." Some firings, as well as some "talking-tos" can feel like interventions. Hell, sometimes they *are* interventions.

No matter how loving and respectful your firing is, you can end up with an enemy. Some folks are just wired that way. They want everything handed to them and rage at anyone who doesn't do their bidding. And playing in a rock band, even at the smallest local level, is often predicated on dreams of "Dude, we're gonna be *huge!*" And when you take that away from King Baby, he gets pissed.

Basically my life experience for dealing with angry lunatics is to do the Judo Jedi thing and step out of their way. Do all the footwork you have to in order to clean up your end of the deal with this person, and then go away. Get their equipment back to them (even if you have to go out of your way to do it), get the practice room key back from them (or change the locks if you have to), and then if they are treating you poorly, stop responding. Don't return their calls, send their e-mail directly into the trash, and so forth. This can be hard and is only for extreme cases, but if someone is genuinely treating you in a creepy manner, step out of their way. This advice also works later when you get popular and have to deal with stalkers.

People like this are angry barnacles who always need to attach themselves to someone. If you stay slick and they can't cling, they'll go find someone else to torment. Almost every time.

And if the person you fired doesn't stop bugging you, keep in mind that old saying, "You're nobody in Hollywood 'til somebody wants you dead." That's kind of overstating it, but if you put yourself out there, more people can see you. And a certain percentage (small if you're an optimist, large if you're a crank like me) of the world are just jerks.

In closing, remember that musicians are your most important resource (after great songs). Without them, you don't have a band and won't get heard as easily.

Treat people the way you'd like to be treated. Don't jump into a musical commitment too early. Have realistic expectations, work hard, and you'll be in a better position than 90 percent of the people out there playing music today.

Outro

Get a good secure place to jam, and get good people you feel secure jamming with. Don't skimp on either, especially the people. You're gonna have to live with these decisions for a while. Once you've got that, we're ready to go on to the *real* core of any band: singing and playing.

Chapter 9

Singing and Playing

Now that you've got your gear, your space, and some songs, what do you do? It may seem like second nature and common sense. In case it's not, we'll break it down here.

- ◆ Tuning
- ◆ Volume
- ◆ Listening
- ◆ Learning
- ◆ Life

I'm not going to cover much on the basic specifics of playing each instrument: "Here's a G chord on the guitar. Now here's the same on a piano." O.K., I will, but only that much. There's a billion books everywhere (any music or record store) on that. It's even on the Internet; just search "guitar tab," along with bands you like, and you'll get it all instantly.

I'm going to cover the general stuff, as well as some stuff that should be obvious but isn't, that you probably won't find anywhere else. Why give a man some drugs when you can teach him to make his own drugs?

I learned to play guitar from listening. Sure I took some lessons (six, to be exact), and I did a little time in church choir singing the praises of their God, (until I got kicked out for smoking), but I'm pretty much self-taught. You can be, too: Once you can tune your instrument, you just play along with records and start writing your own songs and the instrument teaches *you*.

After I took those six guitar lessons, I studied on my own incessantly. That's more or less how I do everything.

I ask lots of questions, too. Never be afraid to look stupid. It's more stupid *not* to ask questions.

Figure 9.1 demonstrates how to hold a guitar pick.

Here's a bunch of very basic chords on guitar and piano. This is about all I learned in my first six lessons, and then I let the guitar and piano teach *me* the rest.

On some of the piano chords I tucked the fingers I'm not using out of the way; this is only so you can see where the other fingers are going. In reality, you would want to just let them hang naturally above the keys, not tuck them under.

Figure 9.1 *How to hold a guitar pick.*

These are not nearly *all* the chords there are, and these are the most basic *voicings* of them. (Voicings are different fingerings and notes to play different flavors of basically the same chord.) But seriously, tune up, try these, and run with it.

Guitar Chords

So...I included each image with both a photograph and a little diagram. I made the diagrams myself in Photoshop, and I am not a designer, so they don't look perfect. But I think they will help you. And I had a lot of fun making them.

With most of these chords, you would strum or pick all six of the strings, with the following exceptions: For the D, A, C and A minor chords you would only strum the thinnest five strings, skipping the fat E string. There are, of course, exceptions you could invent, but that's the basic rule to know and then break.

The word "headstock" just means that that is where the headstock of the guitar is, so you can see which direction is what.

The numbers in the circles are the fingers you use on your left hand (or right hand if you're left handed). Finger one is the index finger. Finger two is the middle finger. Finger three is the ring finger. Finger four is the pinkie.

The letters at the bottom (E, A, D, G, B, E) are the names of the strings.

Enjoy!

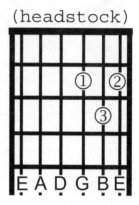

Figure 9.2 *D chord on the guitar.*

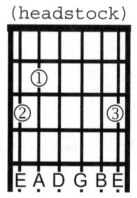

Figure 9.3 *G chord on the guitar.*

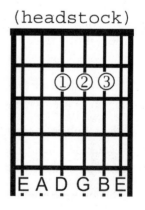

Figure 9.4 *A chord on the guitar.*

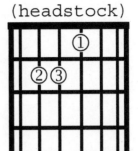

Figure 9.5 *E chord on the guitar.*

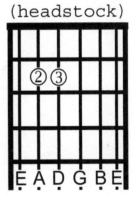

Figure 9.6 *E minor chord on the guitar.*

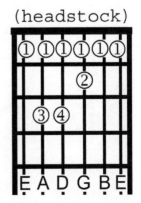

Figure 9.7 *F barred chord on the guitar.*

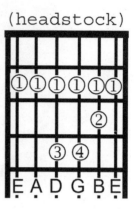

Figure 9.8 *B minor barred chord on the guitar.*

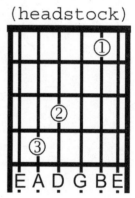

Figure 9.9 *C chord on the guitar.*

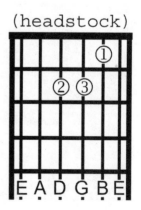

Figure 9.10 *A minor chord on the guitar.*

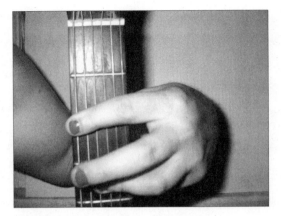 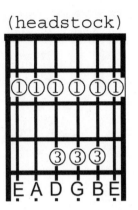

Figure 9.11 *B barred chord on the guitar.*

Keyboard Chords

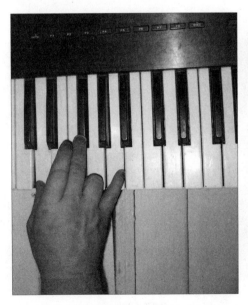

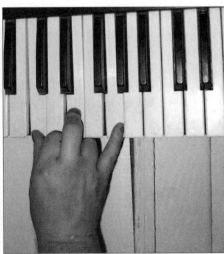

Figure 9.13 *C chord on the piano.*

Figure 9.12 *D chord on the piano.*

Figure 9.14 *E chord on the piano.*

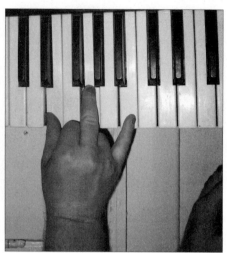

Figure 9.15 *E minor chord on the piano.*

Figure 9.16 *G chord on the piano.*

Figure 9.17 *C minor chord on the piano.*

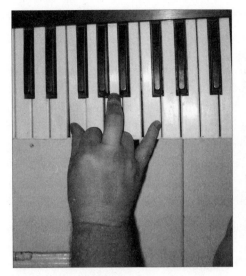

Figure 9.18 *F chord on the piano.*

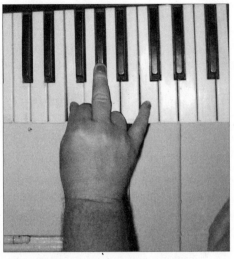

Figure 9.19 *F minor chord on the piano.*

Figure 9.20 *D sharp chord on the piano.*

Let's Get It ON!

Singing and playing are easy. It may not seem like it when you first start out, but it's a natural progression, and if you work at it even a couple of hours a day, you'll grow in your abilities exponentially, at least at first. I started playing guitar when I was 14. By 17, I was amazing. I still play guitar, 22 years later, about as well as I did when I was 17. But it serves me well enough, and I never set out to be a virtuoso anyway. The logarithmic nature of the swift learning curve most people experience with playing and singing is because the more you know, the more you can learn and understand and comprehend more quickly. It's that thing of "standing on the shoulders of giants," but with yourself.

I've heard it said that "If you can talk you can sing," and it's kind of true. Some people are more natural at it than others, but most people can carry a simple melody without a lot of training. There are very few truly tone-deaf humans. If you can sing the four notes to "Mary Had a Little Lamb" and hit them pretty close to correct, you can learn to sing in a band. And the same is true with playing an instrument: Some people are quicker studies than others, but pretty much anyone as smart as a chimp can learn to play three chords, and three chords is the basis of a lot of rock music. The rest is style and what you *do* with those three chords.

My editor Sandy told me, "Woody Guthrie has been quoted as saying that he got by mostly on two chords. He went on to say that every once in a while he'd throw in another one if he wanted to impress some girl."

I did not find it came as naturally to me as it has to others, but I've learned enough on my own to put out a dozen records and tour the world and make a dozen people get my band name tattooed on their bodies.

I always liked to sing, but it took me a long time to get good. In grade school, someone saw me reading Pete Seeger's biography, *How Can I Keep From Singing?* and said, "Good, Michael, you found a book to keep you from singing."

I played guitar in a rock band in high school and tried to sing backup. I wasn't a very good backup singer. Everyone in the band said, "You're a good guitar player. Why don't you just stick to that?" I ignored them and sang on my own, in the shower, in the basement, and in the woods for a decade until I got really good. From then on, whenever I started a band, I was the lead singer, and people loved it.

> **TIP**
>
> Backup singers have to be technically better than lead singers. But there's also something to be said, especially in punk, of everyone in the group, regardless of ability, shouting together on some of the choruses. It's very egalitarian. You sure can do a lot with four chords and four guys (or gals) if you work at it.

Mikes

A microphone (also called "mike," sometimes spelled "mic") can be used handheld or on a mike stand. A mike stand usually has a clip at the top. Mike stands can be adjusted for height and angle by loosening the locking rings, moving the shaft, and tightening the locking rings.

Omnidirectional mikes pick up equally from all sides and are more suited to recording a room full of people talking or recording a whole band rather than isolating individual instruments. They are not good for live sound reinforcement because they tend to feedback more.

There are straight stands and boom stands. I prefer straight stands for singing for some reason, even when playing an instrument, although a boom stand would put everything more out of the way of my hands.

Windscreens are used to reduce the noise of wind when microphones are used outdoors and also to reduce the sound of plosives (sounds of the letters B, D, P) and sibilants (the S sound), which can cause microphones to distort momentarily. Windscreens are also great to help keep you from getting shocked while playing a guitar and singing at the same time.

I bring one in my guitar case and put it on the mike if I get shocked and switching the polarity doesn't fix it, and the club does not provide windscreens. You might want to bring two because as your set progresses and some spit from your mouth makes the windscreen conductive, you will start getting shocked again and may want to change to a fresh one between songs.

A windscreen will also help mask the stink of beer and cigarettes from hundreds of other idiots using the club's mike. You also might want to bring your own mike to prevent this, but make sure yours is clearly marked with your name somehow, and tell the soundman when you are doing soundcheck, so he doesn't think you're stealing one of his at the end of the night. Also, don't forget to take it in the excitement of being drunk on the meager applause!

NOTE

Switching the polarity means switching the polarity switch on the back of your amp or on the P.A. system. This can help keep you from being shocked when you sing and can also minimize audible hum from the speakers. AC current has no positive and negative side. (Actually, it does, but it changes 60 times a second—hence, 60 cycle, a.k.a. 60 Hz, current.) But flipping this switch basically reverses the relationship to the ground. The ground is the third plug on a three-prong plug—the one that looks different from the other two.

Figure 9.21 *Three-prong adapter.*

Figure 9.22 *Another view of a three-prong adapter.*

TIP

Never defeat the ground plug on a three-prong plug on musical equipment by using an adapter to bypass the ground and plug it into a two-prong outlet. You shouldn't even play amplified music in a room without proper grounding. To do so is *asking* for shocks.

Don't switch the ground switch on the guitar *and* the P.A. That's usually the same as not switching it at all.

Electrocution is a possibility, but if the club is properly grounded, you check the polarity, and don't stand in a puddle, you're probably safe. This, coupled with the freedom of mobility, is one reason guitarists sometimes use wireless setups. They make you less susceptible to getting fried.

I have gotten a few shocks in my day but nothing serious. I know thousands of musicians and have seen thousands of shows, and I only know of one who died from a shock, and I wasn't there. Eric Rad, of a San Francisco band called Housecoat Project, was electrocuted while onstage at The Mab (Mabuhay Gardens) playing with his solo project. People thought it was part of the act at first. My friend Jay Crawford, who later played with me in Bomb, was there and told me about it. The Mab was rumored to have had faulty wiring; that is, the stage outlets were perhaps not properly grounded.

You should always have a rehearsal studio that is grounded. Get a ground checker at Radio Shack and check every outlet. If the grounding is bad, look for another studio. Or if you're stuck with it, and can, get an electrician to properly ground it for you.

Also, take the ground checker on the road with you and check clubs. If it's bad, be extra careful, make sure you use windscreens, and make sure there's no water or beer on the stage.

When you are playing a guitar and are about to sing, approach the mike with care. I usually first touch my hand to the mike quickly at sound check, while holding my guitar strings on my plugged-in and turned-on guitar with the other hand. The hand will hurt a lot less than the lips if shocked. If the hand produces no shock, I try my cheek or chin, then my lips. I often take this further by licking the microphone, but I don't recommend it. It's sort of grandstanding and bonding, but you could get a serious shock if the polarity switches for some reason.

Be wary of the possibility that they will have the ground right for you at sound check, then check another band after you and switch it again. Do a quick check with your hand before you start your set.

You'll get a feel for all this mike checking after you do it a bit. Approach electricity with respect but not with fear. It's your friend.

The Process

Basically, get an instrument, learn to tune it, and play along with records you like. Don't plan on copying your heroes for long, but play along enough to really get a feel for what makes music work. It will come surprisingly fast. Learn some simple songs, and learn to play them, at first slowly on your own, and then faster until you can play them as fast as they are written. Concentrate on making all the changes, in time and on the beat at a slower speed, and then work on gradually increasing the speed while maintaining the accuracy. A metronome or drum machine is good for this. Start it at a slower speed and master the changes of the whole song all the way through, and slowly speed up the tempo while maintaining accuracy.

> **TIP**
>
> This is also a good place to point out that a difference of only two or three BPM (beats per minute) in tempo can vastly change the mood of a song. Look at this and try to find the correct tempo where each of your new songs *wants* to be.

When playing along with records, you may find that you'll have to retune a little bit. Most records are made with the guitar tuned to the standard tuning, but sometimes not. Or sometimes your tape drive or turntable will not be exactly at the correct speed due to old worn-out parts. It will usually be correct with a CD because they're digital. In digital realms, you usually get either perfect sound or no sound. Analog units, such as tape recorders and turntables, can give good sound at incorrect speed, and therefore incorrect pitch. You may have to tune your guitar or bass or keyboard a little sharp or flat to play along.

Many people who make music never learn to play complete songs. Go into any music store and you'll hear countless kids playing a riff from a song, but never the whole song. I would encourage you to learn to play complete songs. Practice this early on.

After you've learned to play some songs, try to write one of your own. It needn't be elaborate; you might just start with a good verse and a good chorus. Just make it strong, and make it *you*. Don't try too hard to imitate others. You have your own voice in you; just let it out.

Some people work in spurts, when the mood strikes. Others set aside a time every day to wait and work. They say, "If the muse doesn't show up, at least *I* was there." I'm in the former category.

When you first start writing, your songs probably *will* sound a lot like the music you listen to. But with time, you'll find your own voice and synthesize an original sound out of your influences.

Play with other people early on. This is very important. I've met a lot of hotshot guitar players who sound great in the bedroom but can't play well with others. To me, a big part of musicianship is the ability to play with people. This involves honing your listening ability and respect. Listening and respect are very connected. Some people don't listen to anyone but themselves and don't interact with anyone when they play. This is piggy.

It might even help to turn down a bit so you can hear everyone else, even if you don't feel like it. (Some of the best guitarists I've ever played with had to be told to turn *up*.) You have to be able to not be the "star" a lot of the time, even if you *are* the star. Basically, my feeling is that the *songs* are the star, and even if you are the singer, you should *serve the song*, even if that involves taking a pay cut in the ego department. Let the *song* shine, and you'll get to go along for the ride. And be much cooler, and about 27.898 percent happier.

Mainly, you just have to play. Get in your practice room with your people and play. Learning to play music is a long-term, lifetime commitment. You'll get a lot of it right away and learn more and more as you go on.

Mainly, just ask questions, listen, and remain open. As soon as you think you've got it all, you don't. As soon as you stop being able to learn, you become old, regardless of your age.

Cover Songs

When most bands start out, they usually start doing a lot of songs by other people. I used to go see the 10,000 Maniacs (the top ten band Natalie Merchant used to sing in before she went solo) play in bars before they got famous. We went to the same college in Jamestown, New York, and there wasn't a lot else to do in that town so I saw them about twice a month for about two years. They were basically a Clash cover band at first. But they even did that with their own style and quickly added more and more originals to their set. Back then (especially in small towns) bands usually started out that way, doing a lot of covers and bringing in their own songs gradually. I *hate* the idea of being a human jukebox and would advise against it. The greatest contribution punk rock gave to music, in my mind, was to make it cool to write your own songs. But nowadays, you even have punk cover bands! Yuck!

If you're going to do someone else's song, *make it your own*. That's the way to keep from being a cover band. A big help with this is to *not cover within the genre*. If you're a punk band, do a Johnny Cash song, but make it sound like *you*. If you're a reggae band, don't do a Peter Tosh cover; do a hip hop or jazz number and make it your style of reggae. Ya dig? *Claim it*. Make it *your* song.

That's not copying, that's *collaborating* with the songwriter.

Notation

I don't read music. Well, I do, but about as well as a five-year-old American child reads English. I have a few other ways to notate stuff. I use the standard bonehead guitar system at the beginning of this chapter, either chord diagrams or tablature. I also will just scribble chords above my lyrics, with the chord written over the lyric where the chord changes. In this system, capital letters are the chord, and a small m after means it's minor; a 7 means it's a 7th chord.

Example:

Am, C, Am, G7 means the chords are:

A minor, C major, A minor, G 7th.

I invented a system for notating harmony. Sarah, my backup singer, and I go through each song in my room with an acoustic guitar and figure out which lines and words should be sung alone, which should be unison, and which should be harmony. We do this several times, getting better and better printing out successive versions, singing them, making changes in the computer file, and printing it out again. It's fine tuned each time.

Be sure to recycle your used pages. Or save the old ones and sell 'em on eBay when you get a following.

"ROACH GuRL"

Here's an example. This song is on the CD twice. Once me playing it with a band (roach_gurl.mp3) and once rerecorded with me with Sarah Amstutz singing background (Roach_Gurl_with_Sarah.mp3).

(Engineer and Fruity Loop drums by Mike De Luna)

(Bass, two tracks of acoustic guitar, two tracks of lead vocals, assistant engineer: Michael Dean)

Me and Sarah just sat in my front yard one day and worked out the harmonies. Took about an hour. We wrote them down so we wouldn't forget them or change them. Then practiced a lot.

We use underlines to indicate unison and *italics* to indicate harmony.

No formatting means just I sing.

ROACH GuRL

Every single cockroach in downtown San Francisco
knows you've earned the right to be alive
But no one feels sorry for a twenty-year-old virgin
and I think you'd steal the trophy from a child
And I know you'd take the cane
from a blinded begging lame
and use it for the *kindling on my pyre*
There is a house in New Orleans;
it's burning nightly in my dreams
(*ooh ooh ooh*) You know I shed my soul in your backyard
Obey the voices in your head, dance to static in his bed
Our love died like Dresden on St. Valentines eve

Chorus

I don't want what you've got anymore
You looked so good walking out my door (out my door)
I don't want what you've got any*more*
You shed a lot of *sadness on my floor*

I wish I'd never tasted for then I'd never want
I feel the salt beneath my skin and bones
(*ooooooh*) I'd rather crawl the walls alone than
(*ooooooh*) sit upon your humble throne
I've minions of my own to answer to
I've tasted of the poison wine,
you're tattooed upon my spine
(*ooh ooh ooh*) Sometimes you charge admissions to my dreams
Hang out in another bar, cut yourself another scar
go confuse some other man and fuck the members of my band

Chorus

<u>I don't want what you've got anymore</u>
<u>You looked so good walking out my door (out my door)</u>
<u>I don't want what</u> *you've got anymore*
You bled a lot of sadness on my floor

You bled on my floor
You bled on my floor
You bled on my floor
You bled on my floor

Miscellaneous Stuff

If you look around any practice space, there's tons of stuff and toys and thingies that don't really fit into nice neat categories. So I made this category for them.

Drum Sticks

Learn to grab a new stick mid-song when you drop one. Keep them within reach for when you break them. You can duct tape a map tube (that has a bottom) or a potato chip can to the side of your bass drum to hold them.

TIP

Videotape and audio tape your shows to help you improve. Watch and listen carefully later to see what works. But don't watch them the night of the show. It will kill your buzz from playing, and also the next day you'll be more clear about getting something from it.

Earplugs

Have 'em and wear 'em. At least through the crappy opening band. Save your ears for *your* music.

Taking Care of Your Voice

Don't smoke if you want to sing. If you do smoke, quit. I did, and my voice is better for it. Of course, you're gonna do what you're gonna do. But I'm in this life stuff for the long run.

Figure 9.23 *A pack of earplugs.*

Do vocal warm-ups before your set. This will help your voice not give out, especially on tour where you are singing every night.

Just going up and down the scale is good. I put a few other exercises on the CD (vocalWarmUps.mp3).

Drinking warm tea with a little lemon before a set will help, too. But shy away from drinking something really cold right after you drink something hot. This is bad for your voice.

Sing from deep in your lungs, not from your throat. This will help keep you from developing nodes on your vocal cords.

Calluses

You'll get them from playing guitar. Permanently. On the tips of your fingers on your left hand (if you're right handed). You want them. Doing dishes will get rid of them. So on tour, get the singer to do dishes when you stay at someone's house. My sister, Christiann, once said, "You can stay anywhere in the world as long as you like, rent free, as long as you can do dishes without being asked and converse intelligently in the native tongue."

Advanced Guitar Stuff

Slide

Playing slide is pretty cool. A slide is a round piece of metal or glass you put over a finger on your left hand and slide up and down the neck to produce notes. You don't press down all the way to the neck, just touch the strings a little. And use the fingers behind it on the neck to lightly mute the strings to keep them from ringing out too much. Slide sounds great with a little delay and distortion. Check out David Immergluck's slide playing on the CD on the chorus of "My God Is a Woman" by my band, Slish. And I played slide on "Supergoose," the main guitar riff from 0:13 to 0:30.

Capo

A capo is a little clamp that can go anywhere on the guitar neck to change the key and enable you to play the same chords in different positions without having to rethink or refinger them. These are especially good for accompanying a singer when you want to keep the sound of open (as opposed to barred) chords but without the capo the key is too low or high for that singer. Jeff Buckley used one on his cover of "Hallelujah."

Figure 9.24 *Slide and capo.*

More

See the little movie on the CD-ROM for how to tune a guitar and how to use a P.A.

Everyone in the band should know how to use the P.A. system. Not just the singer. That's rock and roll 101.

Style

Should get its own section but doesn't because there really isn't that much to say. You've either got it or you don't.

HAVE STYLE	AIN'T GOT STYLE
Marilyn Manson	Hootie and the Blowfish
Led Zeppelin	Creed
Iggy Pop	Good Charlotte
Ice-T	P-Diddy
White Stripes	Barenaked Ladies
Public Enemy	Sugar Ray

If you don't have it, don't imitate the style of others; just be yourself and let the music push you along. Don't copy the latest look. That's a losing proposition, if for no other reason than that by the time someone notices you, the Industry will be on to the *next* big thing. I promise you this is true. A lot of dudes in "new metal" bands were in grunge bands 10 years ago and bad hair metal bands a few years before that. And switched style of music *and* dress to match.

They say that in an expensive restaurant, you aren't buying the steak, you are buying the sizzle. Style is the sizzle that is much of what makes a rock and roll band great.

This is an excerpt from my novel, *Starving in the Company of Beautiful Women:*

> The world is fond of the image of the starving artist. People love the archetype of the struggling, brilliant young man or woman, garrisoned away in a garret, slowly going insane while producing a dazzling body of work, and then dying or being consigned to the madhouse or skid row.
>
> The rock fan who works in a gas station cannot afford to trash hotel rooms and snort coke off of a supermodel's breasts, so he pays Mötley

Crüe or Too-Live Crew to do it for him. The yuppie consultant cannot leave his job to pursue madness, so he finances madness in another by purchasing a powerful painting.

We pay our artists to live these lives that we daren't live. When you buy a great rock record, you are acquiring more than music; you are procuring a lifestyle.

This sums it up pretty well. The thing you have to make sure of is that the steak (the music) has to come first, before the sizzle of the style. Because without great, original, groundbreaking music, you're just playing dress up. Like Civil War Recreationists (officially called "Reenactors," but I like " Recreationists" better).

Rock and roll ain't rocket science. All you have to do to be good is be able to play three chords in the same order each time and show up at the same place at the same time a couple times a week. And most people can't even do that! They're too busy playing dress-up in front of a mirror to fucking rock.

TIP

Keep in mind: Many brash "outrageous" rockers, at all levels, are often just scared little kids at heart, overcompensating for a small self-esteem by having a huge ego.

And keep in mind the *Dean Rule of Rock:*

Confident is cool.

Cocky ain't.

And keep in mind the *Corollary to the Dean Rule of Rock:*

The number of tattoos is inversely proportionate to the amount of self-esteem.

Do Your Own Thing

My band Bomb was pretty strikingly original. But because we had a punk energy, we got booked with a lot of punk bands. Usually their audiences loved us. Sometimes there would be a heckler. I recall one 15-year-old who yelled "Hippie!" at me after every song. I finally addressed him over the mike: "When you were four, I was slam dancing to Minor Threat and I was *still* jumping on a dying band-wagon!"

And this was 12 years ago. So you can see how dumb I think it is to start a straight up generic punk band (or pop punk or whatever they're foisting off on the radio this week) in this day and age.

Summation

This is one of the most important parts of being in a band. Your playing and singing are *it*. Well, your playing and singing and the songwriting and the people are *it*. This is way more important than what brand of guitar you use or any of that crap. And anyone who spends more time talking about that crap than the real stuff probably ain't really a musician, at least not in the $30 Way.

Chapter 10

Finding, Playing, and Putting On Gigs

Playing shows is what being in a band is about. Here's how to get out into the clubs, book shows, play shows, and what to expect.

Want to call your own shots and bypass the hassles of begging to play in bars? Want to play to all ages in your shows? Want to be able to choose your opening band? Want to keep *all* the money and not just exist to sell booze for someone else? Here's how to find a space to book your own shows and how to promote them and run them smoothly without wanting to give up after the first try. Logistics and legalities. Insurance. Flyers.

Booking Shows

When you are booking a show, you are fundamentally selling *yourself*. You have to somehow convince the booker (sometimes literally called the "talent buyer") that they should pick you out of the hundreds of bands that approach them each week wanting to play in their venue.

This can feel like begging, but just remember, you're asking on behalf of the art, not for yourself. That makes it easier. It's easier to fight for the art, I've found.

Basically, there are two kinds of bookers, and they have slightly different criteria for what makes them want to book a band. There are professional bookers who work for a club or hall and want to get groups who will draw a crowd, make people dance, and ultimately sell drinks. It's all about the drinks for them. That's what bars are in the business of doing. They do not (usually) exist to promote art, enrich people's lives, or change the world. They exist to sell large quantities of a legal depressant to affluent young people with a lot of disposable income. And when those people are dancing, they drink more.

The other kind of booker is someone who just loves music and likes to promote art. They are usually called promoters rather than bookers. Some people who are called promoters are only into money, not art. Some are even evil. But they are the minority. Promoters are usually independent and put on shows in different bars and in venues that do not serve alcohol. They book bands based on whether they like the band, and sometimes on whether they think the band has an integrity that they respect. They will be more likely than a bar to book someone with cool music but no draw. If they like you, they can form a long relationship and help you build your career. (And don't forget them later if you get bigger!)

Figure 10.1 *Pumped crowd at an Insecto show in Las Vegas.* All Insecto pix courtesy The Insecto News Group, Inc.

Figure 10.2 *Another shot of the pumped crowd at an Insecto show in Las Vegas.*

NOTE

Sometimes both bar bookers and independent bar promoters, male and female, will also try to get dates with people in bands. I'll just mention that and you can do with it what you want. I know some band members who will flirt with bookers to get a show and will have a sexy promo photo, but I don't know anyone who will date a booker for a show.

Contacts

You probably know the names of the clubs in your town that book your type of music. You probably hang out at them. You can either call them during the day and politely ask "Who do I talk to about booking my band?" or ask other bands for a list of their contacts.

After you have your list of clubs, start booking. Call all of them. You might have the bar number, or you might have the booking number. Or, you might be calling some kid who books shows and get his parents. Just say you're trying to get the booker, find out when he'll be in, and what his name is.

The booker will probably say "Send a CD and a press kit," unless they've heard of your band. Don't brag, lie, or berate them. Don't act like you're doing them a favor. You're not. They are doing you a favor. And keep in mind that they talk to bands all day every day, and all of those bands think they're the best band in the history of time. And they act like it. Cut the booker a break, be polite, and do what he tells you.

I find that Excel is a great program for making a database of gigs. (Any spreadsheet program will work; I just use the one that I happened to get, um, free.) You can have separate information in different columns, add rows and columns as needed, and easily extract data from one or more columns as needed to prepare e-mail lists, snail mailing labels, and so forth.

Highlight by holding down the mouse and scrolling down, then copy (Ctrl + C on a PC; Apple Key and C on a Mac) and paste into the other program (Ctrl + V on a PC; Apple Key + V on a Mac).

I usually start by listing the dates I plan to be on tour on the far left column and fill in from there. Once a booking is secure (confirmed—I usually ask, "So, is that

Figure 10.3 *Excel booking sheet.*

	Bold means CONFIRMED bold italic means	venue	contact person	e-mail	cover	split	I play?	PA?	guitar?	projector?
1	Bold means CONFIRMED bold italic means	venue	contact person	e-mail	cover	split	I play?	PA?	guitar?	projector?
2	*Thursday, Tilburg, Holland Oct 2 (south, by*	.013	Japi		1.8 euros	100 euros	x			yes
3	paris	L'universite americain	John Rosania							
4	Saturday oct 4 Bern - switzerland	cinelibre (collective)								
5	*Sunday October 5 , Linz Austria*	Kapu Club	anatol							
6	italy venice (or milan)		sticker guy pete's							
7	switz--bern									
8										
9	thrus oct 9					200 +50% after Break El Guapo				
10	*Fri Oct 10 Nuernberg*	K4	tobi		5 Euros		sure			
11	sat oct 11 Regensburg	Juz Weingasse	sven kellner			all minus expenses.			x	
12	Sunday oct 12 munich	Kafe Kult	tibor							
13	**Monday, Oct 13 Freiburg**	KTS, Basler Str. 103	Steffen			the entrance money, but 150	yes	maybe	yes	
14	tue 14 Strasburg -- north-east france		Francois Girard							
15	wed Oct 15 Trier	Lucky's Luke								
16	*thurs oct 16 Darmstadt*	Oetinger Villa	markus			100 euro guarantee + %			checking	
17	*Friday oct 17 frankfurt*	bauwagenplatz	stephen		5 Euros					
18	*sat oct 18 (near) bielefeld*	jzo	rouven		4 euros	75% from the door-food-sleep				
19	**SUN 19 Braunschweig** (north by hannover)		stephan maeusel		5	200 € plus percentage				yes. From unive
20	Göttingen (near Braunschweig) (sent e-mail onl	Göttingen	JuZi							
21										
22										
23	*Sat 23 berlin*		mark							
24	**Friday24 hamburg**	lichtmess kino	tobi		4 or 5 eur	I get half	?			
25										
26	*Sunday 26 Magdeburg. matinee*	Cafete	Lars-Olle Richter			100 % after expenses	x	x	x	
27	*Monday 27th, Leipzig (he's on the road t*	Zoro	roberto the knife			100 % of door				
28	poland?	emancypunx	emancy punks							
29										

Sheet1 / Sheet2 / Sheet3 /

Figure 10.4 *Highlighting a row in Excel.*

	Bold means CONFIRMED bold italic means	venue	contact person	cover	split	I play?	PA?	guitar?	proje
1	Bold means CONFIRMED bold italic means	venue	contact person	cover	split	I play?	PA?	guitar?	proje
2	*Thursday, Tilburg, Holland Oct 2 (south, by*	.013	Japi	1.8 euros	100 euros	x			yes
3	paris	L'universite americaine de Paris	John Rosania						
4	Saturday oct 4 Bern - switzerland	cinelibre (collective)							
5	*Sunday October 5 , Linz Austria*	Kapu Club	anatol						
6	italy venice (or milan)		sticker guy pete's place						
7	switz--bern								
8									
9	thrus oct 9				200 +50% after Break El Guapo				
10	*Fri Oct 10 Nuernberg*	K4	tobi	5 Euros		sure			
11	sat oct 11 Regensburg	Juz Weingasse	sven kellner		all minus expenses.			x	
12	Sunday oct 12 munich	Kafe Kult	tibor						
13	**Monday, Oct 13 Freiburg**	KTS, Basler Str. 103	Steffen		the entrance money, but 150	yes	maybe	yes	
14	tue 14 Strasburg -- north-east france		Francois Girard						
15	wed Oct 15 Trier	Lucky's Luke							
16	*thurs oct 16 Darmstadt*	Oetinger Villa	markus		100 euro guarantee + %				ched
17	*Friday oct 17 frankfurt*	bauwagenplatz	stephen	5 Euros					
18	*sat oct 18 (near) bielefeld*	jzo	rouven	4 euros	75% from the door-food-sleep				
19	**SUN 19 Braunschweig** (north by hannover)		stephan maeusel	5	200 € plus percentage				yes.
20	Göttingen (near Braunschweig) (sent e-mail onl	Göttingen	JuZi						
21									
22									
23	*Sat 23 berlin*		mark						
24	**Friday24 hamburg**	lichtmess kino	tobi	4 or 5 eur	I get half	?			
25									
26	*Sunday 26 Magdeburg. matinee*	Cafete	Lars-Olle Richter		100 % after expenses	x	x	x	
27	*Monday 27th, Leipzig (he's on the road t*	Zoro	roberto the knife		100 % of door				
28	poland?	emancypunx@poczta.onet.pl	emancy punks						
29									

confirmed now?" to avoid confusion), I bold that entry, so I can see how my progress is going and know where to concentrate my efforts. I also ask them what time the load in, sound check, and our set are. Ask how long a set you should play (very few clubs will ask you to play more than two sets, unless you're the only band). Ask how many guests you get and how many drink tickets you get.

NOTE

You need to learn to multitask, going effortlessly between interfacing with humans and operating on your computer. This is one of my techniques for surviving as an artist in the new economy.

You can make mailing labels in Word. Go to Tools/Envelopes and Labels.

You can set the label number (on the label box somewhere) from Options.

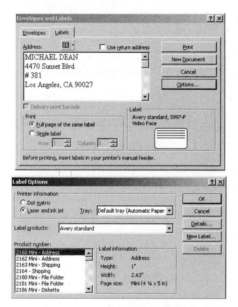

Figure 10.5 *Creating mailing labels in Word.*

You can also set up mail merges in Word to export from other programs, but this is outside the scope of this book. Open the Word Help menu and search for Mail Merge. Or check out *Microsoft Office Word 2003 Fast & Easy* from Premier Press (ISBN 1-59200-080-0).

You should back up all this info regularly. Keep the backup at a band member's house. It also won't hurt to have paper copies of it in case your computer files become corrupted somehow.

Save your info from each contact, and send them all a press kit and CD. There are rare cases where they will book you sight unheard on a first phone call, but you should still send them a kit.

A press kit should consist of several photocopied pages of any press you've received. You should arrange it nicely on pages with the masthead or front cover logo showing the name of the magazine and the date. The press kit should also include a cover letter, short bio, and a photo: 8×10 glossy is best. You can get copies of photos litho screened at local print shops, or ask other bands where they get it done. Litho is cheaper than getting actual photo prints. It doesn't look quite as nice, but it will print fine in a newspaper.

The cover letter should *briefly* state who you are. And it will make a difference if it is addressed to the booker by name, rather than "Dear booking person." Make sure it's typed on a computer. Handwritten letters are hard to read. Signing it by hand is a nice touch, though.

The bio should be less than one page. It should be free of typos and not be written like most rock bios:

> How many typos and misspellings can you find in this excerpt from a band bio?
>
> "…Out of the ashes of too of the finest local powerhouse seminal rock unit's, rising like a phoenix is **_Toilet Town_**, the greatest band to grace the stages of Toledos' club's since Nirvana desimated the stage of the Erie Street Market in 1989."

Frank Zappa said, "Rock journalism is people who can't write writing about people who can't sing for people who can't read."

Get someone who can write (and read!) to write a clear bio. Bios are pretty incidental, and someone who's never heard of you doesn't care that your band came out of two other bands she's never heard of. If one of the bands was popular, mention it. Mention things that are selling points, like competitions you've won, films your songs have been in, popular bands you've opened for, tours you've done, magazines that have covered you (briefly—you'll be attaching copies of the clippings), radio stations that play you, but keep the stuff out that's only interesting to you.

It's good to include a lot of white space and a few bullet points to break up the page so the eye can quickly grok the info without wading into it a lot. Avoid using a lot of fancy fonts. All the rules that would work for the design of a good resume would be applicable here.

What they will mainly judge you by is the photo and, to a lesser extent, the CD. They will listen to the CD, but only for about 20 seconds, so put your best song first, or your best one without a long intro. I used to get used demo tapes from bookers in San Francisco to tape over with my music, and I'll tell ya, those tapes were only played for less than one song. A booker can tell quickly:

◆ If you're good enough to play their club, and

◆ What kind of music you play, so they can tell who to put you on a bill with

Insecto's well-done press kit is included on the CD, in .pdf format (in the EPK folder. EPK—pronounced "E-P-K—stands for "electronic press kit." Sometimes people will tell you, "E-mail me an EPK."). They also have a printed version. It may seem a little long, but it isn't, because it has everything in one file: photo, press, bio, and stage requirements. (Stage requirements could also effectively go in the contract, but I like the way this was done here.)

I've also included a shorter, but still great, press kit (in Microsoft Word format) by Beauty's Confusion.

You can zip files like this before e-mailing them. Zipping doesn't reduce image files or .pdf files, or audio files much in size (these are already basically compressed formats), but it makes them more likely to come through intact. Word files will get a lot smaller from zipping. But unzipping is also one more loop that the person on the other end will have to jump through, and you want as few hoops for them as possible, so it's your call.

Don't pay a professional photographer to take a photo. This costs $100 to $300. You probably have a friend who is good and just getting started who would do it for the cost of the paper and chemicals and credit. (make *sure* you put "photo credit _____" somewhere on the photo. Get in the habit early of crediting *everyone* who helps you. Or trade someone some Web design. Or a few guitar lessons. Or do it yourself. I took almost all the photos in this book myself, and I'm not really a photographer. I used a $220 reconditioned Toshiba 3.2 megapixel digital camera I got off of eBay. Just make sure you use the highest resolution setting.

Bookers can usually gauge your sound and style almost as accurately and far more quickly from the photo, so make sure it's a good one. Look at ALL the photos on www.yourbandsucks.com to see what not to do. You'll learn everything you *shouldn't* do. (By the way, I named the URL for this site.) Then look at bands that have had careers for more than 10 years and look at how they don't bullshit in their photos. Unless it's to the tune of, "We're so sick of promo photos, we're gonna do a dumb one." And NEVER pose your band in front of a brick wall. That is beyond tired.

Don't be cheesy with your photo.

Here are some good photos. Both say a lot about the bands:

Figure 10.6 *Promo photo of Bomb by Ann Stauder.*

Figure 10.7 *Insecto promo photo.*

As for the CD, if it's home burned, make sure that the CD will play on all stereos. Some won't. And make sure that your contact info is clearly marked on the CD itself and on the case. Most bookers make their calls while the CD's in the player, so they want to be able to see the number on the case without taking the CD out and looking at it. You must realize that these people deal with about a hundred demos a week, and any extra work you give them is gonna make them less likely to book you.

Label the CD and the cover well with only pertinent contact info. Use a clear photo on the cover of the CD. Make sure that your contact info is printed (not written).

Carry a couple of promo CDs with you at all times in your purse or backpack. You never know when you'll need them. And don't be stingy with them. Give them to bands, writers, club owners, and potential fans. Trade 'em with your friends, and use them to make new friends.

> **TIP**
>
> I have this, um, friend, who sent all the promo packs out from his work, running them through the postage meter so he wouldn't have to pay the postage. Be careful, though: I have another, um, friend who used the company's corporate FedEx account to send them out, and one of the addresses was not current and the package got returned to work and someone else opened it. This, um, friend, um, lost his job.

So, you've sent your demo out, and they didn't call you. Send your demos out first class mail, and wait two weeks before you call. Politely ask them if they've gotten a chance to listen to it. They probably haven't. Ask when you should call back. Make a note of it in your Excel spreadsheet and call them back when you said you would.

> **TIP**
>
> This may seem like common knowledge, but it isn't. When making calls and leaving a message, you can bypass most answering machine and voicemail outgoing messages and directly leave a message by hitting either # or * or 1 on your phone's keypad.
>
> See? I just added probably a week's worth of minutes to your life span.

So you have them on the phone, they offer you a show. They probably won't offer you a guarantee if you aren't popular.

All-ages shows do not rely on alcohol sales to make money, so they may take even more of the door money. But all-ages shows are sometimes put on by the bands themselves or by promoters who actually do love music, so they are sometimes more sympathetic to giving the touring band a larger cut of the door.

Contracts

If the club will let me, I usually provide my own contract. Here's one I use (already typed up on the CD).

I do *everything* in writing, even with friends. There's nothing wrong with it. And it may actually make people treat you more professionally earlier on. You can act pro from the start, but you *gotta* have the music to back it up. And a lack of a rock star ego helps, too.

You can add or remove what you need. (Keep in mind this does not constitute legal advice. But it works for me.)

You'll need a press kit, complete with clippings. Here's a good one about my old band, although it's from a reunion show. I lost the stuff from our original press kit because I've moved so many times, and that was before I archived things on computers or even had a computer. We're talking late 80s, people.

Anyway, this is the kind of glowing stuff you want written about you so you can put it in your press kit.

If you don't have any clippings yet, you'll still need a photo and a CD (even a home-burned one). And also a bio (not a cheesy one).

PUBLIC PERFORMANCE AGREEMENT

Our band, _____ agrees to perform between 45 and 65

minutes (at the band's discretion) of music at _____ (venue)

on the date(s) of _____.

The venue will allow a sound check, and will pay the soundman.

I will provide some advertising (amount consistent with what is usually done for this venue) and tell all my friends.

The venue will charge a low price at the door (4 dollars or less if our band is the only feature of the evening...6 dollars or less if other films/bands/whatever are featured). I will set aside a fair portion, _____ % (must be between 50 and 90%).

Our band's split will be paid to them promptly within 60 minutes of the end of our set.

All posters, ads, and promo material must contain our band's Website, www._____.com listed.

The band will get _____ drink tickets per band member (good for well drinks and beer and soda only).

The band may have _____ guests admitted free.

NO CORPORATE SPONSORS WILL BE ATTACHED TO THE EVENT WITHOUT WRITTEN PERMISSION OF OUR BAND.

Signed _____

Date _____

Please sign this contract and mail to:

_____

_____

_____

The Bomb

By Don Baird

Pg 28, San Francisco Bay Times Magazine

September 30, 1999

Well, they came, they reunited, they played two shows vowing that they were the last ever, celebrated the release of their posthumous EP Lovesucker (again), made that entire record available for free as a downloadable mp3 file on the Internet (see kittyfeet.com), and had many first-timers transfixed and lots of old fans grinning ear to ear and banging their heads like they hadn't done, oh, since maybe their last reunion show almost two years ago. But this time heads probably banged a bit more fervently with the knowledge that this would indeed be the last show ever by local rock and roll majestics and in my book, one of the truly perfect examples of everything a great rock and roll band can be.

That band is Bomb. For a particular stretch of time they were the ultimate in satisfaction, the definitive rock and roll experience, the forbidden blasphemous renegades. With their raw aural potency and musical depth of genius, the over-the-top ritualistic antics, and the unhinged unpredictable insanity, Bomb was simply the greatest band on my planet. I've written them up many times over the last decade as they've never left me at a loss for words, in fact bassist/vocalist Michael Dean often provided the most amusing anecdotes from on the road by collect phone calls, chronicling the various strange exploits and predicaments encountered on a Bomb tour across the states, which I usually printed verbatim, as they were fascinating and gave a rather graphic indication of so many details that only a demented rock and roll lifestyle could produce.

That of course was many years ago, and we watched Bomb go through many changes over the years. We saw the departure of original guitarist Jay Crawford for life in Europe, being replaced by a young Doug Hilsinger from Philly, then the eventual return of Jay to the continent and the band, creating the super-charged double-guitar line-up that saw the band through its finest moments. Among these high points was the eventual interest of a major label, Warner Brothers, who distributed the band's fourth record, "Hate Fed Love," produced by Bill Laswell. Perhaps their darkest, most dense and complex offering ever, "Hate Fed Love" was of course a big hit with their loyal following created by tireless touring in the states and Europe but it wasn't a big seller for Warner Brothers who eventually dropped them and now the disc is out of print and actually hard to find. If you see it at your local used record store, snatch it up, it's well worth the $3.95 it will set you back, just for their cover of Leonard Cohen's "Suzanne," which I coincidentally overheard coming from the darkened theater of the Century one night as I filled out an application for a DJ position in the lobby of that tenderloin strip joint once. I couldn't believe that a girl was stripping to the mournful version of one of the more depressing songs in pop musical history as rendered by Bomb. If I were in the band, I would have felt like I'd finally made it in some weird sense. And come to think of it, many of Bomb's shows would seem to end with everyone on stage stripped nude anyway.

It was a number of different elements that led to the demise of Bomb, be it personal and professional differences, obligatory rock and roll substance abuses and rehabilitation, Yoko Onos, spontaneous combustion, airplane accidents, etc., the band went their separate ways, pursuing varied interests both inside and outside the realm of rock and roll, including fatherhood, living abroad, new bands, highly developed Internet entities, furthering education, working as bartenders, even working with yours truly as a cook in a restaurant. Guitarist Doug Hilsinger has kept the highest profile in the music department with a variety of bands including Hedonist, Gifthorse and his present band Waycross.

Bassist and vocalist Michael Dean has also been very busy and the fruits of his efforts are best exemplified by a visit to his shamelessly masturbatory yet fully intriguing Website **kittyfeet.com.** Here you will find out everything he's been doing for the past few years, and thanks to certain technological advancements of modern day home computing, you can also download many musical and visual offerings. As well as his own post-Bomb musical projects you can also find all the information you need about Bomb in there too. One incredible offering culled from his Website is an outtake from the first Bomb reunion recording Lovesucker. There was a cut meant to be included on that disc but drummer Tony Fag vetoed that idea for some reason. The song is called "If I Were a Gurl," and the Website explains quite well how the cut came to be and how you can download it for your own listening pleasure. Thankfully, Eugene my fellow Hole in the Wall DJ and huge Bomb fan has a writeable CD thingy (I'm so tech savvy) and has burned copies of it to play at the bar, because it is an unbelievably brilliant piece of music.

Playing on a theme present in other Bomb songs such as Spoked Feet with its opening lyric, "The girl that I miss is just me in a dress," "If I Were a Gurl" explores the realm and possibilities of gender fluidity, something many of rock and roll's most sensational figures have dwelled upon at one time or another. But here Bomb takes the idea for an epic anthemiac 18-minute romp that from beginning to end is utterly powerful and intriguing and most certainly never boring. Each drum beat, guitar foray and resonant throb of the bass line is positively essential and realized and not filler, believe it or not. People frequently ask about it whenever it's played, commenting "It's beautiful," or "It's so satanic," or my favorite, "It's a tranny anthem!" It is definitely one of the finest songs I've heard all year, and to download your own copy of it go to http://kittyfeet.com/mp3.htm; then if you are fortunate enough to have a friend with a CD burner you can have a copy of your very own to impress your friends at parties.

Back to the final Bomb shows: the first took place at the Cocoderie in North Beach and it was amazing. As far as Bomb shows go, this one was particularly dark and powerful and intense beyond belief. I knew we were in for something huge and monumental when after a very leisurely long time setting up and a noodling psychedelic guitar-off intro by Jay and Doug, Michael walked onstage barefoot and wearing just a T-shirt and a pair of black briefs, but the playfulness stopped after the nearly a cappella version of "Mrs. Happiness" from their first LP, *To Elvis in Hell*, when Tony placed himself behind the drum kit. From there on out it was a fucking dark and powerful affair. The crowd was a definite Bomb-loving group of folks, ready to see the sacred wonderkind rip it up, and they did, probably louder and darker and scarier than I've ever seen them play. They also announced before this all started that they would be playing a free show at The Eagle Tavern's second anniversary party that coming Wednesday, a surprise bit of news that nearly put me through the roof. Not only would this show not be their final show after all, but their true final show would be held in a bar that I frequent, have DJed at before, and is one of the few gay bars around that ever plays Bomb's music, or Rock and Roll for that matter. And just for the record here at the onset of the big Folsom Street Fair Weekend and all the Leather Community events, pageants, secret edge-play parties and stylistic stratification symposiums by which you will be judged, read, chewed up and spit out by each other based on how your gear fits and if your "boy" has maintained it properly all weekend long, it is my understanding historically that the original leather bars of yesteryear most definitely featured rock and roll music, not disco, not Cher's new song, but Rock and Roll, the music favored by the bikers whom you model your little outfits after. I'm glad that someone has the sense and sensibilities enough to remain true to that detail and The Eagle Tavern has for two years now, peeling back the many layers and upholding a fundamental and honest sense of tradition that most have forgotten. Faggots are so fickle. Well, they are.

That night at the Eagle was a tremendous party, with the extra treat of owner Joe Banks handling the DJ booth between bands, something he's been doing a bit more of on some Friday nights lately, and his archival knowledge of music and general instinct and tastes have always set the standards of and broadened the scope of all the music played at both The Hole in the Wall and The Eagle. It's always a pleasure to find him in the booth. I've also just learned that Bryon from The Hole, one of my favorite DJs in the city will now be doing every other Friday night at the Eagle, and in spite of his innocent boyish looks, he has a penchant for sick and twisted rock and colorful obscurities.

By the time Bomb took the stage I was feeling pretty festive, satisfied to see that a number of people I had told not to miss this show were there and ready to be dazzled, mystified, and blown away. After a few minor sound bugs were worked out the band roared into a very long set concentrating mostly on selections from Lovesucker and Hate Fed Love, plus a few from their earlier records. The dark and scary tone of the previous show was still somewhat present but the quality that loomed more prominently over this set was one of distinctly solid musicianship. These players created such a finely tuned monstrous machine of a band, everyone shining equally, everyone's timing impeccable, everyone's interplay spellbinding and complex. Michael Dean was in great form, reminding me fully just what a tremendous vocalist/frontperson he is with his great range and clever phrasing and his irresistibly magnetic angelic/demonic persona. The show was like a dream that just gets better and better. I was fully drawn into it and at times felt waves of nostalgia hit me, getting all warm and sentimental and almost teary-eyed but in that happy way. Jay and Doug are definitely two of the best fucking guitar-wizards this town will ever see, and Tony Fag's drumming is like a power bigger than himself, other-worldly, out-of-body even.

Towards the end of the set at least one member, Jay, had disrobed completely, like old times. Just after the show and the following couple of days when I ran into people who were there they kept saying things to me like, "I thought you were gonna snap your head right off your neck," or "You certainly seemed to be in your element that night," or "You were wild! Are you always like that?"

"Well, c'mon; this was Bomb's final show ever," I replied, "But I might be."

Long live Bomb!

What to Expect

You will be told when you book the gig what time the following events will occur:

◆ Load in

◆ Sound check

◆ Doors (what time the doors open to let customers in)

◆ Set

If they don't tell you, you should ask when you are talking to the booker.

TIP

"The Slot" is what musicians call the most desirable time slot of a given evening. It is not always being the last, or "headlining" band. Sometimes, especially on weeknights, it is *second* to last, i.e. third on a four-band bill, or second on a three-band bill.

Load In

The load in is exactly that: the time you load in your gear. Be a few minutes early. You should also ask them ahead of time if you load in through the front, the side, or the back. And if there's free parking for the bands.

Someone will probably check your I.D., maybe before you even load in. If anyone in your band is not yet 21, you should ask the booker about this before you play. Most clubs will let 18 and over (sometimes 16 and over) play, provided they do not drink and are only in the club for sound check and the set. They usually have to leave after. Check with the booker *ahead of time*. If you are under 16, especially if most of the band is, you will probably be only playing all-ages (no alcohol) shows for a while. That ain't a bad thing. We'll talk more about this later.

Drink tickets: You will be given (or ask for and be given) drink tickets for the band members. Usually one or two per member. More if you've played there before and draw a good crowd. They may or may not run a tab for extra drinks. Be careful. Remember, they exist to sell drinks, not to promote art. A hard-drinking band could easily end up spending more than they make. Remember that scene in *The Blues Brothers* where they get presented with a bill at the end of one of the gigs?

You will usually load your gear in to a place right behind the stage. You will be responsible for your own stuff. If they have a guard back there, don't rely on him to keep you from getting ripped off. Take shifts watching it. Bring a paperback or a laptop to kill time.

The drummer will probably want to take the drums out of the cases and set them up, because they take the longest to set up.

Sound Check

You will load your gear on to the stage and set it up to do a sound check. Do it quickly, but do it right. Don't be nervous. Just do your job.

The sound man will be on the stage setting up microphones (and a direct box for the bass and one for the keyboards most likely). Help him out, don't ask unnecessary questions, and *don't play your guitar when his head is in front of the amp setting up a mike!* Same goes for drums. There is no faster way to piss him off, and believe me, you want him on your side, not pissed off at you.

When he's done setting up the mikes, he'll go back to the soundboard at the back of the room and ask you to play your instruments one at a time. He will talk to you over the monitor speakers. *Don't noodle and play when he's checking someone else's sound.* He needs to hear *one at a time* to get the best sound for you. Help him out.

Play and sing at the volume you plan to use in the show.

TIP

Get a small flashlight, and keep it on your key ring so you'll always have it on stage. It's often dark right before the set, and with a flashlight, you'll be able to see stuff easier to set up.

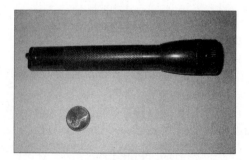

Figure 10.8 *Small Maglite brand flashlight.*

The sound man will ask the drummer to play one drum at a time. He'll probably just say "rack." That means the drummer should just play the rack tom. He'll make some adjustments on the sound board. Then he'll say, "Thank you," which means "stop." Then he'll say "snare," and she just plays her snare drum. And so on. Then he'll say "play the whole kit." She plays the whole kit. Then make some adjustments. He'll tell you to stop. Then he'll ask the guitar player to play. He'll probably just say "guitar." That means the guitar player should play her guitar. Then make some adjustments. He'll tell her to stop. Then he'll ask the bass player to play. He'll probably just say "bass." That means the bass player should play her bass. Then he'll ask the singers to sing one at a time.

When he's all done (this will probably take five or ten minutes total), he'll ask you to play part of a song together as a band. Play a verse and a chorus (or more until he tells you to stop). Pick a song where all the members who do any vocals at all sing. You should find a versatile song with loud parts, quiet parts, and all singers singing in a short space and maybe consider using that to sound check for a while at all the gigs if you want.

Again, this ain't a bad time to check polarity, and maybe put a wind screen on the mike to prevent shocks and improve the sound.

When you all play, if everyone can't hear everything well, stop and ask him to bring up something in the monitors. Depending on the size and complexity of the P.A., you may or may not be able to get individual monitor mixes.

When you're done, ask him if you need to move your gear off the stage or not. Hopefully, you'll just have to move the drums and can leave your amps up there. You'll probably have to push them back so the bands who play before you can put their amps in front of yours.

Big headlining bands at big shows often sound check for a long, long time, even using it as rehearsal or songwriting opportunity on

Figure 10.9 *Microphone with wind screen. Singer Lindsey Gillard of The Sick Lipstick.*

long tours. When you get to this stage (and even before), be considerate of the opening band. It's pretty piggy to sound check for a long time and not give them *any* sound check.

After sound check, you will probably turn in your guest list. This is the list of people who can get in free. Some clubs are very open with this, allowing like five per band member; some are very stingy, allowing like one per *band*. It usually depends on how much they are making on the door. If they were smart, they'd give you unlimited guests to get more drinkers in! But they often aren't and often don't.

When you're in a band, suddenly everyone is your friend (especially if you're opening for the band they actually want to see). *Everyone* will want to be on the guest list, or, as I call it, the "pest list." I recommend reserving it for

◆ People who help you

◆ People who will bring other people in

NOTE

An *old* joke:

Q. How many punkers does it take to change a light bulb?

A. Ten. One to do it and nine to get on the guest list.[1]

1. There is an alternate answer: "Ten. One to do it and nine to write letters to Maximum Rock 'n' Roll complaining that the old one was better."

So.... After your sound check, the other bands will sound check. It's usually in reverse order, with the headlining band first, and the opening band last. This is so when they get to the opening band, they don't have to move their gear; they just leave it there set up ready to play.

Once a band is ready to play their set, the sound man will sometimes have them do a *line check*. (But not the opening band, because they sound checked last, probably right before the doors opened.) This means doing a very abbreviated sound check even though there are people in the club. Sometimes the before-the-doors-open sound check is completely dispensed with in favor of just having everyone do a line check, especially if the club provides *back line*. Back line is when the club has a house bass amp, guitar amp, and drum kit, and all you have to bring is your guitars, effects, bass, and the drummer usually has to (or if he doesn't, he'll probably *want* to) bring his own snare, cymbals, and sticks. You will probably be told this when you book the show. Most showcase clubs provide back line (and they mostly seem to be in Los Angeles, where music is an assembly line and they want everyone on and off as quickly as possible) and won't *let* you bring your own amps, unless you're the headliner and have a draw.

If the club only does line checks and not sound checks proper, I wouldn't worry too much. There's only so much variation on how to mike and amplify guitar, bass, drums, and singing, and a guy who does four bands a night six nights a week is usually pretty good at it.

NOTE

Showcase clubs are clubs that exist to "showcase" bands, allegedly for major labels. They usually have back line, often make you sell tickets, almost never pay bands, and ask everyone who comes in which band they're there to see and book you back only if a lot of people mention you. They also have band-specific audiences; for instance, there can be 10 people for the opening band, 100 people for the second band, no one for the third band, and 50 people for the fourth band. They usually have four or five bands a night. "The Gig" on Melrose in Los Angeles is a good example.

The Set

You will, at some point, be asked by someone to get onstage and actually play your songs. After all, that's why you're there, right?

You should know what time you're playing and get backstage (or whatever passes for backstage at this venue) a few minutes early to tune your guitars, do vocal warm ups, meditate, get drunk, whatever you need to do. You should make sure you have enough water or drinks to get you through the show, though if you run out, you can always say, "Can someone please bring me a _____" from the stage between songs. Someone might, especially if you're doing a great job. Roadies and spouses can also perform this function.

You should play your songs with confidence and love. Don't worry too much about jumping around and being "wild." That will come with time if it's to come at all. Worry about the music.

Actually, just don't worry. Practice is the place to work out all the stuff so you won't have to worry onstage. It should all be a cellular memory, an ingrained response by this time, second nature.

Or be wild. It's up to you. I used to care more about that stuff, but only after the music was really, really good.

If you have trouble hearing an instrument in the monitors, don't hesitate between songs to tell the sound man over the mike, "Could I please have more kick drum in my monitor?" or whatever. But don't get too nitpicky and spend the whole set doing that. You should have it under control to a degree. That's what sound checks are for. Keep in mind that the room sound will change between sound check and the set if people show up. Humans and clothing soak up a lot of sound. A good sound man will accommodate for this.

Encore

When you finish your set, if you are amazing (or if you just have a lot of friends in the room), you may have people yelling for an encore. I usually only do one if it's a *lot* of people. It can seem gratuitous if it's just your boyfriend and your sister screaming "More!," and the other 50 people who are just there to see the other band politely applaud. *Not* doing an encore when one isn't really demanded isn't rude. It's just leaving them wanting more, which is a good thing.

Keep in mind that three people up front yelling for more can look like the whole room is yelling for more. Sometimes it's hard to be honest with yourself.

If anyone is yelling *bad* stuff during the set ("You suck" or something similar), ignore them. If you're particularly witty, you might yell back. This can work to your advantage or not. It kinda depends if you have the crowd behind you or not.

One time Bomb was playing to 500 people (all there for us) and *one* guy up front kept yelling "Fuck you!" to me. (He may actually have been a fan, but it got on my nerves.) I finally said to him over the mike, "Sir, if you do not stop yelling 'Fuck you,' I'm going to climb down there and actually *fuck* you."

Five hundred people laughed at him, and he shut the fuck up.

One time Bomb played in front of 1,500 people who were all there to see the headliner, Primus, and two guys in the audience were throwing ice cubes at my head. I thought the whole room hated us. Keep in mind, one heckler can seem like a room full of them from the stage, too. Keep your head straight and you'll see it all more clearly.

After the Show

Towel off, then get your gear off the stage quickly if there's another band coming on. Put your guitars in their cases, but don't go outside yet. You're all covered with sweat and you'll catch cold.

TIP

Bring an extra T-shirt to every show. Better yet, put on one of your own new band shirts from the merch table and sell the sweaty band shirt off your back. Some types of folks might pay extra. If you put on a good show, you will probably be soaked with sweat when you're done (from rocking out under the hot lights), and you'll appreciate your forethought to have a dry shirt to change into after you play. Also, if you can help it, don't load your gear out from a hot club into the cold night immediately. Let yourself cool down a little bit. You will be less likely to get sick or ruin your voice. And the tubes in your amp will last longer if they avoid going from hot to cold a lot. Extremes in temperature are not good for guitars, either.

Go mingle in the crowd. Shake some hands. Have a drink of something to replenish your body. Rejoice.

After the set, you'll want to get paid if you brought in paying customers and it looks like there's any money to be made.

Thank the sound man, then ask him who to get paid by. A way Tony Fag in Bomb used to broach this was good: "Who do I talk to about the money thing?" It sounds less demanding than "Where's my money?" The sound man will tell you, and you go find that person and say "Hi. I'm _____ from _____. Can we talk about the money thing?" They will probably tell you to come back at the end of the show. They aren't brushing you off; most likely they're really busy. Come back at the end of the night.

Keep an eye on the gear and don't get ripped off. But have fun, support the other bands, and again, have fun.

After the show, get paid, move your gear out, and drive it back to the studio, then go have more fun.

It's best to wait until the next day to start critiquing each other's performances. Don't be a buzz kill. Enjoy the triumph of a job well done before you start tearing it apart.

> **TIP**
>
> When playing a show in your hometown, if there's an out-of-town band on the bill and the show doesn't make much money, consider giving some or all of your band's share to the traveling band. They need it more than you do. And it will come back to you tenfold in goodwill and karma. And they'll probably help you get a gig in their town when you go on tour.
>
> At one show with only about a dozen people there, I even passed a hat and got a few extra bucks for the touring band.
>
> Also, when you're the one paying out the money, always pay the bands, without them asking you, before you leave the venue, even if they're staying at your house. This will avoid them having to feel awkward for asking.

If you made any money at all, make sure you give some to the roadie. Then take some out for the flyers or whatever anyone spent, and split it up *that night*. Don't make people wait for their eight bucks. And unless you're totally broke, don't be too persnickety about paying yourself back your two dollars for the Xerox bill or whatever. The band will stay together longer if everyone soaks up a few of the tiny expenses here and there and never mentions them.

By the way, Tony, you still owe me for that burrito and the ouzo I bought you back in 1986 after our show at the Mab...LOL.

The next day, send an e-mail or make a phone call to the booker. "Hi. This is _____ from _____. Thank you for the show. We had a blast and would love to play again any time. Have a good day."

Believe me, thanking them will make you stand out over 92 percent of the other rude-ass wannabe rock stars they deal with on a daily basis.

Miscellaneous Gigging Stuff

Roadie

You'll have to carry some of your own equipment until you make enough money to pay people. Get a roadie but remember: He's not your slave; he's your helper. And until you make enough to put her on salary, pay her an even split.

Duct Tape

Duct tape is the musician's friend. Duct tape holds rock and roll together. Duct tape can fix a guitar strap, a drum kit, a carburetor, or even a hole in your jeans.

It's available in any hardware store.

Remember, many rolls look alike. Put your name sticker on the inside of the roll.

Figure 10.10 *Duct tape is our friend!*

Stickers

Some clubs are covered with 'em on every available surface, backstage and in the bar itself. Some clubs will charge you 50 bucks for every sticker you stick on the wall. Check before you do. If you're playing the latter type of club, don't give stickers away until people are leaving, or at least tell them from the stage not to stick them up. You might never play there again if people stick them up in the club.

Figure 10.11 *Insecto sticker.*

Figure 10.12 *Band stickers backstage at Spaceland in Los Angeles.*

Autographs

I always have mixed feelings when someone asks me for my autograph. I'm a little flattered and a little embarrassed. Flattered because I'm honored that someone would think that highly to ask me, and embarrassed because the whole idea is pretty zany. I've never asked anyone to give me one.

I recently asked some people I really admire, people not into the "star" bullshit, how they deal with it. They all sign them when asked. Henry Rollins' reply is in his interview at the end of this book. Mike Watt laughed and said, "I have a short name. Doesn't take long to do it." Ian MacKaye said, "Of course I do it. If I say, no, the person feels dumb for asking. If you do sign it, they just stick it in a drawer and years later find it and it makes them happy. It's a snapshot of a good moment."

Set Lists: One for Each Band Member

You don't have to have a set list. You can just have a song list, and band members can take turns starting any song after the last one finishes. This can work well. Bands that don't use set lists have included Fugazi, Flipper, and the Grateful Dead. Each member segues into another song and lets the other members guess which song it is. Bands can get really good at this. You can even jam between songs. Keep it to a minimum though unless you're *really* good at it: Don't bore your audience.

Conversely, some bands rehearse the set as if it were one large piece of music, working out the best order and fine tuning the segues between songs. This is what I usually do, but it can get kinda stale after a while. You get to the point where practice just seems like going through the numbers: Show up, do the set twice (or once), and leave.

If you are going to work the set as a whole piece of music, I would recommend being aware of songs that sound too much alike (because of

Kittyfeet
Set list
Supergoose
Promise
The Web
Hey Louie
Roach Gurl
All My References are Dead
(reprise Promise)
Too Many Babies Grooveyard
Li'l 25

Figure 10.13 *A set list.*

tempo, key, chord changes, styles, and so forth) and not putting them next to each other in the set.

Flyering

You'll want to put up like 100 to 400 flyers for each show. Some towns have laws about this. For a while New York City was fining bands like 100 bucks *per flyer*.

If it's legal in your town, get out there and hit it. Make them catchy and memorable. If you suck at graphic arts, get a friend to do it. Credit them. Thank them. Let them into the show free.

TIP

Stand out. Be true to yourself, but get clever with your promo stuff.

I remember the best rock advertisement I've ever seen. It was from when Jane's Addiction was on an independent label (Triple X Records). It was two photos. The top photo was a young Elvis Presley on stage singing. It said "This rock and roll will never die." Below was a young Perry Farrell onstage singing. It said, "This rock and roll will kill you."

I love that.

Make sure that you can read all the info. And always put a Web URL on there. Say if it's an all-ages show or 21 and over if people will have any doubt.

Remember: It's cheaper and faster to print one flyer on the computer and then Xerox the rest than it is to print them all on the computer.

Getting to know someone who works at a copy shop can be quite helpful.

TIP

The shorter your band name is, the bigger you can put it on the flyer. A four-letter band name, like Bomb or 9353, can be seen from a block away on a flyer made from legal-sized paper.

Use staples or tape on telephone poles. Wheat paste is more permanent but kinda rude and probably illegal. Don't hang them on trees. It's bad for the trees, and we need trees to live. Your band ain't more important than me and my daughter having oxygen.

Hang them up about a week before the show. You will also have to do flyer maintenance, which is coming by a couple of days later and uncovering them and hanging up new ones. Be polite; try not to cover up other flyers unless the show is over. You can find space that stands out by going higher or lower on the pole than the other bands. I used to skateboard around hanging up flyers and lean my board up against the pole and stand on it to get higher up.

TIP

Don't hang eight flyers on one pole, covering up everyone else. If people do that, target them and remove all their flyers, always. It ain't coming from a place of community. It is based on ego and fear. Fuck them. They should be eliminated from the band gene pool.

The Sound Man

As soon as you get there, introduce yourself to him or her. Learn his name. Know him. This is more important than knowing the bartender. Be polite.

Don't ever pay to play a club, but you might tip the sound girl 10 bucks before or after the set. Twenty if you have a good night. That will also help you get booked back, because usually the booker is not there at the show, just during the day. The booker will ask the sound person who drew well, played well (less important to the booker than who drew well), and who kept the audience dancing and drinking. A ten-spot can actually sway their opinion of you.

This isn't "pay to play"; it's tipping the most important person at a show, someone who is usually underpaid and yelled at all night by people who have star complexes. Be cool to them. They are someone you really want on your side.

It will take a while to get a strong following. You may play to just your friends for even a year. But if you're good and have hustle, you will get a crowd after a while. Once you do, you might think about getting your own sound man. Then you'll always sound good at a show. Some clubs won't let you use your own sound girl (check), but if you start making them money, they usually will bend on this if you ask nicely.

Stuff That Sucks

Sometimes clubs will put a clause in the contract where if you cancel, they will actually *charge* you money (usually 100 to 250 bucks)! This is unconscionable in my book. Fuck them. This only, as far as I know, happens in Los Angeles. It is quite indicative of how undervalued music is in this buyer's market.

This attitude is a very good reason to skip bars entirely and just promote your own parties; you know, make your own scene.

How to Make Your Own Scene

Sometimes it's not enough to just be a band. You have to go the extra kilometer and really put out, make it special. I remember when Bomb toured opening up for the Flaming Lips. The Lips would get to the venue early and sound check. But then instead of going back to the hotel or sitting at the bar like most bands would, they would spend like four hours decorating the place. On this particular tour, they had a tank of helium and would blow up hundreds of balloons for the stage. Then they would climb up on ladders and string about a hundred strings of Christmas lights up. And they would have to take them *down* after the show, when most bands would want to do *anything* but that.

And keep in mind this is before the Lips were famous. They were popular, but I believe that it was this kind of care (in addition to writing great songs and touring incessantly) that *made* them famous. In Los Angeles, Jane's Addiction used to decorate warehouses and put on shows that were way more special than just playing in a bar. (This sort of evolved into Lollapalooza.)

Something I would like to see a lot more of is bands doing movie nights. Get together with local filmmakers (or make your own films) and show films between bands. Make it an *event*. Something people will talk about. You could really *hand build* a scene by having your band play every event. Play once a month at a bar, and have different opening bands and films and motifs. Call it "(your band's name) presents _____" or whatever. Just make sure that your portion of it is cool and different enough each time that people don't get sick of you. Maybe add a few new songs each time and vary the presentation and decoration in some way. And do it at different venues maybe. Or if you have a good thing going at one place, keep it there, but just make sure you don't get stale.

Figure 10.14 *An Albatross keyboard.*

Figure 10.15 *An Albatross drums.*

Warehouse Shows

You can even bypass bars entirely and play at youth centers, YMCAs, basements, warehouses, living rooms, backyard BBQ parties, whatever. It helps if you have your own P.A. because most of these places don't have them.

If you do a show in a warehouse and someone gets hurt, you are probably liable. You can get one-day event insurance from most insurance companies. You can also call it a private party and make it donation only and sometimes get around liquor and fire laws, but keep in mind, the authorities can close down anything they want any time they want. And there actually have been cases of communities invoking anti-crack house laws to shut down raves and rock shows. So don't piss off the neighbors.

Get level-headed people to act as security. Make sure NOT to get people that just want to kick ass. Get people who would do anything *but* kick ass, but would if it came down to it. People well into martial arts are usually of a good skill- and mind-set for this task.

Open Mikes

If you can't seem to get a gig *anywhere*, you can try open mikes. These are (usually free) nights at bars where people come in off the street, sign up, wait around, and usually get to play one or two songs. They usually cater more to acoustic acts and people who can set up quickly, but some will allow bands and even have back line for the band.

They work different ways. Some are first come, first serve; that is, you get there at nine, put your name on a list, and that's the order you perform in. Some draw names out of a hat. The one at the Blue Lamp in San Francisco used to book you on a combination of whether you'd played there before, how good you were, if you were a friend of the booker, and if you were a cute girl.

You would think that open mikes would suck and be just a bunch of impatient people waiting for their three minutes of glory, but some are actually great, draw a crowd, and foster a sense of community.

Ask around or check the local entertainment paper.

Editor Sandy adds, "Some places make an absolute business of the open mike night thing and are famous for it. I think the best known one in Nashville is called The Bluebird Café. People come from all over the country, and they actually hold auditions for open mike night (which maybe defeats the purpose), but there are often country music producers and such in the audience. They even publish on their Web page instructions on how to play open mike night at the Bluebird: http://www.bluebirdcafe.com/play/."

I add, "Isn't that the Café in that movie with River Phoenix's brother?"

Press Releases

You should always send a short press release to the appropriate editor at the local entertainment paper when you play somewhere. But wait until you're good. You don't want press coming to your first show if you're still shaky.

Figure 10.16 *DrumFeet.*

Zines

Zines are self-published magazines that people within a given scene make to review and promote each other. You can do a zine yourself to document your scene as it grows. It's a lot of fun.

It's cheaper to just do it online but sometimes more fun to have an actual document for people to hold in their hands. When I was growing up in the hardcore punk scene in Washington, D.C., in the early 80s, an important part of being at a show was passing around zines and reading them.

Conclusion

A sign up at Wild Banana Art Project in Maui reads "Art is a private ritual gone public."

To this, my friend Skip Lunch said "It's that old tree-falls-in-the-forest thing: If an artist makes art and no one sees it, is it art?"

My answer was "Yes. Of course. I often make art alone for the amusement of myself and the Universe. But as soon as I see that *it is good*, my first desire is to run to share it with others."

So get out there and break a leg.[2] Make music, make it good, and then find a way to bring it to the *people*, my brothers and sisters.

---

2. People say "break a leg" because it's considered unlucky to say "good luck" among theater folk.

Everyone says it, and few know what it means. It's an old show biz saying—side curtains are called "legs," and if people hooted and hollered and stamped the floor while screaming for an encore, the vibration would sometimes knock a leg over, or "break a leg." (Tiffany says the old supports weren't as robust, and the people's enthusiasm for live theater was more robust, so the legs did actually break sometimes.) So when someone wishes this to you as you step on stage, they aren't wishing you harm.

I usually tell guitarists "break a string," drummers "break a stick," and everyone else, "break a sweat."

Chapter 11

Hardware Recording

Y ou want to make a document of your music, and you want it to sound as good as humanly possible because a recording is permanent, and you have to live with it forever. Here we will examine the history of hardware recording and what it means to you. How to make the best out of the least. The pros and cons of home recording versus going into a studio. What to expect and what to do in a studio. How to record professional quality demos and albums at home on your own multi-track recorder.

History

Historically, recording of bands was done with hardware: microphones, mixers, and tape recorders, specifically multi-track tape recorders. This method is quickly being replaced by software recording, which we will cover in the next chapter. But there are still reasons to cover hardware recording, not just for historical but for practical reasons.

The tape recorder was invented by Thomas Edison (although his used wire, not tape). He also invented the microphone, the phonograph, and the movie camera (although there is some claim that he stole a lot of ideas from his employee, Nikola Tesla). Regardless, multimedia would be different or non-existent without that Edison dude.

Multi-track recording is generally attributed to jazz-pop guitarist Les Paul, the dude whom the best-selling Gibson guitar is named after. Me and my dear sweet pal of many years, fellow guitarist and writer Deb DeSalvo, once saw him play at a dinner theater called Fat Tuesday's in New York City. The man was amazing. Anyway, he was the first to record tracks and then bounce those tracks (of his guitar and his wife Mary's singing) to another tape recorder, to "orchestrate" the parts, harmonizing with himself and playing off of the previously recorded tracks to produce a thicker, more expansive sound than one or two people could record live. One problem with this bouncing technique, though, is that the more times you bounce back and forth, the more you multiply the amount of tape noise, so there is a limit to how many times you can do it. However, someone came up with a way to make a tape recorder with multiple "tracks" on the same tape running parallel to each other. You can "tell" the tape to record or not record on a given track on a given pass and build your song up with a lot more control and less tape noise.

TIP

Woody adds, "For the record: According to Les Paul himself, he invented the eight-track recorder, the first solid-body electric guitar, the first electric bass guitar, and the use of echo, delay, reverb, and phasing. Check it out at http://www.popmatters.com/music/interviews/paul-les-020514.shtml."

One of the first commercial units was a three-track tape; later came a four-track. For a long time, four-track was the studio standard, but units with 8, 16, 24, and even 48 tracks are common in professional studios and use tapes up to two inches wide to give more space to all those tracks. The more space each track gets and the faster the tape goes, the better the sound quality and lower noise you can get.

It used to be that to get professional studio quality recordings, you needed at least $100,000 worth of gear. But now that software recording is giving studios a run for their money, anyone with a fast computer, a good sound card, and one good microphone basically has a good recording studio. The only thing the professional studio has that you don't is the big room for recording the drums, and you can find one or even just program perfect sounding drums in your bedroom without a drummer.

Four-Track Units

Four-track units are very cool. They are complete self-contained recording studios you can carry anywhere. They have a preamp, input mixer, multi-track recorder, mix down mixer, and headphone amp all in one unit. They use standard, inexpensive cassette tapes as the tape medium. With a little care you can get amazing recordings on them—recordings that are good enough to be pressed into CDs. Or, you can record your basic tracks on your four-track and then input the result into a computer for further overdubs, polish, and mastering.

Best of all, four-tracks are cheap. Since everyone's using computers to record on, four-tracks are considered obsolete. You can get a good used four-track recorder *extremely* cheap. We're kinda at the place where typewriters were a few years ago, and how it's really cheap to get high-8 video cameras because everyone bought mini-DV. Though I think, in a way, high-8 looks cooler. In the same way you can get a used electric typewriter for 10 bucks, you can buy a used four-track in a pawn shop for $75. The Tascam 414 and 424 are common and good, but pretty much any unit is good to start if it works.

Figure 11.1 *Fostex X-28H cassette four-track unit.* Photo by Gary Levitt of the band Setting Sun.

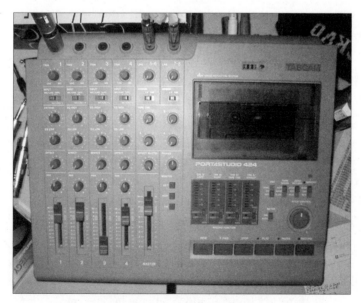

Figure 11.2 *Tascam Portastudio 424.* Photo by E. North.

You can't really buy a typewriter used anymore because they don't make them much because of computers replacing them. But five years ago, you could pick up a bitching electric typewriter in a pawn shop for 20 bucks. You can get a good self-contained recorder-mixer four-track that records on a cassette tape for under a hundred bucks at a pawn shop or on eBay. Or $299 new. I have friends who record *records* that sound *bitchin'* on four-tracks. And they are great to use because they make it easy to learn the basics of recording, which will transfer to recording in a real studio and also transfer to software recording.

TIP

Use name brand tape (Sony, Maxell, TDK, Memorex—you get it at a music store or online) and use a head cleaner tape or kit regularly. Also, buy some canned air and use it to blow dust out of the tape unit and the mixer knobs and sliders. Dust will kill a tape recorder. And don't smoke anything in the control room. Smoke is really bad for the tape heads.

Figure 11.3 *Keep canned air on hand to blow dust out of the mechanisms. (This is kinda fun too!)*

Why Use Multi-Track Systems?

There are two basic things that make multi-track recording (whether done on hardware or software systems) far superior to recording live in the studio with no overdubs. They both involve the amount of control you have over the sound. One is that you can record individual instruments one at a time. This can allow one person to be the whole band or can allow a band to make sure every take on every instrument is as perfect as you want it to be. (Though usually, to ensure a good "feel," the "basics"—guitar, bass, and drums—are recorded all at once.)

You can control every aspect of every instrument on a separate channel from *the mixing desk*. (In a recording studio, a mixer is often called a mixing desk.)

Figure 11.4 *Mixing desk at a friend's big studio. Note computer monitor above and computer keyboard on the desk.*

The second reason that multi-track recording is so powerful is that you can isolate sound. If you use separate microphones on every drum on the drum set, you can isolate them and tweak each one individually. This is more work than just getting a good overall sound and "going with it," but it is a huge improvement. For instance, you can add reverb to the snare only, add digital reverb to the high-hat, analog reverb to the snare drum, and use the bass drum to trigger a sample without affecting the sound of the other instruments. You can add a noise gate as an effect (rather than just as noise reduction) to the snare for a very cool compressed feel. Peter Gabriel did this with Phil Collins and Jerry Marotta's drums on "Biko."

If you record a band live without isolation on a regular stereo recorder, you end up with everything on two tracks, and affecting the drums will also affect the vocals.

This gives you very little control. So, in multi-track recording, we try to get isolation of sound.

This is achieved by two methods: microphone choice and baffling.

The microphones you use for multi-track recording are almost universally going to be unidirectional. These microphones pick up the sound right in front of them and not so much from the sides and rear. Therefore, if you point one at the snare drum from six inches away, it's not going to pick up much of the guitar amp that is six feet away.

The second thing you'll want to do is to baffle the sound. You want to put physical isolation devices between instruments to isolate them further, to avoid "leakage" of one instrument's sound into another instrument's microphone. Perhaps you've noticed that on some TV shows they have Plexiglas up around three sides of the drummer. This is to help isolate the sound of the drums from leaking into the singer's mikes and the guitar mikes and vice versa. Isolation is important live, but more so on a recording. A studio recording does not have the intense energy and interaction with an audience that adds to the live experience.

I've been to shows that blew my mind and later heard recordings of that show that did not blow me away. A lot of what gets you off at a concert is the energy of the crowd and the interaction between band and audience, and this is almost impossible to capture to audio tape. And live bands tend to make more mistakes than in the studio, but we forgive them or don't even notice, because we are enraptured by the kick-ass moment.

This is one reason that on live records bands will still overdub some of the parts of some of the instruments. My old manager, who managed Jane's Addiction, told me that on the Jane's Addiction live record that they did a million years ago on Triple X records, the only thing the band kept was the drums. They overdubbed *everything* else later in the studio. And the audience applause and cheering on that recording was partially from a Los Lobos show and partially from a recording of a bullfight in Spain.

In the studio, in a professional studio, *gobos* are used between the amps. Gobos are little partitions that absorb sound. They are made from wood, covered with fabric, and placed on wheels so that they can be easily moved. You can make them yourself or use very thick blankets to achieve the same thing. You want the amps all isolated as much as possible. And then you just feed everything into headphones and people hear each other for cues to play together mostly through the headphones.

(This takes a little getting used to if you've never done it.) It's always, as I said, a good idea to try and get good "basics" all at the same time. That way you get the feel of a live band but can perfect everything over that, for a best-of-both-worlds synthesis of live and overdubbed.

Usually the vocalist will sing a "guide vocal" to keep the players in time. You can print this to tape if it's exceptional, but usually the singer will do all the vocals over later anyway. Some singers will hold back and not give their all on this, in order to keep their vocal chords from getting burned out, especially if the vocals are being done the next or even the same day.

Since I am not just the singer but usually also the bass player or guitar player when I record with a band, I will do just enough guide vocals (usually the first few or last few words of every few lines and the beginning and end of a chorus) to keep the band and myself confidently knowing where we are in the song, but as little as possible, so I can really concentrate on playing. I'm pretty good at singing and playing at the same time, but can do either one alone better than I can do when doing them at the same time.

Figure 11.5 *Outboard gear at a friend's big studio.*

Figure 11.6 *More outboard gear at a friend's big studio.*

Professional recording studios take care of all this crap for you, so you only have to take care of the music. But they cost between $40 and $400 an hour, plus the cost of the engineer. For what you spend in 10 hours in a top-notch major label studio, you could set yourself up to record at home for life.

In my film, J. Mascis says, "I would stare out the window and I would be paralyzed because I was spending a thousand dollars to stare out the window and I realized I could do that at home." J. has a top-notch studio built into his home so he never has to pay to wait for the muse again.

When you do spend that kind of money in a lush professional studio, a lot of it is going to making you feel like a rock star, to feeding your egos. Sure, you may not have a $5,000 leather couch at home, but is that really going to make you a better musician?

Figure 11.7 *Removable FireWire drives at a friend's big studio. (Note: I really wanted to get a photo for you of their 2-inch 24-track recorder, but they actually just sold it. This studio has gone all software in the past month!)*

Also, if for some reason you *can* justify spending that kind of money (or more likely, someone is spending it on you, but keep in mind, you'll have to pay that back before you see any profit), you would be smart to go into your own studio and do "pre-production" first—making "demos" (demonstration recordings) to work out all the details before you go in and drop bank on the studio with the pool table, the leather couch, and the gold record by some has-been hair metal rockers on the wall.

Figure 11.8 *Leather couch at a friend's big studio.*

Figure 11.9 *Ping-pong table at a friend's big studio.*

Figure 11.10 *Gold records on a friend's studio wall.*

Figure 11.11 *More gold records on a friend's studio wall.*

Figure 11.12 *Yet more gold records on a friend's studio wall.*

NOTE

I was once mastering a Bomb record with the amazing George Horn at Fantasy Studios in Berkeley—the studio and company built from what, in my opinion, was stealing the publishing from Credence Clearwater Revival. They told me I could go into the kitchen and eat anything I wanted free. I thought this was a great deal until I realized that no matter what I ate, the amount of time I spent eating it cost more in studio time than the price of the food. Smart people, those....

TIP

Assistant engineers in big studios are sometimes paid in studio time. You can befriend them and use their studio time free (or do what I did for the first Bomb record—date her). You will probably still have to pay an engineer (the assistant might not be ready to run everything yet), and the time will probably be in the middle of the night, available on short notice, and bumpable (bumped to another day if a paying client shows up), but this is one way to get into a good studio if you're ready.

Some studios use 48 or even 72 tracks, but I think that's overkill. Most great records were recorded on either 24 or 16 tracks, on one- or two-inch tape. (The wider the tape and the faster the tape speed, the higher the fidelity.)

TIP

You can buy inexpensive used *hard disc recorders* (try eBay), which are basically dedicated computers with the software built in and hidden under hardware. They replace both the tape recorder and the mixer and require no tape.

London used one to record the D.I.Y. theme song with me. They are all different, so consult the manual if you get one.

Figure 11.13 *Hard disc recorder.*   **Figure 11.14** *Hard disc recorder close-up.*

To record multi-track, first get your mike levels. Mike your instruments close (but not too close—start at six inches and see how that sounds on tape) and isolate them as much as possible with baffling: gobos, thick blankets, and such. Then plug the microphone inputs into your mixer. If you are using a four-track, use the mixer inputs built into the four-track. If you are using a 24-, 16-, or 8-track tape unit (these can be gotten relatively cheap on eBay), you will probably want to do something like this: On a 16-track unit, I allot six tracks to the drums: one mike each for bass drum, snare, high-hat, floor tom, and two overhead mikes to pick up the cymbals and the whole kit. That leaves two tracks for bass (one direct and one miked—this gives you the deep bass of the direct sound and some warmth of the amp), four tracks for guitar, and four for vocal overdubs and harmonies. Of course, that's a lot of guitar and vocals; you could also give a couple of those tracks to keyboards, DJ, samples, noises, horns, or whatever. Sixteen tracks is a lot, and it's all I could see needing. Some of the greatest records ever were made on two-inch or one-inch tape on a 16-track recorder.

TIP

In the studio, everyone should tune their instrument between *every* take. I can't stress this enough. And it's also *all* I got out of spending $65,000 paying Bill Laswell to record our Warner Brother's album. He taught me that. That's about it.

I would also add that you should all use the same tuner, as some are slightly differently calibrated and will put you in tune with yourself but out of tune with each other.

You may want to use a pre-amp with some microphones. If they're condenser mikes, they will probably need power. Some mixers actually supply power to the mikes, and as we saw earlier, some don't. These need an external power supply box.

You can run the mikes directly into the inputs of the multi-track tape recorder or go through the mixer first. The first way is simpler and usually pretty foolproof as far as getting a pretty good sound right away. Going through the mixer first can complicate things exponentially, but in the hands of someone with experience (you, after you've done it the other way a few times), there's a lot more room for tweaking and fine tuning everything to get it perfect.

The thing to remember though, which is basically the first rule of recording, is: It is easier to add something to a sound later than it is to take it away. Whatever you "print to tape" is what you're stuck with. This is why if you change the EQ through the mixer and print to tape, you will be limited with what you can do to it later. This is especially true with effects: You can always add reverb, but you can't take it away. That's why you want to acoustically deaden the room that you record in and go for a strong but uncolored sound and then mess with it later. This is the reason (other than soundproofing for the neighbors) that you'll want to line your recording studio walls with egg crates and foam rubber and fabric to deaden the sound—to remove all acoustic reflection.

Figure 11.15 *Egg crate-type material on a studio wall.*

There is one exception to this; sometimes guitar amps or drums are miked with two sets of mikes: one close and one at a distance. The *huge* drum sample that Jimmy Page got from John Bonham's drums on the Led Zeppelin records (still the most sampled drum tone on the planet) was gotten like this: They put a mike on every drum on the kit, close up, like one would do. Then they added a couple of mikes on separate tracks like 20 and 40 feet away. One such recording was done in a stone castle. You have the channels miked up close for the individual sounds—the basic power of the kit, and then a couple of ambient mikes picking up the room sound to mix in to give it some more depth.

Guitar amps are usually miked about six inches away from the amp (pointing at one of the individual speakers if there is more than one) and another mike 6 to 10 feet away. This adds a very slight delay (because sound travels at only about a thousand feet per second (check), so the sound hits the second mike a tiny bit later. It's not enough to really be perceived as an actual delay, but it thickens the guitar sound. A lot of metal bands do this, but so did Kurt Cobain. It's a cool sound.

TIP

If you want a thick and heavy rhythm guitar sound, rather than turning up the distortion like you would live, record two identical passes of the guitar with the distortion rolled back a little from what you want. Then put one track a little to the left and the other one a little to the right. This will combine to make a less mushy but heavy-as-hell composite track.

If you only have eight tracks available, I would record a rock band something like this: two for vocals, two for guitar, one for bass guitar, and three for drums. I would keeps the bass drum on its own track because being able to set the bass drum's volume is very important to the sound of the kit. I would put a second mike between the snare and the high hat, picking up both equally on one track. I would use the last track for a sensitive omnidirectional overhead to get the rest of the kit. I would put it right above and in front of the drummer's head, pointing down.

If you are recording a rock band on a four-track, I would use a mixer to get a good sound mixing all the drums (miked as if you were recording to 16 track) and put the drums and bass guitar on one track. I would have one track for guitar, one for vocals, and one left over for additional vocal or guitar.

When recording on only four tracks, you have to get creative. People always say, "Well, the Beatles' *Sargent Pepper* was recorded on only four tracks...," but it was actually recorded on several four track machines synched together, and the sessions were directed by the best producer in the biz; the musicians were geniuses; and they had the BBC orchestra backing them up. You may not be a genius; or you may be, but you probably won't have all that other crap.

TIP

The term *Lo-Fi* is just a marketing term for recorded really cheap. It doesn't mean much. Don't try to sound crappy. Try to sound as good as you can. Don't worry; you won't end up sounding too processed most likely.

You can *bounce* tracks. Basically, this means recording on three tracks, then mixing them down to one track, then freeing up the original tracks to record over. This effectively gives you more than four tracks on a four-track. Specific instruction for how to do this is different for every unit and is covered in the manual.

TIP

If your four-track is used and didn't come with the manual, you can usually search the make, model number, and the word "manual" on Google and find either a downloadable version or someone willing to photocopy theirs for you for five bucks or so. This is true of most equipment.

The problem with bouncing tracks is twofold: First, you add tape hiss every time you bounce. Second, you are stuck with the submix of each bounced track. The sound will behave differently in the whole mix, and you must get good at predicting this. For example, the snare drum on the same track as all the drums and the bass guitar in a submix will have to be a little sharper to cut through when layered later with guitars than if it were on its own track.

You can, however, get amazing performances committed to tape in a great sounding way on a four-track unit that uses a cassette tape as the medium. It just takes a little more care and planning.

You can also record basics on a four-track to get a good tape sound and then dump it into your computer to add more instruments. Software recording, no tape hiss, and virtually unlimited tracks—most programs have at least 99 tracks available, although most programs will crap out before that; it's more limited by your memory and processor. But you can easily get a lot of tracks for sure.

Basically, multi-track recording is pretty simple. All units, from the lowliest consumer four-track to the most expensive studio machine, have very few buttons and two modes for each track: Play and Record. In record mode, you can listen to the other tracks in real time and play along with them. This is the basis for how multi-track recording works. You just have to remember to keep track of what you're doing on each track and keep it together to know if you are recording or playing that track on this particular take, and not accidentally tape over a keeper.

To aid this, engineers usually do two things. One is to put a piece of tape across the track listing on the mixer and the tape recorder and write with a pen what's being recorded on each track. The other is to use *track sheets*. Track sheets are used to write down what was done for a particular song. Track sheets are useful especially if you record and mix on different days (which is highly recommended—most people's ears are only "fresh" for six to eight hours and then need to rest and sleep to be able to have good decision-making capacity again). The sheets are stored in the boxes with the tape. I've included some printable track sheets for different tape and software formats on the CD, in the Goodies folder.

TIP

If you're recording one instrument at a time, start with the drums. Either play along with another instrument in the headphones to guide the drummer or, if she's able to, have her just play the whole song without accompaniment, just counting the whole thing or hearing the whole thing in her head. If you are working this way, have each person listen to what's already recorded and add their part. It's generally best to do the drums, then the bass, then the guitars, then the vocals. If you are recording with a limited number of tracks, you may want to do two instruments at a time on the same track. The disadvantage of this, of course, is that you have to play each one nearly perfectly, starting over if either makes a mistake, even though the other one is fine. You have to get a good sound going to tape, and you're stuck with it. If you raise one or lower one later, it affects both of them.

Mike Levels

You want to test each instrument or each thing going to a separate track to get good levels. Good mike levels are basically the highest levels you can get without going into distortion. Too low and you'll hear a lot of hiss from the tape. Too high and you'll get distortion. Go for a high happy medium.

Most recorders and all mixers have meters for this. They usually have a red line over on the far right or at the top that indicates the distortion zone. This is a good indicator, but the real test is to listen back on headphones and speakers to a little test recording. Have the drummer play each drum and record them. Then have her play the whole kit. And listen to the recording carefully. Do the same for every other instrument, and then do it for the whole band together. Raise or lower the input levels (or move the mikes closer together or farther apart) to get it just right.

The band should not noodle or play when not asked to during this process. The engineer (you) is listening for very subtle things. This is often a good test of the professionalism of musicians—newbies will hit the drums and play wanky solos on the guitar all the time; pros will be able to sit quietly while things that require quiet get done.

I generally start with all the knobs set at seven (on a scale of one to ten) and go up and down from there. For some reason, seven seems to be the good place to start.

Don't rush the band. You are doing this yourself, so you don't *have* to rush. Make them feel comfortable, but try to stay focused and professional.

You are contributing art to the Universe. It's a beautiful thing. It should be fun. Feel the love, baby. Feel the love.

Pantyhose

In *$30 Film School*, we used pantyhose over the lens. This time we're gonna use them between the singer and the microphone to remove plosives, the *P, B,* and *D* sounds, and the sibilants, the *S* sounds. All of these produce short bursts of extra energy that can result in spikes of distortion on the tape. It is generally to be avoided but can actually be left or even exaggerated in some music to retain a rough edge. This is what the Beastie Boys meant when they rapped, "I rock the mike without the pantyhose."

You can also buy a professional thing to cut plosives and sibilants.

Figure 11.16 *Professional thing to cut plosives and sibilants.*

Figure 11.17 *Professional thing to cut plosives and sibilants in use.*

You can also get (or make) a shock mount, which uses strong rubber bands to isolate the microphone from vibrations of people walking.

Figure 11.18 *Shock mount.*

Let's Do This Thing...

Make all your mike and level checks, first just through the headphones and then, when that sounds good, actually record a bit. Have the band (or single performer, if that's what you're doing) play a bit.

TIP

One aspect of big studios that is worth replicating is having an isolation booth with glass between you and the people making noise, to make it so you hear only the sound that's printing to the tape, not the roar of the guitars and drums in the room. This gives you yet more control over the recorded sound.

Record a test. Have the players play about 30 seconds of music, and then have them (or him) stop and play it back. It should sound good and strong but not distorted.

TIP

Have two pairs of speakers to listen to playback on. One should be the best you can afford, but you should also have a crappy set, maybe small computer speakers or even a portable radio speaker. Les Paul used to drive his car up to the studio window and run a wire out to check his final mixes on the little tinny speakers in his car. The theory is that if something sounds good on a crappy little speaker, it will sound good anywhere. So check your final mix on both.

Figure 11.19 *An array of studio monitor speakers to choose from.*

Figure 11.20 *Small monitor speaker.*

Once you get a good sounding recording printed to tape, try a whole song.

Go for the best take you can, but don't overdo it to the point of sapping perfection from the performance. You will quickly find out where this particular band or person's strength lies. Most people, if they are well rehearsed, will get their best take after two or three tries. Keep the first and second one, unless there are horrible mistakes in the basic tracks (drums/bass and maybe guitar). Rewind and go over it if you want, but keep good takes. Tape isn't that expensive.

TIP

If you end up getting a hum sound recorded to tape, stop everything and use the troubleshooting techniques described in Chapter 5, "Microphones, P.A. Systems, and Troubleshooting" (replacing every link in the signal chain with working devices until it is gone) to find it and get rid of it. Hum and buzz have no place on a quality recording.

Don't push a band too hard and make them play past when they sound good. There's no reason in a home studio to hurry. You have all the time in the world. That's the *point* of doing it at home.

When listening to the playbacks, use a critical ear. Go for a good feel, but you also want technically good takes. Mistakes will not fix themselves, you can't really cover them up, and you can't really overdub the drums. Make sure at least that the drums are good. They should have a good "groove," that is, they feel good and make you want to move your feet. They should also not speed up or slow down. A lot of drummers have a problem with this. Sometimes you can get them to fix it by having them play to a click track (quarter notes on a drum machine will work) in headphones, and indeed this may be required for some types of recording, especially if MIDI interfaces are involved. But some rock drummers, who are good, just cannot ever play to a click. Suss out the situation, don't push musicians to be something they aren't. Work to their strengths, not their weaknesses.

TIP

Hand percussion (egg shakers, tambourines, maracas, and so forth) can make a song totally more danceable. Usually they are used only on the chorus, or alternately, only under the guitar solo to make it shine a little more. But make sure that the person playing it is *totally* in the pocket. If they aren't as tight or tighter with the rhythm than the drummer, they will make the song sound *worse*, not better.

Figure 11.21 *Bongos.*

Figure 11.22 *Egg-shaped shaker.*

Figure 11.23 *Maracas.*

Figure 11.24 *Tambourine.*

Figure 11.25 *Conga drum.*

> **TIP**
>
> Don't let your singer play hand percussion on stage if he can't keep a beat, no matter how cool he thinks it looks.

Once you have a good sounding take of the basic tracks, try some overdubs. Add the guitar, vocals, and whatnot until the song is built up to where you like. Keep in mind to take the track off Record and put it on Play; you don't want to tape over a good take. Multi-track recording requires a good bit of left-brained geek think to keep track of all this crap, which is why, historically, one person only did this and someone else actually played the music—that is, someone else did the right-brained stuff. But the $30 Way is to develop the *whole* brain so you don't have to depend on others.

> **TIP**
>
> You can use background sounds if you like. These are quiet things, not quite subliminal, but almost—noises, sound effects, voices—that will not be heard the first time someone listens, but will be revealed upon subsequent spins, especially with headphones. It gives your music more depth and perhaps a longer shelf life.

You can "punch in" a part of a take if the take is mostly good except for one part. Punching in means taping over part of one take on one channel and leaving the part of the take that was good. But you'll need a place before and after where there is nothing (like space between vocal lines if you're doing a punch on the vocal track) to punch in and punch out.

Once you've got all the stuff recorded for the song, it's time to *mix*. Mixing is the process of taking all the stuff that you did in the recording process and assembling it into a coherent and polished song.

Actually, it's already a lot more ready than you think. In filmmaking, the analogous process would be *editing*, where you wouldn't be nearly as done as you are now. In filmmaking, you'd have a bunch of tapes you've shot of raw scenes that wouldn't even resemble a movie.

TIP

With some systems, you can use the mixer to assign submixes, so you can have different mixes for each person's headphones; that is, the singer can have more of herself, the drummer can have more of the bass player, and so forth. With very basic systems, such as a four-track, however, you only have one mix. You can use a splitter box (cheap at Radio Shack) to send this signal to four or more headphones.

Make a *rough mix* of your song. This basically means getting everything about the same volume and making a cassette or CD of it to listen to for a day or two so that you can start making notes. Don't worry about the details; don't worry about EQ or reverb or anything like that. Just make a quick mix, put the tape back in the box, store it in a cool dry dark place, and go do something else for a day.

Listen to the rough mix a bit, but keep an open mind. Don't get too attached to or critical of it. Look for any places that you need to overdub to fix any minor mistakes, but if all that stuff's fine, just listen to what it needs in order to get it perfect, as far as levels, EQ, and reverb are concerned.

I have actually heard rough mixes of records that sounded better than the record ended up sounding. Sometimes in the mixing, people overdo it. This can be part of what is commonly called "overproducing" a band—that which takes away too much of the "edge" that makes them perfect.

If you're doing a record, you can either record all the basics for the whole record or record and mix one song at a time. It's generally best to do all the basics at once because:

◆ You only have to get the sound once.

◆ The band may not want to leave their equipment set up if they have other gigs.

◆ Once a band starts cranking out the tunes, they often get in a zone and can lay down basics for a whole album, or at least half an album, in one day.

You might not want to do all the vocal overdubs the same day, as people tend to strain their voices and will need a day to sound as good as new after.

TIP

The old-fashioned headphones that completely cover the ear and seal out a lot of the room sound are generally better for the band members, especially the drummer, when recording the band all at once. They seal out the sound better and allow you to just concentrate on the recorder sound. I have even seen people wrap duct tape around them and their head to form a tighter seal with the ears!

Other people prefer Walkman-type lighter open-sound models. If you have money for both, keep both on hand, so people will have a choice.

Final Mix

So, after a day or two of not recording or listening to loud music, your ears should be rested and ready to try some mixing.

Reload the tape onto the recorder (or pop the cassette in if you're using a cassette) and pull the tracks all up so you can hear each of them. You can probably *solo* (only hear that track without the others) or *mute* (not hear that track but hear all the others) if your recorder or mixer has buttons for each track labeled like that. This will help in seeing what each track needs. Keep in mind that changes that sound intense when soloed will sound less so when they are "sitting in the track" (played with the other instruments in the song). Keep in mind here that track can mean either the individual channel or the song. For some reason track is used for both; but you are smart and can tell from the context which one I mean. If you make the snare drum really bright and ringing with the EQ on the drum track while you solo it, it's not going to stand out as much once you bring up the guitars and bass. You will get used to this with time and eventually automatically adjust accordingly. Keep in mind that your first bunch of recordings is not going to be perfect, and that all art is a learning process.

Mess around with the different instruments in a soloed state and also sitting in the track with all the other instruments. There should be at least three knobs of EQ (equalization) to raise and lower the different frequency components of each track (the lows, the mids, and the highs).

The lows (or low end or bass) control affects the bass frequencies, the parts of the sound that you feel more than hear. You'll need speakers with good bass response to even notice these differences.

Music with too much low sounds muddy; too little sounds thin.

The mids (or midrange) knob controls the middle frequencies. This is where a lot of the program material lives. It is the "punch" of the music, and it is where a lot of the guitar tone and most human vocal sits. Too much mid sounds woody, too little lacks "presence."

The high (or high end or treble) control affects the amount of high frequency. This is where the "breath" of the music lives. Too much of this sounds tinny; too little, muffled.

So, you wanna mess with these three or more knobs to boost (add) or cut these from the sound. Straight up (on a knob) or in the middle (on a slider) on these knobs will usually be no boost and no cut. This will usually be labeled with a zero. The numbers on a mixer are sometimes arbitrary but are usually decibels of boost or cut, depending on whether there is a + sign or − sign next to it. To the left (on a knob) or down (on a slider) is usually a cut. To the right or up is usually a boost. Mess with these until you get the sound you like.

Then experiment with reverb. Reverb is usually a knob built into the mixer, or if not, you'll have to hook a reverb unit (hardware or software) through the Effects Sends, which is similar to the input and output for the effects send on some P.A. systems that we discussed in Chapter 5 or the effects loop we saw in some guitar amps in Chapter 4, "Effects."

You will hook the output and input of the reverb unit through the Effects Send jacks on the mixer and use the mixer's Reverb or Effects Send knob to control the amount of reverb in your mix. Some four-track recorders or mixers have reverb built in.

Some people tend to overuse reverb, especially to try to drown bad vocals. I don't do this. I try to have only enough reverb to make things sit well in the track but don't use it to polish turds. I try not to record with turds to begin with.

TIP

You can leave "out-takes" like false starts or flubbed endings on songs on the final record. This adds to the feel of the record as a "document" of an organic, living session, rather than an airbrushed snapshot of an impossibly perfect thing. I did this on the song "Golden Gate Bridge" on the CD. The drummer started the song a little fast, I stopped him, and we started over.

Don't put too many of these on a record, maybe two, tops. And don't leave them in the middle of the song. That's a mistake, not an interesting quirk.

Sometimes one clam on a record is okay, especially an otherwise great live record. (*Clams* are wrong notes. As in, "I sure hit a few clams on that one!") I always thought it was kind of neat when otherwise very good bands leave them in on records. Makes them seem a little more human. Like at 2:48 in Nirvana's cover of "Man Who Sold the World" from the MTV *Unplugged* album.

It usually sounds best to put some reverb on the drums (particularly the snare) and a little on the vocals, but overall, I don't use a lot of it. You may choose to use more, and in some forms of music (like reggae) it is actually used as an effect. But it's your call. This is your music. Do what you want. Also remember that, like everything else, reverb that is very prominent on a soloed track is not so much so when you add the other instruments back into the mix.

Once you've got all this, you need only get the mix (volume) between the individual instruments to a good point and then get a good balance of stereo mix. Stereo mix is where each instrument sits in the stereo field, left or right. This button is usually called Pan. Experiment with this; putting it all the way to the left will usually pan that track all the way into the left speaker. To the right will be all the way in the right speaker. In the middle will be equally in both.

1960s recordings tended to be extreme with the stereo separation; putting one instrument all the way to the left and another all the way to the right (check out the first couple of Doors records in headphones and you'll see what I mean). But stereo was new then (previous recordings were *mono*—meant to be played through one speaker only), and they were still trying to figure out what to do with it. But modern recordings tend to not have such an extreme stereo field. Usually the vocals, snare drum, and bass drum are dead center. The drums on the left of the kit are partially to the left, the drums on the right partially to the right. The guitars are usually a little left and a little right of center. Listen to how your favorite records are recorded and you'll get a feel for what works how and such. Again, experiment.

TIP

You can use the stereo mix to pan the two channels (dry and wet) of a stereo chorus or delay. It will add a lot of depth to the mix.

You can do a million other things with effects and such to mix the record the way you want it, but the basics of a good mix are getting these basics right: volume, EQ, reverb, and a good stereo mix. Get that all right (it's different for every song) and you've got it.

When the mix sounds good, mix down your master to tape or to a hard drive (or best of all a *DAT*—digital audio tape). You may or may not have to ride some of the faders at certain points during the output. It's your call, and you'll figure that all out with experience.

Then listen to that for a couple of days and see how you like living with it. If it works for you, you're done. If not, it doesn't cost anything to go change it.

Conclusion

I once heard someone say that when you're paying for studio time, it's easy to make a record on no money, and easy on a lot of money, but hard to make it for a budget that lies somewhere in the middle. This is because if you have no money, you just get a great sound and go for it. If you have unlimited money, you try all the tricks that you've always wanted to try. If you've got a medium budget, you *try* to get the big budget record with all the tricks you've always wanted to try, but you fall short and forget to even get a good basic sound. There is some truth to this, but if you're recording in your home studio, it shouldn't be an issue. Work at first at trying to get a great basic sound, and with experience, learn to get a great sound with all the bells and thistles and fun crap. But remember that none of that stuff makes up for poor songwriting or playing. Great songs recorded in a good basic manner will always beat crappy songs recorded on an unlimited budget. That's the secret of the $30 Way, no matter if it's film, music, writing, or whatever.

That's where we have the advantage that no money can buy: talent.

Chapter 12

Software Recording

Software is really just bunches of strings of zeros and ones. But oh boy, can it do a lot. It's the instructions that enable your computer to do pretty much *anything*.

Software is no replacement for songwriting skills. The better you understand the fundamentals of writing a chorus, hook, and verse and structuring things with variations on a theme, the more likely you will make music that's great, even with software that makes anyone sound good. And it sure is cheaper than a hardware-only studio, just as good, and in some ways, better.

Software recording allows you to do everything (and more) that you can do with hardware recording. And all without tape hiss, maintenance of moving parts, the expense of tape, or even the need for a tape recorder.

I remember the first time I heard the top-ten pop hit "Tubthumping" on the radio with its perky pub party lyrics:

> "He drinks a whisky drink
> He drinks a vodka drink
> He drinks a lager drink
> He drinks a cider drink
> He sings the songs that remind him
> Of the good times
> He sings the songs that remind him
> Of the better times."

I thought to myself, "Ah, a cute pop song for people who like to drink. How quaint." (As a side note, I also thought, "…and it borrows heavily from Bonzo Dog Band's "Give Booze A Chance," which also borrows heavily from a John Lennon song.[1]

Then the DJ announced the name of the band. Chumbawamba. I was like, "My God! Them? Who let *them* on the radio??"

---

1. *Reminds me of my line in* Starving in the Company of Beautiful Women*: "Everything that can be done has been done. Being a great artist now consists simply of being a good editor."*

See, I remember Chumbawamba from their first go round as a bunch of squatting British anarchists who demanded the immediate overthrow of all governments and wrote scathing, screeching atonal dirge music. I think they described themselves as "Situationists." Or at least that's what the filthy, smelly, penniless, vegan crusty crass punks with "Chumbawamba" scrawled on their filthy leather jackets were called in 1987.

A batch of them took over my apartment that summer and would not leave. I think "Situationist" means you find yourself in a good situation, like my living room, and stay there. And when asked to chip in money to pay the phone bill or buy some food or beer, they yell that you're "exploiting the workers."[2]

Anyway, in 1987 if you'd told me that Chumbawamba, a collective of shrieking, squealing, squalling limeys would have a number-one hit by 1997, I would have thought you daft and said, "Shut up and do some dishes, you lazy poofter!"

So, how did this band that might have blown up a major label in 1987 end up on a major label in 1997?

A large part of the answer is: software recording.

Just as a word processing program makes a good writer much more able to organize her thoughts, software recording solutions like Vegas, Sound Forge, Acid, FL Studio, and Pro Tools can take the most marginally tuneful rough musical draft and make it easy for someone with a good sense of pacing to rearrange his output into a passable pop song. You only have to sing the chorus correctly once, then it's just cutting and pasting. And that chorus, and each line and note and every beat in the song, can be pasted from the best parts of dozens of other takes. All this studio glitz is one reason groups that sound great on record don't always sound great live.

It also enables individuals to make music easily without even having a band.

Computer recording can make the lame rock. But in the hands of a someone who's already talented, it can polish the raw unrefined diamond and make it shine. In the hands of someone who's extremely talented, like Trent Reznor of Nine Inch Nails, it can produce new music that passes beyond the ordinary and is actually acutely amazing.

---

2. For some reason, most people I've met who rail about "the system exploiting the worker" never seem to do much working themselves.

We don't need to reinvent the wheel (just the reel to reel). Most of what we learned in the last chapter applies here. You still want to use good mikes, baffle them for better sound isolation, and not hurry or pressure the musicians. Tune your instruments. Get good levels. Record tests and listen to them before starting. All that stuff is the same in software recording. So if you didn't read the last chapter because you just want to jump ahead to software recording, go read it now. Ninety-three percent of it will be relevant here. The only stuff that isn't is the actual other end of the recording chain. You'll be going into the computer rather than into a tape recorder, and the mixer and effects will probably be software on the screen, although the smartest software recording engineers still use a hardware mixer too, and probably some outboard hardware pre-amps, and effects like reverb and delay.

Let's Get It ON

Sonic Foundry's Vegas is my tool of choice for multi-track software recording.

It is now actually a video program with multi-track audio support, but when I first used it shortly after it came out in 1998, it was audio only. It is an excellent program, with a very intuitive interface that sort of imitates the look, feel, and functionality of a multi-track recorder *and* a mixing desk. The metaphor is complete, even down to the Arm for Record button you would have on a hardware multi-track recorder.

> **NOTE**
>
> Some of these tutorials are re-purposed from my film school book. I apologize, but there's no need to reinvent the wheel here. You can jump ahead to the Vegas one if you want. It contains new information.

Using Acid

Sonic Foundry (recently purchased by Sony Pictures) makes three great programs that I highly recommend you get somehow: Acid, Sound Forge, and Vegas.

Acid is a very simple-to-use software utility that can easily allow even non-musicians to make great-sounding background music for films or even basic tracks to record a band over.

Acid does one thing only, but it does that one thing very well: It takes different audio loops and stretches them to match each other in a coherent manner. Acid will do in seconds what people used to spend all day trying to do with two turntables and a tape machine.

You can take the result into Sound Forge, Vegas, or ProTools to edit and then bring it into Vegas and add other sounds, live instruments, or even vocals. There are several different levels of Acid, one for any budget. Acid Pro is the high-end version with the most depth. Acid Music is the mid-level version. Acid Style is the beginner (and least expensive) version.

Here's a lesson on using Acid (a demo version is included on the CD—although it times out at two minutes and has to be restarted). Try to get a full version somehow to make a rhythm track.

Open Acid. Save the project with a descriptive name.

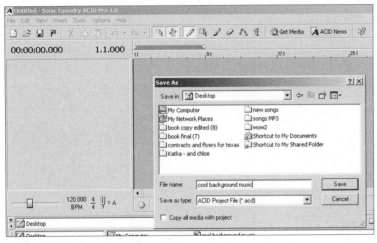

Figure 12.1 *Save the Acid project.*

You should always save a project (in any program) as soon as you start it and then save periodically as you go in case the program or machine crashes. Make this second nature. I use the Ctrl + S keyboard function to do this (Apple + S on a Mac).

Select File, Open. Open all the files in the Noises/Acid file folder on the CD-ROM that comes with this book (see Figures 12.2 and 12.3). I made these sample audio loops in Sonic Foundry's Sound Forge using parts of previously existing songs of mine, but you can use any audio sample in Acid. Acid recognizes both .wav and .aiff format files. You can even buy ready-made CDs of great rhythm tracks from Sonic Foundry. These are specially prepared and have special internal meta information that makes them loop better and gives better results when matching tempos.

There are also some cooler ones that you can use in your songs in the folder "sample loops." These were created by www.monochromevision.net.

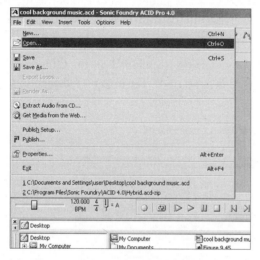

Figure 12.2 *Open all the files in the folder.*

Figure 12.3 *Open all the files in the folder, continued.*

> ### NOTE
>
> .wav (wave) files are a standard Windows media format. .aiff (pronounced "A-I-F-F") is a standard Apple format. Most computers and almost all audio and video programs can read both formats nowadays. For all practical purposes, one format does not have any large advantage over the other. They both sound almost identical and have almost the same file size.

The Acid interface will automatically create tracks for each sound file.

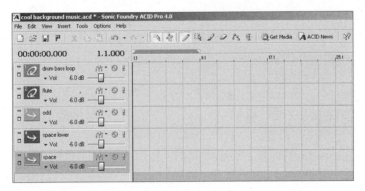

Figure 12.4 *Tracks in Acid.*

We will use two tools in this demonstration, the Draw Tool and the Erase Tool (see Figure 12.5).

Click on the Draw tool button. Using the Draw tool (it looks like a pencil), hold the left mouse button down and draw a line across the drum bass loop track. Then release the mouse. You will get a track of solid drum bass loop (see Figure 12.6).

Hit the spacebar to begin playback. You will notice that Acid has looped the short audio track to create a longer rhythm track.

If it seems slower or faster than you like, you can adjust the Project Tempo slider to the desired speed. Note that a variance of only a few BPM (beats per minute) can make a big difference in the mood of a piece. I brought this project from the default of 120 BPM up to 159 BPM. This gave it a hard industrial sound.

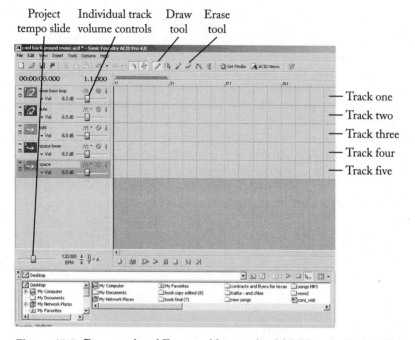

Project tempo slide   Individual track volume controls   Draw tool   Erase tool

Track one
Track two
Track three
Track four
Track five

Figure 12.5 *Draw tool and Erase tool buttons in Acid. Note the Project Tempo slider and the individual track volume controls. We will use those, too.*

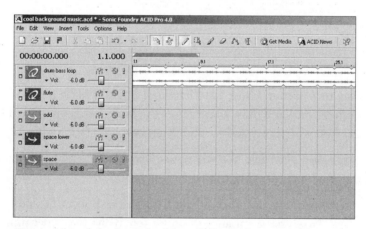

Figure 12.6 *A single track with audio in Acid.*

Now, using the Draw tool, draw some more audio in the rest of the tracks (see Figure 12.7). But this time, lift and release it here and there to allow the sound to start and stop.

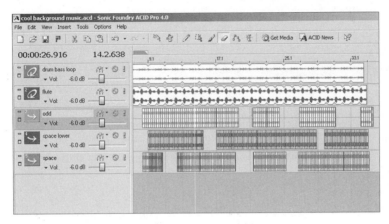

Figure 12.7 *Several tracks with audio in Acid.*

After making changes, press the Home key on your keyboard to return to the beginning of the piece. Listen to the changes again by pressing the spacebar again. Keep making changes until it sounds the way you want it.

Don't forget to periodically save your project as you go. Just press Ctrl + S.

A good way to work is to have the basic track you are using for the beat, usually the one with the most rhythmic sound (in this case the drum bass loop) go all the way through, or almost all the way through. (It can be interesting to have it drop out for a few measures, as it does here near the end. Note in Figure 12.7 that other tracks take up the beat at that point until the drum bass loop comes back in. I usually build on the basic beat by having other tracks come in and out. It is often a good rule of thumb to have the rest of the tracks build in a way that there's not much at first but more as the song goes on. Of course there are infinite variations, but this is a good formula to start with. So now that you've got some tracks down, you can remove parts by using the Erase tool. That's how I build in Acid—I put down a lot, then take away.

You can adjust the individual track volumes by using the individual track volume controls. This will help give you a balance you like.

When we get a sound we're satisfied with, it's time to render it, close Acid. Select File, Render As and then from the drop-down menu, select Mixed Wave file.

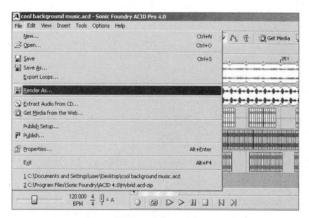

Figure 12.8 *Pick Render As from the File menu.*

Figure 12.9 *Type a filename to save your new Acid soundtrack.*

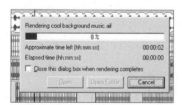

Figure 12.10 *Acid soundtrack rendering.*

Close the Dialog Window.

TIP

You'll need some good computer speakers. These are pretty cheap, and you can get them anywhere.

Figure 12.11 *Computer speakers.*

You will now have a complete piece you can use as basic tracks to record over in another program like Vegas.

TIP

Muska & Lipman has two great books that explore Acid and Sound Forge in much more detail than we had room for here: *ACID Power!* by David Franks, and *Sound Forge 6 Power!* by Scott Garrigus.

Using Sound Forge

Sonic Foundry's Sound Forge is a much more robust program than Acid. I think of it as the audio equivalent of Photoshop—an incredibly deep program with a 500-page manual and dozens of menus and plug-ins that can be used for an almost unlimited number of sound manipulations. But it is also, on a basic level, easy to use. For the first part of this tutorial, we will open the file we just made in Acid (see Figures 12.12 and 12.13), apply a little EQ, reverb, and flange, and then save the file.

First, use File/Open to bring in the file we just made.

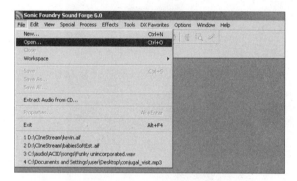

Figure 12.12 *Opening a file in Sound Forge.*

Figure 12.13 *Opening a file in Sound Forge, continued.*

Note that you can see the actual wave form of the file (look at Figure 12.14). This takes the place of having a dedicated hardware oscilloscope. This is useful in advanced editing for finding altering regions and finding looping points.

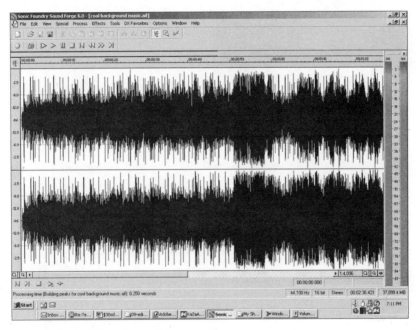

Figure 12.14 *Wave form of the open file.*

Hit the spacebar to begin playback. As we've learned, in almost all audio and media programs, this will stop and start playback. As in Acid, hitting the Home key on the keyboard when the program is stopped brings you back to the beginning of the file.

Now let's do a little EQ. EQ stands for *equalization*, which is the mix of different frequencies present in the overall sound of a file. If there's too much low end, it will sound muffled. Too much high, and the sound is shrill. Changing the EQ of a sound file is a useful technique for making any file sound better.

Select Process/EQ/Graphic (see Figure 12.15). A dialog box will appear (see Figure 12.16).

Hit the Reset button. This returns all the frequency bands to zero, which is no boost and no cut. At this setting, no EQ is applied.

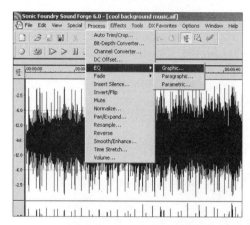

Figure 12.15 *Accessing the EQ dialog box.*

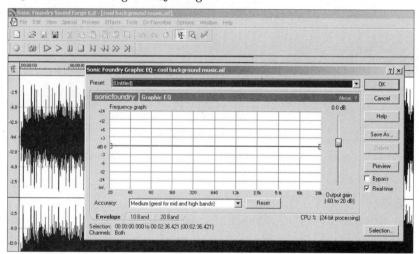

Figure 12.16 *EQ dialog box.*

Try boosting the bass by sliding the left hand (lower) end of the frequency line up a bit (see Figure 12.17). Click on OK to apply. It will take a little while for the file to render. The speed will depend on the power of your computer. You will see a little taskbar in the lower left corner showing the progress.

After the file finishes redrawing, play it again, and notice that it sounds a lot deeper because it now has more bass.

There is a drop-down menu with several useful presets (see Figure 12.18).

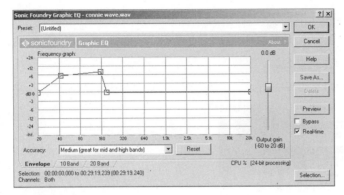

Figure 12.17 *Boosting bass EQ.*

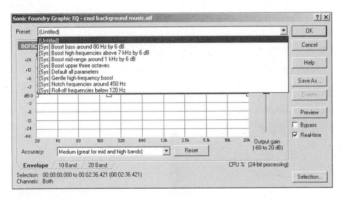

Figure 12.18 *EQ drop-down menu.*

Experiment with these later and listen to how the sound is altered. Make copies of each file before altering it in Sound Forge, because it will overwrite the file and you will not be able to go back to your original once you've saved the changes.

Now click on OK, click Save As from the File menu, and save the altered file with a new filename.

Now we will apply some reverb. *Reverb* (short for *reverberation*) adds depth and warmth to a sound by imitating the sound of short echoes. If you clap your hands in a large empty auditorium, you will hear some reverb. If you do the same in a small closet full of clothes, you will hear none.

Select Effects/Reverb to access the Reverb dialog box (see Figures 12.19 and 12.20).

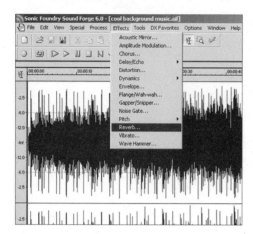

Figure 12.19 *Accessing the Reverb dialog box.*

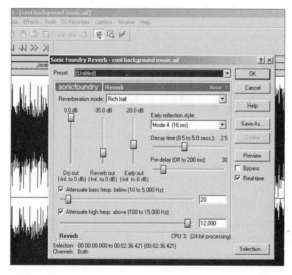

Figure 12.20 *The Reverb dialog box.*

Go to the drop-down menu and select Long Hall. Click on the Preview button for a real-time preview of what it will sound like. If you like it, click on OK, wait for the changes to render, then play the file. Notice how different it now sounds.

By the way, the Real-Time Preview button is available for all the effects in Sound Forge.

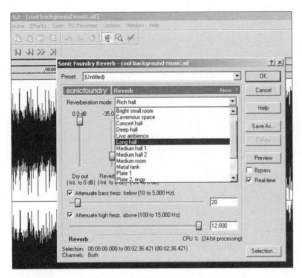

Figure 12.21 *The Reverb dialog box drop-down menu.*

Now click on Save As, give the file a new name, and save it.

Finally, we'll add a little flange. Flange is an effect that makes a file sort of sound like it's inside a jet engine, in a really cool way. It's used on a lot of rock records to make them sound trippy. As soon as you hear it, I'm sure you'll go "Oh, *that's* what that is."

Select Effects/Flange-Wah-Wah to open the Flange dialog box.

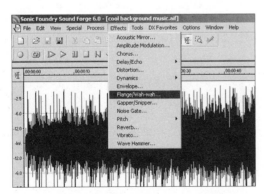

Figure 12.22 *Opening the Flange dialog box.*

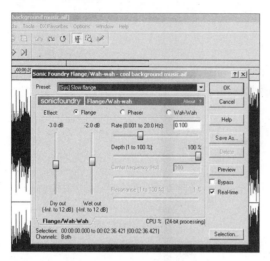

Figure 12.23 *The Flange dialog box.*

Get the preset Slow Flange 2 from the drop-down menu, and click OK. Listen to the file. Save.

You can repeat these steps for even more flange. You can do this with any of the controls in Sound Forge. Doing any of these processes twice will add twice as much of the effect.

You can also highlight just a part of a file and process only that part (see Figure 12.24). (If you highlight none, the entire file is affected.) You highlight by holding down the mouse button and sweeping the cursor over just part of the file.

NOTE

You may have some extraneous new small .skf and .sfl files in the same folder as your final product. They will have file names like cool background music.sfk and cool background music.aif.sfl. They are just meta disc image files created by Sound Forge (and Acid and Vegas) to help them work. They are sort of digital poop left behind and can safely be deleted.

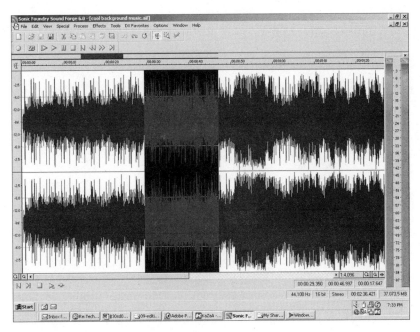

Figure 12.24 *Part of a file highlighted.*

You can adjust the volume of your music in Sound Forge (Process/Volume). Experiment until you get a volume you like.

Move the slider to get the desired effect. If the number is above 100 percent, you are raising the volume. Below 100 percent, you are lowering it. When you get what you want, click OK and save the file.

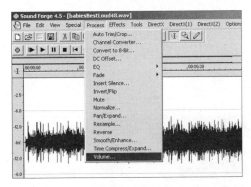

Figure 12.25 *Accessing Volume dialog box in Sound Forge.*

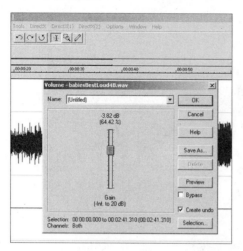

Figure 12.26 *Altering volume in Sound Forge.*

You want the highest volume you can get without clipping. Clipping is distortion. If the wave form goes outside the top of the waveform window, it is clipped.

Once a waveform is clipped, you can't unclip it, even if you lower the volume.

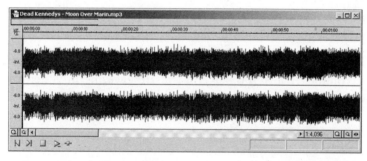

Figure 12.27 *Audio not clipped.*

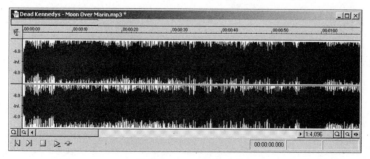

Figure 12.28 *Audio clipped.*

Note the square and bottoms and tops of the wave form in the second example. That's the actual clipping.

Advanced Sound Program Use

I'm not going to get extremely deep into any of these programs. Each one would be a book unto itself. But I'll cover a few more techniques and programs that you may find useful.

Acid, Sound Forge, and Vegas Video are all separate programs made by Sonic Foundry, but they all work well in concert with each other. It is sort of reminiscent of how a graphic designer would use Photoshop and Illustrator.

For instance, you can right-click on a track in Vegas and have the option to open that track in Sound Forge and edit it without even leaving Vegas. Keep in mind that this will be destructive editing; it will overwrite the original track, so you should save backup copies until you become very adept at using it and know exactly what the results of each action will be.

There are other programs like ProTools that are even deeper. I'm not going to go into them other than to mention them. ProTools does most of what Acid, Sound Forge, and Vegas do combined, but it is harder to use. There is a free version of ProTools available at Digidesign.com.

Mastering

You can master a record in Sound Forge. Mastering is the process of taking all the final mixed songs for an album and doing a last bit of fluffing and tweaking to make them perfect. Mastering is often the difference between an amateur sounding record and a professional sounding one. Even something that is recorded really lo-fi sounds more pro after being mastered.

You can add a tiny bit of EQ. You can balance the volume level from song to song to make the album a more consistent listening experience. Some people add a tiny bit of compression and a tiny bit of limiting. The default settings for both compression and limiting are pretty darned good, but you can experiment with both if you find it affecting the sound too much or too little.

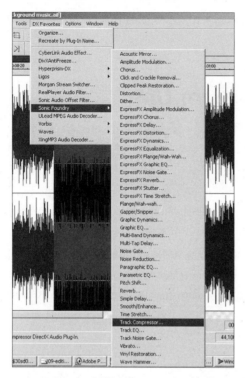

Figure 12.29 *Adding compression in Sound Forge.*

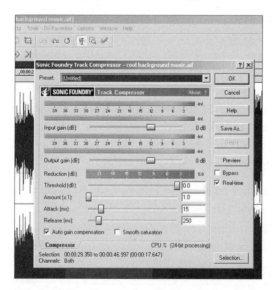

Figure12.30 *Compression dialog window in Sound Forge.*

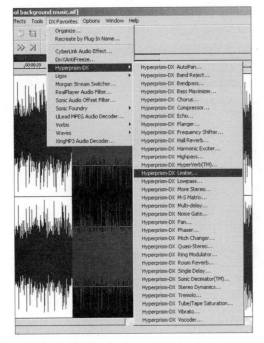

Figure 12.31 *Adding limiting in Sound Forge.*

Note that the drop-down menu here is the Hyperprism DX menu, which is not available in Sound Forge out of the box. Hyperprism DX is a set of third-party plug-ins. More on plug-ins in a moment.

There is some limiting available as a drop-down option from the Compression dialog window, but it is not as robust as the Hyperprism DX plug-in.

Experiment to find the best settings. You might have to do it in sections: Music has different needs than voice, and music with voice has still other needs. There are also presets you might try. For some operations, noise reduction in Sound Forge, for instance, you may need a plug-in. A *plug-in* is a little add-on program that extends the functionality of another program. Some are made by the same company that makes the main program; some are third-party add-ons.

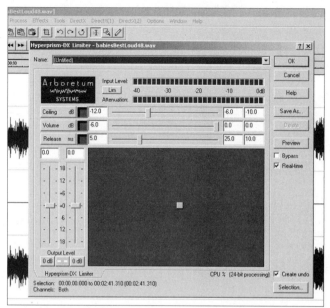

Figure 12.32 *Limiting dialog window in Sound Forge.*

TIP

WITH MASTERING: DON'T OVER DO IT! Too much will ruin the sound, not improve it. Start with very small adjustments and always keep backup copies you can revert to if you fuck it up. Also, as with all audio operations, don't try to do too much in one day. You will get done faster if you go slower sometimes: When you get frustrated, go outside and play in the sun and talk to actual humans. Then come back tomorrow with a fresh set of ears and no frustration.

Noise Reduction

The Sound Forge Noise Reduction plug-in can work wonders, but using this utility takes some experience and skill. Otherwise it makes your program material sound overprocessed. My friend Adam Hauck recently sent me some music taken off of one of my records, and I e-mailed him back and said "You're using too much Sound Forge Noise Reduction plug-in. He wrote back "How the heck did you know? I'm downright baffled."

Basically, I said "Because I have it, I've used it, and I've decided not to use it much. Most of the time when I use it, it sounds like there are robots whispering under the music." I used a little too much on the Maggie Estep interview on the *D.I.Y.* DVD, for example.

Actually, in the hands of a skilled pro, it can work wonders. I had a friend in San Fran who was making a good bit of scratch restoring bootleg tapes of sixties hippie music live shows for some bootleg record producer. You really have to work with it, though. It tends to work really well on constant sounds like motor or electrical hum and really poorly on non-constant sounds, like wind.

After you install the plug-in, (there is a demo on the CD) it will appear in one of the Direct-X drop-down menus in Sound Forge (alphabetically as Sonic Foundry Noise Reduction).

You open it while you already have a file open, check the Capture noiseprint checkbox (near the bottom left of the Noise-Reduction plug-in dialog box), and you find a place in the file with no music or talking, and hold the mouse down and drag across the wave form to highlight and sample a short bit of silence by hitting the Preview button.

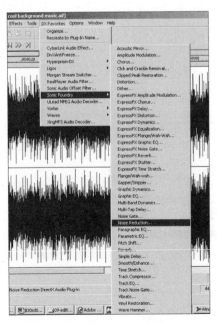

Figure 12.33 *Opening the Noise-Reduction plug-in in Sound Forge.*

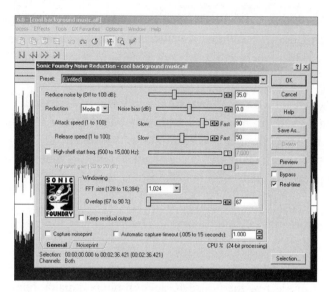

Figure 12.34 *Noise-Reduction plug-in dialog box.*

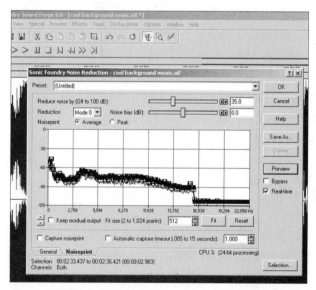

Figure 12.35 *Capture Noiseprint pane of Noise-Reduction plug-in dialog box.*

A quarter-second to two seconds is good. It takes a *noiseprint* of the background noise in that selection. Then you Save As and name it (you might want to use the same preset again) (see Figure 12.36).

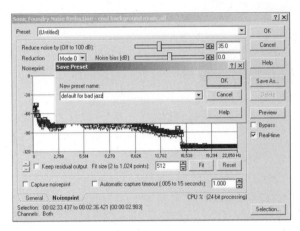

Figure 12.36 *Saving noiseprint settings.*

Then close the plug-in, deselect the silent part, and click anywhere in the file. Reopen the plug-in, and click OK to apply it to the whole file.

You can control the amount of noise reduction with the Reduce Noise By slider at the top of the Noiseprint pane. Too little, and it doesn't do much. Too much, and you get the "whispering robot" digital artifacts. Experiment until you find the right amount.

Pitch Change

You can change the pitch of a file in Sound Forge (Effects/Pitch/Shift). (See Figures 12.37 and 12.38.) Note that the Set the Sample Rate Only box must be checked.

Usually bringing it up or down 2 semitones (use the slider, or type 2 for up and -2 for down) will correct this when going from 44.1k to 48k or vice versa.

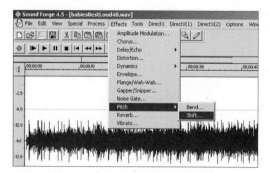

Figure 12.37 *Opening the Pitch/Shift dialog box.*

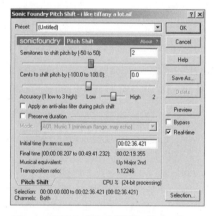

Figure 12.38 *Pitch/Shift dialog box.*

Experiment with the right number of semitones to raise or lower until it sounds like it did before resampling. Be sure to save a copy of the original file to revert to, especially if resampling and shifting changes the file length, which it sometimes does. This may or may not matter, depending on what you're doing with it. It won't be by much. It will probably only matter if you need to synch it up to existing audio or video files.

You can see the exact length of a file, as well as the sampling rate, file size, and other properties in Sound Forge by looking in the bottom right corner of the main display in Sound Forge.

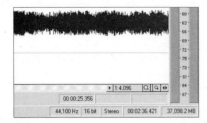

Figure 12.39 *The Properties display in the bottom right corner of Sound Forge.*

Making Audio Loops in Sound Forge

As we've seen, loops are good for importing into other programs like Acid. You can then construct rhythms and soundtracks out of them by combining other sounds.

In Sound Forge, select part of the waveform by holding down your mouse cursor and moving it along the file.

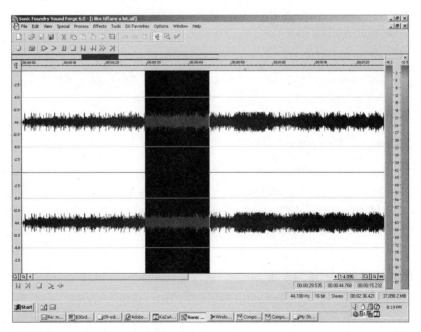

Figure 12.40 *Select part of the waveform.*

Loop tool
button

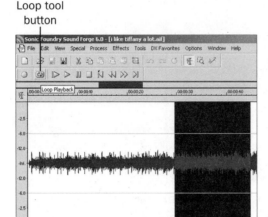

Figure 12.41 *Sound Forge's Loop Tool button.*

Click the Loop button, and move the mouse curser back and forth while holding down the left mouse button. Play around until you find a section that loops well. Then copy that section to a new file and save.

This is how I did the looping menu audio backgrounds for the *D.I.Y.* DVD menus and the "Acid files" on the CD used in the tutorial at the beginning of this chapter. You can also make drum loops from drum parts on records.

Video in Sound Forge

You can open a video file in Sound Forge and in Acid; it's just like opening an audio file. You can't do much to edit the video, but you can edit the audio and then resave it. The video will display key frames at the top of the window so you can follow where the video is in relation to the audio.

Multitracking in Vegas

Vegas Video is an NLE (non-linear editing) video editing system that also supports multitracking audio capabilities. You can record a whole band one instrument at a time. Or bring in existing files and add vocals.

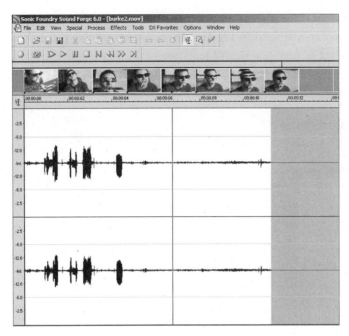

Figure 12.42 *A Quicktime file of director Burke Roberts opened up in Sound Forge.*

Scribble   Timecode   Mute button on   Arm for
strip   window   original vocal   Record button

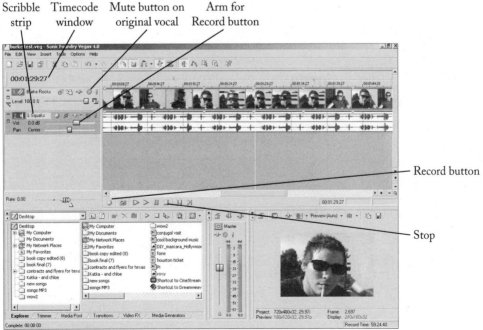

Record button

Stop

Figure 12.43 *Vegas interface.*

Vegas Video can be used for editing video, audio, or both at the same time. The audio portion is easy to use, with a very intuitive interface. Basically, the audio portion has all the tools that you would have on an analog multi-track recorder combined with a mixing board. Vegas Video just adds an extra line to the timeline and two editing windows, just like any other NLE system.

Figure 12.44 *Inserting a new audio track in Vegas.*

Add a new audio track and name it by double-clicking on the scribble strip (see Figure 12.45) and typing a descriptive name (like "Squawk 2").

Click the red Arm for Record button (see Figure 12.46).

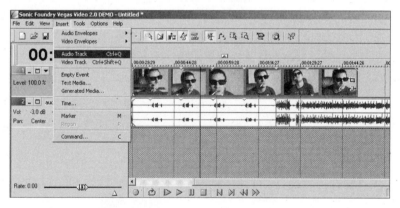

Figure 12.45 *Adding an audio track in Vegas Video.*

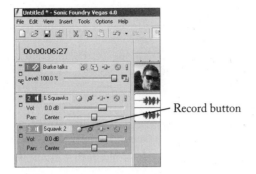

Figure 12.46 *Click the red Arm for Record button.*

Vegas will ask you where to save the file. Pick a location from the Browse button and name the file.

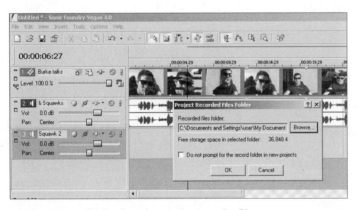

Figure 12.47 *Pick a location and name the file.*

When you are ready to record, you still need to set the audio levels. Have your subject speak into the microphone while you watch the meters where it says Master. You want to have the average rate come as close to going into the red without going up into the red very often. Red means clipping (distortion). You don't want distortion. Conversely, if it's too far below the red, you don't have a high enough signal-to-noise ratio, which will result in poor sound.

When you get a good level, hit the red Record button and have the singer sing (or guitarist play, or whatever). As with hardware recording, it's best to start with drums, or at least a click track if you're recording one instrument at a time.

TIP

If you get a multi-track soundcard—about $150 to $1000; at least $300 for a good one—you can record the whole band on separate tracks at the same time. Get one that's at least 20-bit and has a breakout box.

The singer will also be able to hear any previously recorded audio on the other tracks in the headphones unless you press the Mute button on that track. In that case, he'll hear only the new music as he records it. You can build a whole band one track at a time this way.

When you are done recording, click Stop. A dialog box will appear, and you can save the new take (see Figures 12.48 and 12.49).

If you don't like it, you don't need to save it. Click Done to save (see Figure 12.49).

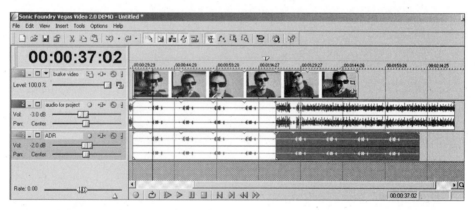

Figure 12.48 *New track of music.*

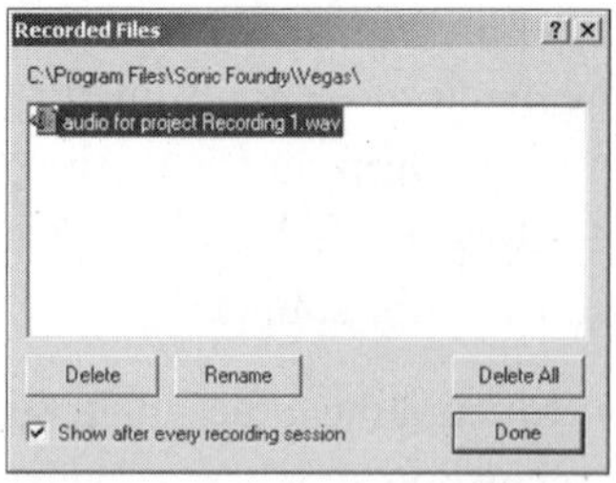

Figure 12.49 *Save Take dialog box.*

Then you can mix and replace between the old and new vocal take and export to a new track. You can try as often as you need and save the new takes or record over them.

You can use the numbers in the Timecode window to mark a particular part so you can come back to it exactly.

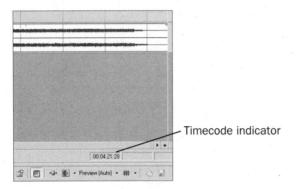
Timecode indicator

Figure 12.50 *Timecode indicator in Vegas.*

Timecode is a way for finding specific points in an audio or video timeline. It consists of hours, minutes, seconds, and frames (resets at 30; it's a video thing), separated by semicolons. This:

> 00:04:28:21

means that the point where the cursor rests in the timeline at that instant is zero hours, four minutes, twenty-eight seconds, and twenty-one frames from the beginning of the song.

TIP

You can download Vegas Video 3.0 LE, a free, working lite version. It has four tracks of audio, and you can bounce one track to another.

They move the download page sometimes, so search "Vegas Video 3.0 LE, a free" on Google.

Vegas Video 3.0 LE also comes with Sound Forge in some cases.

Mixing in Vegas

To mix down your song, change the settings of the track volume and track pan for each track until you have a good balance that you like. Then go to File/Render As and pick the wave format default (unless you want to export as one of the compressed formats from the drop-down menu). Hit Save and it will render.

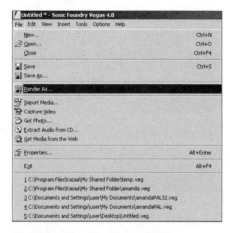

Figure 12.51 *Rendering in Vegas.*

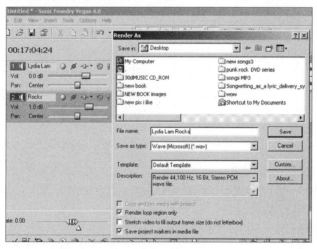

Figure 12.52 *More rendering in Vegas.*

Recording in Acid

You can also multi-track in Acid. It's not as robust for this as Vegas, but the interface and process are almost identical. The above info will work for Acid, except that you needn't create a new audio track. Just hit the red Record button, and a new track will automatically be created.

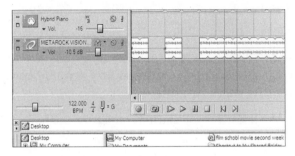

Figure 12.53 *Record button in Acid.*

Pro Tools

I'm not offering a tutorial of ProTools because they did not respond to my request for a working copy of the program to review, and their free version runs on just about every operating system in use except mine (Windows 2000 Professional—the BEST OS for media production, *hands down.*

But all these programs, even from different companies, have very similar actions and interfaces. The ProTools Web site, www.protools.com, offers a free *working* version (and a downloadable manual!) that is limited to eight tracks. But you can still bounce several tracks down to one or two to free up more virtual tracks, just like you can do on a hardware four-track or eight-track recorder. This is very in keeping with the $30 Way and is also a good alternative to bootlegging the programs we mention here, no matter how easy it is to bootleg them. Nod nod, wink wink.

> **TIP**
>
> A lot of times, when you go to type in the serial number to register a piece of software, you'll have the issue of "Is that a zero or the letter 'O'?" They do look a lot alike, but in my experience, *it's always a zero.* I've never found a letter O in a serial number yet.
>
> A call to programmers: Go one further and eliminate zeros from serial numbers. Installing your damn software is time consuming enough without the extra confusion.

FL Studio

FL Studio (formerly Fruity Loops) from Image Line Software is a pretty amazing piece of software. People with no musical experience can do sequencing and looping and produce pretty robust pieces of music in minutes. People with musical experience can create masterpieces with it.

The full product, FL Studio Fruityloops, is available for $99 from www.Flstudio.com. Their e-mail is info@flstudio.com.

It is especially well suited to producing electronica and dance music and industrial, but with a little finesse, can produce mellower trippy very rhythmic backings for hip-hop, trip-hop, rock, jazz, in short, anything.

This is a very deep program. We'll just get you started and let you see how to do a simple beat (that you could then import into any other program to record over top of) to inspire you. Then you can run with it from there.

The Web site contains a demo, but the Save function is disabled.

Try to get a full version somehow.

Begin by opening the program. Close the demo that automatically opens. Hit File/New to open a new project. Go under File/Templates and pick a drum machine emulator. I've picked the old reliable 808 (simulating a Roland 808 analog drum machine).

Figure 12.54 *Pick a drum template.*

What looks like a switchboard will pop up. Make sure you are in pattern mode (pat) not song mode (song) and that pattern 1 is lit up on the pattern number chooser. If these aren't showing that value, click once on the buttons until they are.

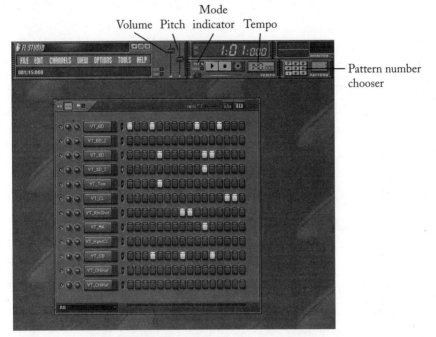

Figure 12.55 *Drum emulator switchboard in FL Studio.*

Notice the sliders at the top to change the pitch of the project. And you can right-click on the tempo display to change the tempo options.

Figure 12.56 *Right-click tempo numbers to change tempo.*

Click on various squares in the switchboard to enable that tone and beat to activate. Left-clicking a square adds the tone there; right-clicking removes it. Then hit the spacebar to play what you've got. Hitting the spacebar again will stop playback.

You can turn a track off by clicking the little green button on the far left of the track.

The horizontal rows represent different components of the beat. Left-to-right represents time. The whole sequence, left to right, represents one measure.

Experiment with different combinations. When you get one you like the sound of, hit Save and go on to define your number two pattern. Click the pattern number chooser over to 2, and start over.

Figure 12.57 *Pattern number chooser set to 2.*

This time, click the little icon near the upper-right corner that says PR to reveal the piano roll. This will allow you to assign actual notes to different voices.

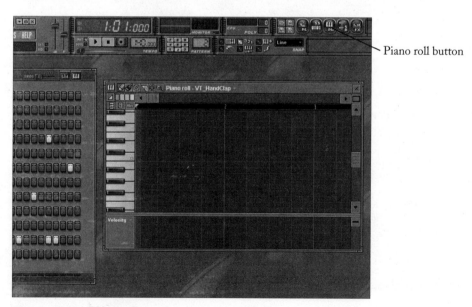

Piano roll button

Figure 12.58 *Piano roll.*

Click some different patterns on the switchboard and also on the piano roll and hit the spacebar. Make changes until you're happy and move on to define pattern three. You can choose which voicing is controlled by the piano roll by right-clicking on that voice name in the switchboard and then hitting Send to Piano Roll from under the right-click menu.

A very useful technique is to copy one pattern to another and then make small variations in the new pattern. Copying makes it so you don't have to reinvent the mousetrap each time. To copy a pattern:

Figure 12.59 *VT_SD enabled to send to piano roll.*

Hold your mouse down and scroll down this row of green buttons until they are all lit up.

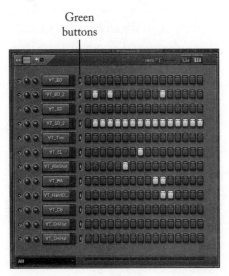

Figure 12.60 *Light up this row of green buttons.*

Then click anywhere on the pattern switchboard and press Ctrl + C to copy. Enable a new pattern number, click anywhere in that pattern switchboard, and press Ctrl + V to paste it in. Then alter as needed.

Repeat all these above steps until you have six or more patterns defined.

Then click over to Song mode on the mode picker and start stringing these patterns into songs.

Hit the button near the upper-right corner labeled PL to reveal the playlist.

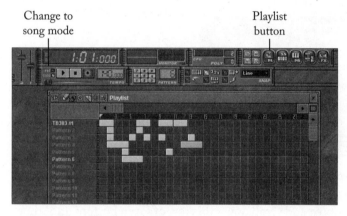

Figure 12.61 *Playlist revealed.*

Now you are using the patterns you created previously to string together into longer units that will be used as the basis for songs. Try to hear the other instruments over the top of them as you are going along, and remember the basic precepts and tenets of good songwriting we learned earlier, particularly finding a good balance between repetition and variation, and building and releasing tension as you go.

Note that the metaphor is again time equals left to right, and patterns equal up and down. Also note that you can have more than one pattern play at a time.

Left-clicking a square adds the pattern there, right-clicking removes it.

Play and change until you're happy. When you're happy, save the song, then export by going to File/Export Wave and then hit Go in the bottom right of the dialog box to render.

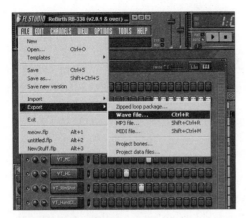

Figure 12.62 *Exporting the final song in FL Studio.*

Figure 12.63 *Hit Go to render.*

In the Noises folder of the CD, I've included the final mixed version, meow_rendered_from_FL_studio.wav. Also there is Skinny_dippin_in_the_Gulf_with_my_Tiff_Kitty.wav. It's kinda cool. (Both are used as background music on "I Left My Band In San Francisco" on the CD.)

My forte is rock instruments, not electronic compositions. There's a very good chance you'll be making stuff much cooler than these two humble efforts within very little time of working in this program.

Miscellaneous Stuff

There are a lot of little things that help make a person a better recording engineer or producer in the digital realm. And it's the little things that count in life, right? So, here I'll give you some tiny tips that may not seem all that big but might just save your butt at some point.

Backing Up

I am a fastidious backer-upper. I started using computers for my writing a long time ago. I actually did write with a typewriter at first, before word processors were common. I was born in 1964, and I've been writing almost every day since 1978. I used to take a copy of the latest version of my latest project once a week and bring the discs over to a friend's house. This was in case my house burned down or my computer died or was stolen.

Later, when I was writing my novel, I would upload the last copy every night to an unlinked spot on several servers (usually extra space on servers of people I had done Web design work for). A novel doesn't take up much space, and those people are unaware of what you have on their server, and they will never know. There are probably STILL copies of various drafts of my novel on unlinked spots on other people's Web sites. I don't remember. I would make sure to use servers in different cities, in case my city (San Francisco at the time) were destroyed by an earthquake. This is sort of the reason the Internet was invented: The United States Army made the Internet to have a computer system that would survive a nuclear war.

If you don't do Web design and don't know how to FTP files, you can do the same effect with e-mailing a copy to yourself on some Web-based mail service like Hotmail or Yahoo!. Then a copy of your file is stored on their server.

TIP

Yahoo! gets a lot less spam than Hotmail.

I recall talking to some girl at a party about my fastidious backing up. She pretty much told me that I was an idiot, and an anal retentive idiot at that.

Two months later, her completed novel was lost when her laptop was stolen out of her car. She had no backup copy. Three months after that, *this* anal retentive's novel hit the shelves.

The thing that got me into making backups was this: When I went to community college—John Adams campus at City College of San Francisco—kids from the neighborhood would sneak into the building and mess with whole computer labs by flipping the breakers in the hall. I started hitting Ctrl + S every two minutes to save, in any program. I still do.

I back up important audio and video projects on an external FireWire drive, daily if I'm working a lot. I also back them up to re-recordable data DVDs (password-protected in case I lose them) and keep them somewhere else, in case my house gets burned down or robbed. Sometimes, I even make daily DVD backups and carry them with me. To me, my data is my *life*. While I am working on this book right now, I would rather lose everything in my apartment (including family heir-looms and about $10,000 worth of electronic and musical equipment and cameras and such) than lose all the data on the $80 hard drive on my computer.

That's why I back up constantly.

If there were a fire, I'd just grab my cat and my computer. Or even just the kitty and today's backup. Computers are so cheap that they barely matter. It's the work on them that I venerate. When traveling abroad, I bring my best work on a couple DVDs in my backpack. That way, if I decide not to return, I'm set.[3]

My life exists as multiple copies of art that affect people. It lives out in the world, not in my town or my car or my bank account or any of that shit. My apartment need only function as a place to sleep, love, and make art. I could live anywhere and do what I do. I don't care about amassing stuff, unless it is for making music, video, art, whatever. Basically, I could take a laptop and leave anytime.

---

3. I don't love Los Angeles and I'm maybe looking for a cool place to move. If you have any suggestions, in the U.S. or otherwise, please e-mail me at MD@kittyfeet.com and tell me where I should move and why. Bid for it. It's a contest. Whoever sells me on their town with the best of everything wins me in their town for a year or more.

Figure 12.64 *A copy of my novel,* Starving in the Company of Beautiful Women, *holding up a broken side of my bed⁴ (me and a gal broke it, somehow). See, books are not sacred: The object that contains the art is not sacred. Only the content is. And there's plenty more copies of this content out in the world.*

TIP

You can use FireWire or even regular removable hard drives for going from studio to studio. You could record the drum tracks in the big room of an expensive studio and save money by taking the project home to finish in your home studio.

Telecommuting for Art

You can record over distances with other people. The song "Smelly Piano" on the CD was recorded as a snail mail collaboration with Mike Pickle. My friend Dave Majka programmed the drums and did the engineering. I played piano and bass

---

4. *This is kinda cute because one of the only bad reviews this book every got was a consumer review on Amazon.com where someone wrote something like, "I had to rate this one star to be able to post the review, but even that's generous. Couldn't there be a lower rating, like maybe an icon of a book holding up the short leg of a table?"*

and did the singing. We mixed it and mailed a CD to Mike Pickle, who added the lead guitar and mailed a new CD back to me.

Theoretically, with DSL, you might almost be able to do this in real time over the Internet, but I've not yet tried it.

You could certainly e-mail FL Studio projects. Since they are basically just the sheet music (like MIDI), they are tiny.

TIP

Troubleshooting Tip: Just because the Device Manager on your PC says "This device is working properly" doesn't mean it is. It simply means that the hardware is still responding electrically. One day Tiffany couldn't use her computer to connect to the Internet. The Device Manager said that her modem was working correctly. I went over there and pulled the modem out and there was a big electrical burn mark near where the phone plugs in to it. We went to Good Guys, spent 19 bucks on a new modem, slipped it in, and she was instantly in business again.

To Culminate

Computers are great, but don't forget to step away from the computer from time to time and *live life*. Then you'll have something meaningful to write songs about. There is no software to imitate *heart*.

I look at a computer merely as a tool, an extension of my brain. When I wake up, I turn the computer on, make coffee, and start my day. And the computer is on until I fall asleep. I sit down at it for a minute or an hour here and there all day and all night.

But I somehow lived life quite well for the 28 years before I even touched a computer, and wrote and recorded many damn fine songs before then.

A physical machine is an amplifier for your muscles, to increase the strength and breadth of the tasks you can do. A computer is an amplifier for your brain. It increases the amount of work you are able to do with your mind power, and it exponentially intensifies your ability to get that work out to the world.

Next, we'll learn how to do exactly that.

Chapter 13

Make and Promote
Your Own CDs

Why wait for a record deal? Do it yourself. Here are tutorials on making your own CDs. Also, advice on getting the world to notice.

Once you've spent a zillion hours writing, rehearsing, and committing your art to tape or hard drive and then mastering, you'll probably want to duplicate a whole mess o' copies and get your blood, sweat, and bytes out to the world. You'll need to create a CD master to do this.

You'll need a good CD burner. They ship built in to almost all new computers now. If you don't have one, go buy one at Fry's, Circuit City, or some place like that, or online.

Figure 13.1 *Blank CDs in a local store (and some blank DVDs, too).*

Figure 13.2 *Blank CD labels in a local store.*

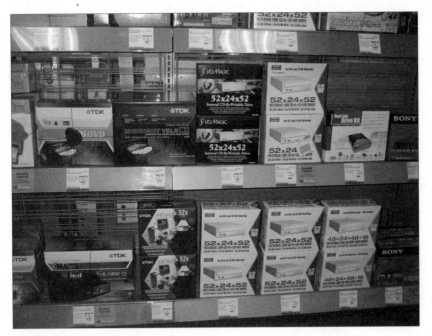

Figure 13.3 *CD burners in a local store.*

They're all a little different to install, so follow the directions.

Nero

You'll also need a CD burning program. I use Stomp RecordNow Max (which ships free with many CD burners) to make simple audio CDs. It's easy to use, powerful, and comes free with most burners. I use the wizard. Just follow the prompts and create a new audio CD by dragging the song files into the left side, and then hitting the Burn icon at the top (eight icons from the left, just below the Window menu).

The status bar at the bottom will tell you how much room you have left on a blank CD.

Before burning, if you like, you can rearrange the song order by dragging them around in the list with your mouse.

You can burn one CD or many. (You can save the configuration, so you don't have to re-do it each time.) Many people, when starting out, make records on CD with print runs of as little as 10 or 20 and just burn more as they run out.

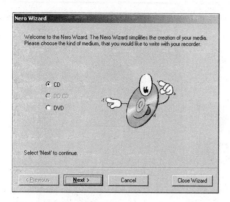

Figure 13.4 *Nero.*

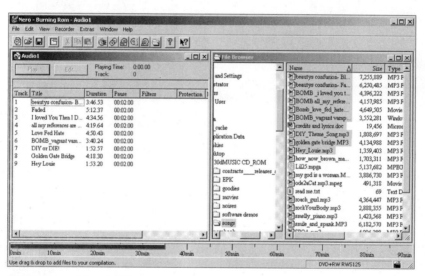

Figure 13.5 *More of Nero.*

You can burn one copy and use it as a master to take to a CD duplication place and get hundreds (or thousands) of copies made.

Some stores (particularly chains) won't carry burned CDs because they won't play on every machine. Ones replicated by a duplication house (even if created from a burned CD) will.

Close other programs (especially memory hogs like Photoshop and interrupt hogs like audio and video players) while burning CDs. Go offline. The burner may put skips on the CD if it runs out of memory at any point in the burn.

If you do this and still end up with skips, you may need more RAM or a faster processor.

Also, you might turn off air conditioners and other power suckers. If they're running on the same circuit as your computer, it can cause energy fluctuations that can affect burning adversely.

RecordNow Max

You can also burn CDs with Stomp RecordNow Max (there is a 30-day *working* demo on the CD with this book).

Open the program. Close the wizard. You'll get the window seen in Figure 13.6.

Drag your audio files onto the window on the right. You can then rearrange the order by dragging the files around if you want.

Hit the red Burn button. Your CD burner tray should open up when the burn is done and politely hand you your disc.

Again, you can save the list to make more copies or use this as a master to take to a duplicator.

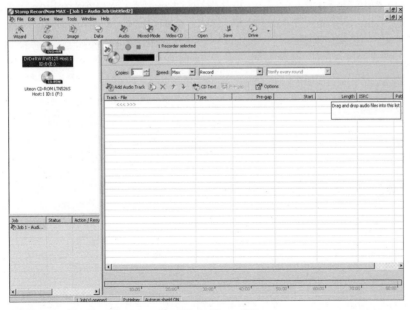

Figure 13.6 *Burning an audio CD in RecordNow.*

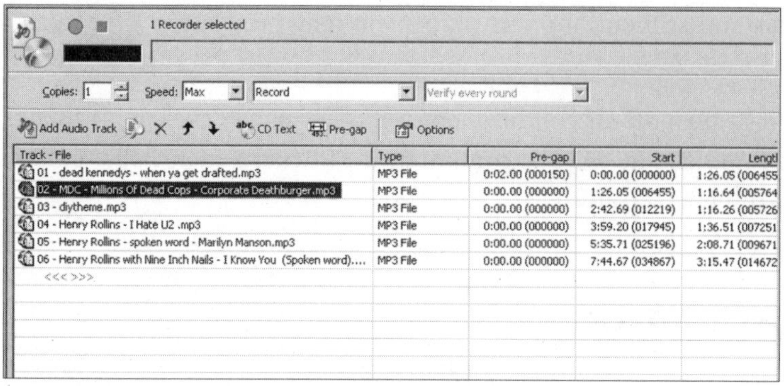

Figure 13.7 *Burning another audio CD in RecordNow.*

"Watson, Come Here. I Need You!"

The first time I burned a CD of my music, I felt powerful. Doesn't burning CDs make you feel a little good? It's fun, no?

Love it. This is why we make art. It feels good.

Look at putting art out into the world as putting a message in a bottle. It's communication with the unknown. Tapping into the Universe through people you may never meet. Though when you go on tour, you may actually get to meet them! One cool thing about the art I do is: Though I may not move a million "units," I do touch people's souls. I get at least five e-mails a week from strangers saying, "Dude, your movie/book/CD rocks. If you're ever in _____, you can stay with us."

TIP

You don't have to sell a billion copies of a release to be making good music and affecting people. Mike Switzer of the Hawthorne Improv Music Collective in Houston has one extra dedicated computer running all the time burning CDs. The collective has about 100 releases, in runs of approximately 30 copies each. They sell them for between one and five bucks each. They swap with other players and even give them away. The point is just to get them out there.

CD-Extra CD

One thing that never caught on, but I think should have and still could, is *CD-Extra* CDs. These are CDs that contain both audio and data material. These will play in an audio CD player and also display data when read on a computer.

I did this with my 1998 commercial release *Living Vicariously Through Michael Dean* (on the Direct Hit Records label out of Dallas). Thanks Kelly! Only 1,000 were pressed, but it was pretty flucking kewl.

To create one with Stomp RecordNow Max, insert a CD into your burner, open the program, and close the wizard. Click the Mixed Mode button in the middle top.

You will get a window that looks like this:

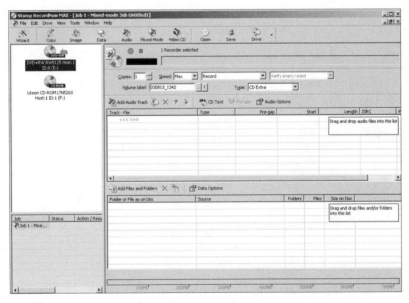

Figure 13.8 *Making a CD-Extra in RecordNow.*

Drag audio files into the top right quadrant, and the data files into the bottom right quadrant.

Hit the red Record button. Ignore the little prompt that comes up. It will begin recording anyway.

A few minutes later, voila! You'll have a CD with data and music on the same disc.

When you're done, make sure you test it on various audio players and different computers (both Mac and PC) before committing to having a whole mess o' copies manufactured.

You will also probably have to put instructions on the back of the jewel case that say something like:

> "This split session disc will play in any audio CD player. It also contains extra program material, videos, and goodies that you access by placing it in your computer and clicking on the file called Index.htm."

One thing you can do is have the navigation of the data part surf like a Web site. It will load instantly because it will not have to download the files. If there are HTML files on the disc, the person's Web browser will open when the index.htm file is clicked.

You can also create the navigational interface using Macromedia Director (like on the data-only CD that comes with this book).

Again, test the final product before committing to making a lot of them.

To create a CD-Extra with Nero, insert a CD into your burner, hit File/New, and close the wizard. You will get a window that looks like this:

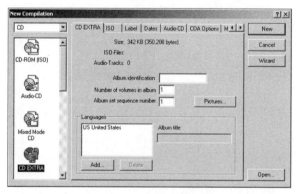

Figure 13.9 *Making a CD-Extra in Nero.*

If you want, you can type in the album name. This will then show up on some CD players' digital readouts while it plays.

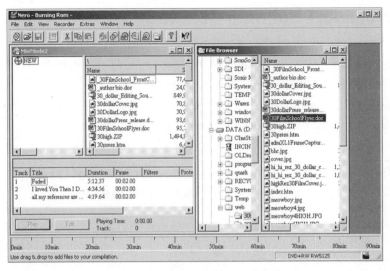

Figure 13.10 *Making another CD-Extra in Nero.*

Drag the data into the top left quadrant. Ignore the Pictures and CDPlus folders—they need to be there but you don't need to deal with them. And they will not be seen by the end user. Drag the songs into the bottom left quadrant and burn as usual.

Sometimes the creation of a CD-extra will fail for no reason, and you'll have to waste a few blank CDs until it works.

If you get the message shown in Figure 13.11 while burning, click on No.

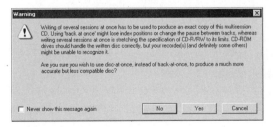

Figure 13.11 *Nero error.*

There. Done. Although I've had to do a few tries on Nero to get it to work. On RecordNow max, it worked the first time.

What Data Should I Put on a CD-Extra?

Anything. But keep in mind that it will take away the amount of room you have for music on the audio-only portion. The total capacity of a CD is about 700 megs, no matter how you slice it.

Serve up your CD-Extra with MP3s. A Web site. Flash animations. Printable high-rez images of the band. Press clippings. EPKs. Videos.

Michael Woody on the production of Michael Dean's "Whore Love Song" video (on the CD)

"Michael Dean performing 'Whore Love Song' was shot at an in-store appearance with all manner of distracting crap in the background. One of the challenges of D.I.Y. is making do with what you've got (and haven't got, like a green-screen studio) when you know what you want to accomplish, so I exported the movie out of Premiere as a filmstrip and opened it in Photoshop to paint over the background.

"If you've never done it before, be careful! A filmstrip export produces one potentially enormous image file containing all of the frames from the video stacked vertically, like a filmstrip. It takes a considerable amount of RAM to be able to work on a filmstrip, so be prepared to break your video clip into smaller files that can then be turned into multiple filmstrips that can be reassembled later.

"The original background was comprised of too many shapes and colors, including colors in Michael's clothing, so I couldn't use the color selector for a simple color-replace command so I scrolled down the file and, frame by frame, painted out the background with a color that I could replace. I then imported it back into Premiere, keyed the background out, and added the various background patterns. Of course, it could have been done more easily under the right circumstances but, lacking those, I basically did what I had to do to get the effect I wanted."

Covers

Amtech, who did my DVD pressing in Canada (www.amtechdisc.com) was kind enough to provide CD Quark cover and label templates for our CD. (The DVD label should work for CD.)

There is an excellent tutorial on page layout, pre-press, and making things print ready on their site at:

www.amtechdisc.com/printspecs/cd-label-film-spec.htm.

I also highly recommend them for all your CD, CD-Extra, and DVD pressing needs. They're great folks, reasonably priced, attentive, and do good work. Tell George I sent ya.

They are in Canada, so if you're not there, you will have to pay shipping, but they are cheaper than most places in the States. And you may save with a few other aspects of the whole job overall from going down the street.

With print (covers, flyers, and such), always use high-rez (high-resolution: between 150 and 300 dpi, or dots per inch) images. Printing low-rez (Web-rez— 72 dpi) looks crappy. And I'm seeing a *lot* more of this, as bands and clubs just take images from Web sites, including their own. In the old days, we cut and pasted (with scissors and real paste!) from magazines. All high rez.

Look in the Goodies folder on the CD for examples. One is called high-rez-example.jpg, and one is called low-rez-example.jpg. The high rez one's file size is 970K; the low-rez is about 65K. They are both 72 dpi, but the high-rez one is huge (2048 × 1536 pixels), so the relative resolution is way higher than the low-rez one (600 × 450 pixels).

Conversely, use low-rez on the Web. High-rez images have higher file sizes and take longer to download. I am seeing a lot of goofballs who don't understand this and just use the resize function in the HTML to make an image look smaller (and scrunched). Idiots. It still takes as long to download! I've seen single pages with two *megs* of images. A page should have less than 100K of images *and* HTML most of the time. The exception is giving a clickable link to a high-rez version of an image marked "high-rez version to download and use for print." Go to www.30dollarfilmschool.com and click on the link, Bio, press release, and high-rez photos of author and cover, for a good example of how to do this.

Giving Back

Somewhere on the cover or the lyric sheet, thank *everyone* who helped in any way. Shout out to your homies and also to people who did *anything*, no matter how small, for you. One thing I always *loved* about old-school punk bands was they usually thanked over a hundred people in the liner notes. Fuck yeah!

Make thanks a habit in all aspects of your art. For instance, when you send out a press release with a photo, make sure that you tell them who the photographer is, and ask the publication to please make sure to credit the photographer.

Conversely, some punk bands used to follow their "thanks" section with a "no thanks" section for people they didn't like. I did this on my first record and haven't done it since. 'Cause like Momma said, "If you can't say something nice, don't say nothin' at all." And we all know that rock and roll is all about being nice, right? Tee hee hee.

Anyway, be totally on top of it, and don't worry about being a pest: While doing a project, I e-mailed one band and asked them the names of all the members and asked for specifics. The singer wrote back saying something like, "Why am I even doing this if you can't keep track?" I wrote her back this:

> That sounds kinda rude, no?
>
> I'm just trying to be totally on top of helping everyone get credit.
>
> Some people don't ask all these questions that I do, and believe me, you'd probably rather I ask too many than too few.
>
> Doing a project that involves over 300 people is a logistical nightmare.
>
> I appreciate your help.

She and I kissed and made up and are both cool with it now.

Audio Subterfuge

Audio subterfuge is mostly entertainment for yourself, but here are a couple of things you can do if you want to play around with noise.

Hidden Sounds

You can put a hidden track on a CD. This is kinda neat and maybe even a little cheesy. But it's fun.

You can put up to 99 tracks on a CD. Say your CD has 12 songs on it. You could make the hidden track a later track, say, song number 69. Then you put a bunch of blank songs between track 13 and 68. You can use the blank five-second song on the CD called 5_second_blank.wav (in the Noises folder) and just put it on there as many times as you like to fill space. (Or if you're really twisted, put slices of the Brown Sound instead.)

When the CD you burn (or a CD replicated by a pressing plant from the CD master you produce) is played, after the last of the main tracks, it will silently play all of the five-second blank songs until it gets to the hidden song.

Hidden tracks are usually not listed on the track listing. They are a fun thing that the fans have to discover on their own—either by word of mouth or by forgetting to turn the CD off and then the song starts on its own after a period of silence. It usually surprises the listener.

Brown Sound

On the second pressing of the *D.I.Y. or Die* DVD, the audio background under the Scenes menu has 3:41 of my music, then a minute of silence, then three more minutes of music. But the silence isn't silent. It's *very loud* subsonic bass. From 3:42 to 4:42, it's a loud sine wave at 3Hz, 7Hz, then 17Hz for 10 seconds each, then repeated.

Talk about bass! All three are frequencies then reputed to cause loss of bowel function at high volumes. It didn't work on myself or test subjects, though. Just makes them feel creepy. Just makes me feel drunk, but not in a fun way.

The U.S. Army actually experimented at one point with using frequencies like this as a *weapon*.

This is only on the second pressing, but you probably have it. The first is the Canada-only release pressing. If it says MVD on the back, it's the second pressing, even though it still says "Manufactured in Canada." It's also on the end of some of the VHS, although VHS may not have the audio capability to transmit bass this low. It's a couple of octaves lower than Watt.

I've included this sound on the CD for you to use wherever you see fit: noises/brownSound.

Peace, love, and gastrointestinal disturbances,

Michael Dean, Mad Scientist

Visual Subterfuge

To get your stuff into most stores, you will need a barcode. You can pay a service bureau 15 to 50 bucks to generate one for you or do it yourself in Quark with an extension called "Azalea" which you can, um, find on the Internet. The barcode has the retail price, publisher, and (with a book) ISBN number encoded for the scanner to read.

I've included on the CD two images I created; one is BarCodeppBoy.tiff, and the reversal is ppBoy –Reverse.tiff. Either of these will work with the included DVD or VHS or CD Quark templates to have a guy peeing on your barcode on the product. This is my protest, because you can't really buy or sell anything these days without this Mark of the Digital Beast. So I like to pee on it. I did this on "D.I.Y. or Die."

Feel free to use with credit.

Make Sure…

…that you make stuff look *good*. Just because you're low budget doesn't mean it has to look like it. With computers, you can look as great as you like; quality is only limited by imagination.

Figure 13.12 is a cool promo photo/piece of art that my friend Beau took back in the day. The day being a fine fall day in 1987.

This was actually taken with a 35 mm film camera, but scanned and all that stuff on a computer.

Figure 13.12 *Bomb promo photo by Beau Brashares.*

Promotion

Now that you've made your own records (and videos, if you're smart and read *$30 Film School*), here's how to get them out to the world. Finding a distributor. Self-distribution. Consignment.

Priorities in Promotion and Art

"Opportunity is missed by most people because it is dressed in overalls and looks like work."

—Thomas Edison, inventor of the microphone, phonograph, and motion pictures.

You have to be relentless to do this stuff for a living. I am.

A cute girl recently told me that I'm cool and talented and that she's attracted to me, but she doesn't like the fact that I'm not spontaneous and that I require 24 hours notice to do anything, and I get mad when people flake.

I sent her this e-mail:

> Subject: I do more by 1:54 p.m. than most people do all month.
>
> What I did today: Set up sales of my film for the merch tent on Warped tour. Set up a paid showing of my film in Alabama. Confirmed a show in Germany and a show in Poland that I'll be at. Talked to a friend who is having a bad day. Went to the gym. Answered at least 40 e-mails. proofread something for someone. Set up band practice. Faxed press releases for my film book to 20 magazines. Negotiated the terms for my new book deal. Negotiated with the school I'm teaching for in Houston. Got someone to buy me a free plane ticket for doing Web design. Petted my cat. Talked on the phone. Restrung my guitar. Worked on my next book. Went shopping. Made calls.
>
> Now do you see why I can't be spontaneous? This is a typical day for me, and it's not yet half over. I'll be up until 3 a.m. doing more similar crap.
>
> You said you are inspired by the things I do. But please know that I wouldn't get them done if I weren't careful with my time.
>
> Love, m.d.

I remember reading an interview with Ian MacKaye where he said something like, "People ask me all the time, 'How do you make a living at music?' and I tell them 'I don't make a living at music. I've been up for twelve hours today, I've been busy all day. I've faxed, I've talked on the phone, I've answered e-mails, and I haven't played any music at all.'"

Basically, the way to make a living at D.I.Y. art is to be great, spend as much time working on your art as most people spend on their day jobs, and then also spend six or eight hours a day *administering* your art. It's very frustrating. But you gotta do it. Assume that no one else is going to do it for you.

Figure 13.13 *This is what my calendar looks like.*

TIP

I would never recommend that you make a stencil of your band's name or logo and spray paint it around town (or other towns on tour), because that, of course, would be illegal.

Using the Internet

"Whoever has their art on the most people's hard drives when he dies, wins."

—Me

The Internet is the best way to cheaply promote your music worldwide. But keep in mind that everyone else is doing it, too. Here's how to do it, how to stand out, and how to make, not lose, money in the process. Do your own promotion and distribution online, without spamming.

A Web site should at least be a brochure. I hate sites that beep and flash and spin and do a whole bunch of crazy crap, but I can't even find the contact info quickly! Also, you don't want to make people jump through a bunch of hoops to get to your stuff. It takes long enough to download a song; I don't wanna have to look at Pepsi and Britney Spears ads to get to your music, ya know?

You can sell your art directly from your site by adding a PayPal button for payment (paypal.com). They don't take much money out on each sale and will put the rest directly in your bank account. I used to sell stuff on amazon.com, but they take almost half the retail price (although they do fulfill the orders) *plus* they have started charging on top of that! (My books are still on there, but my publisher pays the fees, not me.)

If you're personally responsible for fulfilling (shipping) product when people order it, do it in a timely manner. You should be honored when anyone spends hard-earned cake on your art. Get it out there quickly.

Cdbaby.com gets your CDs on www.towerrecords.com (complete with streaming two-minute MP3s). Cdstreet.com is another one some of my friends use.

I also put my stuff on eBay. And you not only can sell your regular new CDs of your band on there, you can sell your personal memorabilia. Gwar sells props from old tours. I've sold the rough drafts of my books with handwritten margin notes (after the books come out, of course). It's all good.

You should also spend a good bit of time scanning and linking all the press you get. And share the same with your e-mail list. Keep people up on what you're doing. You probably don't have to send out an e-mail for every little thing you do, but I let people keep track. When I got interviewed on NPR, you can be sure I let my peeps know so they could tune in.

Also, periodically check any links to stuff linked from your Web site to make sure the page hasn't disappeared or the info on it hasn't moved.

TIP

A lot of what I know about the care and feeding of computers and dealing with the Internet and such is already covered in my book *$30 Film School*. If I repeated it all here, this book would be about a thousand pages long. So I would recommend reading that book, too, even if you never plan to make videos, although I'd say any musician who doesn't plan to make videos, in this day and age, is insane, or at least denying her art a huge whole 'nother dimension. Mark my words: DVDs, in some form, will replace CDs as the thing you buy when you buy a band's latest release. If you can't afford both books, do what I do: Sometimes I go sit in a chain bookstore and read it without paying.

Figure 13.14 *Mini-DV video cameras.*

You might want to get a digital still camera to take photos for your Web site or for CD and DVD covers, or importing as stills in videos. (I love this look, by the way—I do it with the drum drill photo in the credits of "Left My Band in San Francisco.") They are cheap and good. I took most of the photos in this book myself with a Toshiba PDR-332. It was $210 from www.refurbdepot.com.

Figure 13.15 *Digital cameras.*

There are more of these right now, on eBay, complete with guarantee. So look around.

It's 3.2 megapixel, and I spent 60 bucks extra for a 128-meg memory card so I can take 200 high-rez photos, or 1200 Web-rez ones. It's very easy to use.

I love it. I got it to take the photos for this book, but I'm having a blast learning to use it. I guess that's because I'm making art (even though I'm not trying to—I'm just trying to learn to use the camera). It's been a while; I've been so busy *teaching* art this past year (writing these books, touring to do seminars, speaking at schools, squats, bars, and museums) that my big ole art heart has gotten a little cranky from lack of use.

I'm not going to teach you Web design here. Everyone pretty much knows how to do that already. If you don't know, get your 12-year-old sister to teach you.

I will tell you what programs I use. I do my basic Web design and uploading in Dreamweaver and use Photoshop to manipulate images.

I will cover some basic important concepts that aren't so much second nature, and show a few music-specific programs and techniques that will aid your desire to be heard.

MP3s

MP3s are 1/10 the file size of uncompressed audio files and sound almost as good. They are the format of choice for sharing music across the Internet.

You'll want to upload a few MP3s of your songs to the Internet so people can download them.

You can create MP3s with a freestanding utility like AudioCatalyst (shareware from www.xingtech.com). Also, many other programs, like Sound Forge, allow you to use a drop-down menu to choose to save as MP3 format.

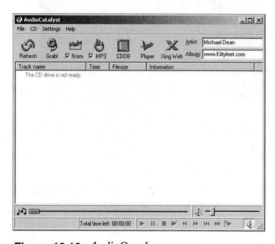

Figure 13.16 *AudioCatalyst.*

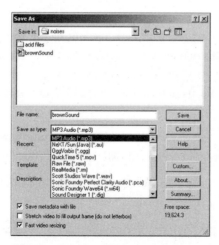

Figure 13.17 *Sound Forge drop-down menu for Save as File Type.*

TIP

If there are things you can set for different criteria in your MP3s, 128K Joint Stereo is generally the accepted standard. Most programs do this as a matter of default, but if they don't and you have to set it manually, set it to 128K.

Make sure to *tag* your MP3s with meta information. This can be done with just artist and song title info in AudioCatalyst as you make the MP3. Type it in the spaces in the top right corner. Or do it later in more detail with a stand-alone utility, such as Easy Tagger (shareware from www.istoksoft.com). I've included a working demo on the CD. This will make it so your band name, album, and URL appear on the MP3 player (software or hardware) when your song is played. MP3s tend to get e-mailed, re-linked, and shared with programs like Kazaa, and you want people to be able to contact you or at least know what they are listening to if they didn't get it from your site.

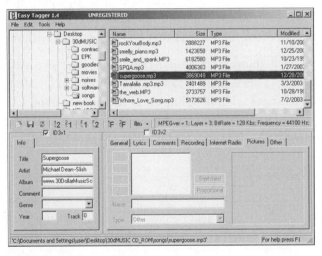

Figure 13.18 *Easy Tagger.*

To use Easy Tagger, just open it, ignore the nag screen—the demands to pay and register—you're just trying it out, remember? You can pay later if you like it. Open the program. Dig the cool translucent look...pretty damn psychodelic if'n you ask me. Hit the little tic mark next to 1D3v1 on the next screen, and enter your info like I did here. Then hit the little Save icon (the thing that looks like a floppy disc above and just to the left of the 1D3v1 tic box), and you're set.

Then it will scroll the information somewhere in any MP3 player to show the listener the song title, name, artist, and album.

Figure 13.19 *Tagged song displaying info as it plays in WMP.*

With stuff that isn't from an album (or sometimes even if it is), I put my URL. That's more important than the album name, in my book. My Web sites are my window onto the World and often the World's first point of contact with me.

You can also set the song style (punk, jazz, choral, classic rock, and so forth) from a drop-down list if you want. This is kind of against my gut feeling. I hate to categorize my art, and the fact that I am not willing to do this is one reason I have to operate outside "the biz," but doing so will make it easier for the listener to organize their favorites in some MP3 players. It's your call.

TIP

When you install programs, if your firewall asks permission for the program to access the Internet, mark the tic box Remember This Answer Next Time I Use This Program and hit No, unless it has a reason or need to access the Internet. Otherwise, you're giving "them" access to info they have no right to be accessing. Be especially wary of programs that ask to "act as a server."

The exception, of course, is programs like browsers, FTP utilities, etc, that by definition *need* to access the Internet, i.e. it is their *job* to access the Internet.

And note that Kazaa and other file-sharing utilities *are* servers, so they will need permission to *act* like a server, damn it.

Figure 13.20 *Firewall asking for permission to access the Internet.*

I was one of the first people to use MP3s on the Internet (in 1996), and I was one of the first users of MP3.com. I used to love this service, but now they limit the number of MP3s you can upload free, charge for more, and bombard you with ads and demand your sales profiles with every download. Ain't these folks ever heard of cookies? It seems like a doomed business plan to me.

www.besonic.com is a site I like. And Zebox.com is good, too (and I don't just say that because I've been their featured artist three times). They don't have as many ads, don't charge you, there's no limit on number of songs, no demand for demographic info with each download, and they are not (yet) owned by Vivendi.

I try to put at least one MP3 somewhere with a direct URL so people don't have to jump through hoops to get it.

Like this:

http://www.kittyfeet.com/pj.mp3

Bandwidth ain't that expensive any more. Just put stuff on your own site.

I avoid Geocities and places that don't allow use of direct URL downloads and that add banner ads and crap like that. Server space is cheap or free.

I have a…friend…who says, "One thing I do is when I do Web design for people, I host MP3 files on their extra server space, then link from my site. They never know."

Photoshop Web Gallery

A really good way to put a bunch of photos up on your Web site without a lot of work is the one-click utility in Photoshop 6 or later called Web Photo Gallery.

Figure 13.21 *Make Web Photo Gallery in Photoshop.*

This brings up a dialog box to set the style and font, as well as to choose the folder to be processed and the destination folder.

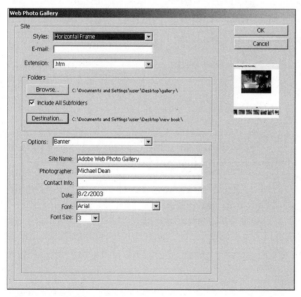

Figure 13.22 *Setting style, input, and destination folders.*

This instantly generates a set of Web pages (which you can later alter in your Web design program if you want) that look pretty damn good. It includes automatically generated clickable thumbnails so people can see what they're gonna get before they bother to click on something.

Note that this process also resizes your actual images and makes them smaller. But still, it's a nice way to share a bunch of photos (like all the photos from a given show) quickly and without a lot of work.

Figure 13.23 shows what the result looks like.

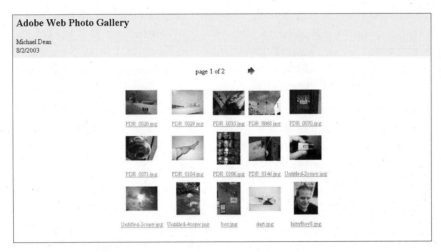

Figure 13.23 *Automatically generated Web page.*

When you're done, just upload the entire new folder and link the index page elsewhere on your site.

See the final result at www.kittyfeet.com/gallery.

The actual file path of this is www.kittyfeet.com/gallery/index.htm—a Web site automatically opens index.htm or index.html in a given folder by default if none is specified.

TIP

You can also batch process large print-rez images to Web-rez size automatically in Photoshop. It's kind of tricky and outside the scope of this book. But it's in the Help menu of Photoshop. Just search using the Batch command in the Help menu.

Why I Love the Internet

When I was a kid I felt really isolated and not accepted by other kids. The thing that saved me was making a little micropower FM radio transmitter. It had two transistors, three capacitors, a diode, and a battery. I built it into the handset of an old telephone. I would go into the woods behind our house and hike and talk. I felt almost like I had a direct line to God. I would ramble in typical, yet advanced, little-boy poetry and smash my psyche into the sky. I would write my mile-high invisible graffiti skywriting that could only be known to anyone with an FM radio within a quarter-mile.

At first, I made sure to only transmit when far enough into the woods that there was a great chance no one was listening. After a bit, I got more adventurous and brought my weird science to school. Some of the kids teased me aloud for "talking to himself on that stupid broken phone," 'til one day, someone had snuck in a little radio (the principal hated rock n' roll and had tacitly banned radios, but broken phones were okay) and happened to be tuned into that frequency. They found out I was actually broadcasting.

It didn't even matter before that no one was listening. It was the *possibility* that someone *might* be listening that made it more interesting than just reading or watching TV. I was not just passively *consuming*; I was *doing*.

As a kid I was also really into sending away for things—free samples, record clubs, writing letters to the editor (and fan letters to artists and scientists I admired). I felt really trapped in my little town and felt that *anything* I could do to get my mind to extend out into the world was more powerful than sitting around accepting the stuff that the TV spoon fed me.

This is the reason that when I first discovered punk rock firsthand (at age 18, in 1982) and got on the Internet (in 1996), I was totally taken by both of them. Punk seemed powerful because it was all about doing it yourself and not waiting for permission from anyone to do it. The Internet seemed the same but more so, it was like, "Wow, I can publish my own stuff and anyone in the world can read it."

I was hooked.

I spend at least eight hours a day now on a computer. Granted, I'm not looking at the Internet all that time, but I do have a high-speed connection open all that time and do stuff on the Internet often. But it's rarely surfing the Web (unless I'm looking for specific information). It's more likely *making* the Web. I am less into consuming media and more into *being* the media.

I hope you are, too. If you're reading this book, chances are that you are. It's the $30 Way.

AddWeb

AddWeb (shareware from www.cyberspacehq.com) is a great utility for adding your site to a number of search engines at once. You simply type in the URL, site name, a description, and your meta words (the words you've included in the HTML head that are seen by the search engine but not the Web surfer—unless they click View/Source).

The full version submits to about a thousand engines, but the free version submits to the 12 engines that most people use anyway. So that's almost as good. Buy the other version if you want; it's best to cover all your bases when you can.

I use the wizard and allow it to Populate from Web page; that way you don't have to type all the meta info in yourself. But to do so, you first have to upload the Web page. This is obviously one of those programs you *are* going to want to allow your firewall to access the Internet with. Otherwise, it won't work!

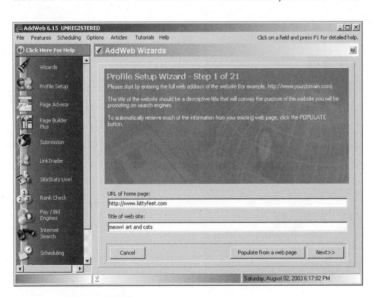

Figure 13.24 *AddWeb.*

By way of explanation, here's the meta tags in the HTML head that I added by hand when I did the coding for a music page on my site. (The site is all my music. I bootleg myself.)

```
<html><head><title>Free bootleg rock! MP3s! Yes! Fuck yes!</title><meta
name="description" content="THE BEST FREE MUSIC ON THE NET. MP3s FROM HELL!">
```

```
<meta name="keywords" content="art, free, rock, Bomb, mp3, mpeg, michael dean, punk,
love, los angeles, San Francisco, mp3, computer, warez, counter culture, quicktime, on-
line, Rock, n', Roll, kittyfeet, Anarchy, meow, movies, food, coffee, fun, joy, pleasure,
lust for life, grrrl, grrl, grrrrl, poetry, literature, alternative">
</head><body background="blue.jpg" TEXT="#00FFFF" BGCOLOR="#0000FF" vlink="#FFFF00"
LINK="#FFFFFF"></head>
```

TIP

It's best *not* to put unrelated keywords in your meta tags. It may seem cool, like it will
bring more people to your site. And it will, but it defeats the usefulness of the Web,
and you'll end up pissing off a lot of people, and it will work against you. You'll also get
way more spam (some spam companies make lists of e-mail addresses harvested off
of sites based on keywords). Some search engines will actually remove you if they figure out you're doing this.

emailSTRIPPER

emailSTRIPPER is a very cool tiny freeware program from www.papercut.biz/
emailStripper.htm. It's included on the CD with this book. It removes all that
junk formatting that you get from cutting and pasting from e-mails sent from one
person to another. Removes all the extraneous >>>>>> as well as other symbols
and junk carriage returns.

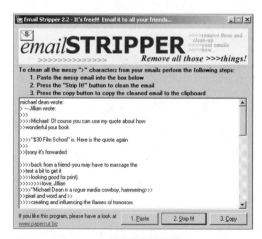

Figure 13.25 *emailSTRIPPER.*

Here's some forwarded e-mail text:

michael dean wrote:

>-- Jillian wrote:

>>>

>>>>Michael: Of course you can use my quote about how

>>wonderful your book

>>>>"$30 Film School" is. Here is the quote again

>>>

>>(sorry it's forwarded

>>>>back from a friend--you may have to massage the

>>text a bit to get it

>>>>looking good for print).

>>>>>>>love, Jillian

>>>>>>>>>>>>>>>>>>>>>>>>>>>>>>>>

>>>>"Michael Dean is a rogue media cowboy, hammering>>>

>>pixel and word and >>

>>>>creating and influencing the flames of tomorrow.

>>>>>He sits in his room

>>>>>>rocking away on his computer harder than Tony

>>>>>Iommi does his guitar.

>>

>>>>While you're out getting drunk and bragging about

>>>

>>how you're gonna be

>>

>>>>somebody someday, he's quietly DOING it.

>>>>

>>>>"Michael's film book and his D.I.Y. movie changed my

>>>

>>life. I quit my job

>>

>>>>because of them and now have the courage to make

>>>

>>art full time.

>>

>>>>Michael, I really want to meet you! If you ever

>>>

>>come to Seattle, you

```
>>
>>>>have a place to stay and unlimited back rubs (and
>>>
>>more)."
>>
>>>>--Jillian Bronly,
>>>>Seattle, WA
> _____
> Do you Yahoo!?
> Yahoo! SiteBuilder - Free, easy-to-use Website design software
> http://sitebuilder.yahoo.com
```

Here's the same after stripping it with emailSTRIPPER:

```
Michael: Of course you can use my quote about how wonderful your book "$30 Film School"
is. Here is the quote again (sorry it's forwarded back from a friend--you may have to
massage the text a bit to get it looking good for print).
love, Jillian
"Michael Dean is a rogue media cowboy, hammering pixel and word and creating and
influencing the flames of tomorrow. He sits in his room rocking away on his computer
harder than Tony Iommi does his guitar. While you're out getting drunk and bragging about
how you're gonna be somebody someday, he's quietly DOING it.
"Michael's film book and his D.I.Y. movie changed my life. I quit my job because of them
and now have the courage to make art full time. Michael, I really want to meet you! If
you ever come to Seattle, you have a place to stay and unlimited back rubs (and more)."
--Jillian Bronly, Seattle, WA

---------≈
```

Make sure you delete the line it adds at the bottom:

"This email was cleaned by emailStripper, available for free from http://www.papercut.biz/emailStripper.htm."

TIP

When you put a URL (Web address or e-mail address) in any outgoing communication (e-mail, Web site, flyer, or press release), always test it first! Little is worse than sending out press kits (e-mail or printed) with a non-working URL in them. I always type it into the title bar of an active browser, make sure the page loads, and then cut and paste from the title bar.

Linking

I have heard of people getting upset about being linked, but I think they are insane. If they don't want to be linked, they shouldn't be on the Internet. I think links are always okay, and I don't ever ask permission. The nature of the Web is such that it invites linking. It is *based* on linking.

If you want to cover your ass, just don't link anyone in a way that implies a partnership or endorsement that does not exist. For instance, if you have a page on your site that says "We like Gretsch guitars," with a link, then you're probably cool. If you say "Joe Blow and the Nobodies use Gretsch Guitars exclusively" and have a link with their corporate logo, it kind of looks like *they* have signed *you* to an endorsement, which is misleading.

The only linking that upsets me is leeching, which is where people link a file on their site without linking the page, like putting one of my songs for download on their site, or especially an image. It's basically using my art (and bandwidth!) as theirs without credit.

Some guy named Kevin leeched images from my site, the photos of people in "D.I.Y. or Die," and gave them dumb names and captions on his site. But he still was serving them from my site. (I discovered this from my Web logs.) I changed the filenames and HTML on my end and made new image files with the old file names (so they would show up on his site) My new image files said "Kevin is a leech and a thief." They stayed up on his site for two weeks with people viewing them every day them before he noticed and took the page down!

TIP

I always use the HTML command `open in new browser target=_Blank`"—easily done with right-clicking `make link` command in Dreamweaver—so people don't leave my site when they look at an external page.

Web Boards and Mailing List Services

You will probably want to have a Web board so people can post things. You will need to weekly (or in my case, daily) maintain it and delete stuff: You'll probably get some board spam, commercial posts unrelated to your cause, and people saying mean things. (The more I get recognized for my art in the public eye, the more I find less-celebrated former "friends" coming out to talk smack about me.)

I usually leave mean stuff up if it's ridiculous enough to be funny and if the person signs it. If they're a jerk and don't sign it, I delete it. And I always delete unrelated "get rich quick" crap.

Yahoo Groups (http://groups.yahoo.com) is good, but they put ads on every page. You can get one that you serve on your own site called wwwboard free from www.scriptarchive.com. This is the one I used on my site. But it involves a tiny bit of scripting that almost borders on programming. If you are not computer intuitive, I suggest going with the Yahoo! solution. One advantage of Yahoo! is that you will be able to be searched by people on Yahoo! by keywords easier.

I put this disclaimer on my Web board:

"And anything posted here becomes property of Michael Dean and may be used in any way he sees fit. And he thanks you."

That way people know that I might use it later elsewhere as advertising or whatever if I like it.

Topica.com

Topica is a very good way to maintain and administer your mailing list. People sign up by sending an e-mail; it's automatic. I put this line as my sig line (signature) at the bottom of all my e-mails, and I have it on a few places on my Web site:

If you want on my mailing list send an email to kittyfeet69-subscribe@topica.com

You can block people later and remove them from your list if you need to or just turn their receiving of e-mails on for a particular mailing, then turn it back off. They can unsubscribe themselves without bugging you. Topica does not sell or trade or abuse your list. You can search and export your database, and it is secure, and they don't trade e-mails. They do put an ad at the top and bottom of each mailing, but I get around it by putting:

(Ignore the ad above. Topica puts it there) at the top of every outgoing message and

(Ignore the ad below. Topica puts it there) at the bottom.

For some reason, Topica won't display e-mail addresses in a mass e-mail; it's probably an anti-spam legality thing. So when I have to send an e-mail with an e-mail address somewhere in it, I do a workaround of just linking an HTML page with the URL displayed, or the URL of an image file with the address. (I heard they may be fixing this, so run a test.)

Using an image file for an e-mail URL on a Web site is good also to prevent spam. An image (unlike text or HTML) cannot be scanned by a roving mail-gathering bot. People actually have to *type* the e-mail address rather than just click to e-mail you, but if they really want to talk to you, they'll take the five seconds to do that.

TIP

Send out stuff about your friends and people you don't know on your e-mail list. If it's all you, it's kinda piggy. But if you toot other people's horns, too, you're just being a cheerleader for art: yours and everyone else's.

Testimonials

Get people, especially famous people, to write blurbs for your books, Web sites, records, all your art. I do. It helps. Also, when you get a fan letter or e-mail, ask the person to post a review on your Web board and on Amazon.com if you're selling your stuff there.

I always did this and sort of felt like a loser for it sometimes, like "No one who really has their shit together would do this," until I wrote a fan letter to Lloyd Kaufman of Troma films and he asked me to post a review on Amazon! That dude is totally famous and rich and successful and makes cool art on his own terms.

Don't *ever* post the contents of someone's e-mail on the Web without permission. One time I told a guy I really liked his music and was a little dismayed to find my letter reprinted on his Web site. E-mails are personal one-to-one communiqués and should not be shared unless you ask. Most people (including me) would say "sure" if asked in that situation, too.

Promotional Zest and Artistic Zeal

In order to really get yourself out there, you have to:

Have great stuff

and

Have a religious fervor for your own output.

Remember the movie *The Blues Brothers*? A recurrent line in that film was the leaders of the band saying (and believing), "We're on a mission from God."

I sort of believe that about myself and my art. I must—I have worked for over 20 years making about 50 cents an hour doing art. (This year was the first time I've actually made enough money to be above the poverty line, and that includes the year and a half that I was on Warner Brothers.)

I just believe that what I do is important enough to give up security and creature comforts to work on. I am very intelligent (my I.Q. is 143—genius on some scales and almost genius on others), and I could have had all-expenses-paid scholarships to any college I wanted when I was younger. Instead, I dropped out of high school (got kicked out, actually) and went to live on the streets in Washington, D.C., at age 19 and played in a punk rock band.

That set the pace for my life. I definitely could have been a lawyer, doctor, or scientist making over $100,000 a year. (I could be making twice that if I'd gone into marketing. I'm very good at it. Except that I get suicidal when I'm trying to market something I don't believe in.)

Instead I've devoted my life to making art in every medium I can, and I've averaged under ten grand a year my whole life. And I love my life!

To really get the world to believe what you believe, you first have to really believe it yourself. And I don't mean being pumped up with ego and convincing yourself that you're great, even if you suck. (Think everyone on *American Idol* or *Live at the Apollo*, but *especially* the losers.)

I guess what I'm getting at is if you're great, if you have that indefinable spark that makes people stand out from the crowd, if you are truly talented *and* original (if not outright visionary!), you *still* have to be driven and relentless to get the world to notice. And this is true from the most integrity-filled indie punk rock icon to the person in the number one spot on the charts. They both believe in themselves to the point where they do not even question when someone questions them— they just sidestep it and move on. They trust their vision, drive, and internal mission statement with an unfaltering accuracy.

I've taken a lot of heat for being like this. A lot of people *hate* me because I toot my own horn. But I figure that if I don't toot my own horn, no one else will.

(As I was just sitting in the Dallas airport typing this, Tiffany called to tell me that there's a huge article about my upcoming Houston B. Dalton bookstore book signing in the weekly entertainment paper there. It kinda proved my point *and* made my day.)

Figure 13.26 *My sweet, smart, talented helluva cool friend, Tiffany Couser.*

Anyway, you have to believe in your art to get it out to the Universe.

> **TIP**
>
> I don't mind if I only sell a few of a piece of art. I don't look at it as "moving units." Major labels do. They would just as soon sell soap as art if it paid as well.
>
> I'm like Johnny Appleseed. Each sale is not just a unit shipped, it is the potential to change a life.

So, how do you do this without stepping on people's toes and without being a violently self-serving egomaniac? Easy. Other than living a virtuous life (and my idea of virtue is probably far more decadent than most people who use that term), you give up your part in it. You make it about the *art*, not about the *artist*. Sure, you put your name alongside the art, sign it, get to go along for the ride, and cash the checks at the end of the day, but it ain't about you.

It's about the art. You're bragging for the art. Not yourself. The art is the star, not you.

This little shift in attitudinal behavior allows one to be a hellfire and brimstone pulpit pounder for the cause of good without being too much of a brat. It's about the art. Period.

I go through an airport and I see blank food tubes selling out to the corporate ideal. Yuck, man, it's shallow. And it's totally the Peter Principle. Today in first class (I fly all the time, but today was the first time I've ever flown in first class—on a standby ticket donated by an airline employee who believes in my art), the goon sitting next to me was some well-paid, doughy, white, middle-aged, middle management type. I put on my eye shades and tried to sleep, but I nosed my peepers out the edge of the shades to see what he was writing. He was writing an evaluation of the 120 employees below him, and in about 20 words each, deciding their fate—who should get promoted and who should get fired. And this guy's English skills were about equivalent to an eighth grader—typos everywhere!

He probably has a secretary to edit his crap and make him look good. Hope he doesn't have her fired, too.

Getting Your Stuff into Stores

Many local stores will take stuff on consignment. This means no money up front, and you get some later if and when they sell.

This is covered in detail in *$30 Film School*, but basically it works like this: You approach local merchants and *nicely* ask them to take a few units on consignment. You sign a little form. You go out and hang flyers. You go promote. Then you go back in 90 days and *nicely* ask them if they sold your art and get some money if they did.

As far as getting your stuff distributed in chain stores and stuff like that, it's very difficult. I tried with my records and books that were on independent labels. The result was spotty coverage at best. The one record I did on Warner Brothers got into every store in America (only one copy in some cases, but at least it was there). These books, the *$30 School* series, get into Borders, B. Dalton, and Barnes & Noble, everywhere. I tried hard to get that done myself with my self-published novel to no avail. Like I said, people can get the job done when their job is getting their job done. But it's rare that people are as smart as my publisher and put out something good like this. More often, you have a better chance of selling another damn cat book than successfully pitching something that will actually help people. I *love* cats but hate cat books. They are very nearly the lowest common denominator of the publishing industry.

I think the best win-win situation is somewhere between being totally independent and being on a major. I like to make what I love for *myself* and then find a distributor. I did this with my *D.I.Y. or DIE* movie.

This methodology gives you the most control and the most money, too.

Here are a few of the bigger independent distributors: Mordam Records, Red Distribution, Alternative Distro Alliance (ADA), Choke Distribution, Very Distro, Midheaven Mailorder, Interpunk and Dischord. They are all very easy to find online. Most of them take CDs and DVDs. Some of them are very picky about what they take, not just musically, but ideologically.

For DVD-only *distro* (distribution), try Facets Multimedia, Music Video Distributors (MVD); and for Europe, Quantum Leap.

For any of them, you'll have to send a sample, a polite, short cover letter, and a press kit. Then wait six weeks and follow up with a polite phone call.

In music you will usually go through as many as you can. With film, sometimes they will give you an advance and want an exclusive. I did that with MVD with the *D.I.Y. or DIE* DVD. Sometimes the film rules work with music, sometimes vice versa. Feel it out.

Just make what you can, make it great, and get it out there.

TIP

Big chain stores like Tower usually won't take home-burned CDs. Because home-burns will play on most, but not all CD players, these places have a policy of not taking them. They don't want to deal with the returned copies. To get into these stores, you have to have a manufactured CD. Something about having them pressed from a glass master, rather than burned on a computer, ups the playability rate past 99.9 percent, so stores don't have to deal with returns.

Endcap

Endcap is a retail sales term (equally at home in the cheese section of Whole Foods as it is in Tower Records or Borders Books or a tiny, spunky indie punk store) for those little displays of select product that stores have at the end of aisles. It's the first thing the consumer sees when she walks into the store or section. The record company/publisher/cheese manufacturer pays the store to put them up there. It's basically advertising.

You can pay independent promoters to do the same for you, but it's not gonna work as well as it will for the big boys. You're better off putting your money into other things—cheap ads in magazines your people actually read, going on tour, and sending out promo copies to radio stations.

Some independent promoters are a total scam—it's old fashioned illegal payola under a new legal name. Big labels hire them and basically pay stations through them. The coolest indie artists don't hire them, so why bother?

Here's the Web address of an article explaining this in detail: www.stereo-phile.com/shownews.cgi?1623.

Wrap Up

What goes around comes around: The other day, my friend Blaine Grayboyes was moderately bragging to me that he had 25 helpers working for free on his upcoming movie project. I was quite impressed because I've never been able to get nearly that many people to help with anything at one time. I said, "How'd you do it?"

He was incredulous that I didn't know. He replied, "I read your book!" and thumped the copy of *$30 Film School* sitting between us on his table.

I was amused at the interesting bit of cyclical coincidence surrounding this because Blaine is *quoted* in *$30 Film School*.

So…if you use the techniques and suggestions here to become incredibly famous with your band, feel free to invite my band to open for you.

Chapter 14

Business

Making art your full-time job is a full-time job.

—Me

Things covered in this chapter:

What to name your band. How to make sure the name is unique, and says something about you and your music. How to protect your name. How to protect your songs. How to protect yourself from the multitudes of talentless fools who want to make a buck off of you without really doing anything useful. When you don't need a manager, and when you do. Do you need an agent? When you actually *should* get a lawyer. How to negotiate

Figure 14.1 *Business.* Photo by Lydia Lam.

win-win situations with industry professionals, from local bars to major labels. Understanding contracts and making them work for you (including examples). Not getting screwed by clubs. Not getting screwed by labels. Getting what you want and getting paid.

Band Names

After great songs, your group name is your #2 asset. Here we will learn how to pick a good name. How to stand out as a band. How to see if the name's already being used. How to make sure no one else uses it.

There are two schools of thought on band names. One says, "The name doesn't matter; it's all about the music." The other says, "The name is very important. It should say something about you because it's often the first (or last) thing people will know you by."

I'm kind of a subscriber to the third school. I believe a band name is important, but not as important as the songs. I feel people will forgive a dumb name more than crappy songs. If you have great songs, the name is less important. But it still matters.

Basically, you want a catchy name that isn't a joke (if you want to be taken seriously) and people will be happy to say, "I like _____ a lot." One test is to picture someone saying to their friend, "Check out this new band _____" and see if it rings true to you. Also picture it on a T-shirt.

Naming a band is one of the most fun parts of being in a band. Most bands start out with a long list that they have a lot of fun coming up with. Then they go through that and winnow it down to a short list of five or so that they could seriously be attached to for a few years. Then they usually take a vote and do a certain amount of focus group testing on their friends.

Naming the band is often done before all the songs are written or the lineup is even solidified. I think this is putting the cat before the mouse, but do what you want.

I put this part later in the book. It was originally earlier, but I wanted to stress that the music is *way* more important than the name.

The most important thing is that your band name be original. If there are two bands with the same name, it's gonna be a problem. And this gets tough, because there are so many bands out there now. Plus there have been so many bands in the past, and you can't use any of their names either.

When checking out potential names to see if they're being used, I would first recommend looking on MP3.com. Pretty much every band in the world is on this site. Type www.mp3.com/(band name) into your browser and see if something comes up. By this, I mean, if you want to call your band "devil kitty," type www.mp3.com/devilkitty. (Of course, this name is already taken by me. And I had it years before the all-girl band in Japan started to put out records under that name. But I don't really care, because I am not doing anything with it currently, and they're cute.) Or just go to the main page of www.mp3.com and type in the band name you want to use. If it doesn't come up, there's a good chance it's available. I would also run a search on Google, with the term both in quotes and not. Then check at www.netsol.com and see if the domain name is available. If your name passes all these tests, it's probably available. You also might check with some vinyl nerd at an indie record store, one of those people who prides himself on knowing about every band that has ever existed, no matter how obscure.

Any name that is one word, especially a common noun, is probably taken: Pavement, Bottlecap, Shellac, Television, Flour, Flower, and so forth. Same thing with any common phrase, movie title, or book title. (Literary band names are usually pretty dumb; they end up over-intellectualizing something that isn't intellectual by nature.) I was pretty surprised in 1986 when my band Bomb started that the name was *not* taken. (Of course, a few people, a hip-hop band and a solo drummer, stole it later. But we came up with it.) I would also tend to avoid the punk rock cliché of an adjective-noun band name. Most of them are pretty dumb, though there are some pretty cool exceptions, like Angelic Upstarts, Reagan Youth, and Naked Raygun. There were a lot of bands who used Reagan in their name when that guy was president. It kinda limited their viability to last past his presidency. Though Naked Raygun did invent and contribute the "Oh, oh oh oh" backup vocal that was stolen by everyone from Perry Farrell to Pennywise. Naked Raygun, unlike a lot of punk bands, could also write a hell of a catchy tune.

You want to stand out. A name can help. Then we come up against the "Should we go with a vulgar name?" conundrum. I always thought the name Butthole Surfers was pretty dumb, even though I loved that band from the first time I saw them (opening for Dead Kennedys in Washington, D.C., in 1983). I also think that by the time they were writing songs like "Pepper," they had outlived that name but were still stuck with it. They had lost some members, too. They obviously did not subscribe to the Dischord Records ethic of "Make up a new band name, write new songs, and start over when someone leaves the band." But I don't either. Unless it's the singer. The only band that was strong enough to keep the name with different singers was Black Flag. Rollins wasn't even their first singer.

I don't even think that Butthole Surfers is a vulgar name. I've heard *far* more offensive. But when they used to tour in a van in the early 80s, they were usually listed in ads in most local papers as the B_____ Surfers, or the B-Hole Surfers. I remember their singer, Gibby Haynes said, "Jeez, I don't know why everyone's so uptight. Even my 84-year-old grandma can say 'Butthole Surfers' out loud with no problem."

Basically, what I'm getting at is if you pick a badass name, you're gonna have to deal with the baggage that comes with a badass name. And also, a name that sounds clever at first is gonna sound pretty unclever with time.

CAUTION

This book is all educational/speculative only. Nothing here constitutes legal advice. The guy who wrote this book is not a lawyer. He is a high school dropout. He may be right, and probably is, but we'd be remiss to not tell you to consult with an attorney. Even though they'll probably, by definition, try to take all your money if they can.

Avoid naming your band after trademarked products or famous movies. That's just asking for trouble. And the attention that comes with the trouble will not, despite what you think, help you. It will not be "free publicity." It will be legal fees you cannot afford.

So, after you've come up with a truly original name you can all live with, you should protect it. The first thing I would do is get the domain name and develop a Web site. Then I would offer something for sale on the Web site that has the band name on it. If you don't have a tape yet, at least a T-shirt. Because by selling over the Internet, you are "engaging in interstate commerce," which is one of the indicators used to define the date of something first being trademarked. And once you're offering tapes or CDs for sale, have a little available for download. For some reason, this "enticement" helps establish the music recording's class of trademark.

I would put a little ™ trademark symbol next to the band name. Do not use the R in a circle, ®; this is reserved for a registered trademark. More on this later. Put the date you started selling on the Web site and print the page out. You may need this later to help establish "first use in commerce." You might think that's not very air-tight; anyone can put any date on a Web site and lie, but all Web sites are actually cached daily by all the major search engines, as well as by the government, and this can be used to prove what was up there on a certain date. Your printed copy of the Web page is just to include in the trademark application.

You can do this through a lawyer, but I personally don't. I save lawyers for stuff I absolutely cannot do myself. So, if you actually want to pursue a solid trademark, go to www.uspto.gov and run a search for the name. Click on Trademarks in the left column, then go to the first choice on the next page. (It says "TESS," which stands for Trademark Electronic Search System.[1]) Then go to New User Form Search (Basic) and enter your band name. If nothing comes up, you can go ahead and apply to register it. It will cost $335 on your credit card to start, and a year

---

1. *This is not the first time I've seen a database named after a woman. Gotta love them nurds.*

later, if approved, will cost another hundred to finalize. If you get turned down and cannot successfully appeal it (usually because someone else has a solid prior claim to the name), you do *not* get the $335 back.

The cost of trademarking your band name is a good reason to make sure you do your Web search first. You don't want to waste $335 on something that isn't going to work out.

And keep in mind that just because a name does not show up in TESS does not mean it is not in the process of being trademarked by someone else. It can take a month or more to show up there after someone begins the process. This is another reason to come up with absolutely unique names.

You will usually get turned down the first time, usually about eight months after you apply. That's when you'll send in your printed Web site and any new merchandise you have—when they ask for more proof. Only after you get the paperwork back from the trademark office saying that it is a registered trademark (this takes about a year) can you use the little ® symbol.

Note that you cannot "park" a trademark the way you can "park" a domain name. You have to actually be selling or in the process of getting ready to use it to sell something. But you don't have to be selling on a big scale.

Note that it's $335 *per class*. Eventually, if you're planning on making money on your band, you will want to register it in at least two classes, Class 9 (sound recordings featuring music) and Class 25 (clothing, namely T-shirts, sport shirts, sweat shirts, hats and shorts). But for now, if you can't afford both, one is a good start. My trademark lawyer friend that used to play in my band tells me that it's far better to have a registered trademark in one class than none.

I have my band name, Kittyfeet, trademarked, (go ahead and run the search) but in a different class (042; software). This is from a previous business venture that did not make much money. I use it only occasionally nowadays for that venture. So the name is still active. One of these days I'll get around to registering it in the other two classes. "So many gerbils, so little time."

The test of a trademark in court is often simply, "Who has more money for lawyers?" But basically, it's also, "Can someone be confused?" Which brings up an interesting fact. You can't play music under the name of a famous musician, even if it's your real name. If your name is David Bowie, you're gonna have to find a variation on that. Sorry, but that's the way it is. I use my middle initial, W, and sometimes middle name, Wareham, because Michael Dean is such a common name.

When I was touring, there were three guys with the same name in the same scene: me, the bass player from Corrosion of Conformity, and the drummer in Gang Green. There's a singer named Dean Wareham, but I ain't him. There are no other humans on this planet named Michael Wareham Dean, according to my Web searches.

Once you get approved by the trademark office, you pay them another 100 bucks, then you can add the R in a circle, ®, after your name or logo.

Get a good name that you can live with and that says something about your band. Make sure it's unique and all yours and protect it. A little bit of attention to these details now will save a lot of hassle later.

Copyrights

Song thieves aren't nearly as common as most people might worry, but they do exist. Songs are worth money. Here you'll learn how to protect your prized possessions. We will also cover the options of *not* worrying too much about copyright.

I see artists spending a lot more time worrying about this than they probably need to. I actually see people who have yet to create *anything* worrying about how they're gonna protect this thing that they *might* come up with sooner or later. I find that this is common among the wannabes: They will do *anything* but get down to it, roll up their sleeves, and *work*.

But you ain't a wannabe. How do I know? Because the *$30 School* books ain't for wannabes. There were probably plenty of books on the same shelf in the bookstore next to this one that offered overnight success. Those books exist only for the commerce of helping books. They don't help people become stars. Or artists.

So if you're reading this book, I can properly assume that you're a sensible person who is not afraid of a little work. So you will understand that it's putting the pipe before the crack to worry too much about copyrights before you've actually *written* anything to copyright.

But if you have started writing songs, then you're ready.

Here's my experience on the matter: I've put out 12 or 13 records (I can't even remember exactly how many—that should give you some insight into how much more I am a process-oriented artist than I am a goal-oriented artist). Most of these records have been on small cool indie labels. A couple I put out myself. The first one I even had a party with friends to put the covers together. One was on a major label. So you can see I've done pretty much every kind of record deal that it is possible to do. And I've *never* had anyone steal a song in any way. It ain't that much of a worry. And I've written some great songs. People just don't really steal much. There is too much vanity probably…people have their own ideas, there are a million ideas out there and why *would* someone bother stealing a song? I don't even know anyone who's had it happen.

Now I should probably cover a bit here of what is actually copyrightable.

What Is Not Covered by Copyright?

Ideas are *not* covered by copyright. If I do a concept album about the phases of the moon or a musical about the mating habits of the Nutria rats of Louisiana swamps, you can too, and I can't stop you.

Titles of songs and records are not covered by copyright. There are a hundred songs called "I Love You" and a dozen called "Money." Titles of huge-selling records might be covered by trademark (especially if done in conjunction with a movie release), but that's not going to be a problem for you. Band names, as we have seen, are covered by trademark. But not copyright.

What Is Covered?

Works of art and intellectual property: songs. Melodies and lyrics. Collections of songs. Arrangements of songs. CDs of samples to be used to create new music. The individual samples themselves. Movies. Screenplays. Software. Photographs. Books. Magazines, newspapers, pamphlets, poems, plays, articles (even on the Internet). Anything written and published.

How Long Does a Copyright Last?

The life of the author plus 50 years.

After this time, they enter what is called *public domain*, which means that it's fair play to be covered without paying the writer royalties.

Not everything you'd think would be public domain actually is. "Happy Birthday to You" is owned by Michael Jackson. He also, somehow, owns the Beatles' songs. (Don't get me started on that.)

How Do You Get a Copyright?

Unlike patents and trademarks, which have to be *granted* by the government, you grant copyrights to yourself simply by putting a copyright notice on the art and then publishing it. A copyright notice consists of the little c in a circle copyright symbol (©) and/or the word *copyright*, then the year and your name. Like:

© 2003 Michael W. Dean

or

Copyright 2003 Michael W. Dean

or

Copyright © 2003 Michael W. Dean

Any of these three is acceptable. Then you publish it. This can mean either making copies of it or putting it on the Internet. Both constitute publishing. You just have to make multiple copies of it and make it available to the public.

The U.S. government will, however, *register* a copyright. And this is worth doing. The easiest way to do this is to copyright a collection of songs at the same time. This costs $20, and all you do is send in a cassette tape or a CD of the songs (you could also send a data CD with the lyrics on there in electronic format for extra protection). You can get all the forms to do so from the Library of Congress site: www.loc.gov/copyright.

There is a rumor that you can do a "poor man's copyright," which consists of mailing a tape to yourself and then later, if needed, using the postmark date to establish first authorship. This is not very airtight, as it's too easy to just alter a piece of mail. The government is better.

Some countries honor the copyrights of other jurisdictions. Some do not. Check your local laws if you are not in the U.S. And keep in mind that if you are in the U.S., your copyright may not apply in other countries.

There are several private organizations, like ProtectRight.com, that claim to be able to do the same thing that the government does, as far as keeping a copy on hand for a fee, but since the fee is the same as the government price, I go directly to the source, the U.S. Copyright office.

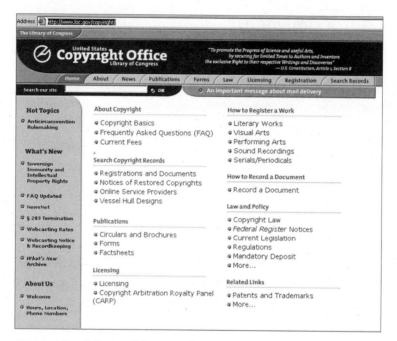

Figure 14.2 *Library of Congress site.*

Publishing Rights

This is that weird bit of commerce voodoo that is extremely complicated and beyond the scope of this book. If you get signed to a major label, your lawyer will be glad to explain it to you and charge you $350 an hour to do so. They did that to me, and I'm smart, and I didn't get it. I do know that I got small checks (like 200 bucks a pop, three times a year) in the mail for a few years after I got dropped from Warner Brothers. After a while, they tapered off. We did get a publishing advance, which is basically you betting the company that you'll fail. We won, because we didn't sell that many records (about 10,000 of the Warner Brothers record). That's nothing on a major label, and they gave us a $65,000 advance. Of course, after that was split with the band, the lawyer, the manager, and all, it worked out to minimum wage.

The Flip Side

You don't really have to deal with copyrights and all that crap at all. Dischord Records does not copyright their work. Sometimes the individual bands do, but the label does not add a copyright. When you sell your art through most media corporations, the corporation, not the artist, owns the copyright. Look at the copyright in the beginning of this book. It's not in my name; it's in the name of Muska & Lipman. This is something you usually are asked to give up in exchange for a good advance.

Dischord works more like a repository or public library for documenting music they love, rather than a conventional media concern. And their two biggest selling bands, Minor Threat (who sold over a half-million copies of one record—an amazing number for an indie label) and Fugazi have never charged anyone for covering their music. And they're covered by everyone from The Red Hot Chili Peppers to Slayer to Silverchair. Bands that sell *millions*. Dischord is not interested in dealing with the commercial trappings of art, just the art itself, but somehow they do commercially better than most indie and some major labels. And actually pay health insurance for all their employees.

I am somewhere in the middle. I throw a copyright notice on everything I do (unless a company pays me to let them own the copyright[2]), but I never really bother much beyond that. I have never registered a copyright with the Copyright office. I was a member of ASCAP (a performing rights organization that allegedly collects royalties due to musicians and takes a tax off the top for doing so) but only because I was dumb and on a major label and my lawyer told me to. I dunno…seems like a lot of paperwork to me. (If you contact www.ascap.com or www.bmi.com, I'm sure either will give you a compelling case for how they will try to get you lots of money).

If you want to play that game, feel free. It doesn't interest me at this point in my life though.

To Wind Up So Far

Protect yourself, but don't trip on it too much. As we said at the end of the last chapter, the music should *always* come first. Everything else is just administration.

---

2. *It may seem antithetical to the thesis of this book to do so, but it's really not. Muska not only lets me print pretty much anything I want, they provide excellent editorial support and get my books into stores everywhere that I could probably not get them into on my own. Their editors are really smart and close to my ethic and don't dilute me. They work with me, back and forth, making suggestions for small changes in focus that only make my words stronger without diluting my intent. Being able to take suggestions is part of the growing-up process, in my book.*

Slick Guys in Suits and Ties with Little Ponytails

Agent or Not? Manager or Not?

Basically, my experience is that when you need an agent or a manager, one will find you. If you're just starting out, you probably don't need one. And what you *really* don't need is a well-meaning friend with no business skills or experience who basically wants to be a part of something and call himself a manager. You're probably better off doing it yourself. There are exceptions, and I'm sure that many great managers and agents started out as well-meaning unknown friends of some band, but it's been my experience that these folks can cause more harm than good.

A lot of people who want to be managers or agents don't even know the difference. A manager does *not* book your shows. An agent does. A manager oversees all aspects of your career; an agent gets you jobs. In California, it's actually illegal for a manager to book you shows. (This is a throwback to a Hollywood studio system thing to protect against conflicts of interest.)

We'll cover getting an agent later in Chapter 16, "Touring."

Figure 14.3 *Some of Babyland's gear. Yes, that is an Apple Macintosh SE. (It had a whole 1000K of RAM!) One man's doorstop is another man's sequencer.* Photo by Michael Dean.

"The Deal"

The idea of record deals is sold to the public in a very misleading way: like the company is doing you a favor, and like your life is going to change for the better in intense and immense ways if you get The Deal. Like the fairy godmother, in the form of a corporation, is going to wave her funded-debt wand and whisk you sky high in a tornado of adulation, love, money, sex, and happiness. They even propagate this, literally, with shows like *American Idol*, where the contestants "win" a record deal. (I'm not sure that's even legal. Isn't that a violation of gaming or labor or even usury laws?)

My old band, Bomb, started in 1986 out of a love of music. We had a blast and we were great—way better than most bands, and we got recognized and built a following quickly. But we would have laughed if you had told us we'd end up on a major label, not because we hated "the Biz," but because no one was signing weird bands back then.

But then the industry changed a bit (because Jane's Addiction got popular), and Bomb was signed to Warner Brothers.

In retrospect, The Label's dealings with us were like a sinister man wooing a simple woman into bed: all love and promises before we signed. Then it was like pulling teeth on a wolverine to get them to come through on the other end and fulfill any of those promises after we'd inked the contract. I even had to pay out of my own pocket to send out promo copies that I had to beg for when we went on tour. Everyone made money except the band: the lawyers, the producer, The Label, the manager, the agent. The members of the band made a sub-McDonalds wage for 12 months and were then dropped without even being told we were dropped. Our lawyer told us we were dropped, and he'd heard it by reading it in a trade paper.

At this point, I felt like the simple woman who is lying on the bed alone, next to her prettiest dress, crying after having just been used by the sinister man. After he's satisfied himself and is on to some younger, prettier girl, I'm lying there, wondering if I'm pregnant, saying, "But he said he loves me. He'll be back."

I became obsessed with the idea of The Deal. I could still write great songs. But my band was breaking up. We were all daunted by the whole ordeal. Before The Deal, we'd been really happy making cool music, putting out powerful records, and rocking the nation's clubs out of a van. After The Deal, I sank hard into drug addiction, and the band said, "It's the drugs or the band. Choose."

I told the band (who were my good friends), "You're all fired," because I had been told by The Label that I was the star. I figured I could get anybody to be my backup players and rock to the top.

And I found players easily. I started a band called Drive-By Crucifixion.[3] Nice guys and good musicians (our song "Ivy" is on the CD), but we didn't have the same spark and magic that the first group had. And my efforts were fueled less by the love of music and more by the need for The Deal.

Figure 14.4 *Drive-By Crucifixion.* Photo by Warner Williams.

I got my publishing company to give me money, and we cut a demo. I made the mistake of recording 12 songs too quickly rather than three songs really well. I did some showcases for the few industry people who were still returning my calls. They showed up, saw our earnest-yet-slapdash efforts, said "thanks," and left. I sank harder into drugs.

Okay, since I was never more than a footnote in the grand scheme of the history of music, the above story is the closest to a "Behind the Music" I'll ever see, but it's

---

3. *My mother told me at the time that it was a bad omen to have a promo photo with a gun to my head. She was so right. This was the beginning of the end for me, career-wise at least. Lydia says the photo looks very* Apocalypse Now. *I agree.*

got value for you. The moral is: Put the music and your friends first. The Deal should be the last thing on your mind.

Remember that this was all back in 1990 when they were handing out deals more easily than today. Nowadays, file sharing has decimated the industry, and the economy is bad anyway, so they're extremely reserved with bringing on new talent. The major labels are, with few exceptions, only signing people under 24 who are very cute, have very catchy songs, and have already sold 10,000 records. But if you can sell 10,000 records on your own, you don't *need* a major label! You can run your own ship, do it tight, tour, develop a fan base, and keep *all* the money. And you'd probably make more selling 10,000 records yourself than 100,000 on a major.

I have to refer here to the article, "The Problem with Music," by Steve Albini[4] (www.electrical.com), reprinted with permission in the appendix of this book. It shows why you shouldn't bother. I love this. Steve knows what he's talking about. He's engineered some hit records, including Nirvana and Bush.

TIP

Keep receipts for everything. All equipment, all travel, even buying videos, tapes, CDs, books (including this one) may be able to be written off if you make money at some point.

I look at the media in general (movie companies, book publishers, magazines, TV, and major labels specifically) as a pipeline that needs to be filled. In this business model, *the pipeline* is important; *what you fill it with* isn't. The only thing that matters is that it gets filled.

This pipeline can work really well if you're trying to sell something. *They* have amazingly aggressive and effective mechanisms already in place to be all ready to pump their sludge into every home in the world on a few days' notice. It can also work horribly if you're an artist. They don't care how you want your art to be

---

4. *Steve Albini is an independent musician and record producer who played in the band Big Black (and helped create the "hard industrial" sound that is making millions for others). He produced Nirvana's "In Utero" record, but turned down a Producer credit because he feels that elevates the engineer above the band. He did this knowing he would have made several million dollars in royalties just by allowing those two words "produced by" to be added to the record cover. He used the term "Recorded by Steve Albini," instead.*

Figure 14.5 *Energy 2.* Photo by Michael Dean.

Figure 14.6 *Singer in An Albatross (cool indie band).* Photo by Michael Dean.

presented and represented, although they'll lie and tell you they do; they care how it will fit into the existing template that they use to sell stuff.

The nature of a pipeline is such that it costs an incredible amount to construct, but the price is amortized across all the billions of barrels of oil pumped across it each year. In the real pipeline world of oil, this means that you need to keep people burning oil. Thus, all the car commercials and wars to keep that machine going.

You've probably heard all the stories of the scientists who occasionally come up with a carburetor that yields a hundred miles to the gallon. They are all allegedly bought out or murdered by the oil companies. Who knows if this is true? I do know for a fact, however, that Los Angeles used to have a great public transportation system, but the light rail was bought up by General Motors (with help from an oil company and a tire company), who in turn ripped up all the tracks and destroyed the system so everyone would have to buy cars.

This is the same logic running most of the major labels. The problem is they are operating on an old business model, one that was put out to pasture by the advent of online file sharing. They just refuse to let go.

It is also my opinion that they treat artists like shit.

TIP

I think *American Idol* and anything else with a "battle of the bands" mentality is stupid. I think that people who would do *anything* to be famous are idiots. That's not art; it's insecurity. True artists are capable of being insecure, but they don't let it get in the way. We just make art. We are so busy creating that we don't get involved in petty squabbles.

There's enough room for everyone with talent. You don't have to destroy anyone else to get heard. You may not end up a rock star, but you can make great art and maybe even make a living.

Cities used to have a style. There used to be Boston-style hardcore punk and D.C. style and LA style and Orange County punk. Now, every city, every mall, every kid, it's all pumped through the pipeline of the media and the associated companies owned by the same conglomerate. They can tweak the formula 1.82 percent and have the new record/video/outfit/cologne in every town literally overnight.

I think that all people are equal, but I love the differences that make them unique. We're all headed away from that, to a place where we're all equally bland.

Fight this.

Figure 14.7 *Left to right: Michael Dean, Tony Fag, Hilsinger, Jay Morgan Crawford.* Promo photo of Bomb by Ann Stauder.

Figure 14.8 *Another promo photo of Bomb by Ann Stauder.*

These photographs are two of a series that contained a different (but similar) shot that was used by Warner Brothers as our promo photo. The poster of this was used in the movie *Demolition Man* as decoration on Sandra Bullock's character's office wall. Not only were we not paid for that (it was in the contract that they could "exploit our image" in any way they saw fit), but I was not able to get use of that image for this book. And I wasn't even able to get one song of our music, which I wrote and sang, to use as an example on the CD of this book. When I contacted them, some new lawyer (who was 12 years old in 1990 when I was on The Label) told me, "We can work out a deal to lease use of your music to you at a reasonable rate." So I just used the stuff we did on indie labels, which we still have the rights to.

So how do we not get screwed? How do we do it right? Well…here's something that worked for me:

The Art of Business

An excerpt from my last book:

> **How a nobody negotiated without a lawyer to get a good literary agent on his own terms (a parable for any negotiation):**
>
> When I was finishing up my first movie, some kid heard about it. He wrote me an e-mail and said, "I wanna make movies too. How do you do

it?" I spent about an hour writing everything I could think of and sent it to him. I kept a copy of it.

A few weeks later, someone else wrote me and asked me how to promote a movie. I spent about two hours writing everything I could think of and sent it to her. I kept a copy of it. I expanded it into a Web site called 99CentFilmSchool.com. People read it, but no one went to PayPal to pay the 99-cent tip I asked for.

I decided to expand it into a book with a CD-ROM. I expanded the Web site into the first two chapters of the book and took the Web site down. I called the book-in-progress *$30 Film School*.

I studied online how non-fiction is sold. I realized that it is often sold with only a proposal and a sample chapter or two written. I wrote a 28-page proposal following this format exactly. It included my "credentials," which basically were nothing more than an interview on the front page of the San Francisco *Examiner* and the fact that I had made one film, had booked a shoestring tour, and had a lot of moxie.

I wrote a two-page query and e-mailed it to 40 agents that I found from online research. Most never wrote back. Ten wrote back and said "Not for us." Six wrote back and said "Please send us your proposal." I wrote back and said "e-mail or snail mail?" Four said e-mail; two said snail mail. I sent them all out that day.

Two days later, one e-mailed back and said "We love it and want to represent you." They attached a contract. I checked them out online. They didn't have much of a track record, and I considered them a last resort in case the other five said "no."

I e-mailed the other five agents looking at my query and said, "So-and-so sent me a contract, but I wanted to talk to you before I signed it. Have you had a chance to look at my proposal yet?" The ones who had opted for e-mail all said "No, but I'll look at it tonight." Knowing that someone else was interested lit a fire under them.

I looked at the last-resort agent's contract and noticed that they wanted me to sign over my entire literary career, forever: non-fiction, fiction, screenplays, articles, everything. I e-mailed them back, "I have a lawyer who is acting as my agent for screenplays, so those rights are not available to sign over. As for everything else, I would be much more likely to consider this if you did this on a project-by-project basis, rather than everything I write. My old agent did this for my novel." (This is true. But he never sold my novel, and we went our separate ways. I self-published my novel, D.I.Y. style. I didn't tell them that he didn't sell my book, but I wasn't lying.)

Three of the five other agents wrote back and all said, "We are interested in representing you. All three sent contracts. The two who didn't reply were the two that had insisted that I send it by snail mail rather than e-mail. They had just gotten my stuff and were not operating at Internet speed…a common problem with people in the publishing industry…still stuck in an all-paper mindset. They lost out because of it. One later sent me a contract, two weeks after I'd already signed with my agent.

All three of the contracts wanted me to sign over my entire literary career, forever: non-fiction, fiction, screenplays, articles, everything. But two of the agencies were heavy players with huge batting records. One was my absolute number-one choice of all—Waterside. They are one of the most powerful agents for non-fiction how-to tech books in the world. They even agented *HTML for Dummies*, which I bought in 1996 and learned Web design from.

I wrote back to all three and again said "I have a lawyer who is acting as my agent for screenplays, so those rights are not available to sign over.[5] As for everything else, I would be much more likely to consider this if you did this on a project-by-project basis, rather than everything I write. My old agent did this for my novel. And right now you and three other agencies (I named them all) have all sent me contracts, and one has agreed to do it only for this project. If you did that also, it would likely sway me in your direction."

My number-one choice wrote back and said "Okay." And sent an amended contract. (I wanted them so badly I would have signed their original contract, but played my cards right.) I read the contract for a day, thought about it, signed it, and faxed it to them on a Saturday, e-mailed them confirmation, and snail mailed them the signed contract.

So, this is how I got a great agent, on my terms, in a week. In all of this, I was humble and calm, not cocky, and I didn't lie. Everything I told

---

5. *It's a good idea to use different agents and distributors. If you have a monopoly in any one area, you can get screwed. If they mess up, you're stuck with them. Remember Prince writing the word "SLAVE" on his cheek for photos because he said that's what Warner Brothers was treating him like?*

Figure 14.9 *An Albatross.* Photo by Michael Dean.

Figure 14.10 *Pat—Rosemary's Billy Goat.* Photo by Newtron Foto.

everyone was true, and I got what I wanted. This is a good working model for negotiations. But the only way you can do this is if you have some kick-ass art to back it up.

Keep in mind that negotiations aren't always events. They are sometimes conversations. And these conversations can happen in one sitting, but usually happen over a period of time. And people are more into negotiating with people who respect them than with people who are trying to "play them." Always go for win/win, my friend, win/win.

TIP

Here's more advice on conducting business, and this goes with the "sell what you know and love" logic and also the "let it flow through you" thing: Business needn't be a glum, cheerless affair. I chitty chat with people I do business with if they're into it. And it's not just "How's the kids? The wife? Good, let's rip each other off now." It's genuine interest in a fellow human being. For example, every time I e-mail my Canadian DVD distributor, George (from Analogue Media Technologies or *Amtech*), we chitty chat about everything from the weather (usually me teasing him…I'm in LA, he's in Montreal, it's often 70 degrees Fahrenheit warmer at my house than at his house) to parenting, punk rock, whatever. I've never met him, never talked on the phone, can never remember his last name, but he genuinely seems like a real friend. There's more than just money slipping between us. And he's one of the most reliable, punctual businessmen I've ever had the pleasure of dealing with.

When you have an agent or a manager, it's standard (and probably in your contract) that all checks that come in go to *her* first, and she writes you a check after taking out her 15 percent. Hopefully, they will do this promptly. My literary agent FedExes me my cut the day after she gets a check. This is unheard of cool. Most people take up to a month.

Be on top of getting paid (corporations often misfile stuff), but don't hassle them. If a check is late, make a polite call.

So, if you make something stellar that can sell on the first try, get several people interested, and sweetly and politely and humbly play them against each other, you can get what you want and get a deal that is equitable for the artist and not just the un-artistic old fat man who owns the factory.

You can use my example above for ideas on how to keep your soul and some of your cash.

The State of the Business of Art

Music and art have become devalued. First, there are simply many more people making art, and most of them are not very good. This is true everywhere, but more so in America, especially in Los Angeles. *Everyone* in LA is trying to "make it," and it makes it hard for people like me who just want to make good art. I'm currently booking a tour for my film in Europe, and there are some gigs with me playing music. It's easier to book a show in Europe, sight unheard, than to get a gig in my own town! And chances are, more people will show up at the shows in Europe!

Another reason art has become devalued: The same aspects of being able to digitize art that make it so easy to make and move around the globe the way we want to also make it easy to copy without paying. And there's *nothing* we can really do about it. We have to embrace this.

You have to be really, really good to make a living, and basically work two jobs. You need to spend six to eight hours a day, six or seven days a week making art, and six to eight hours a day, five or six days a week promoting that art to make a living. You need to not rely on the idea of someone "discovering you" and just do it yourself. You can still avail yourself with managers and agents *when the time comes to need them,* but you will still have to do a lot yourself. And you *still* might not get to quit your day job. And if you do (I have), you have to know it may not last forever. Sure, I make art for a living, but I haven't thrown away my suits and ties. I know I could have to go back to temping in offices *any time.*

About 20 years ago, Robert Fripp (who has sold millions of records and still makes a living at music) said that the way to make sure you make a living in the 21st century as an artist is to still do your own laundry.

Figure 14.11 *Mike—Pigmy Love Circus.* Photo by Newtron Foto.

Making a Living

Part of the way to make a living is to give up the idea of waiting for that corporation to hand you a huge cash settlement for all your hard years of being a artist and a dreamer and a genius. The rest of the formula is to *diversify*. Most of the people I know who make a living at music, even the ones you've heard of, don't *just* play or sing in a band.

Check out my friends interviewed at the end of this book and other people I've worked with: Peter DiStefano, who played guitar in Porno for Pyros, does soundtrack work on (big- and small-budget) films from his home studio. He still plays gigs, but he has a family now, and it suits him better to work at home so he can be close to his family, and it allows him to make a living on his own terms and still make cool music. My friend Warren Huart is a great guitarist but works as a record producer. Janis Tanaka gets excellent touring work playing bass with the likes of Pink and L7, but still has to go work sometimes at an office job between tours. Ian MacKaye runs a record company. Eric McFadden gives guitar lessons. Michael Woody subsidizes his real work by producing sound design for theater companies and flashy GUIs for self-congratulatory corporate intranets.

If you keep your day job and like it, you never have to compromise. Storm Large is a bartender. London May is a pediatric nurse. They both dig their jobs, and both make *great* music and *never* compromise.

Contracts

I do nothing on a handshake for the same reason I do nothing any more on a long, bad contract or a short, bad letter of intent.

NOTE

A "letter of intent" is a pre-contract contract that major labels use to screw bands. It is basically a one-page contract that says "The artist agrees to sign a longer contract at some later point, and the terms of this longer contract are up to the label." A&R (*artist and repertoire* guys—basically talent scouts) keep 'em in their pocket at all times.

I do everything on a short written agreement. Even between friends. And no one's ever sued me. Or had reason to. Be honest, get it in writing, keep your word, keep your side of the street clean, and you cannot lose.

My contracts are short and to the point, and they cover both parties. Some examples are on the CD.

NOTE

Again, I have to tell you that nothing here constitutes legal advice, but I will say that I've done better as my own D.I.Y. counsel than I've done paying entertainment attorneys $400 an hour.

My problem with most contracts is that they are very one-sided in favor of the corporation. And needlessly complicated and long. Of course they are. They are written by lawyers who get paid by the hour.

Many contracts are written in a way that's impossible for the artist to understand alone. You have to pay a lawyer (often a guy secretly on the side of the guys who wrote it) to basically say "yes" or "no" to you. And you have to trust him.

Lawyers should charge by the pound rather than the hour to write contracts. My band's contract when we were on a major label was 75 pages long! And it was written in a way that I almost gave up reading it before I got to the small print hidden on pages 56 and 68 where I gave up all my rights.

And a lot of these contracts, especially those from large corporations, are written in a very punitive tone—very Angry God: "We, The Corporation, are all. You, the lowly 'artist', are lucky to have us." It's built up to make you feel bad. And contracts don't need to be this long, complicated, or mean. The relationships they define aren't that complicated or sacred.

Some corporations basically rip off artists by appealing to a combination of vanity and the need to be seen. And it isn't personal. It's business. But it feels personal when you're the artist. Artists have a need to be validated, because they rarely are. We also have an innate need to have our work felt and seen by the world, even if we are not credited for it. That's why we make art. We make things that we feel the world needs to see, and we will sometimes sell out many rights and most money to get them seen.

TIP

If you can help it, don't let The Label cross-collateralize royalties. Cross-collateralizing is when if one record fails and one does well, they pay themselves for the one that fails out of the successful one before you get any money.

Look in the folder contracts_releases_and extras on the CD. There are a few *actual* contracts and dunning letters to and from attorneys. People I know donated use of them to show what to do (and in some cases what *not* to do) with regard to contracts. (I censored out the names of the parties, but trust me. These are some *big* bands. You probably have some of their records.)

Artists are usually treated with distrust. They are a necessary evil of the film, music, and publishing industries. But we have wild hearts and tend to be less predictable than the suits who run and profit from those industries. The people running these industries often have never created anything, and they feel fear and jealousy at our ability to create. The people who own the means of distribution know that they've got the artist strung out on the services of the corporation and can charge drug-pusher percentages in exploiting the artists.

People who run a major label have usually never written a song, have no ability to, and feel small and impotent when confronted with true creatives. However, the lower echelon people, the A&R folks who actually deal with the artist and present a human face to get the artist to sign the horribly one-sided contract, are often former musicians themselves. This is how they hook the artist in.

Media corporations (all of them: film studios, TV networks, book publishers, record labels, ad nauseam) should be a lot less one-sided in dealing with the people who create the content for them. Copyright laws (including fair use) and patents were created by our founding fathers to encourage artistic and scientific progress. They knew that this D.I.Y. self-starting ingenuity is what would make America strong and great.

It's un-American (in the original Jeffersonian definition of what America was to be) and piggy to do otherwise. Treating content providers poorly is seditious and borders on treason.

What's good for the artist is good for America.

Media corporations perpetrate this "we're-doing-you-a-favor" sweatshop mentality to keep artists scared and hungry. It's kind of like how male society at large pays women less and keeps women down so women are hungry enough that they can be paid to take off their clothes and have sex.

Think "Whitey buying Manhattan from the Indians for $24 in beads, some smallpox-filled blankets, and a few pipes of tobacco."

Most artist management contracts basically say somewhere in them that the manager is actually required to do *nothing* and that the artist can never sue the manager, and that if the artist does dare to sue, she has to pay the legal expenses for *both sides*! This is common in label contracts, too.

Take, for example, music publishing deals. The publishing companies pay a ghetto-rich amount to a starving artist, usually when he gets signed, in exchange for half or more of the future "publishing" rights (the payment a songwriter gets every time a song is played on the radio, a juke box, used in a movie, and so forth). The publishing company is often a subsidiary of The Label signing you. Which gives incentive to The Label to give you a low advance. So you'll be hungry enough to give more of your soul to the monster.

Bomb was on Warner Brothers. Our publishing company was Warner-Chappell, a subsidiary of Warner Brothers. Fancy that.

Some would say that this might constitute an illegal conflict of interest. Not me, though. It might not be legal for me to say that.

It is my opinion that when you deal with these people, you're screwed. And a lawyer won't help much. There are only a handful of big media corporations. No matter what he tells you, a lawyer isn't gonna fight too hard for an unknown artist and piss off a conglomerate that he has to deal with all the time. (Even many of the "indies" are somehow connected to either Sony, Bertelsman, Time/Warner/AOL, Vivendi, Newscorp, Viacom, Disney/ABC, GE/NBC, Hearst. And this includes music, film, books, magazine, and TV. See "Who Owns What" at www.cjr.org/owners/index.asp. Also check out www.thenation.com/special/bigten.html.

> **TIP**
>
> Lloyd Kaufman says that for most stuff where you need a lawyer, you don't have to pay $400 an hour for an entertainment lawyer. You can pay your family lawyer $125 an hour to look over and approve or change a contract. It's all the same stuff. The entertainment guys don't necessarily do a better job, but they do charge *way* more.

I think the music publishing deal idea might be based on that dude in the Old Testament, Esau, who sold his birthright (future inheritance plus all rights as firstborn son) to his brother Jacob for a bowl of soup when he was down and out. (Genesis 25:29-34) In this analogy, Esau is the artist and Jacob is the publishing company. And the mother who set up the scam would be the entertainment attorney, I suppose.

Basically, publishing deals are you betting the company that you'll fail. Only if your record is a commercial flop do you win the publishing bet. If you sell a million records, they win.

> **TIP**
>
> Even if you give your music away, say to a cool indie film by your friends, you should still do a contract, like they can use it in the film but have to pay royalties if they do a soundtrack record or whatever. It's okay (and good art karma) to give music away sometimes, but don't do it in an unlimited way (or all the time). Limit it to the project at hand. Otherwise, it might hurt you later if you want to sign to a label (or any number of other possibilities and scenarios). And at least get it in writing that everyone in the band gets credit, a link on their Web site, and two DVDs of the final project without having to ask for them.

Someone told me that the reason labels "have to" screw the bands is that so many bands "fail." I replied:

They fail (to make money) because:

1. The entertainment industry is fraught with waste. A huge amount of money was spent by five labels just flying from LA and New York to San Francisco to check out/court Bomb—first-class airline tickets, first-class hotels, expensive meals, unlimited expense accounts, lawyers, cocaine, and more; all this to sign a band, not promote them, and sell 10,000 records. For that money, Touch and Go Records or Dischord Records could have signed 20 bands, paid the bands better, and promoted them, and half of them would have sold 75,000 records and all made a profit.

2. A&R people have tin ears. They don't know what people want. Only one in ten bands signed gets their contract renewed for a second record.

I don't measure success only by sales, but I'll bet you I could pick five bands and three of them would be hits. And I'm just a fan.

Like I said in my last book, "The Universe doesn't care how many records you sell. The Universe cares how sweetly you sing. Art helps people. So, pass it on."

Don't misjudge me. The last few pages of screed spiel is not typical armchair commie "The-Capitalists-will-sell-us-the-rope-we'll-hang-them-with" Berkeley Luddite-with-a-vengeance rhetoric. I do actually value free enterprise, and I really dig a lot of the fruits of corporate technology (like stuff that enables art and communication—like computers and digital video cameras). I just think "they" could toss "us" a few more doggie bones while they screw us out of our money and our style.

A True Cautionary Example

I was recently talking to a talented singer in a really cool band. I thought this band could benefit from being on a major label. I rarely think that, but they had great songs, looked cool, had a powerful stage show, a charismatic and striking singer, but had no audience. These and other factors made me think that they would be a good candidate for The Deal.

I know one person who works at a major label. I used to know a lot, when I was on a major, but that was over a decade ago. I told this singer that I was going to call this label dude up and invite him to see the singer's band. The singer thanked me, but seemed a little bitter at the mention of a label. Probably because he had already had three major label deals, lost them all, and was broke. And he's now 40, which severely lessens the chance of a fourth deal.

The singer said, "I totally appreciate that, Mike." (You can tell we aren't really close, because my real friends all call me Michael.) "You're a true friend." He took my hand and shook it. He didn't let go. He added, "But you know what I'm gonna tell that guy when I meet him?" He held my hand tighter and pulled me close so no one else in the room could hear what he was saying. He hissed through bad beer breath into my frightened ear, while not releasing my hand, "I'm gonna tell him, 'I'd love to be on your label, sir. But if you screw me, I'm gonna kill you. I'm gonna kill your wife. I'm gonna kill your children. Then I'm gonna kill your dog.' That's what I'm going to tell him."

Needless to say, I decided not to invite the guy from the label to see the singer's band. The singer's level of insanity is toxic and indicative of personality streaks in humans that I live to avoid, even if it's all talk, which it quite possibly was in this case. But the hatred that had festered in him for decades does prove one thing (other than the fact that rock music tends to attract unstable, chemically dependent people with low self-esteem and huge egos): Relying on corporations causes frustration. You will most likely not get your way.

If you never deal with a corporation to sell your art, you will never end up wanting to kill the family of people at that corporation. This is just one more reason to *do it yourself*. "Deals" set up expectations, and expectations are appointments with resentments. And resentments hurt us. We don't suffer because we make mistakes. We suffer because we defend them. Most self-improvement ideas are based on changing your thinking to change your actions. I'm into changing my actions to change my thinking. Don't hold on to your hatred. Forgiving people frees up mental space to live and create. Resentment is fun for a minute, but it'll kill you.

The Antidote

To continue the story about my band, Bomb that we started earlier…anyway, somehow my band got signed, and suddenly we had a manager. He was big on giving us pep talks. It is my opinion that he was better at that than at business, actually. So he told us about when he managed Jane's Addiction…how a lot of bands get lazy when they get signed, but not Jane's. Most groups feel like they've "arrived" and their days of paying dues are finished once they've inked the contract. *Jane's Addiction looked at this as being the opposite.* They'd always worked hard, but once they got signed, they worked harder. They hit the streets more, put up more flyers. They still set up and promoted their own warehouse shows and tried to make it more than just a rock show, even adding circus-like attractions.

Years later, a friend of mine, Candacy, told me how back in 1988 she was working at a small record store in Columbus, Ohio when some guy named Perry Farrell. called her up and chatted for a long time. He had a new record out on Warner Brothers with some band called Jane's Addiction. She'd never heard of them. By the end of the conversation, she felt like they were friends and she was willing to do all their local promotion, from setting up radio interviews to taking it to the streets with flyers, to playing their record non-stop in the store.

Getting any kind of deal doesn't mean you can now you can just lay back, cruise down Sunset Boulevard in the back of a limo and snort coke off a supermodel's breasts. Jane's Addiction did several grueling tours in a van, opening for everybody—Big Black, Love, Iggy Pop, The Ramones, X, Red Hot Chili Peppers, Love and Rockets—after getting signed.

When you get a deal of any kind, it just means you have a job. The work isn't over; it's just begun.

If Jane's Addiction had sucked, they wouldn't have taken off. The fact that they were amazing, both on record and live, made it possible for this type of hypnotic moxie to work. And the band had the personal touch. Without that, and without their work ethic, they might not have taken off.

Our manager told me that Madonna took a similar approach when she got signed to Warner Brothers. She made up press kits and spent a week going to everyone in the corporation, from the CEO to the mail room, and hanging out with them. Smart. And remember, the guy in the mail room could be the CEO some day. Or you could just want to make sure that your packages get where they're going. No one is too small to help you. And it's just good karma to not overlook the little guy.

One of my favorite scenes in my *D.I.Y. or DIE* film is Ian MacKaye[6] saying that Fugazi was offered a million dollars by a major label and they said "No" because it "Just wasn't something that was for sale."

Ian owns his house but hasn't painted the front porch since I met him in 1984. He wears the same ten-dollar tennis shoes I do. His priorities are about his work, not outward appearances. I think that's cool.

One thing I love about Fugazi that ties in with this is they say they don't feel that everyone in the world has to like their band, or even hear them. Contrast this with major labels, or with Nike and Coca-Cola. McDonalds offends me because they destroy the rainforest, but they also offend me because I feel that they are culturally bereft *and* have to be every gosh darned place I look.

Conclusion

Act the way you'd want to be treated. Business needn't be a "screw you before you screw me" state of affairs. When done the $30 Way, it's a win-win exchange. More of a conversation than an event, and everyone should end up happy. Work at making this happen every time.

Art and commerce can coexist without compromise. There are many valid ways to do this, but it all pretty much comes down to this: Don't be piggy. Don't stockpile. Just let life, fame, money, whatever flow *through* you. There's enough of all those resources in the Universe for *every talented and driven person in the world to have as much as they need.*

6. *Are you sick of hearing about Ian yet? I've mentioned him a lot, but I just think he really has a good thing going, and that it's worth looking at. And I first met him and saw his scene when I was 20 and looking for something that made sense. And I found it. And no, despite what one article said, I don't worship him. I don't run everything by a WWID test, either. I just think he's a swell cat.*

Chapter 15

**Starting Labels and
Production Companies**

How to start and run your own successful media concerns. Starting a label. Doing it to get your music heard, doing it to help other bands. Making, rather than losing, money. Also, starting your own *production company*. **Why this is the secret new business model that is going to replace major labels.** What a production company is, how to run one, and how to stand out.

Running a Record Label

I've run a couple of record labels. They only existed to put out my stuff.

I would have liked, at various times in my life, to have expanded that to include other artists, but I got sidetracked by various other things.

My label, Cloaca Records, only put out the first 7-inch E.P.[1] of my band Baby Opaque. The disc was called "Pain, Fears and Insects." Later, my band Bomb's label, Boogadigga Records (named after the sound of our drummer's trademark beat), only put out the first Bomb record, "To Elvis in Hell." With each of these, we only pressed a thousand copies and probably only broke even. I have no idea, and it would be impossible to really tell, because we did what you *should* do when you run your own label: We sold them, but we also traded them for places to stay, food, gas, swapped for other bands' records, and gave them away as thank-yous on the road. We also sold many at somewhere between cost and full retail if someone really wanted it but didn't have the whole amount.

Both of those records are *way* out of print. If you can find them in a used record store, they are either 50 cents or 50 dollars, depending on if the person has listened to them and knows about the bands. We still have rabid fans, and I still get fan e-mails from strangers. A decade later! *That* is why I play music—to touch people *for life*. Like a virus. I'm in art and life for the long run.

I make the music and art I wish existed. I make art I see a need for. If Bomb had already existed, I wouldn't have started another band: I would have been Bomb's roadie.

1. Extended play *single—a primarily defunct format of putting about four songs at 33 1/3 RPM on a vinyl record that would normally hold two songs at 45 RPM. This was a popular format with punk and punk-ethic bands because it maximized the amount you could say on a limited budget.*

So basically, to start a label all you have to do is get a P.O. box and put out a CD or DVD. Then you send copies to every magazine that might review you and every station that might play you, and you place a few ads. Start a Web site. Keep records of customers and transactions, build a database of customers, don't spam, don't sell or trade the list, be spectacular enough to get word-of-mouth buzz, and try to make your money back.

TIP

Dischord Records has a policy where if they have a $2,000 advertising budget, they take out 200 ten-dollar ads, one in almost every small fanzine in the country, rather than one $2,000 ad in a national magazine. This is smart for two reasons. First—it probably reaches more people. And second—it supports the scene, which in turn supports them.

Take any money you make on the first record, put out a second record, repeat ad nauseum.

You might want to write up a single-page agreement with any bands you "sign" so they don't sue you if you don't make them famous. And mainly so things are solidly understood. Even (especially) with your friends.

TIP

Don't blame people for stuff that's not their fault.

The most equitable contract I've signed was the one that Bomb had with Boner Records. Boner paid our recording bill ($800)[2] and kept the money from the first thousand copies they sold to cover their expenses. After that, they split the profit with the band, 50/50. They only owned those masters, not the songs and not any rights to future recordings. We were free to go to another label any time.[3]

2. Recorded at Inner Ear Studios by Eli Janney, who later went on to form Girls Against Boys, remix David Bowie, and played on the amazing soundtrack for "Hedwig and the Angry Inch."

3. Contrast this with tiny Sub Pop records who made millions when Nirvana hit it big. But only because Chris Novoselic was drunk one evening and realized, "We don't have a contract with Sub Pop! We need to protect ourselves" and woke up the guy who ran Sub Pop in the middle of the night and made him write up a contract at his kitchen table.

Every three months Boner automatically sent a check and an accurate, detailed statement. They never stiffed us. They're still in business after almost 20 years because of that sort of ethic. And they started as a band putting out one record of their own. The label owner, Tom Flynn, was in Fang and put out their "Land Shark" record as Boner 001.

It goes without saying, but if people send you checks, cash them promptly. (It goes without saying for me, because I'm often so broke that I'll ride my bicycle to the bank to deposit a single $15 check.) Not everyone balances their checkbook. And while it's technically their fault, not yours, if you wait six months and it bounces, they will hold it against you and your company. Good companies do good business, and this entails promptly cashing checks.

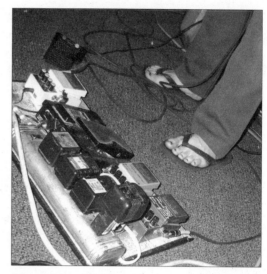

Figure 15.1 *Footie pedals.*

Most businesses that succeed go to the bank and deposit checks *every night*. And they ship orders within 24 hours.

Keep money *moving*. Let it flow through you. It is not only the art karma secret part of the $30 Way, but it also makes the local and global economies stronger.

Fan Mail

Snail mail *and* e-mail. Answer it. Be prompt and kind. Think about how you'd feel writing your favorite star, especially when you were younger and more impressionable. Getting fan mail is an honor. Treat it like that.

As with all e-mail, read your outgoing fan mail replies out loud before sending. Maybe keep them in your drafts folder and sleep on them before sending. Keep in mind that what does not sound stern in your head when you write it lacks inflection when they get it and may sound meaner than you intended.

Running a Production Company

The big business of the record industry is screwed. Napster started killing it and Kazaa is finishing the job.

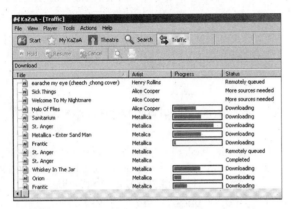

Figure 15.2 *What Kazaa would look like illegally downloading audio files. This is a simulation that I, um, created in Illustrator.*

Record companies prosecuting file sharers is like if horse buggy manufacturers had gone after the first car drivers. Record companies are acting dumber than a bowl of mice and twice as cranky.

They're so backwards that they're shooting their own grave and digging their own foot by going after their customers. The horse is out of the burning barn and there's no putting her back.

You can't stop file sharing by arresting folks. There's too many tens of millions of people doing it. And many of them consider the arrests a challenge. It's war. And The Man will lose.

You can't stop file sharing by technological means, either. The Internet, by design, routes around interference. It was designed by the U.S. Army to be a communication system that could survive a nuclear war. Any software or hardware that attempts to block free use is perceived by the system as a cranky little obstacle far less detrimental than an A-bomb and easily ignored. Byte packets are slipperier than water. They will *always* find the path of least resistance.

Some media conglomerates are even considering or taking steps toward divesting themselves of their music units. Sony is finding that they are making far more money in their home computers, MP3 players, and MP3-enabled cell phones than they are in putting out music. And these MP3 hardware divisions *encourage* (or at least enable) people to bootleg music. So they have come to be in direct competition with themselves!

I think that part of the appeal of file sharing is that it makes you feel involved. It is more active than simply buying a CD and passively consuming it. I think that people are tired of being passive consumers.

TIP

There's nothing you can do about bootlegs. It's part of doing business in today's digital economy.

I have a girlfriend who speaks Chinese very well. She offered to do translation subtitles for a DVD I did so that I could have them sold in China and Hong Kong. I asked a distributor if he could market there effectively. He said, "I had a sub-distributor there and I only had one order from them. They bought one copy each of 15 titles."

I said, "Was it by chance your 15 best selling titles?"

He said, "Yeah. How did you know?"

"I'll bet they pressed a hundred thousand copies of each one."

He said, "I think I'm gonna be sick."

By the way, the best way to copy protect DVDs is no copy protection at all: Make them DVD-9 format (with dummy data if you need, to make them more than 4.7 megs). Home burners can't copy them easily.

I've met[4] a huge record producer who has done a lot of top ten records, including two records I love. One of them more or less changed rock and roll forever. The guy's a multimillionaire.

He doesn't want people to know this, but he's almost been put out of business by Napster and Kazaa. He hates them.

I'm not going to name him, because I have a lot of respect for him as an artist and a person. But I'm not going to feel too sorry for him going from making millions a year to just having the millions he's already made.

But here's what he's doing: He's starting a production company.

---

4. Notice I didn't say, I know him, even though I didn't drop his name. But he has been to my house. He's sat in the chair I'm sitting in right now.

This kind of takes the business model used in film and applies it to music. You know how when you go see a movie nowadays, there are often four or five or six company logos in the opening and closing credits? Films are now usually produced as big independents by ad hoc corporations that come together and kick ass for a year, go their separate ways, and sell the result to a major studio. Sometimes directly, sometimes through one of those other logos swimming on the screen.

My Prediction

The new business model will sidestep the big centralized intermediary of the huge record company. They will still be in business, but basically as distributors and marketers, which is what they do best anyway.

They are basically going to let the independent production companies farm out the A&R, development, and creative (recording and producing) side of it, which they aren't very good at anyway. This is where you can come in. And *shine.*

The old business model (think car companies, oil companies, and beer companies, as well as media concerns) is outmoded. You don't need a brick-and-mortar office or factory. That can always be outsourced.

A centralized system is vulnerable to all manner of attack and attrition—economic and otherwise. Information *is* business, and today a business can be one person with a laptop in her backpack. You can even leave the country at any time. (I *always* keep my passport up to date. *Especially* in the last couple of years.)

One or two people (or a few more) can change the world, and they don't even have to be in the same place. Take for instance this book: I'm writing this in Los Angeles. I sent *all* the files this time to my editor by FTP (including 500+ megs of high-rez image files—all the photos and screenshots in the book). I didn't even mail him a CD. I will be making changes from Internet cafés in Europe while I'm on tour next month. My acquisitions editor is in Indianapolis. My agent is in San Diego. The copy editor is in the Midwest somewhere (I don't know where—we only deal via e-mail). The tech editor is in Northern California somewhere (ibid). Most of these people work out of their homes. The company headquarters is in Boston. The books are printed in and shipped worldwide from Kentucky.

A similar methodology can *and will* work for audio and video production and dissemination. Basically to do this, you need to be smart, talented, hard working, and a little lucky.

I do almost everything across the Internet these days. Here are some MP3 files I temporarily loaded on my site for one of my assistants to grab and transcribe in a different city. I've never *met* the guy who did this for me:

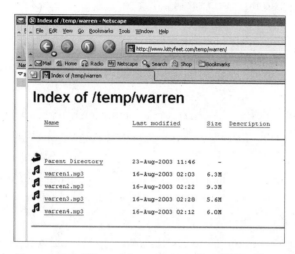

Figure 15.3 *Warren's interview as four MP3 files on my server.*

I do stuff like this all day every day. It's my life.

TIP

You could make records over the Internet, but the file sizes are a little large, even for DSL. But you can *easily* write and even record music through the mail. Death Cab for Cutie side project The Postal Service even gets their name this way. It's two guys. One guy writes and records the music and mails a CD to the singer, who writes lyrics and melodies, sings them and records them to the backing track. The results are very cool.

How to Stand Out as a Production Company

You need to be *excellent* at the creative side *and* the business side to pull this off. If you're only good at one of these, get a partner to do the other part. And put your relationship in writing. This is one of those things where it wouldn't hurt to go to the family lawyer to help draft a short, equitable contract. And make sure that either party can get out if it turns out you hate working with each other. And you might consider forming a limited liability corporation (LLC) to cover all your asses (and assets).

CAUTION

AGAIN, NOTHING IN THIS BOOK CONSTITUTES LEGAL ADVICE. ALL INFO IS PROVIDED FOR ENTERTAINMENT PURPOSES ONLY.

You find a great band and sign them to an equitable contract. Produce the band, record them, and work with them to design the packaging and videos. You deliver two data CDs to the distributor for lots of money. (One CD of music, one of the artwork page layout file. Or better yet, a data DVD with the album, video, and page layout!) You split the money with the band and move on.

You don't even need to think in terms of albums. I think that *songs* are going to take the place of albums. This is a by-product of file sharing, also a result of labels charging 20 bucks for one hit and nine crappy filler songs. Apple has the right idea: They have actual physical brick-and-mortar stores that have no physical product. They only exist to sell 99-cent files downloaded to your iPod. Heck yeah!

You can be a production company that operates a *song bank*. A song bank is a repository of songs to be perused and licensed by people for films, compilations, and so forth. You just need to work out your own unique interface and payment methodology. And get *one hit* so you'll be in demand. Don't sign crap. Be picky. Don't follow trends. Start them. You will become known for your quality.

It's a decentralized world. Don't have an old-school centralized mindset if you want to survive.

Figure 15.4 *Rock energy onstage.*

What Makes a Good Producer?

A good producer makes things work out a lot better overall with your art. They aren't someone to meddle with things; they are someone to make you shine.

A lot of young people refuse to be produced, but that's kind of foolish. I think that being teachable *keeps* you young. When you stop being teachable, you start getting old.

Figure 15.5 *Rock rock rock rock rock and roll high school.*

A good relationship with a producer polishes a diamond in the rough. And you get to utilize the experience of someone older and more adept and get to use it while you're still young and cute enough to sell records.

Below is a flipside of the whole "do it yourself" argument. It's a letter (reprinted with permission) from my friend Beau Brashares. It was part of a conversation between the two of us talking about a band we loved back in the old days in D.C. The band name has been removed to protect the egos of the guilty.

I've known Beau for 23 years, and I know he's being pretty facetious in a *Modest Proposal* kind of way about the gun in the second and tenth paragraphs, but I wholeheartedly see his point. After all, one of the sayings I made up back when I started making (good) records on my own in 1984 was "The problem with *every-one* being able to make a record is that *everyone* makes a record."

Beau is an extremely talented person, and very smart. And I don't just say this because he broke up a band (Amplifier, from San Francisco) that had *everything* to make it: excellent songs, great singing, great playing, unique arrangements and production, major management, even stunning good looks. He was about to get signed and walked away and went to law school. He is now a practicing attorney in New York City and records music and takes fine art photographs for fun.

This may seem like it runs counter to my D.I.Y. ethos, but in some way, it doesn't. I agree with all of this:

Michael—

XXXXX was one of those bands that never made a definitive record. That first tape was a classic, but their first EP (called "YYYYY") was merely a few butchered remixes of randomly chosen songs from that tape. Long after they broke up they recorded (their first LP[5]), which again recycled songs from the classic tape but remixed even more poorly. For instance, the cheesy drum machine beats that were somehow perfect on the tape were replaced with booming beats from an 80s-sounding drum machine. The songs were so good to begin with that a few people bought and liked that record despite its failures, and it started a little ZZZZZ cottage industry for (the singer). He went on to form a whole bunch of really shitty bands that were also called ZZZZZ, and in them his vocal schtick, without the context of (the guitar player)'s and (the bass player)'s playing, gets incredibly tiresome.

So the post-mortem on XXXXX is as follows: That first tape and their early live shows are a great memory for those of us that were there, but that's all there really is. If someone like you or me could go back in time with a gun, point it at the band and say, "We're releasing this whole demo tape, exactly as is, on an LP and then you are going to tour the world and play those same songs for a year," they would have become hugely and justly famous.

Unfortunately, nobody outside the band took control of the situation and they were their own worst enemy (and not just from the drugs).

You know, there's a lesson in all this. It starts with the fact that almost all artists, musicians, and writers are utterly clueless as to what others find appealing about their

---

5. Long Playing record. *Archaic vinyl format. Full-length 12-inch record with about 45 minutes of music on it.*

work. In fact, they are usually embarrassed about the very elements that make their work unique and special.

A great editor, producer, A&R person, or manager can recognize the artist's charm and originality and emphasize those features to the public despite the artist's wishes. In the same way, a band can have a balance of power that enables each member to filter the work of the other members (the Beatles being the classic example). Almost all great art involves some kind of intermediary between the individual artist and the public, and as an ironic consequence, the creative minds behind such art usually are bitter because the end result doesn't reflect their exact intentions. (Artists are very insecure and narcissistic, as we know, and intuitively they think the best possible art is that which most closely resembles what's going on in their own heads.)

Unfortunately, many artists eventually get enough power to take control of their work and force *their* idea on the world, and that's usually when it starts to suck. Frequently, this same thing happens when one member of a band gets the ability to shout down the other members. What XXXXX had in the early days was:

(I) A productive balance of power between the members

and

(II) A very talented producer/engineer in VVVVV.

Before they got a single record out though, (the guitar player) sort of took over the production and creative direction of the group, and of course everything went to hell. Now, (the guitar player) is still a hugely talented person—possibly the most talented person I know. But his very strong personality has been his downfall in some respects, because he's always been able to bully others into doing things his way, and even though his way has a lot of merit, that filtering effect is lost when one person is in charge of the whole artistic process. So what we've gotten on XXXXX's records is basically (the guitar player)'s take on what that band had to offer, which is vastly different from what the rest of us liked about them.

You may already have thought about all this stuff, I realize. As a big proponent of the whole "D.I.Y." thing, it's probably occurred to you that most artists who truly do everything themselves have a very, very limited appeal. On the other hand, they are very happy with the art they make, because it really does display the artist as he or she wishes to be seen by others. So the D.I.Y. thing usually leads to bad art and happy artists, whereas the commercial art world, with its more collaborative process, tends to make the artists unhappy but, when the right mix of talents coincides, generates the occasional masterpiece. (Of course, usually the commercial art world causes the *wrong* mix of talents to coincide, so it's usually the worst of all worlds, leading many to decide on going totally in their own, D.I.Y. direction.)

What the world needs is more talented artists who understand how this all works and have the maturity to recognize when an editor or band member or producer is changing their art for the better, even if it's diverging from their personal vision. We don't necessarily have to rely on the business interests to shove this idea down our throats in their clumsy and scattershot way, but unfortunately for many, getting free of the business interests also means getting free of *any* intrusion on their personal artistic vision, which in turn means a lot of art fails to strike any meaningful resonance with a broad cross-section of people.

Perhaps you and I should start an armed management/production team and force great bands at gunpoint to do exactly as we say.

Beau

Large Hollywood movie studios and record companies are not going to be replaced this week. But they are going to have to reckon with the lone eccentric genius working in his or her bedroom or garage. Microsoft and Apple started in garages. This archetype has also worked for media companies.

Now that you are strong and excellent enough to go up against the Goliaths, consider not going up against them at all. Create a better, *parallel* universe that does not include the Goliaths. You can do it yourself and keep it *all* for yourself—all

Figure 15.6 *An Albatross guitar.*

Figure 15.7 *Keys.*

the control and all the money. Independent music can be more than just a farm system for the big guys. It can truly be the alternative.[6]

Know your options. It's your call. Make sure it *stays* your call.

Importance of Follow Through

Someone said to me, "I wish I'd had your movie idea."

Ideas ain't much. I have 50 ideas this good each year; I just follow through on two or three of them at a time.

When I was a drug addict, I had *notebooks* full of great ideas that never came to fruition. Ideas are nothing. They are free. It's the work that counts.

The Universe rewards hard work, but you have to be *ready*.

Be the Ninja: Practice daily at follow through so you can become excellent at being able to jump in the correct direction at will.

When opportunity falls in your lap, stick a twenty in her garter and watch her wiggle.

Slow and Steady Wins the Race

I've lived in LA for two years. When I first got here, I hung out with some people who talked *constantly* about how they were gonna get a huge record deal and a huge movie deal and a huge book deal and all kinds of deals. They were all about The Deal. I got sick of their boasting, name dropping, and desperation; quietly quit hanging out with them; and went home to work on *art*, not deals.

The deals pretty much found me. I now have a good movie and two new books that I've finished in that time. I have a small cool movie deal and a small cool multiple-book deal. None of those boasters have anything. Several have moved back to Ohio and now hate LA. None of those people remember that I exist because my deals are below their radar—not big enough to count. And some of it was stuff I put out myself. And to people with stars in their eyes, that means you do not exist.

---

6. *That's what "alternative music" used to mean, when I helped start it, before it got co-opted as a marketing term by very un-alternative corporations.*

I'm living a small, reasonable, happy reality. These people are miserable and still living vast spectacular fantasies.

I've heard a Hollywood saying that you should "Do six things each day to further your career."

Forget that. I'd rather do 137 things a day to make *art* and get it out the door. There *is* a difference.

The Final Analysis

The recording industry is collapsing. Why hitch your star to a drowning wagon? The future does not belong to the lumbering behemoths of the old-money corporations. It belongs to small, potent, highly mobile networks of creative people telecommuting as peers from their homes and on the road.

You don't need a factory, you just need a good plan, good help, and a good laptop.

You can, and should, do it yourself.

$30 Music School

Chapter 16

Touring

Going on tour with a rock and roll band is about the most fun you will ever have in your life. Here's what you'll know by the time you finish reading this chapter: How to set up shows and make, not lose, money. Promotion. Travel and accommodations. How to book and do interviews. Advancing the show. The show itself. Collecting the money at the end of the night. Getting asked back.

Touring with a rock band is an American rite of passage. Time was when a boy would join the Army and come home a man. Then we realized that in joining the Army, we were just laying our life out to die for the banking interests of fat, old, rich, white men. So nowadays, boys and girls just start a band, put out a record, get in the van, and bring their song to the gin mills and basements of the world.

You can book your own tour. I recommend this. If you wait for someone to do it for you, it may never happen. Sure, on the off chance that someone does do it for you, it may be on a slightly bigger scale, but like I said, it also just might never happen. Do it yourself. Now.

It's also tough. You probably won't make money on your first tour. You'll be lucky to break even and might lose some money. You might lose your apartment. You might come back to find your girlfriend or boyfriend is seeing someone else or has left you. A lot can change in two months. But hell, you're a young, devil-may-care pip and can weather anything.

I remember the first day of my first tour. My band, Bomb, somehow booked a U.S. tour, using contacts from *Maximum Rock and Roll* magazine. This, um, friend of mine made the calls from payphones using stolen telephone credit card numbers that, um, he bought from crack heads on Sixth and Mission in San Francisco.

We packed four guys and equipment into a borrowed station wagon and set out to cover 10,000 miles and play 30 shows in 29 days in 22 different states.

Our first gig, the car broke down on the way. We fixed the engine with parts from a ballpoint pen and made it to the gig very late. It was an outdoor show at Rouge Valley Community College in Oregon. There had been 500 people, but since the headlining band, us, didn't show, people started milling out. When we pulled up, I ran up the hill and told the soundman we'd made it. He made the announcement over the P.A., and people stopped leaving. We set up in five minutes and started playing to the half of the crowd that hadn't left. After two songs, the police and the fire marshal cut the power and stopped the show.

We got paid 50 bucks and went back to the promoter's house. As I fell asleep on his dirty floor with two teenage girls in a puddle of beer, I thought, "I have never felt so alive."

I was 22 then. I'm almost 40 now. I still like playing music, but the thought of driving thousands of miles to battle cops and skinheads and get paid in beer does not appeal to me much. But I'm sure glad I did it.

In the time Bomb was together, we played over 500 shows in 35 states and 6 countries. I traveled the world for free; I met a lot of cool people. I have friends for life and a place to stay any time, all over the world. I made music that touched people to the core of their soul, influenced the music on the radio today, found out what I was made of, and somehow lived to tell the tale. And I wouldn't trade that for anything in the world.

So how does a band go on tour and thrive? I'll tell ya....

First, you have to be great. I wouldn't go on tour until you've played a bunch of shows and have a following in your home town. You also have to have some "product," something to send bookers so they know what you sound like. You'll also want to have product to sell at the shows.

Make sure that everyone in the band *wants* to go on tour and *can* do it, that is, is able to get away from work, school, spouse, and so forth. If you're underage, you'll need your parents' permission, and someone will have to be over 18 to drive.

When you decide you're ready to tour, decide a time block and start working toward that goal. A good amount is to be gone for a month on your first tour, and book three or four months in advance.

It sometimes makes more sense to do a regional tour before attempting the whole country. Maybe from where you live, a thousand miles away and back. Or in a circle and back. And go for a week or two. Like maybe the West or East Coast. Or the Midwest. Or Texas, Louisiana, and Florida.

Booking

You'll need contacts, and you'll need a press kit. Contacts can be gotten from a variety of sources. *Maximum Rock and Roll* magazine is great, but only if you are a punk band or are some type of music that can play with punk bands. The book called *Book Your Own Fucking Life* is good too. (Their Web site, byofl.org, is lame. Get the book.)

This Web site rocks also: www.herosseverum.com/resources.htm.

I find that the best thing is to just befriend another band that tours and try to get them to share their phone list or database. They will usually be reserved about doing this unless they trust you. Too many idiots having it (and many musicians are idiots) makes it harder for everyone. Only give your info out to people who aren't going to make you wish you hadn't.

Once you start booking, if you have trouble finding a contact in a particular city, you can always call the college radio station. Someone there will know where you should play. You might have to call back though, because the way college radio stations fill their day, you might get the book review show or the Sunday prayer show when you call. Just ask them when the DJ who plays your type of music is back. Also, if the phone is ringing off the hook, call back in 10 minutes. It probably means that the DJ is talking on the air at that moment.

If you do get a sympathetic DJ, find out her name and address to send her promo material. She might be quite helpful in getting people to come to your show once you book it.

If you have the name of the club you want to play but don't have the number, just look it up on the Internet. That will save you 50 cents or more a pop for calling information. I find that Google.com is the best engine for most searches.

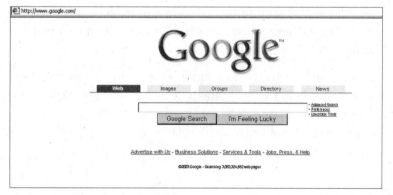

Figure 16.1 *Google.com rocks.*

I just type the name of the club in quotes, type a space, and then type the name of the city in quotes. That usually yields pretty refined results. You can also search on phonebook.com.

TIP

A lot of what we covered about booking local gigs in Chapter 10, "Finding, Playing, and Putting On Gigs," will apply here also, especially with record keeping and thanking people.

Tell the booker your name, the name of your band, what city you're in, and when you're going on tour. Ask how to get a show. Don't be surprised if they haven't heard of you, even if you're big in your hometown.

You'll probably still have to send out a CD and photo and press kit. As with local shows, you should include a cover letter. The cover letter should *briefly* state who you are, why they should care, and when you want to come through their town.

So you've sent your press kit and CD to them, and they didn't call back. Call after two weeks and gently remind them that you're booking a tour and ask when you should call back. Make a note of it in your Excel spreadsheet and call them back when you said you would.

When they finally have heard the CD, they are hopefully ready to give you a show. They might not be willing to give you the night you want, and sometimes you'll have to choose between backtracking and not having a show. I remember this was Bomb's MO. We would play anywhere, any time. We went on tour in the Pacific Northwest in the dead of winter. We booked shows on consecutive nights with 22-hour drives between them. We booked a matinee show in Toledo and an evening show in Detroit for the same night. It's your call whether or not you wanna be this insane with booking. It's certainly fun when you're young.

After securing a gig, you should also ask them for contacts for press and radio in their town, and you should follow that up with kits and a cover letter, even if the club says they'll do it for you. You can't rely on busy people to do everything they say, and it can't hurt to have it done twice. Better that than not at all.

Make another column in your Excel spreadsheet and add the local press info for that town. If you go back on tour, this stuff will help you later.

Be sure to find out if the venue provides food for the band, drinks, and a place to stay. Mark this on your Excel spreadsheet, and then ask if you should fax or mail a contract.

Some places will not do a contract, but most will. Sometimes they'll let you use yours; sometimes they insist on using their own contract. The former is usually preferable, but on your first few tours, you probably don't have a choice.

They will probably offer you a percentage of the door. I suggest you take it. Unless it's some kind of pay-to-play ticket sales thing. That stuff is insane in your own city, but beyond dumb if you have to do it from another city. A reasonable offer for an out of town band would be 1/3 or _ of the evening's take if there are a few other bands. Usually the club will take some off the top to make sure they break even and then some. Bars are in the business of making money, not of supporting the arts. They do make a lot of money off liquor, but wanna make sure they make enough money to pay the soundman, extra door people, security, and so forth that's required to put on a show.

Figure 16.2 *An Albatross guitar.* (Photo by Michael Dean. As we said in the first chapter, unless otherwise indicated, all photos in this book are by Michael Dean.)

Figure 16.3 *An Albatross keyboard.*

Ideally, you want to make $300 or $400 a night, but this is rare the first time out. But all is not a wash—I find that a band with modest needs, if they budget their money and have a low per diem (amount each person is allotted each day for expenses) of $10 or $15, can effectively tour grossing as low as $100 a day.

TIP

Try to book as many shows as you can (especially since a few tentative dates probably won't come through at the last minute, and a few confirmed dates might cancel during the tour). Days off are expensive. It's like Mike Watt says, "If ya ain't playin', you're payin'!"

While an occasional day of rest is good, too many shows is better than too few. Too many shows is what I call a "quality problem."

I try to book 30 gigs in 30 days and end up booking 27. Probably two of those will cancel. This leaves 25 shows in 30 days, which is perfect.

Merch

It helps to have things to sell at your shows. Merchandise, or *merch*, is often the difference between making enough money to make it to the next city or not. I remember on Bomb's first tour, pulling into Omaha and running out of gas, hours before the club opened. We were starving. We saw some punk rocker kids on the street, jumped out, and sold them two T-shirts. This gave us enough gas to make it to the show; we bought macaroni and cheese and went over to one of the punker's mom's house and cooked the mack and jack and hung out until sound check.

You should have T-shirts, stickers, and CDs. It is usually the roadie's job to sell them while the band's onstage, but if so, he should be set up somewhere that he can still see the stage and run up and attend to it if something falls apart while the band is playing. And he should keep the money in a money belt or butt pack (harder to steal than a wallet) when he leaves the merch table.

If you find that it's easier, you might just set up after your set. Unless your merch is amazingly cool looking or you've been in that town before or have a following, it's unlikely you'll sell much before you play. You'll have to wow 'em first.

Be willing to cut deals on merch, but have your bottom line that you'll not go below. It should be slightly above wholesale.

Well before you leave, find a good place locally to get merch made up ahead of time in your town and deal with someone who's going to get it done in time so you have it to take with you. Some bands that sell a lot of merch on tour have working relationships with people who exclusively deal with bands and will make up more T-shirts quickly and overnight stuff to you on tour. Make sure that you have it shipped to someone you trust a few towns ahead. Shipping to the club is a last resort.

Bands that do a lot of merch business, like Gwar, who probably sell more T-shirts than they do records, sometimes have someone whose dedicated job on tour is to man the merch table. And they bring an actual table. Or two.

NOTE

My friend Newt with Insecto has a cool portable display case built into a closable carrying case to show the wares available. It is easy to carry, sets up in a few seconds, and has blinking lights to attract attention. He usually sets this up to show what kind of Insecto panties and baby-Ts are for sale and then does the actual selling himself off the side of the stage after they play.

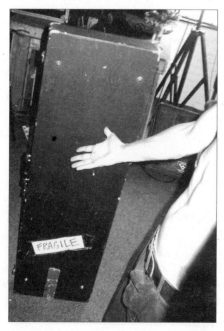

Figure 16.4 *Insecto merch booth, folded up.*

Figure 16.5 *Insecto merch booth, set up in a bar.*

Some clubs will try to take a percentage of the merch sales. I feel this is unethical. Find out ahead of time and use this as one of the points to take out if you have any ability to bargain, especially on your second tour if you did well on your first.

You can always just sell the stuff later out of your van when they aren't looking.

My recommendations for merchandise:

- Buttons
- Photo reproductions. You can get them printed up at any print shop in Hollywood (look for the big signs that say HEAD SHOTS in the window. But if you don't live in Hollywood, most print shops can make them. Get a friend to take the photo, or do it yourself.
- Stickers (including bumper stickers): www.stickerguy.com. Best prices, best quality—vinyl stickers that last a long time, but long turn-around—about six weeks. They will not do work for major label bands. Indie only.
- T-shirts

Make sure you work with high-rez graphics files only. I am *so* sick of people making flyers, and especially stickers, from the 72 dpi images they take from their Web site—that look like crap. Graphics for print must be 150 dpi or more. 300 or 600 is best. It's not that hard to do. Conversely, I am sick of seeing high-rez graphics on Web sites. They take forever to load. A good way to do this is the way I do it on www.kittyfeet.com/30bucks/30press.htm.

It's low-rez Web images that link to printable high-rez ones. That is how you do it, people.

TIP

I have a "friend" who bootlegged 100 copies of his own documentary film and sold burned DVDs on tour because the company he had his exclusive deal with wouldn't give him any tour support. He did it to make enough money to get to the next show each night, and it worked. It was the difference between losing and making money on his European tour, and it didn't take any bread out of anyone's mouth. If anything, the tour made money for the company by increasing awareness of his film.

TIP

Some bands, particularly in Europe, take small quantities (between one and ten) of merch items from other bands and labels and sell each other's wares at all their shows. They call this their "distro," as in, "Help me set up the distro, please." It's a table where they sell their own and their friends' T-shirts, CDs, fanzines, DVDs, and so forth. They trade their stuff to each other or sell it to each other for this purpose dirt cheap.

These distros help everyone; each band has more exposure, and fans get more options. It also gives them more stuff to sell, which makes them more money. It also makes you look more legit if you are just starting out and only have one or two products of your own.

Roadies

You need a good roadie. The roadie is basically a person who is not in the band who comes along and helps you along. On a big band's tour, with lots of money, this is a salaried position, and there are several or many of them. There are also a separate salaried driver, guitar tech, drum tech, road manager (person who asks for the money at the end of the night and deals with moment-to-moment logistics, "finding mandolin strings," and so on) as well as probably a cook, nutritionist, personal trainer, and even a masseuse.

On your first no-budget tour, this will often all fall on one person—the roadie. You want someone who can drive, stay sane, lift and even fix equipment and the engine on the van, as well as perform the duties of bodyguard and psychologist. Choose this person wisely. She can be either a great help or a big drag.

TIP

If you are sober and the people in your band aren't, it might be a good idea to bring a sober roadie. Then you won't feel totally alone in your sobriety. It's not hard to find sober folks who would love to go on tour. A lot of times when people get sober, they don't really have a clear image right away of what to do with their lives.

Even if you *do* drink, a sober (or relatively sober) roadie ain't a bad idea. At least as a designated driver.

On your first tour, the roadie is not on salary and is probably paid the same per diem as the band members. But don't treat her like a slave. She ain't. She is your friend and your peer. She can make or break your tour.

Money

One person should be in charge of collecting and holding and doling out the money. Make sure it's someone who is level headed and honest. You need someone who is able to deal with club owners and get the money without being a prick but also without getting stepped on. Also, he should be able to do simple math and not skim off the till, even if he feels justified because he's fighting hard to get the band's money at the end of the night. One way this person can get compensated for this task is to not have to move equipment at the end of the night. He still moves it at the beginning, but when it's time for load out, he'll probably be in the manager's office anyway.

This person should keep written records and should also bring copies of the contracts for each show on tour. Often, the booker you did the contract with many weeks ago during the day will not be working that night. And the goon who runs

Figure 16.6 *Insecto bass.*

Figure 16.7 *Guitar at Spaceland.*

the place will say, "We never waive the 15 percent charge we take of the band's merch sales," or "We never give guarantees, only a percentage." If you have made contrary arrangements, you can pull out written proof.

One time Bomb played a club called The Electric Banana in Pittsburgh (don't look for it; it's not there anymore). The manager at that time had a reputation for pulling guns on bands when they went to get the money at the end of the night. Tony was like, "Good. I'm gonna tell him 'Go ahead and shoot me'." We didn't even get to the point of asking for the money; the manager cut our electricity three songs into the set to take a phone call, and then left. If you deal with a reputable booking agent, crap like this is less likely to happen.

Van

You need a good van to go on tour. Something that won't break down and something that gets good mileage. It helps if your roadie or someone in the band is a mechanic. And make sure you have Triple-A. That will pay for itself in your first tow, and you get discounts on hotels, and they will do TripTiks for you to map out your driving, as well as suggest swimming holes, amusement parks, museums, and fun stuff to do on days off.

The van *must* be fitted with a loft. Basically this is two-fold: One, it provides a place to sleep on those long drives. It also protects the equipment. Basically, you or someone you know who is good at carpentry builds a box in the back of the van. It's only open from the back, which adds to security. Even if someone breaks into the front of the van, they can't easily steal your guitars.

There's an art to building these things. Whoever builds it should have a good visual mind to picture how to make it so all the band's equipment, in cases, will fit together like a jigsaw puzzle in the least amount of space. Experiment with different configurations first, and make a diagram of what goes in where in what order after you perfect it. Then draw your plans and build it using two by fours and sheet plywood. Watch out for exposed nails, and make sure it's sturdy. If it's done right, you probably won't be able to take it out without dismantling it, so make it right the first time.

You should be able to fit some merch under there, too. And make sure not to put CDs, or god forbid, vinyl, where they will get too hot from the engine or the sun and melt.

If your engine starts to overheat and you wanna try to make it to the next town, turn on the heater. This sounds insane, but it actually draws heat *away* from the engine. *Don't* turn on the air conditioner. That will overheat you quicker. Bomb actually drove 100 miles like this on the desert in 120-degree heat. We were in our underwear with our heads out the window, but we made it to a service station.

Bomb's first tour was done in a station wagon. This is *not* recommended, because with all your gear in the back, there's no way to lie down. It's hard enough to get good sleep in a moving van, but it's almost impossible sitting up in a car. And lack of sleep will make the road suck instead of be fun.

Get a tune-up before you leave, and make sure your tags and insurance are up to date. Cops, especially in the South, love to pull over freaky looking vans full of weirdoes with out-of-state tags (especially if that state is California!).

TIP

You can drill a hole in the floor of the van and use a funnel to pee through on long drives.

There is always the impulse to spray paint the band van and personalize it with a lot of stickers, but I'll tell you, you're asking for trouble. It's better to blend in. Bomb had a normal Ford Econoline van with only one bumper sticker, and we never got pulled over once in years of touring. The sticker said, "If it ain't country, it ain't music." Take whatever chances you want, though; just be willing to lose shows over the consequences. The band MDC got pulled over a lot and detained on any charge the cops could think of, probably because the van was always full of a bunch of merch with the band's name on it, and the band's name was Millions of Dead Cops. But on the other hand, Mojo Nixon is rumored to have toured for years with no registration or insurance or even plates without getting pulled over. His plates were fake "Elvis-1" Tennessee plates he bought at Graceland. But some people lead charmed lives....

TIP

Take turns driving. Don't drive drunk or stoned, and don't die. Someone's going to have to write the sequel to this book, and I'm gonna be too busy with other stuff to do it. Maybe it will be you. So don't die.

Cheap Tickets

Sometimes, tours will take you to other countries. Or it will make more sense to fly to a location, rent equipment, and drive from there.

STA Travel (www.statravel.com) sells student tickets *very* cheap, especially overseas. And they sell you the student I.D. for 20 bucks online. And they don't check. And you'll need to enter a 12-digit student ID number. And the student can be of any age, up to 99. And you *are* a student of *$30 Music School*, but one could mention a different, accredited, school, though I would never suggest you do anything *illegal*.

The airlines might check, though, so it might be better to enroll in one class in your local community college and get a legit ID number. (They didn't check with a, um, friend of mine who recently went to Europe this way.)

Idiot Checks

When staying at someone's house or in a hotel, each person would be wise to stake out one corner to call your own and keep all your stuff there. You never really know when you'll have to split if plans change, and it sucks leaving something behind on the road. (If you do though, you might get someone to Fed-Ex[1] it to you a couple of stops ahead. And when you leave a gig or any other place, do an idiot check. This is true not only of the band's equipment, but also of personal things.

Pack as lightly as possible on tour. There really is no need to bring a whole mess of crap with you on the road. Bringing too much stuff will only prove the Zen thing about how possessions weigh you down. I don't even always bring toothpaste or shampoo. I just use it at the houses or hotels I stay at.

I just bring my cell phone, laptop, and very few changes of clothes. I usually wear the same stuff for a couple of days, and then trade with some girl. I get her stuff; she gets my stuff. She gets a memento, and I get new (to me) stuff. What more do you need?

Figure 16.8 *Babyland guy.*

Figure 16.9 *An Albatross keyboard.*

1. *Don't stalk celebrities, but if you really feel the need to get something into the hands of a famous performer, your best bet is to FedEx it to them care of a venue where they'll be performing. Best if it arrives the day before their show. This actually works.*

Getting Along

A tour is a good test of whether or not you want to keep playing music with these people. Some folks' true coloration doesn't surface until you've smelled their socks and farts in a van for a few weeks. It immediately becomes obvious who the creep is. And like a four-way marriage, everyone's petty jealousies and annoying peccadilloes will become less, not more, tolerable with time. It really separates the women from the little girls.

Of course, most bands have two people who fit the asshole/pussy formula. It's often the two main songwriters. A lot of great creative pairs consist of one asshole and one pussy.

Jagger, pussy. Richards, asshole.

McCartney, pussy. Lennon, asshole.

Jones, Pussy. Strummer, asshole.

In Bomb, Tony Fag was the asshole and I was the pussy.

I love Tony now that I'm not in a band with him. We should do commercials for the phone company…keeping in touch to talk about the good old days. Okay, maybe not. But I do like him now that I'm not in a van with him.

TIP

Bring earplugs and eye shades[2] everywhere. I once did a whole tour with eye shades on. When I wasn't sleeping, I just pushed them up on my forehead. Good for quick catnaps backstage and in the van, and also not a bad look. Kinda sleepy and sexy. Very un-corporate America for sure. Earplugs rock. Not just to blot out the crappy opening band from ruining what little hearing you have left, but to stomp out humans and their yammering. Same on a plane. If you're wearing earplugs, strangers won't go out of their way to try to annoy you with their inane chatter about food and the mating habits of celebrities. Banter sucks. For a guy who talks a hell of a lot, I sure spend a lot of the day not talking. There's often no reason to, and I save my energy and thoughts to direct them where they matter. This is a way to not waste your life and to maximize your everything—only talk when there's a reason. If you really like the sound of your own voice, get a Dictaphone (great for jotting down thoughts and melodies by the way) and practice with yourself to get really good at being interviewed. You can damn well bet I did a bit of that when I was younger.

---

2. I call them "eye squish" for some reason. And ear plugs are "ear squish."

If you find yourself without earplugs when you need them, in a pinch you can use a (hopefully unused) cigarette filter. Flare it out a bit first.

If you only have one earplug, you can rip it in two to make two earplugs if you have that cheap spongy type.

Toilet paper can be used to keep out some noise when nothing else is available.

A T-shirt can work as an eye squish if you need.

Figure 16.10 *Earplugs—bring your own.*

I once recorded with Mark Needham, an engineer who had worked with Rancid. I already liked that band a lot, but I started to love 'em after he told me that Rancid was totally the most brotherly loving band he'd ever worked with. He said they never argued, seemed on a common goal with everything, talked through disagreements calmly, never let the ego get in the way, and always saved a piece of pizza for the guy who stepped out for a minute. I loved that.

If music ain't fun, why bother?

Everyone in the band should get sleeping bags. You won't always be able to afford a hotel room, and more often than not on your first few tours you will end up sleeping on the promoter's or a fan's floor.

TIP

I implied it a few chapters back, but it bears repeating: When you stay at people's houses, if you do *all* their dishes (not just the ones you dirtied), I *guarantee* you'll get asked back to not only stay, but to play.

Voltage Conversion

When touring outside North America, you will find that most wall sockets are 220 volts, not the 110 we have here. This will fry your amp. Or it would it you could get your plug into their weird wall sockets, which you can't.

You'll need converters. And you have to make sure that they can handle the wattage that your amp draws (which is more than it puts out to the speakers. A 300-watt bass amp can draw 750 watts or more from the wall). Don't get the little ones they sell at airports, which can only handle a laptop or an electric razor.

Note that most new laptops can take 110 or 220 volts into the power supply. But read the specs to keep from frying yours. If yours does take 220, you won't need the heavy converter transformer, but you still will need the little plug adapter so you can fit your plug in the European socket. They come in sets for each country, and usually only come with the transformer.

Even with the right converter, you can still encounter problems with amps or especially with keyboards or anything with a computer built in it. I would recommend renting or borrowing equipment in the country of destination. Bomb did this.

There are a million garage bands in Europe that will host you, drive you, provide gear, let you stay in their house, eat their food, get drunk with their girlfriends, and probably even book the tour to get to go on the road with an American band. And in some countries (like Switzerland and Germany), rock clubs are even sponsored by the government to keep kids off the street! These folks pay really well and treat you well.

One person should always sleep in the van to keep the equipment from getting ripped off.

It's better to stay in motels than hotels, unless the hotel has secured parking with a guard. In a motel, you can park the van full of gear, with one member sleeping in it right outside the door. If anyone tries to break in, that person can yell and hopefully someone will come out and help.

Take turns with van sleep duty, unless there's one person who really likes it.

NOTE

One of my favorite true rock 'n' roll stories is this: When my friend Bean was playing bass with Helios Creed, one club they played was in such a bad neighborhood that the venue had a guy on the roof with a shotgun guarding the bands as they loaded out.

You don't want to carry weapons on tour, as they will get you in trouble if you're searched, but a tire iron or something that can double as something else is not a bad idea to keep handy, for defensive purposes only. An exception is that women can usually get away with carrying Mace easier than guys. Cops will usually let that one slide. Usually. But don't use a weapon, even in defense, if there's a way not to. These are hard decisions to make on the spot, which is why you probably shouldn't trust this guard duty to someone who's been drinking.

You can usually get a room for one or two people and sneak the rest in. Some of you might have to duck down in the van when someone goes and signs in.

Don't trash the room. You can't afford it. Just have fun, do what you will, make a mess, but don't break stuff. And leave a few bucks tip for the maid. You owe her.

TIP

Always brush your teeth often on tour. Bring toothpaste, keep it in the van, and go in a bathroom and freshen up. You're gonna be talking to a lot of people close up.

Take your vitamins. Bring some with you, but in the original container so no one thinks they are narcotics if you get searched at an airport or a border.

Advancing Shows

After you book a show, send promo material to the club and to the local press. Send a press kit plus a poster design if they will use it. Some clubs will deal with electronic files, but most won't. Ask ahead of time. A few places will even book based on an MP3, but ask first. And make sure it's an easy download, direct URL, not some service (like MP3.com or worse) where you have to jump through a bunch of hoops and give a bunch of demographic info to download. Because they won't do it.

Then advance the show. This means calling and e-mailing four weeks, two weeks, one week, and two days before the gig and letting them know you're on the way, and making sure the club hasn't been burned down by fundamentalist Christians. (You laugh? It happened to Bomb.) Call them when you're pulling in to town, too, about a half hour away, so they can let the soundman know. And if you're gonna be late at all (you did get the time for load in and the time for soundcheck on your Excel spreadsheet when you booked the show, right?), call. Call if you're going to be late for *anything with anyone*, for any appointment, not just on tour.

All this advancing of shows may seem like overkill, but it's not. It all makes things flow better. And if you find out that the show is cancelled four or five days in advance (they won't always call you if it is), you can either scramble for a replacement or at least re-route your driving to something more comfortable.

And make sure you get good directions from the freeway to the club. And bring maps. You don't want to get lost pulling into town. Especially since a lot of clubs are in less than good neighborhoods because the rents are cheaper.

Figure 16.11 *An Albatross bass.*

Figure 16.12 *An Albatross singer.*

TIP
Be early for everything: interviews, gigs, practice, whatever. Get to that end of town, check in with the people, and then kill some time there. Eat lunch near your destination. It's the way to always be on time.

Booking Agents

Of course, if all of the above sounds like a hell of a lot of work, it is. A booking agent will do it for you and usually charge 15 percent of your gross to do so. But they usually won't deal with you until you have a following, and hell, your band might break up by then. If you do it yourself, you'll at least get to go on one tour and not miss this important coming of age ritual of growing up in modern society.

But booking agents already have the contacts, deal with the same clubs every day, and have relationships with the bookers. Some booking agents will deal with bands that aren't proven yet by charging money up front. This is not very reputable, but might be the only way. A compromise might be to offer to put up a $300 deposit to cover expenses until you get on the road. It does cost them time and money to book you, and they don't know if you'll even be together when it comes time to tour. Bands break up a lot, usually because they have unrealistic expectations and people get frustrated when the Universe does not instantly grant their wishes.

Some booking agents will book shows that will send you on long drives to play for people who may not like you simply because they get a percentage on each booking. It's easier for a booking agent to just look at a map and see a long drive and make a phone call than it is for you to have to actually make the drive. And if you're a pop band, you might not want to get booked on a punk bill, but if your agent gets her cut either way, you might get booked like that. (See the Steve Albini interview on the Extras section of the *D.I.Y. or DIE* DVD for more on this.)

You approach a booking agent the same way you approach anyone you want to do business with: make a call or send a short letter with that all-important press kit and CD, and follow up and ask them nicely.

You can ask other bands for recommendations of who they book through. If they're your friends and have faith in you, they might even put in a good word.

If you're really happening scene-wise, packin' 'em in, the booker will probably approach *you*. Just beware of slick promises and don't sign long-term contracts with anyone who can't deliver something huge. And even then, don't sign long-term contracts. The way bookers work is, if they do a great job, you'll go back again and again. They don't need to force you to do so in writing. It's all relationships, like anything in the entertainment business.

TIP

Don't forget to thank people, anyone who helps you—clubs, bookers, radio DJs, writers, fans, friends, everyone. Take lots of pictures, keep a journal. Get out and stretch, run around the parking lot, don't eat too much junk food, and be sure to buy lots of postcards to send home to everyone.

If you're paid a percentage of the door and not a guarantee, and you don't make much, you're stuck with it. You can ask for a little more, but don't whine.

If you do have a money guarantee, and they claim they didn't make it and can't pay you, make them pay it. Have them empty out the pool table or cigarette machine. They shouldn't make real written guarantees if they can't pay them. Don't take a check; don't accept "come back tomorrow"; get paid before you leave. If they seem like Mafioso types and pull some power crap on you, calmly tell them you know the headlining bands they have listed next month (if you do) and you'll tell those bands that the club doesn't pay up. Play hardball only if you have to, but play if you need to and it looks like it might help.

One good thing about working with a booking agent is that since she deals with the same club bookers all the time, the clubs are less likely to screw you if you came through someone who brings them a lot of business than if you book yourself.

AlphaSmart

I don't do paid endorsements, but I will wholeheartedly advise the use of something that works for me. I highly recommend that if you're going on tour you check out AlphaSmart.com. They have two products that might be highly useful for the traveling literate artist. The AlphaSmart is a durable little portable word processor that weighs two pounds, costs 200 bucks, runs 300 hours on three AA batteries, and saves text as soon as you turn it off. It also saves and shuts off automatically after a few minutes of inactivity. I am typing on one right now. I typed this whole chapter on one, in the back of a van on the way to go see some friends in San Francisco. The AlphaSmart is great if, like me, most of what you do on a computer is just typing text.

I love writing technical manuals on a device made for small children.

Sometimes people laugh at it and say, "Is that a toy?" They start bragging about and show me their Pentium IV, 3 GHz laptop. I say, "What do you do with it?" and they don't even really know. They can't give me a concrete answer. And I say, "I'm working on a really good book that will change people's lives and it's already sold." They stop laughing. One particularly annoying blank corporate food tube was trying to cut me down on a plane and going on and on about his "advanced spreadsheet capability." This prompted me to retort, "At least I'm doing something interesting with my life."

I especially love the AlphaSmart's "no boot time, no shut-down time, no need to hit save" feature, because I think and write in spurts. I tend to turn an AlphaSmart on, type a paragraph (or even just a sentence), and turn it off. I will do that five or ten times in one airplane or car trip.

I actually just accidentally proved the premise of that last paragraph as I wrote it. I am in the Dallas airport and was waiting for the train that goes from one terminal to the next. It arrived as I was typing. I turned it off, threw it in my bag, jumped on the train (that only stops for about 45 seconds), and started typing as soon as I got on the train. Try that, even with the fastest laptop.

AlphaSmarts are way lighter than a laptop, which is cool because you don't have to think, "Am I going to need this today?" and decide whether or not to take it when you leave the house. A six-pound laptop will be a burden after eight hours of running around. A two-pound AlphaSmart will barely be noticed.

The AlphaSmart Dana, which lists for $399 ($469 with a modem), is sort of an AlphaSmart on steroids. It is the same size and weight as an AlphaSmart but runs on a

Palm OS, so it can do a lot more. It can run spreadsheets, do e-mail, do formatted word processing, and play games (great for long drives). And it can (slowly) surf the Web. It's way cheaper and lighter than a laptop and runs 25 hours on a charge (the most any laptop runs is about 6 hours, and even that's rare).

The next model is even going to be enabled for wireless use.

AlphaSmarts and Danas both can upload text easily to a computer via infrared, USB, or through a keyboard port that will load into any application, including the oldest computer running DOS, but even better on any Windows or Mac application. They will even work with Linux-based systems. They also boot up and close down almost instantly, so if you find yourself with two minutes to kill somewhere, you can be typing while most laptops will still be booting.

I *love* these devices and have one of each.

If you get one, get the carrying case, too. I also add a piece of Plexiglas inside the case to offer a little protection against bumps.

Figure 16.13 *I wrote some of this book on this AlphaSmart.*

General Random Advice

Get a good cell phone plan with nationwide roaming. You'll need it to advance the shows and just keep in touch with people. I pay about 70 bucks for mine, and that includes a 10-mile tow anywhere in the U.S., up to six times a year. (I hate phone companies and refuse to endorse one. You'll have to find you own plan.)

Bring a walkman, earplugs, and mixed tapes for long drives. It will help you keep sane. I have a cheap ($35 new on eBay—way cheaper than an iPod) portable CD player that also plays burned MP3 data CDs. This is huge: You can put up to 150 songs on a single CD!

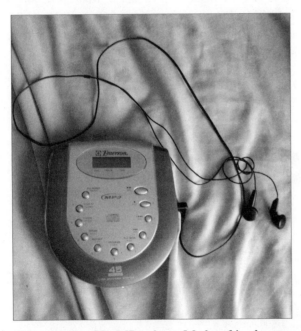

Figure 16.14 *CD-MP3 player. My best friend on tour.*

If you must do drugs, check the drug laws of every state. In some states you can lose your van and gear if one person gets caught with dope. And be honest with each other; it's no good for one person to drag down another person.

Be careful about bringing people from one gig to another. People will want you to do this because you have an exciting life compared to them. But if they are under

18 (they might lie—ask for ID), even if you don't sleep with them, you can get arrested for contributing to the delinquency of a minor, especially if you cross state lines.

Conclusion

Basically, the final word is that touring should be fun. You may not get to do this for the rest of your life. Or you may. Look at touring as an end, not a means. Enjoy each one like it's your last. You are doing this because it seems more interesting than working in an office to you. Why make it as dreary as that office job? Have fun. Get out and see the world. Take lots of photos. Keep a journal. Make friends. Get drunk. Have sex. But use condoms and be so nice to your fellow starving musicians that you are all pals when it's over.

Chapter 17

Closing Arguments

Before we set you loose, here's a last-minute fine-tuning of your spirit. How to be confident but not cocky. How to not let rock and roll kill you. How to deal with criticism. How to use art karma, how to network, and how to make people want to go *way* out of their way to help you. Dealing with adversity. And integrity—how to keep it real and still get paid.

Figure 17.2. *T-Fairy from Insecto*. Photo by Newtron Foto.

Figure 17.1 *The Sick Lipstick's keyboard guy.*

In "Rebel Without a Crew," Robert Rodriguez talks about subjecting himself to paid medical research to finance his first film. I had never heard of him in 1986, but I did the same thing that year to pay to press the 1,000 vinyl copies of the only pressing of Bomb's first record, "To Elvis in Hell." I did a government-funded drug study: drinking grain alcohol in orange juice for breakfast alongside intravenous cocaine(!) at UC Parnassus hospital in San Francisco. I was paid $500 for four days of coming in on an empty stomach at 6 a.m. and getting "injected, infected, and de-tected—and rejected"—in a laboratory setting.

Now I know that some people think cocaine is fun. But it isn't really fun when they shoot you up with sub-lethal doses of it. Sure, it feels like God is tickling you in special places for about 20 minutes. But then you come down and feel suicidally despondent and have an alcohol hangover to boot. Then they keep you there for another 7 hours and 40 minutes and bug you and take regular blood draws and don't let you eat or smoke and make you take hand-eye coordination tests and answer quizzes, and you have EKG pads attached to your chest and an itchy EEG wire bonnet attached to your scalp with conductive ooze.[1]

Yum. I've suffered for my art. Have you?

This book is for people who want to be heard. And you're gonna have to be willing to make some sacrifices. You don't have to go to the lengths I did. But if you are into music just for money or fame, you're reading the wrong book.

Still with us? Good.

Spouses and Kids and Jobs

This is a tough one. I don't know what to tell people who have kids to take care of. I guess I am a little traditional on this one. I say, "Don't quit your day job." I think if you gotta take care of someone else, you are doing them a disservice by trying to make a living at music, unless you're already on your way. The chances of starting at peg one and "making it" are astronomically against you. You should buy lottery tickets instead, and work a job, and play music as a hobby.

Playing music as a hobby ain't all that bad. Maintaining your amateur status can be a noble thing. Some of my favorite musicians don't make a living; they just make great music.

Who says everyone has to be a star? I find that whole line of reasoning specious. It don't hold water. It's just a lie propagated by the music-support industry, the people who make a living off the hopefuls.

An old joke:

Q. What do you call a musician without a girlfriend?

A. Homeless.

---

1. Kids: Don't try this at home. These are trained professionals.

I prefer not to have a girlfriend, at least in my own city. I like freedom, don't need constant reassurance (any more—I did back in the day), and would rather quietly sit in my room and change the world. I wouldn't have finished *$30 Film School* or *D.I.Y. or DIE* or this book if I'd had a girlfriend in Los Angeles, and I'm fine with it.

Kids? Personally, I'm fixed. I got snipped five years ago. I'm happy just living with my fur children (cats).

I already have an adult teen daughter in college, and she's so cool that one's enough, and I don't want more.

The world population has doubled in my lifetime, from three billion to six billion. Now that's pretty scary. I think that almost all of society's problems (especially pollution and crime) are traceable directly to that.

Polyamory

There is no such thing as free love. Sex always comes with consequences. But we still look for free love. "Maybe next time it won't be more trouble than it's worth...."

But it's always trouble. I always get attached or the person turns out psycho. Or both.

Resentments, Enemies, and Stalkers

There *is* such a thing as reasonable criticism. Then there's the fact that some people are just creeps. It's like my very smart friend Liza Matlack says in *D.I.Y. or DIE*, "People making worthwhile art themselves almost never dispense mean-spirited criticism."

But it's easier to write a bad review than a good review because there are more negative adjectives than positive ones. And many published pop-culture "writers" can't really write. It's easier to tear something down than to build something up.

Anyone in the public eye gets crap from lots of losers. Search the name of your favorite famous artist with the word "sucks" after it on any search engine and you'll get dozens, if not hundreds, of hits. Kurt Cobain said he was terrified when

Nirvana got on the cover of Rolling Stone because "Now every gun nut in the country knows what I look like."[2]

A lot of mean-spirited criticism stems from jealousy. People who can't (or won't) create or can't (or won't) get attention for their creativity (usually because it isn't good, isn't focused, or their motives are selfish and people can smell that) are content to get *any* attention, even attention for trying to tear down something good.

I've encountered several people in my life (usually males) who get near me for a while and then later turn on me and try anything they can to mess with me. This can range from threatening e-mails to public slander to trying to have me arrested for no good reason.

So, what to do? Well, there is an old show business saying, "Read the bad reviews once and the good reviews twice." Don't dwell on reviews. Even the positive ones. They really aren't that representative of reality. Oh, it's nice to know you're having an effect on people, but good or bad, keep this in mind: People who write for a living have to write about *something*. This week it's you. Next week, it's about someone else. Frank Zappa said, "Most rock journalism is people who can't write, interviewing people who can't talk, for people who can't read."

A lot of magazine writers are magazine writers because they couldn't get their books published. And rock critics are usually in bands that aren't very good. Keep that in mind. A lot of them have a chip on their shoulders and are ready to take out anyone who does something cool.

Those who can, do.

Those who can't, teach.

Those who can't teach become critics.

(And "those who can't teach, teach teachers"!)

Those who can't become critics, stalk celebrities.

Restraining orders are a bitch to get and are usually only for when someone's seriously dangerous and unrelenting. And they don't even block people, only set a precedent to have them arrested more easily later.

2. Unfortunately, there was one gun nut that poor beautiful bastard couldn't get away from: Kurt Cobain.

The only place you can *really* block someone is at your own head. If someone wants to terrorize you and you don't react, they will usually go terrorize someone else. Just like bullies in grade school. (It's the same people, actually—just older.)

One of the best ways to clear out your head when it's full of some mental attacker's hate is to go do something good for someone else. When you're listening to a friend's problem or helping her, it's harder to remember your own problem.

Just concentrate on the good. Mark Twain said "I could live a week on one kind word." (I would have to add, "and two if it's from a pretty girl.") Just keep creating, and keep walking with good. My pal Phil Sudo, who is now dead, believed that "If you always tell the truth, you'll never have to keep track of what lie you told to whom. If you live a life of integrity, you'll always have the appropriate response in *any* situation."

Figure 17.3 *Phil Sudo.*

So if you are honest and keep your side of the street clean, there really isn't much someone can do to "get" you if you don't let them. None of what they try to do to you really works. It just ends up dragging *them* down, not you, if you ignore them.

My friend Warner Harrison, who is now dead, once told me that everything is based on either fear or love. And that when a person is acting in fear, he cannot live in love. And when he is acting in love, there is no fear.

Eric Drooker said that his friend Allen Ginsberg, who is now dead, once told him, "Everyone's a prophet if they listen to their heart."

Figure 17.4 *Warner Harrison and Michael Dean.* Photo by Eric Circle A. 1992.

Dead Ends

You don't wanna shoot yourself in the foot, face, or any other body part, figuratively or literally. The dirty hallowed halls of rock music are a pantheon of otherwise brilliant people who sometimes made horrible decisions. You needn't join that stupid club to be cool or great. These people did dumb shit despite, not because of, their talent.

Drugs

Drugs are a dead end.

A partial list of dead people I know can be found at www.kittyfeet.com/dead.htm. At this writing, there are 62 people on the list. Over half of them died directly (overdose) or indirectly (car crashes, AIDS) from drugs and alcohol.

Many of them were musicians.[3] You've never heard of most of them: They did not make a dent because they died way too soon.

No matter how successful you are, you won't be happy if you're an addict. I had a friend who played bass in one of the headlining bands at Woodstock (the second Woodstock, not the first or third) and said he was miserable the whole time because he just wanted to go get high. And that should have been the highest moment of any musician's life. *Woodstock!*

A drug habit makes it really hard to enjoy touring or all the fun things that you get to do in a rock band.

The sidewalks and the ceilings look the same in every town.

Shortly after Kurt Cobain died, I was talking to Dale Crover (the drummer in the Melvins) at a Flipper concert in a park in San Francisco. He also used to play drums in Nirvana. I said, "My theory is that Kurt probably killed himself because he couldn't get off heroin." Dale said, "Michael, I think you're right."

Drugs may be useful to some as a tool, in small amounts over a short period of time, to retrain the neural pathways of one's brain to see things differently. Generally, however, we "get it" the first few times, and everything after that is self-destructive masturbation.

---

3. The two buds mentioned above, Phil Sudo and Warner Harrison, did not die from drugs. Phil had cancer, and Warner had a brain aneurysm.

Don't buy the lie. The lie is, "Since some of the greatest artists were addicts and drunks, being an addict or drunk must make you a great artist."

Not so. Those people were great *despite* the substances, not because of them.

It takes more than a six-pack and a typewriter to be great. For every original like Hendrix or Bukowski, there are two million junkie/drunk hacks clutching their pens while they die in the gutter, claiming to be artists.[4]

Drugs and alcohol appeal to musicians because musicians often have low self-esteem and large egos. The same things that attract people to the fleeting glory of being onstage are the same things that attract them to the fleeting stimulation of drugs.

Pot makes you stupid. Alcohol makes you fat and ugly, inside and out. Psychedelics and stimulants make you insane, and not in a cute way. Their use imitates the symptoms of schizophrenia. My friend, whose mother is schizophrenic, described it as, "You remember the bullies that followed you around in school? A schizophrenic feels like that *all the time.*" Jesus, I spent 20 years putting those bullies behind me. Why would I want to take something that brings that feeling back?

There is *no* such thing as recreational use of hard drugs. Anyone using heroin, speed, or any form of cocaine will not keep doing them "once in a while" over a long enough time line.

I say all of this from personal experience.

The problem with drugs is that they borrow energy and happiness from tomorrow and use it today. Eventually you have to pay tomorrow back for today. They also come with a lot of denial. Someone using them doesn't notice that they are progressing into a pit of addiction and despair. It happens so gradually that you can compare today to yesterday and not see a difference. You get tunnel vision and forget to compare yourself to yourself a year ago.

A lot of musicians are clean, completely clean, and very successful. Most older musicians that have been making a living for over 10 years are either in recovery[5] or never liked drugs and alcohol. No one can maintain a career *and* an addiction.

---

4. *From my novel,* Starving in the Company of Beautiful Women.

5. *Hell, in Los Angeles, one fellowship often even ends up being a networking system for musicians. That's not the primary purpose, but it is a byproduct. And why not? People help people they know.*

Drugs are like an extremely jealous lover. They resent anything that gets in the way. At first music is aided by drugs. Then drugs are aided by the musician's career. But eventually, even the career gets in the way of the drugs. That's probably why I've seen a gold record in a pawn shop.

Denial is so powerful. Even a skid row drunk with a bloated liver or a homeless junkie with flesh-eating bacteria on both arms can lie to himself and say "It's okay." Or even "It's not okay, but I'll deal with it later. After my next hit…."

If you need help, don't wait nearly that long. And don't use the "I'll get help after this gig" excuse.

Hell, give up your band and job and go inpatient to a rehab if you have to. Most cities have a place you can go for free, *today*, if you want to. It may not be pleasant, but it will help. Sometimes you can go outpatient to a day treatment place. I know people who have gotten clean that way. People at meetings will know where these places are. Don't say "I would go in, but I don't want to lose my band (job, girl, house, whatever) and let that keep you from seeking help. Because the nature of addiction (including alcohol) is that you will always end up losing all that stuff eventually anyway if you don't nip it in the bud. And no one is ever "cured" in the sense of you never have to deal with it again. Staying clean, I've heard, involves a little daily work for the rest of your life. But some of this work is fun, and it actually helps you become a happier person. It's all about treating the reasons you had to get high or drunk in the first place.

Or so I've heard.

Suicide

I tried it when I was 20. Failed. Thought my life's work was done because my first record came out. What a loser. Damn, I'm glad I failed.

Don't kick yourself off the planet. Whatever pain you are experiencing is less permanent than death.

Or if you're killing yourself to hurt others, stay here for a minute and consider that you can hurt far more people for far longer alive than dead!

"If you commit suicide, you're probably killing the wrong person."

—some guy

TIP

Andre Dubus said, "We don't have to live great lives, we just have to understand and survive the ones we've got."

AIDS

Use rubbers when you do it, and bleach the needles if you must shoot up. I did, and I lived to tell the tale.

TIP

Don't drink or shoot the bleach.

Humility and Work Ethic

A lot of successful independent artists think like humble rock stars. (Yes, there is such a thing.) This is a model worthy of emulation.

Jimi Hendrix said "Find yourself, then your art." George Clinton said, "Free your ass and your mind will follow." Here's some tough love: You need to know who you are, or at least be on the way, before you can "make it" as an artist. Of course, this is a task that takes a whole lifetime. But the trip can start now. Right now. Right where you're sitting.

When I started doing touring with my movie last year, I was suddenly treated like a low-rent rockstar for the first time in 10 years (10 years ago was when I actually *was* a low-rent rock star). People were again suddenly hanging on my every word, wanting to meet me, girls wanted to sleep with me, boys wanted to be me (and vice versa on both counts). And I got kinda cocky with it. I lost a friend of 12 years over it.

The lesson I immediately deduced (that I was too young/drunk/selfish to learn the first time around) was: It's okay for me to be treated like a rock star, but it's not okay for me to *act* like a rock star.

Do art for the love of the art. I've been doing art all my life. I did a monochromatic watercolor when I was three years old, called "Thunder and Lightning" and my mother, God rest her pretty soul, bought an antique frame at a yard sale, framed my humble art, and hung it on the wall. That's why I make art.

Another inspiration for me was my father, who chose to run his own company and work 80 hours a week for a salary he could have earned working 40 hours a week for someone else. He's 83 and still very physically active and busy with several cool projects.

I recently said to him, "Hey, Dad, I tell everyone I got my D.I.Y ethic from you."

He says "You couldn't have, because I still have mine!"

I was also totally influenced by the D.C. punk scene. I lived in D.C. in the early 80s, when Minor Threat was still together. I gave up college scholarships and the promise of good schools to run away from home at 19 and live in an abandoned building and sing in a band because that seemed more real to me.

I loved the teen-run D.C. record labels, the no-nonsense attitude, and idea of everyone in the band shouting backup on the chorus in true egalitarian spirit. They were pulling rabbit after rabbit out of all their hats and working their asses off[6] (at art and usually also at some crappy day job). They were creating something from nothing and having a blast doing it. It wasn't about money: It was bigger than that.

Art Karma—And Green Karma (Money)

A member of the band Kiss says in the movie *Decline of Western Civilization: The Metal Years,* "Money only makes you not care about money."

I feel that if you're doing it right, that's true.

My friend Mike Kelley says, "I try to think of money as a resource, like water or electricity. Somehow it goes away and then somehow it comes around again."

I got a parking ticket for 50 bucks today. So I just wrote a check, sent it off the same day, and let 50 bucks worth of green karma flow through me.

---

6. *Dischord even answers my e-mail on holidays. Still. I love that. The same way that to me a birthday is just another day, and even better if I'm working my ass off. I don't party on my birthday. I just work. That's my party and my devotion to life. Labor Day? A day for me to labor. Christmas? Just an irritation because the banks and post office are closed.*

Money is not a measure of worth; it's a utility. It's a form of energy. And if you get some, don't gloat. You wouldn't feel bad if you had less static electricity in your hair than your friend or brag if you had more. Treat money the same way.

I particularly love the money karma "let it flow *through* you" idea. It works for everything, not just money.

As much as Hollywood is an easy target about which to complain, there is a beautiful magic to it. I'm not just speaking of the false magic whereby talentless people walk around and imagine what Jo Moskow calls "the sidewalks speaking to them"… implying that *they're* the next big thing. I call this "Dilution of Grandeur."

No, there is an elegant spirituality to this place. It's probably a combination of Old Testament mysticism, 12-step ideology, California Hippie Zen, and traditional Ye Olde American Dream, back from when the American dream worked.

The more money you spend on others, the better you are. Donate. Fund. Hire. Give. Spend green, spend locally, spend well. When you travel, consider the town you're in to be your hometown for that day. Tip big, even if you can't afford it.

Get rich and then spread it around where it's needed.

Donate old equipment to schools when you upgrade. Or if you can, buy them new stuff. Historically, companies that give things away thrive. Ones that don't, don't. Even fat cats like the Rockefellers knew this. They supported orchestras and ballets and continue to help the arts today.

Art karma, man, art karma.

It doesn't matter how much money you have, but rather what you do with it. You can be a millionaire and still be pure. Just let the money flow through you; give it away; hire cool, talented people; pay them when you can; and treat people the way you'd like to be treated.

A long time ago a musician friend once did a really boss thing for me. I was about to get evicted and he gave me $200, which helped save the farm. But he said "You have to pay it to someone else, not me." (This was five years before that *Pay It Forward* movie.) Good plan if you ask me. And I did pay it forward. But I gave 50 bucks each to four people who needed money for food. Friends and strangers. Mostly artists, but not all. Good people, just broke. And I told them the same.

And it all came back tenfold or more.[7] Art Karma.

---

7. *Maybe for him, too. His band went platinum a few years ago.*

TIP

When I have some money and go shopping, I usually buy a few cans of something I don't like very much. That way I'll have *something* to eat on those rare occasions when I'm *really* hungry and *really* broke.

Figure 17.5 *Roach from Groovie Ghoulies.* Photo by Newtron Foto.

"As long as there are 99-Cent Stores, we will never have to sell out."

—Lydia Lam

The Seven Habits of Highly Effective Punk Rockers

1. Pass it on.

Share information, resources, equipment, and opportunities. Especially opportunities. Some people hold their contacts close to their chest, afraid that if they help someone else, it will bump them out of the running. Nothing can be further from the truth. People remember help they've received, and what goes around, comes around.

And some folks have this illusion that there is a finite amount of exposure or "fame" available. This is horse hockey. There is enough for everyone who deserves it. If you *calmly* think you deserve it, you're right. You will get your chance.

> **TIP**
>
> "Share your knowledge. It's a way to achieve immortality."
>
> —The Dali Lama

> **TIP**
>
> Food bought from money made playing music actually tastes better than day-job purchased food.

If you only look out for Number One, people will try to push you out of their way and knock you down.

If you look out for others and not just yourself, people will get behind you and push you along.

But if riches are all you're looking for, you're in the wrong school.

Conversely, don't give your contacts to self-seeking idiots or spammers who will dilute the power by harassing people and make you look bad. Protect the scene, and work to *foster* a scene.

2. Do what you love.

Do what you do and love it, but know that not everyone will get it. Once I was in line at the 99-Cent Store buying a dozen blank VHS tapes. A kid smiled and said, "You gonna tape the Olympics?"

I said "No, I'm sending out copies of a film I made to festivals." He grunted and looked disappointed. Seems that a lot of people would rather *consume* media than *be* the media.

Don't freak out. Just live to make art. You may not make a million dollars, but you will move people. That's what it's all about. And you *will* get laid. By very interesting, very cool, very creative people that you can know for a long time. I do.

I said in my novel, "It's all about art. All artists just wanna reach beyond the mundane and scratch into something real. Whether you're painting the ceiling of the chapel or banging out three shaky chords in the garage, you are declaring your intentions to smear your fingerprints on the veil of the infinite…. And things just might work out all right."

And remember:

> All art is just an attempt to augment or imitate God.
>
> Follow the spark and the rest will follow.
>
> We're not suffering. We're celebrating.

Figure 17.6 *An Albatross bass.*

3. Try not to lie.

At least to humans. Music making attracts a lot of liars because it attracts people who *need* to be seen and heard, even if they have nothing to say. And they will do anything to get seen and heard. Any time anyone tells you anything, run it through your own internal B.S. filter and ask yourself if this person has any reason to lie to you. Don't be paranoid and mistrusting; just listen with your heart. You'll get good at spotting the creeps.

I mentioned it in my film book, but I'll reiterate it here because it's just as important in music if not more so: Don't pretend you know people you don't.

The last time I played in Seattle, Dave Grohl was up front singing along with all my words and we had a drink after. But that doesn't mean we're buddies. I don't know him. I'd met him only a couple of times before (before he was in Nirvana, when he played in Scream, an amazing band that never got their due), but I'd be lying to say, "He's my friend." He seems like a nice guy, but I don't know him.

When people say, "I'm friends with _____" and try to impress you with it, ask them, "Did she invite you to her wedding?" "Did he help you when you moved?" I think those are accurate tests of friendship. Don't lie. It's tacky, and you don't need to. And if you do, people will catch you.

4. Don't be piggy.

I was out walking the other day on Sunset Blvd. This guy was hanging up really cool looking big sticker flyers for his band. I stopped to compliment him and asked him if he made them. He was really cocky and said, "Naw, my record company did."

Then I started to walk away and saw the other side of the pole. I noticed that he had gone out of his way to cover up someone else's flyer, (a flyer that I had seen on my way up that street, for an independent film that looked really cool), when he *totally* had room on the pole not to cover anyone else up.

TIP

Be humble. Death abhors a braggart. Death takes the loud talkers.

One thing that's wrong with the world is that a lot of people are willing to do *anything* to get famous. I like being on TV but am not willing to lie, steal, cheat, cover up flyers, or go to bed with someone I wouldn't go to lunch with in order to do it.

That's everything that's wrong with the a lot of artists. Everywhere, but *especially* in Hollywood. It's not like there isn't enough fame to go around. It's not like if you crush the other guy it's gonna give you an advantage. Just be great. If you're great, you're gonna rise. That's a law of physics.

Cream does not destroy milk to get to the top, it just slides by it.

A lot of up-and-coming artists demand that people in positions of distribution power pay attention:

"Here's my tape. Listen to it now!"

"Why should I?"

"If you heard it, you'd love it."

It's better to try to get to know people and get to know them for the sake of knowing them without expecting anything in return; then they'll just naturally want to help you. It seems like a catch-22, and you might wonder, "Well, isn't it a hustle if I go out of my way to know those people?" It's not. Figure a way to do it and keep integrity. Just be a people person. Cultivate individual relationships. Music is all based on relationships. Not in a scam way, but in a *real* way. People want to help people they know.

There's something to be said for taking the "I think I can" tenacity and stick-to-itiveness of punk rock and applying it to your art, but don't bug people or screw people over. Again: **Have hustle, but don't be a hustler.**

There's a thin line between getting your work out there and trying to control things you cannot control. I don't always get it right, but I'm learning.

As I get older, I realize that I am powerless over reality. I can do my best to do the footwork to get stuff done, but then I have to walk away. The best solution is to work hard for your art on a daily basis and don't get caught up in the results.

Be so busy with the next thing that you don't care about the results of the last thing.

If you do what you do well, the Universe will eventually part her legs on your behalf.

5. Don't limit your self-definition.

I am less about self-definition and more about spirit. I didn't set out to make films to be able to call myself "a filmmaker." I just had a story to tell, and film seemed like a good way. So I endeavored to learn film. I'm a better guitar player than those

Figure 17.8 *Guitar.*

in a lot of bands I see, and I sometimes play gigs, but I don't consider myself a guitar player.

I just do art and want to be able to do it well in every medium. And I don't want to be stuck with any one art form. That way I'm not limited. When a spirit moves me, I don't have to say, "I'll write a song," but conversely, "Hmmmm...should I write a song, or make a Web page, or make a film, or write a screenplay, or a novel, or a poem, design some software, make a Flash animation, or paint a picture?"

Basically, my attitude is San Francisco-meets-Hollywood. And it's working out fine for me. I have the San Fran love of art and beauty. I spent 16 years there. Then I moved to Los Angeles and applied in the real world the stuff I'd learned up north.

Live this.

It doesn't matter where you are. You can make art anywhere. I really don't define myself as a resident of Los Angeles. I don't get out much, so it doesn't really matter what city I'm in. I live here because it's cheap and it's warm. A city is just a place to park my bed and my computer and get my mail. My life exists more between my ears and out in the entire world than in the few miles around my physical body. My view of Los Angeles is not Hollywood glitz. It's me staring at a computer screen in my apartment or standing in line at the Echo Park Post office on Glendale Ave. That's all I do everyday it seems like.

I remember being in a band on tour. My impression of a town was the bar we played in and the person's house we crashed at after the show. And a lot of my image of a place was based on whether or not we had a good turnout at the gig and whether or not I got with a girl. For a long time I thought Toledo was a great town and New York City sucked.

Figure 17.9 *Josh from Insecto. He took my place when I left the band. He rocks.*

You have to give up to get. I had to learn to give up wanting to be a rock star. Actually, it would be more accurate to say I am learning to not need to be a rock star. In doing so, I've come closer to being a rock star than ever. It's like the *Tao of Steve* or *Fight Club*. You have to give up wanting something before you can get it. It's total Zen Guitar.

I also had to give up wanting to be a rock star socialite so I could have more time and focus—to realign my spirit so I would have more to say. As a result, the Universe gave me opportunities to say it and be heard.

D.I.Y. requires constant vigilance. There are no vacations. I had the social life of a monk during my first 18 months in Los Angeles, by choice. *D.I.Y. or DIE* and *$30 Film School* and *$30 Music School* were things that I felt people had to see. That made it easy to give my all, and I didn't feel like I was giving anything up. I didn't feel like a martyr staying home on a Saturday night when my friends were out partying and had invited me. In a different mindset, years earlier, I did feel like a martyr in my band because I was doing more work than anyone else, and I had a cranky "nobody loves me" attitude.

True D.I.Y. ethic is about loving what you do, not about getting pity for doing it. When I'm broke, but out spreading art, my rich patent attorney friend and my rich government economist friend who both own big houses in the suburbs envy me. They tell me this.

There's nothing wrong with being a nurd at home alone working on art on a Saturday night.[8]

People who change the world aren't out partying on a Saturday night. They're home changing it.

6. Hone your drive.

Artists have to keep moving their hands. That's what makes them artists. Look at the hands of the subjects in *D.I.Y*—always moving.

I'm fidgety. Can't stop twitching. Sometimes people think I'm on drugs, but I'm not. I just always flow. I'm like a shark: I have to keep moving or I'll die.

---

8. *Nurds rule the world these days. I'd bet my bottom forbidden donut that when the cool kids were out getting laid, Trent Reznor was at home in front of the mirror, wearing a Devo flower pot hat, a Pink Floyd's* The Wall *T-shirt, and playing air keytar along with "Foreplay/Longtime" by Boston.*

Bassist Mike Watt is a big inspiration for me. That motherfluffer beat cancer that would have killed three other men. He was touring six months after his surgery. The guy never rests. Same with his frequent collaborator, Peter DiStefano. Beat cancer, too. I love that guy. And Peter also works all the time making great stuff.

Spared. We're Spared.

Little Mike treats me like a quitter when I sleep. "Sleep is for quitters. You're quitting the day! You can sleep when you're dead." But I love sleep and need it. It's part of my artistic process...to process the day and prepare for the next one...and to get ideas. What is all art except an attempt to make sense of dreams? Except documentaries, which are an attempt to explain waking life.

Art for me is an attempt to capture the way my thoughts worked when I was a child. My art is just me painting the sunny windy cloudy days that remind me of a cross-section of a sliver of the Polaroid sky of my childhood. And doing it in any and all media.

I *have* to make stuff. And I have to show it to people.

My studio apartment is a cramped art factory. A one-man voluntary sweatshop. It's a system, an equation. It exists only for eating, sleeping, loving, and making art. D.H. Peligro jokingly/lovingly called me a "Legend in my own room." But I spend a lot of time in there making the legend seep out into the world.

Genesis P-Orridge says, "Change your own bedroom and you can change the world."

My goal is to make art, and then get the product *out* of my apartment. That's why I'll sometimes sell CDs/VHS tapes/books/records/DVDs of my work cheaper than retail or even give them away. I still make a profit in the long run, but I feel my art is of no use to the world stacked up in my apartment. It has to get *out!*

I keep my office in my house because my life and my work are the same thing. I don't have an office or workspace separate from my home. This is partially out of economic necessity, but I actually believe that if I had the luxury of a bigger space, I'd still do it all in the same room. Or at least the same building. I can't go somewhere else to get this done. I work in spurts. I'll sit on my back porch staring at the sky with my feet up, come in and type one word or one sentence, and go back out to stare at the sky and pet my cat.

Figure 17.10 *Me at work.*

I have reverse insomnia. I fall asleep easily but get up too early. Sometimes I awake at 4 a.m. after a disturbing and/or wonderful dream and work until I fall back to sleep. It's in my DNA. My dad is like this, also. Sometimes he gets up too early and can't fall back to sleep and he just goes to his desk and works and starts his day. He's a businessman and I'm an artist, but it's the same.

And, like him, I nap. Every afternoon, starting when I turned 30. I eat lunch, take a burrito nap, then get up, drink coffee, and start over. It's like living two days in one. And then I'm good to go until I fall asleep watching old movies at 4 a.m.

This sleep schedule is just my rhythm. Don't try to imitate it; find your own rhythm and live it. Nurture it. Find a way to not meld to someone else's rhythm. That's the beauty of not having a 9-to-5 job. It allows me to work on art 24/7.

I've always put art first…spent every cent on art. I've often gone without buying nice things, going to movies, and such.

Sometimes I really get a kick outa being me. I think that this is what makes me successful. I think I'm totally successful…flying around the world and then coming home and having to wash my socks out in the sink because I can't afford to do laundry. Dig my life!

I am what the band MDC called a Soup Kitchen Celebrity. And I'm fine with it.

A lot of people never have lived like this. And it isn't something to pity; it's something to envy. I could get a job and have a nice car and a mortgage. But I don't want to.

I always paid my rent and phone bill somehow, though. Having a place to do my art is more important to me than eating.

I was never really *starving*, but I was often worried. I often had like $3, pending bills, and only a little food. And I'd spent $100 that day on computer upgrades or postage.

Sure, you will still have doubts, but it's always there, as close as your heartbeat.

7. Don't rest on the past.

I love this thing Ian MacKaye said. Someone asked him in an interview about the D.C. punk book *Dance of Days*. He said, "I have not read it. I don't read books about myself. ...(these are) history books, and history is about what has been done. I am not done. I am doing. I'm not there yet. I've got too much work to do."

Ian is mentioned on about ever other page of *Dance of Days*. I don't think I could not at least glance at a book like that about me, but I love his sentiment.

Music is a very ephemeral experience and is sensitive to trends, and fans are very fickle. I talked to this guy, Aaron Nemoyten, the other day on the phone. He's 18 years old and playing in bands in Northern California, playing clubs I used to sell out with my band 10 years ago. He's never heard of my band and goes to shows in the same clubs with happenin' new bands that are packing the place.

TIP

I have a friend in Hollywood who is a pretty good songwriter, but really hung up on trying to be a *star*. He desperately wants a record deal. Only he's about 36 and probably too old to get signed.

When you stand at his kitchen sink, the view out the window is entirely blocked by the Capitol Records building. He lives about three blocks away. How demoralizing must *that* be?

This is a good place to remind you for a third time: *"Be fair to everyone. You meet the same people on the way up that you meet on the way down."* I found this to be *so* true. When I was in a happening band, I was cocky with the bookers at these clubs. When they'd call and offer me a paid show headlining on a Saturday night, I'd treat them crappy. They'd sometimes give me the gig because we were hot at the time, but they'd remember my pissy 'tude. Then, after that band broke up and I started a new band, the new band didn't have a following. I thought the band's fans would follow me to the next group because I was ego driven and thought I was the *star*. But people actually liked the *band*, not just me. So I'd call the club trying to get my new band a gig opening for a free show on a Tuesday night. They'd be like, "Don't call us; we'll call you."

Another (happier) parable on the fickleness of fans, on a larger level, is the story of T-Ride. T-Ride (Telluride) was a band from San Francisco in the late 80s and early 90s. They were kinda pretty-boy glammy looking but exceptional musicians. They got signed to Zoo Entertainment or Hollywood Records or one of those huge synthetic major labels[9] that bled money and never had a hit. I forget which one. Anyway, T-Ride was the first unknown band to ever be given a million dollars to sign with *any* label.

Instead of blowing it on limos and strippers, they built a recording studio. They *still* have that studio today. I've recorded there (with Slish), and it kicks ass. They were very smart. That was the first moral of this story.

So, they spent *four years* in their studio crafting their debut record. Four freaking years! That's about eight times as long as most bands spend. Or more.

They recorded about 20 layers of guitar harmonies. They recorded about 20 tracks of vocal harmonies. They ended up sounding very much like Queen: incredibly polished and technical. The whole time, the label kept saying, "Give us the record. Give us the record. Give us the record. Give us the record." But the band stuck to their guns and waited until they felt it was perfect.

Finally, they turned the masters in to the label. The record hit the stores. And one week later, Nirvana's *Nevermind* album hit the world and completely erased any market for polished symphonic rock music.

T-Ride went on tour opening for White Zombie and got booed and pelted with bottles. Don't ask me how they got on that tour. Most likely the way this always happens. Some business partnership…same manager or something.

---

9. Synthetic in the sense that the label didn't grow and evolve. It just sprang up overnight as an already huge entity that splintered off from some huge film company.

T-Ride is long since broken up, but Eric Dodd and the guys still have the studio and are still happily making their own music and anonymously making a good living recording for other people. I think, in some ways, they are more successful than Kurt Cobain, who is famous and dead.

Parable three:

One decision I regret, which I add as a cautionary example, is this: My band used to practice down the hall from another band, The Himalayans. They had no following yet, while my band did. Their very earnest singer approached me one day and said "We're starting this loosely organized thing where different bands will agree to come see each other's shows. If 10 bands all do this, we'll all have a following, and it can only grow from there."

I told him "Forget it. My band already has a following," and stormed off. I would never do this now to anyone, but I was a lot stupider and a little bit mean back then.

The following year that guy started a new band called Counting Crows. Two years later, my band was broken up and I was scrambling for gigs with a solo project. He was going triple-platinum and giving a leg-up to all those unknown bands that had helped him with his project.

Parable Four:

I remember when my friend David Immergluck was in Counting Crows. They offered him a choice when he recorded their first record: Either some ghetto-rich amount now and no points later or no money up front and points on sales later. He took the money now.

Six months later the money was gone and he was working the counter at Tower Records in San Francisco, selling 100 copies of that record a day and seeing nary a cent.

Parable Five:

Another friend was once toiling in the hot sun laying tar on a roof. His co-worker was a former top ten singer from the 60s. One of the singer's songs came on the radio while they were working. The singer said "Well, there's another nickel for my ex-wife and the taxman.

Conclusion

To recap:

> Pass it on.
>
> Do what you love.
>
> Try not to lie.
>
> Don't be piggy.
>
> Don't limit your self-definition.
>
> Hone your drive.
>
> Don't rest on the past.

There's nothing like standing in front of a Marshall stack with a Les Paul, slamming with a tight rhythm section. It feels immense. But a lot of people hit something new (like music) really hard at first and then lose interest with time. Music just takes perseverance. If you're committed to an hour a day for many years, you can probably do everything you want in music. I have.

Don't worry about all the other cool bands in the world. Music ain't competition; it's communication. Just make great music. There can never be too much good art. That's like there being too much love or sex or happiness. The Universe loves you every time you write, sing, record, sell, or give away a great song.

And most likely it won't come as one big "break"; it will come as a continuum of small things that add up to a lifetime of successfully sharing art and maybe making a little money.

If your art has wings, it will fly.

—some guy

Chapter 18

Interviews

I have found that I can basically get *anyone* on the phone. It ain't that hard for me for some reason. I could have interviewed a lot more people who sold a lot more records, but chose not to. I was more concerned with integrity and attitude than record sales.[1]

I'm also personally a fan of all these people's music.

I'm mainly into interviewing people who have had between 10 and 20 years of what I consider success, on their *own* terms, and am avoiding top-ten kiddies no one will remember in a year.

These people are in it for the long run, in music and in life.

> Henry Rollins
>
> London May
>
> Janis Tanaka
>
> Dave Brockie
>
> Joan Jett
>
> Peter DiStefano
>
> Jonathan Richman

The opinions in this chapter belong to the interviewees and do not reflect the opinions of Michael W. Dean, his publisher, editor, agent, or cat.

Henry Rollins

Web site: www.two1361.com

May 13, 2003, at Rollins' office.

Henry Rollins is a workaholic. I've admired him since SOA, the band Henry sang for in D.C. in 1980 and 1981, before he moved to California and joined Black Flag. The man simply does not stop: making records and books, acting in films, doing spoken word shows and

---

1. *It's funny—Someone actually criticized me for having about seven percent of my last book interviews and quotes, like it was cheating. In reality, I consider it* collaboration *and expanding on my limited world view, and it's not cheating. It actually takes me more time (and care) to proof and format the work of others than to just barf up more of my stuff. Writing's easy for me (my editor cut 90 pages out of* $30 Film School *to trim it down to a svelte 520 pages!). Editing takes work. I just think using outside opinions and interviews make the whole thing stronger.*

records. Few know this, but he actually won a Grammy for his *Get in the Van* spoken word album.

He is one of the few people I see who operates in the Hollywood system but keeps his integrity as well as his sanity. It was a pleasure to interview him.

In my opinion, this interview contains almost everything an aspiring musician needs to hear. It's an hour of mad science.

Figure 18.1 *Henry Rollins.* Photo by Michael Dean.

I got Henry Rollins' e-mail from Ian MacKaye. Sent Rollins an e-mail asking to interview him for this book. The e-mail had the subject line "Got your e-mail address from Ian MacKaye." I only dropped Ian's name because I figured Henry probably gets an ungodly amount of e-mail and I know that he and Ian have been friends since they were teens.

Within 90 seconds Henry wrote back, saying "M, sure I guess, since Ian sent you. I am in LA; you can come by the office if you like. Today is okay, sooner the better as I am jetlagging, and things are starting to get very busy here. Henry"

He sent his phone number. When he said, "office" I'd expected a receptionist, but he answered the phone himself.

Damn cool….so easy, no nonsense…25 minutes later I was sitting in his office. There was no receptionist. He answered the door and was alone. We got right to it.

His office is a modest duplex in a residential neighborhood in Hollywood. The other side has his record and book company; he lives nearby in a second house. Pretty nice by punk rock standards, but would be shabby by most Hollywood media business standards.

In my mind, this guy has it going on. He's totally in charge of his own game, a workaholic, and doesn't give a damn about the image. It's all about the work for him.

I barely spoke. He's an amazing interview—one of those guys you ask one question and they drop mad science for 20 minutes. Then you ask another question and they talk for 10 more.

Henry Rollins: So, what do you want to know?

Michael Dean: Why do you do what you do? Why did you take the road you did instead of working for someone else?

HR: Well, I had normal jobs from when I was a little kid throwing newspapers until I left Washington, D.C. to move out here to be in Black Flag in the summer of 1981. Right before I came out here was the last time I had a straight job with a time clock working for someone else.

Then I came out here and worked for SST, Greg Ginn's label, as part of being in Black Flag. We were living on the floor of the place, and I ended up working there. You learn a lot about the independent record thing by living knee-deep in a label. I learned a lot in those five years in Black Flag, and from there I formed my own companies, combining what I learned there with what I learned at retail jobs as a kid. You know, working the cash register and whatnot.

Having a normal job again—I've never considered it. Does that answer your question?

MD: Sort of. I meant in relation to being in a band. Why do you do most of it yourself?

HR: The nature of what I do: books, records, the more cooks you have in the kitchen, when you throw them into the mix, often their ideas aren't your ideas and their idea gets on the cover of your record. Somehow all of the sudden there's a tambourine in the mix of your record and you're like, "What's that about?" and they're like "Well, you should have showed up to the mix of your recording session." So I learned early on that the way to keep your artistic integrity intact is to learn the mechanics of how this is done and get ownership of it and be in control of it as much as possible as much of the time as you can.

At this point I record all my own records and own all the music publishing rights, and I own my own companies. Next door is my book and record company and this is my office. We are a little factory, like any small independent label. We're pretty much similar to any label like Dischord or Touch and Go. Probably a fraction of the releases and a fraction of the sales, but the same kind of spirit in that we do what we like to do. Hopefully, some people like it, and if not, oh well. We're still gonna keep putting out what we think is cool rather than what we think will sell. Us liking it is the basic criterion for doing it.

MD: How many employees do you have?

HR: Two full time, and sometimes when we have a lot of mail order we have someone who comes in and helps, but we run it pretty efficiently with two people.

MD: When you record, do you ever employ outside producers, you know, take anyone else's suggestions on it?

HR: The last several Rollins Band records I've produced, except our live one, the guy who's engineered our records for years, Clif Norrell, he produced it. I mixed it with him, but he got all the sounds. But most of our stuff I produced, not because I'm the only person in the world who could do it, but because I had a very clear idea of what I wanted to hear on those records, and I didn't want to do a lot of explaining. I'd rather just have an engineer that I know very well that I can tell what I want and he can get it, rather than bring in a producer whose job it is to take the music down *his* street. And the last few records I've wanted a really clear sound, just a live band in a room hitting it. Very unproduced in a way. Just kind of documented.

MD: Did you sell part of your music publishing at one point?

HR: I was on a label called Imago for two records from 1991 to 1994. And they said in the contract that the only way to sign with this label was to also do a publishing deal with them. We found out later that other bands didn't have to do this. But it was a sticking point with the signing. They take part of the publishing and for that you get an advance.

Now I do the publishing in my band, and I give the guys in the band an advance, and I administer the music.

MD: Did you come to regret that decision you made to sell your publishing back then?

HR: Yeah, sure, in that…

MD: Do they have a share in what you do now?

HR: No, no no no, NO! Just those two records. And after that I've never done a publishing deal again. To do your publishing with somebody is not a bad thing, because hopefully they're looking to get you into movie soundtracks and such—they're looking to *administer*— that's the active verb, they *admin* your music. Dentyne comes calling and wants to…. That's how you see some travel cruise commercial with an Iggy Pop song in it. He has a music publisher who goes and gets it, and he probably gets an amazing chunk of change for that.

We've been in a lot of movie soundtracks, but it's always been the director coming to me or my manager, so the music publisher never did anything that we weren't doing. I don't need the money, why would I give away the rights to anything? When we're getting the opportunities, and the publisher was doing nothing except making money. So we decided not to do that anymore.

MD: I know that Ian (MacKaye) turns down a lot of things like that; you seem like one of the few people who has integrity still but lives in both worlds: writing for *Details Magazine* and being in big Hollywood movies, but still running your own label. How do you jibe that? Do you see it as a contradiction?

HR: No. That brings up that whole thing of "selling out." To me, selling out is when you make your record and the label says "We would prefer if you did this other song instead, and you cave in. That's selling out.

There is this imaginary rule book written by someone at *Maximum Rock 'N' Roll Magazine* that says "If you're in a band you can't do this and this…." (*MD bursts out laughing.*) "If you come from this kind of music you can't do this… I've never seen it in print, and I've never been handcuffed for these charges. I do what the fuck I want to do.

The problem is when you physically try to impede my progress—then it moves up to a whole 'nother level that you probably can't handle me on. If it's just words, mean little things, I'm not Stalin, say what you want. Get in my way, it's a whole 'nother thing.

I come from a very Nietzschean Darwinian proclivity: The straightest, most direct line between two points is a broken nose. I live by that. I've lived by that. I'm not a violent person. It's all fun and games until someone tries to physically bar you from going somewhere. And then it's some Cro-Magnon watering hole bullshit.

So I do what I want. I live in Hollywood. I go for some Hollywood auditions. I get in a few movies. If someone doesn't like that…like I give a fuck.

It's how I've funded a lot of things that I knew wouldn't make money. I used someone else's money. Like a lot of really expensive books we've put out. Like photo books that I wanted to do because I believed in the art. I could have never afforded these playing music in the little clubs I play in. Some of these books I've put out and most of the records I put out. I will dip into that mainstream world. It's the same idea as a poet working at McDonald's. You get some bread so you can put out your chapbook. For me, that's Hollywood, where I can go into a movie and do something that's fun and interesting and get a paycheck from it and do something interesting with it. I quite enjoy dabbling in the mainstream. I don't think there's an integrity thing there. I think if I were in some bag running around with 17-year-old girls, I think that's losing the plot. But I'm quite grounded and I know what I'm doing. On the outside it's contradiction, but for me it's subversion.

I've done a lot of movies, a lot of voiceovers, but I don't have anybody's phone number. I don't keep in touch with them, I don't really think of it after I'm done.

MD: What advice do you have for people in bands with regards to finding, keeping, and firing musicians?

HR: I've only been in one situation, well, two, where there is someone in the band we didn't want in the band anymore. One because he had an alcohol problem. And no one in the band had the backbone to call the guy and tell him that it was over. So I called the guy and dispatched him. He was cool about it and said, "Fine."

The other time the guy was such a day-to-day nightmare that when we got home from the tour he said, "I quit," at the same time we said, "You're fired." And it wasn't like we said, "You're not employed by us anymore." It was like breaking up with a girlfriend; you can't be around that person anymore—Velcro rip yourself away from them, can't be around that person anymore.

Those were the only times I've ever been in that position, and I don't know what to recommend other than be honest, be direct, and never lose your will to confront.

MD: How do you deal with mean-spirited, non-constructive criticism? Does it get you down?

HR: Yeah, sure, as much as it would bother any human. Say someone is mean to your record. It happens. It comes with the territory.

But, everybody, from the band you hate the most to the band you love the most, they have one thing in common. They worked really hard on that record. Every band, whatever you're into, they all worked hard on it. So you give it everything you have and someone rips your baby a new one. It's hard to not take it personally because you sweated blood and lost sleep to make that record. You birthed it and it was hard. So when someone gratuitously swipes it, you're like, "Fuck! We bled through the *eyes* for this." So it hurts, but it's, so what? You stop breathing? No. You just keep jamming.

It happens. I've been panned.

MD: The art, or you?

HR: Both. A lot of times they leave the music alone and just go after me. Maybe I'm a bad person. Or maybe a lot of people who write for publications are people who make a living by getting Jiffy Packs of CDs that they hastily write reviews of and then take them down to record stores and sell them so they can supplement their Top Ramen diet with Budweiser.

To me, to be a music writer, you should have a record collection that looks like mine.

(Rollins gets up and leads me through two rooms with shelves on every wall, floor to ceiling—probably 10,000 CDs and cassettes total.)

MD: Where's the vinyl?

HR: Next door. So when these people are kind of, "Neyhhhhhhhhhhhhh…," I can see a lot of their record collection in what they write. At the end of the day, you make these records because you want to make them. If you put them out in the world, unleash them from the garage into the world, not everyone in the world is going to think that the pictures of your baby are pretty. They're gonna go, "What an ugly kid you have." It hurts.

And I know I'm not that bad a person. I've never raped anybody. I've never killed anybody. I wouldn't steal from you, nor would I hurt your child. More often than not, I'd go out of my way to help you. So when I get slammed every once in a while, I look at why I'm doing all this stuff. I do it because I like what I do. I give it everything I have, and I work hard at it. So if someone doesn't like what I do, tough on me, gotta keep jamming.

But to say that that kind of thing doesn't hurt would be lying.

MD: Do you get enough sleep most nights?

HR: Um, I get an adequate amount. My body kind of keeled over last night. I just got back from 89 shows. I've been on the road since January 7th. I got back from Australia Friday afternoon, slept three hours, came here and started working. Saturday and Sunday, same thing. Yesterday, I was up at 3:00 a.m., came in, went back to the house and made a protein shake, drank it, figured I'd sit and let the shake assimilate, laid down on the couch, woke up three hours later, and it was dark. Managed to stagger to bed and slept another seven hours. So I guess I needed sleep. But I usually get between four and six hours.

MD: Is that enough?

HR: Some days it feels like enough. Some days it doesn't. What usually determines sleep for me is the workout I've done that evening. Legs or back is going to put me down on the mat for a couple of extra hours. Like I did legs at 5:30 this morning, so I'll be feeling it later so I'll sleep harder. On the road with the band, I sleep longer because it's such a physical outlay. I'll walk off stage and get right to my bunk pretty quickly afterwards.

MD: I've been to your shows and a lot of people want to know you afterwards. They want to talk to you and hang out and give you stuff. How do you deal with that?

HR: Well, I get a lot of mail. I answer all the letters. That's what I've been doing the last three nights, these things (Rollins points to mail bins) were full of mail. I answer every e-mail I can. At shows I sign everything that's put in front of me, do every photo, and answer every question I can, and just do the best I can.

People talk to me every day. Here I am. I go to the store. I don't hide. I fix the roof when it leaks, I go to the hardware store, I stand in line. More often than not, I talk to someone within five minutes of being on any street anywhere. Someone starts talking to me. I just treat them like I'd like to be treated.

Sometimes it can be a little invasive. We've had stalkers here. We've had people camping out here (gestures out to the bushes) for weeks at a time. It gets pretty intense. But I've been doing this for a long time. I've been doing shows for 23 years. Without an audience I don't have a job. So these people mean everything to me. So if they want to ask me something, I can make some time for that because I can respect the fact that they've been checking me out. I'm blown away that they keep coming after so long. I gotta think I'm at least three of the seven days past the thing stamped on the side of the milk. I can't believe that people keep showing up.

MD: Yeah, when you were in SOA what did you think you were going to be doing in five years?

HR: I've never gotten very far away from that whole mentality. I work very hard every day. I live way below my means. That's one of the reasons that the Hollywood thing…it's like getting a free pencil to me. Warner Brothers, Sony, they're all right here. If they're handing out auditions, shit yeah, I'm going.

MD: Where do you live?

HR: I live in Hollywood, up the hill. I used to live here (in the office) but I bought another place a few years ago. I still have that I-work-for-a-living mindset. Music and entertainment for me have always been a journeyman's voyage. We come to town, we play, we'll see you in eight months if you show up again. It's not like some big tour to promote a single; we're not waiting for radio to do something for us. It's like Lemmy said to me once, "We're a journeyman band. We're Motörhead. We come to your town, we kick your ass, and we leave." That's kind of what I do. That's why in the 80s I started looking at learning a few other things to do. Because I started looking at a lot of other musicians who actually had talent—I never considered myself really talented, I just think I have a lot of tenacity and I think that counts for something—but I saw a lot of people with real talent not being able to pay their rent. So I said, "Okay. It's a survival situation. I'd better learn to do more than this music stuff. That's when I started going to auditions for voiceover work and acting and really working on the talking shows in an effort to stay lively.

One of my heroes is a fellow named Man Ray, who I'm sure you're familiar with. He sculpted, painted, drew, arted out. If you saw interviews with him, you'd think he was a cab driver. You wouldn't believe this was the great Man Ray. He was just this guy—like when you listen to Henry Miller, he sounded like he was this guy who came in to fix your toilet. (Effects Brooklyn accent.) "I'm a writtah…" You look at a guy like that, he lived, and he painted, and he wrote; that's kind of like what I go after.

MD: Do you have any advice for musicians who wanna do what they want to do?

HR: To do what you want to do, you have to be very tough. Especially in this day and age. Not tough like being insensitive; you have to be tough like Miles Davis who protected his art. He was very protective of that thing that he had; he was like a swan—it's this very graceful creature but if you mess with it, it gets very pugnacious. So on some level you have to have a bit of that. If you're going to take this kind of sensitivity into the brutality of the entertainment business, you'll take some knocks. Because if you're any good, down the road a piece, you're going to be fairly into rising to the occasion.

I think these days a lot of bands who do their first tour on a Privo bus with shiny new gear are missing out on a lot of things that will keep them in the game after the blush is off the rose. Because you never maintain your popularity—everyone has an arc. Or ebbs and flows. Guys like Neil Young, they just keep making records and it's never like an up or down thing, it's like a high-tide, low-tide thing. He's just going to keep making records whether you buy them or not. Neil Young makes records. That's what he does. He doesn't care. He's busy making records and doing tours. It's not an up and down thing for him: It's an ebb and flow thing. But you just have to stay tough through the vicissitude. All the greats, no matter what, they just keep working. Those bands that were hydro-grown through the Clear Channel thing, they have no roots to the ground, so when push comes to shove, they have no anchor.

Take a guy like Fred Durst, who I've got no problem with, I'm not trying to make fun. Here's a guy who's not untalented, but he just came out and BAM! He was huge. No one stays that huge for that long. You have your moment, and your demographic grows up and starts breeding and moves to the suburbs, and you're left to either cross over to a new audience or not. There will be a time when he plays to half of the people he played to at his peak. Then a third. It will be interesting to see how guys like Marilyn Manson...will he be in love with music enough...there again, another guy I'm not putting down. I think he's amazing, but when you're born and bred on MTV, will you have enough love of music to be back in little clubs where they may have not even started or were there for a tiny bit of time? And to me, that's the measure of the musician—if you're still into it enough to ride that wave down, enough to do it even when you're not fab anymore. That I think is a real measure. Lemmy—he fascinates me. I'm no expert on Motörhead, but this guy, who lives right up this street, he saw the Beatles play at the Cavern Club. Who roadied for Hendrix. He once said something to me that was mind blowing. He said, "I remember before there was rock and roll." I said "What do you mean?" He said, "I remember before there was rock and roll. There were just Rosemary Clooney records. And then there was Elvis. And WHAM! Our lives changed."

Lemmy was there for that. And then all these decades. And there was a time when Motörhead was on everyone's shirt. Now? No. But he still goes out and does it. That's the real thing. Guys like Iggy, that's what they do.

These days, the current culture that's directed at young people...the audience is acting the way the record companies want them to...in that, it's very easy to find a pretty girl to sing, or a pretty boy to sing, with cheekbones that can jump up and down. Boys and girls look like that for about three summers. Pert, lean, handsome, or whatever—the things that make their age group flock towards them. So instead of finding them talented, the record companies have discovered that it's easier to find pretty people than talented people. So they've created this popular culture that's a Menudo effect. This Avril Levine—who I have no problems with—but here's this teenage girl with her big record—will they still love her tomorrow? We'll see. Or is she just this thing that was just hydro-grown by the industry to look good for a couple of summers and then be trotted away and dropped so they can install the next one that has a one-and-a-half or two album career arc. (Claps his hands together.) Gone! And these days you have an audience that downloads music because they get so much overpriced mediocre stuff thrown at them. "Twenty-two dollars for this? Fuck you!" Then they go to the computer and download it.

MD: Does it bother you when people download your music?

HR: No. Not at all. It means at least someone's hearing it.

People come up to me and go, "Dude, I downloaded your new talking record…and, oops! Oh shit!" (*Rollins laughs.*) And I'm like, "It's okay. It's fine."

MD: Avril Levine complains in interviews about Britney Spears, saying "She's not the real deal; I am." But Avril's songs are co-written by the same people who write Britney's songs. It's like that whole Coke vs. Pepsi, Nike vs. Adidas bullshit.

HR: The major label industry and major entertainment industry are turning everything into Coke and Pepsi. Thankfully, there's people like Dischord Records, Touch and Go, and Ipecac—Mike Patton's label. People like Cory Rusk of Touch and Go, and Ian MacKaye, the real deal, the real guys who are putting out amazing records on their labels. The best stuff Dischord has ever done is out this year. The new El Guapo record is amazing; the Q and not U record is amazing. The Black Eyes record is amazing. Have you heard this stuff?

MD: No. I did get the remixed "Flex Your Head" and listened to that stuff for the first time in eight or nine years.

HR: They're putting out some stuff that's like…you've never heard music like this. It's new music. They're doing great stuff. They're selling great music for really cheap.

That's a thing we do here. We sell a double CD of a talking record for 10 bucks with one dollar of it going to a different charity. Our company—we work five days a week here and we contribute money five days a week. The Southern Poverty Law Center, who battles the Klan through litigation; the Hollygrove Children's Shelter down the street from here for kids; we work with Partnership for a Drug-Free America, The West Memphis Three, and continually put in a dollar from each thing we sell.

There's a lot of labels that put out a lot of cool stuff for the right price to turn people on to good things and not bilk them and not take their money. So all is not lost. There are good bands playing in every city every night. There are cool labels in every state in America. And a lot of honest, switched-on people who do well, mean well, and are dedicated to keeping that good thing happening. So for all the Avrils and Britney Spears in the world, there is another choice. The danger is, in my opinion, young people who only see their access to music, and I specify music, being MTV or some Clear Channel mafia.

MD: They're buying it all up.

HR: They own it all. You'll wake up tomorrow morning with a Clear Channel chip in you that they installed while you were sleeping.

I was just in Europe, and Clear Channel is buying up venues there. Venues I've been playing in for 21 years are now Clear Channel venues. I'm like, "Come on! What are you doing?"

(*Laughs.*) Now the Clear Channel rep in Amsterdam is telling me how it is. I'm like, "Thanks. I've been playing this place since you were eight years old. And you're telling me how it is now? All right." (*Laughs more.*) "Meet the new boss, same as the old boss."

For me there is a danger with young people, and I'll specify young people, who will not get the chance to check out *Blonde on Blonde* by Dylan, or check out Leadbelly or Coltrane. Or a tenth of what's in that room (points at his record collection): King Crimson, Black Sabbath, all kinds of neat stuff, all kinds of great reggae, jazz, big band; there's so much good music in the world, you're never gonna hear one percent of it. From every country, there's musicians who will blow your mind.

The idea that this young person who's like 17 years old who should be this intellectual sponge, just uploading knowledge and culture and having this amazing emotional roller coaster would be into three bands because he liked their video…. That to me is losing the plot. When there's a lot more great stuff out there to read, not just Stephen King, not just a book with a movie still on the front. When there's great music to be heard, from before your mama was born. Music that people actually got razored in the face for playing because they were black. Wrong color in this country to be Ornette Coleman, to be a musical genius. So a lot of people bled through the eyes to make a lot of good music and a lot of great culture. A lot of great writers were killed by Stalin for stuff they wrote….

[At this point the tape ran out on my Dictaphone. Rollins did something very cool that I've never seen an interviewee do: As he heard the tape recorder snap off after 45 minutes, he picked it up without looking at it (he kept his eyes on me the entire interview), turned the tape over without pausing in his story, pressed Record (again without looking at it), and set it back down and talked for 20 more minutes.]

…for a while. That sucks. And I think at the end of the day, culture loses. Watering hole culture…the water starts receding. Record companies with less life span for an artist, in the present day, major labels, which is now kinda the last place you want to be in music, like the last place you want to effect political change is in political office. Here's a situation that seems to be a working engine for the anti-music anti-culture. It seems to be using less colors, less nuance, less flavoring in the food. It's more strip-mall culture. I think Americans buy into that. It's how we're raised. And the way the music industry now feeds into American consumerist culture. You propose something different and you'll be surprised how conservative young people can be. You get some really amazing attitudes coming back at you, real conservative plot loss. I'm like, "Gee, who have *you* been listening to?"

But thankfully there's a lot of cool independent people. Like a lot of the people who are on here…(gestures to a copy of *DIY or DIE: How To Survive as an Independent Artist.*) The attitude to put something else across. To run counter to what's going on.

Like J Mascis who has never made a bad record. He's a great songwriter who writes beautiful music. There's people like that all over the place. A guy like J, if he sent in the record that got him on Warner Brothers, "Green Mind," if he sent that in now, they would just go, "Who is this guy?"

MD: Some artists have done that as a test. Platinum artists, just for kicks, have sent in a demo under a different name to their labels and gotten rejected.

You read that "Problem with Music" article by Steve Albini?

HR: No.

To me, one of the problems with music *is* Steve Albini. I just think he makes all his records sound the same. An asexual insect with no balls. How he can emasculate rock music is incredible, with the same scalpel every time. And you can tell him I said that.

Pretty talented, smart guy, and he fights the good fight. I just think his production is bullshit. He's definitely on the good side of things. He hates the corporate crap. I just think his production's really corny.

MD: I'm out of questions. Thanks.

When we were finished, I turned the Dictaphone off and we talked for about 15 more minutes.

Part of it was him saying that "Any young people who are reading your book should know that you can make great records without spending a fortune." He mentioned Inner Ear Studios in Virginia.

I told him that I'd recorded four records there myself, and got on his computer and showed him where to download my cover of "Long Black Veil" with Ian singing backup on it. He said it was great.

He smiled and said, "I've never downloaded a song before in my life."

NOTE

Tiffany Couser and I proofread this article a few times and then I e-mailed Rollins back and asked if he wanted to take a pass through it to check to make sure we got it all right.

He wrote right back and said "Sure." An hour later I had the final result back.

It was Memorial Day. That's one thing I've noticed about most thriving self-employed D.I.Y. folk: they don't really take vacations.

London May

London May is pretty much my best friend in Los Angeles. I love working with him, and he's also a great guy.

He befriended me when I first moved here, and we talk a lot. I think there's a good chance I would have left to move back to San Francisco if I hadn't met him.

I also saw him play with Reptile House back in 1984. He was a monster on the drums then, and still is now. (Be sure to watch the movie on the CD that he stars in, *I Left My Band in San Francisco*. His segment is the "London May 99-Cent Drum Clinic." He drops mad science).

Figure 18.2 *London May.* Photo by Michael Dean.

A few of the bands/artists he's played/jammed with (at one time or another): Rueben and Dave from Dain Bramage (replacing a pre-Nirvana Dave Grohl), Asa and Dan Higgs (Lungfish), The Circle Jerks, Ron Emory and Jack Grisham (from TSOL), Glenn Danzig and Samhain (played both drums and bass), Son of Sam (featuring Davey Havok of AFI), Tiger Army, Reptile House, Dag Nasty, Dead, White and Blue, Lunch Box, Distorted Pony, Rat Patrol, Sheppard Pratt (drums and guitar), Amazing Chan Clan (guitar), Duane Peters and The Hunns (with Nashville Pussy's Corey Parks), Michael W. Dean ("D.I.Y. or Die" soundtrack), Jeremy Stacey (Echo and the Bunnymen), Treephort (guitar-Warped Tour '03), Mark Phillips (Down by Law, Joy Killer) and many more.

Producers he's worked with: Michael Bienhorn (Red Hot Chili Peppers, Soundgarden), Rick Rubin (Slayer, The Cult), Mark Van Hecke (Violent Femmes, Smithereens), Paul Stacey (Oasis, Madonna), Steve Albini (Nirvana, Page & Plant), Kid Congo Powers (The Bad Seeds, The Cramps), Ian Mackaye (Minor Threat, Fugazi).

Interview with London May

August 9, 2003, in the café of a Barnes and Noble, Manhattan Beach, California, before Michael Dean's book signing for *$30 Film School*.

London May: This is a hub of awkwardness.

Michael Dean: If we start talking, people will go away sooner or later. So, what bands have you been in?

LM: I'll narrow it down to the well-known ones or the ones that did records. Reptile House did a record on Dischord. I was in a band called Samhain that did quite a few records on quite a few labels. I drummed and toured with Dag Nasty that did some records on Dischord. I played with Ron Emory, from TSOL, in Lunchbox for a couple of years. Played in a band called Distorted Pony who put out a couple of records on a label called Trance out of Texas, King Coffee from the Butthole's label. Then what else? I had a band called Shepard Pratt that recorded a record for a label called Tim Kerr out of Portland. I did the Son of Sam project on Nitro Records. And then I did the second Tiger Army record, which is on Hellcat/Epitaph. And that about brings me up to speed. There's a bunch of singles and various things I guested on, but those are the main records.

MD: Did you play drums on all those?

LM: I played drums on all of them. Some of them, like the Shepard Pratt record, I played guitar also. On the Samhain reunion tour in '99, I also played bass.

MD: Do you make a living at music?

LM: No. Ever since I started playing I've always wanted to support myself at it, but the money was…it was just never consistent. You had to rely on too many flaky people. If you thought you would be okay financially because you had a tour coming up, the tour could get cancelled. Somebody could quit. It was always so sketchy, and you never make any money as the drummer anyway.

MD: Why not?

LM: Because you're eternally regarded as a sideman, which is just the nature of the beast. It's really hard to get more than a pittance for your efforts. So, I always worked a side job, in a restaurant, a bookstore, a video store. I was always supporting myself primarily through working a 9 to 5 job, and hopefully I could do something flexible enough that I could go on tour and play shows and they wouldn't flip out. But after 10 years of making minimum wage and getting later into my 20s, I started realizing why they call them "dead-end jobs."

Any money that I made from band stuff was always just fun money, just a gift. I never got into music for money. I never counted on the money I made in music to support myself. I graduated high school and went right on tour, holding down shit jobs along the way. Never had another thought of going back to school.

But then one day I just had this epiphany that I should get involved with some type of academia where I could learn a marketable trade that I could use whether I'm playing or not. So I got into the medical field and went to nursing school about eight years ago. All the time, I was still playing and touring and recording, but I also managed to go to classes in between. So now I'm a pediatric nurse here in Los Angeles. That's something I can pretty much rely on, whereas music is very, very fickle.

MD: Do they let you leave to go on tour?

LM: Yeah. It's good to have a career in an area that has a shortage. And for my particular field, there are not enough people to do all the work. There's always going to be sick people. There's always going to be sick kids. And the number of people to handle it is just dwindling. And because I have this particular skill, they are very accommodating to what I do with my art, whether it's traveling or touring or recording. So, I'm not saying that's going to work for everybody in every situation, but if you do specialize in something, you might have more flexibility to make your own schedule.

MD: You just did something on the Warped Tour, right? And you did a tour of Southern California, 'cause LA's so big, you can do that. And you came home every night, right? Can you tell us about that? And what else you're up to?

LM: Besides music, I'm working on a film project on the unsolved murders of women in Juarez, Mexico.

MD: What's the Web site?

LM: www.decimalmedia.com I was filming some stuff in Texas and Mexico a couple of months ago. While I was in Texas, I stumbled on this band who I just thought were amazing. I wasn't even thinking about music or bands. It was just weird and random. I was one of about eight people at this dreadful bar and this punk band from Atlanta called Treephort played. They were on a little tour. It's very rare that I see anything that gives me any sort of belief in punk rock, but this band was the exception.

They eventually came to Los Angeles, and they stayed with me for a couple of weeks while they were playing. I went to see them play a couple of times while they were doing club shows around, and I got that taste for wanting to play a little bit...so I took over the rhythm guitar parts from the lead singer so he didn't have to carry a guitar around. I did his guitar parts and we did...I did a stint on the Warped Tour. Treephort being there was the best thing about it. They were not scheduled; we crashed the Warped Tour at 6:30 in the morning and rode in with the vendors. And ended up getting a chance to play and became kind of the underdog favorites of the people running the Warped Tour and were allowed to stay.

MD: What do you mean you crashed the tour? Is this something any band could do? (*Laughs.*)

LM: After this tour I imagine there are going to be stricter guidelines. There's going to be the Treephort rule. I doubt it'll ever be allowed to happen again.

Security is pretty lax at 6:30 in the morning. You've got a lot of sleepy people not checking passes. We got in and set up on a friend's stage.

MD: Another band?

LM: On the Troma Films stage. Troma knew about Treephort and they were kind of, "Well, if you can get in with your equipment, you can play." And so....

So we did that every day. We thought our ad hoc guerilla performances were really on the down low, but word had spread quickly. Our shows became such an event that we became kind of the bastard child of the Warped Tour. And everybody in charge kind of looked the other way when we were sneaking in and out, and we got to play every day. By the time we played in Pomona, California, the fellow who runs the Warped Tour, this guy named Kevin Lyman, actually sent the local news crew over to film us.

Sometimes we'd do four shows a day. I was playing guitar and it was great. It was the most fun I've had in a long time. And then I left the tour to go back to my life, which...working and you know I have a lot of stuff here in LA that I have to take care of. So I wasn't able to finish the tour with them.

MD: And these guys were playing to eight people when you saw them a month or two earlier?

LM: And by the time we had finished, there were 500 people. And we weren't even supposed to be there.

MD: And you were playing four times a day?

LM: Yes, but sometimes the set would last only 15 minutes. Maybe we would do one song and everything would get destroyed. One time the generator ran out of gas. It was really exciting. To me it really *was* punk rock. It was warfare. It had nothing to do with the corporations, you know.

MD: Like Vans....

LM: ...Target brand, Vans brand...just the mall rock that punk is now.

MD: As someone who's been playing punk rock since '78, '79...

LM: '80.

MD: '80. Okay, since 1980. For 23 years you've been playing punk rock, starting back when there was no way to make a living out of it, there was no way in hell a major corporation would touch it. What do you think about how it's changed to become kiddie punk, cookie-cutter, mall culture now?

LM: I think, like everything that's fairly superficial and bland, it'll just run its course. It's just the way our culture is. There will always be an underground that will never be in the spotlight. So the stuff in the spotlight, to me, is not underground. It's the factory version of what the underground was. It's the safe version. It's not for me.

MD: My friend calls 'em "Civil War re-creationists."

They're just puttin' on the uniform and going through the already established motions. Like being in a play, but not as interesting.

LM: Well, it's very...being at these big punk shows these days for me, it's not like "Oh, I'm so much older, so it's weird for me." It's just weird because things are so different.

MD: How old are you?

LM: Just turned 36. It's weird to see just how...how...what's the word I'm looking for?...just how *family-oriented* this new punk rock stuff is.

MD: PG-rated Punk.

LM: PG Punk. And it's just... those words don't go together. Punk has nothing to do with taking your family to a rock festival. What are they *thinking*?

MD: Yeah, the people that used to beat us up for being into punk rock are into punk rock now. That's kind of weird to me.

LM: It's all jocks and I hate jocks. I hate jocks. I think jocks are the...Nazis in Nike.

MD: Jocks are the reason punk rock had to be created!

LM: And they're still there. Now jocks are 80 percent of the audience and even make up the bands. It just makes me uncomfortable. It makes me uncomfortable to see what is being touted as punk rock.

MD: I always wondered what the next generation what would be into that would shock me and thought everything has to get more offensive, but it's actually gone the other way. Good Charlotte offends me.

LM: Yes, but I don't want to spend this whole thing talking about what I like and don't like about popular music. It doesn't really matter. If you're happy out there, and the kids love you, and you're playing and selling records, that's fine. It's just a shiny machine that's not for me. Most of the musicians I associate with are pretty much unphased by anything that's happening now in popular music. So just as it's always been, we don't waste time spittin' in the wind. We just make our own music.

MD: What's the biggest audience you've ever played to? The smallest you've ever played to? And the average?

LM: The biggest would be 5000 with the Samhain reunion tour in Detroit. It was a great show to play and a terrific place to dislocate my shoulder halfway through the set and wind up in the emergency room. I'll never forget that.

MD: You didn't play any festivals in Europe that were bigger than that?

LM: Lots of small shows in Europe but no, no Wembley. No, not yet. Not yet. The smallest would be certainly…

MD: Nobody.

LM: Nobody. The soundman and the club owner.

MD: And the pissed-off bartender who's not making any tips and hates you.

How many times has that happened?

LM: More than I would like to admit. I can't remember the last time, though.

That stuff never bothered me. If there was nobody there, then it was a chance to stretch out musically or practice a new song.

MD: So you play anyway, even if no one shows up.

LM: Absolutely.

MD: Me too. It's a matter of honor.

LM: Yes, you show up like you said you would, and you play every night like it's the last show of your life. A take-no-prisoners/take-no-shit kind of attitude.

You have to earn your right to rock, and it's by doing the turd town tours. The dog-food tours.

MD: I played a show to three people in Tucson one time and it got written up favorably in *Spin* magazine. Even when that doesn't happen, the three people there love it and remember it if you're great and you do your best.

I read once that The Police were playing to three people in a bar in West Virginia the day they first had a song chart in England.

LM: You know, I see new bands now get onstage in front of thousands of people and then they bitch about the monitors or they don't have the right guitar and they are apologizing for this and that. They've got a runny nose or something and I just can't believe it. What sort of *audacity*? These kids don't deserve to be playing outside of the garage and then they get onstage and you know…I don't think even the Rolling Stones would do that prima donna crap. These kids just scowl all night if the side fill is not pumping the floor tom enough, and that's just bullshit.

I can play with the lights off and boxing gloves on. Every band I've been in, I can play the entire set by myself, completely isolated. You've got these guys onstage now who, unless it sounds like a fucking record onstage, they can't play. And they're completely pissed. And they treat their crews like little worker ants. And it's gonna make or break their night because the sample didn't trigger at the right time or the lights went out at the wrong cue. That's ridiculous. Michael, you know what it's like. You've played with nothing and you're happy with it. You sing out of a guitar amp. You play whatever you have and if you're good, it comes through. If you suck, there's no amount of tech that can make it any better.

MD: Average size crowd you've played to?

LM: Average would be all the shows all together, right? Boy, there's a lot of stinkers (attendance-wise) and then there are a lot a huge ones too. So it would be right in the middle. It would be like 500. But there's a lot of club shows that were 40 people, but there were a lot of hall shows where there were 2,000 people.

MD: Have you had as much fun at a 40-person show as at a 2,000-person show before?

LM: Oh, of course. Honestly, I always have a good time playing. I look forward to it. I prepare for it. It's a big part of why I do what I do, and I take it very seriously. I try to give everything, every time I play.

But other people can drain that away from you, if other people get pissy and act unappreciative of the fact that anybody even showed up. Nobody has to show up anyway. If *anybody* shows up, that's a reason to go crazy and you don't put on half a show. I've been in situations where that's happened. If it's not a big show where the room is going crazy, then some players only put on half a show.

MD: You mean half as long or half…

LM: Half the effort. And that's not what I'm about.

MD: What have you had to do to get paid money you're owed before?

LM: Well, it starts with some phone calls. Nice phone calls, reminders. Then it goes to letters. Nice letters. "This is what we agreed on and that hasn't happened."

And then, if you still don't hear back, make the letters more stern and formal, and of course, you save copies of all the letters. And you send them all certified mail.

MD: So you have a signature confirmation.

LM: Yeah. And make sure that you get…whomever you're sending to, …get their home address. At one point, I had to actually go to the person's house and…

MD: Cause you've been there but you didn't know the actual street address....

LM: Exactly. Had to go to the person's house and write it down so I could send them a letter to their home address.

MD: Because if you send it to an office, they can say they never got it.

LM: Right. Then, if you're still not getting their attention, go to the next step, which is an even tougher letter saying that you have an attorney now and you are ready to get legal on their lame asses.

MD: You write that or does an attorney write that?

LM: In the past I'd have a lawyer do it, but now I'm so familiar with this game, I pretty much have a form letter ready: Insert band name, insert record company name. Today I use my attorney as a last resort.

MD: We should put the template on the CD-ROM with the book. (*Laughs.*)

LM: That'd be great. I've got the original. (*Laughs.*)

(We did put it on the CD.)

What will finally happen—after this letter campaign, you'll get a call that says, "Hey, we gotta talk about this." Usually someone on their end has advised them to straighten this out. But don't count on them to be amicable or agreeable. You are probably still a long way away from resolution.

MD: And you keep records of when they call and what...

LM: You prepare yourself for that conversation. You write some stuff down. You go back and you talk to your friends and you go, "Do you remember this and do you remember that?" "Yeah, I was there when he said this." You get some people to back up your claims because the people who owe you will act like they don't fucking know you. People that you have been with in a band with for years will act like, "What did you do for us?" or "You were just the..."

MD: Drummer.

LM: Yeah, "You were just the drummer." So you really have to get your paperwork in order. Documentation, documentation. "You said this, and he was here to verify that. You said this on this date. You promised me this but you gave me that." Be ready when these cheats call to "discuss" your "misunderstandings." He or she is going to say everything to discourage you and frustrate you from getting what's yours.

I look at a band like building a house. They build a house and they need a special person to come put the roof on. They call me, and I put my special roof on. And then they sell the house and don't give me any money. And that's when I have to go back and say, "No...."

MD: Or they live in the house but won't let you live in it.

LM: Exactly. Or they'll almost force you to quit. Then they can feel justified in not paying you. The scenario is common; they promise you the world when things are getting started, and then when things get rolling and the money's flowin,' they'll vibe key members out so they can replace them with yes men (usually fans) who are happy to play for nothing. Then the remaining guy gets to keep a bigger share of the pie.

Fuck that.

MD: It's also an issue of left-brain versus right-brain. Art versus commerce, and a lot of people don't have the capacity for both of those. I think you kind of need to develop both to survive as an independent artist.

LM: Most artist/performers know just enough about the music business to protect their own ass but not yours. They know just enough to say the right phrase, here or there, that makes you think they know what they're talking about. Don't count on someone else looking out for your best interests.

There's always going to be a guy in the band who's getting more than everyone else, and that's fine. But there comes a level of arrogance and greed that those people get, that they want to give you an actual penny on the dollar and think that you should be happy. I can't accept that. Punk and alternative bands may not be Fortune 500 companies, but a small, savvy group can make a killing and provide decently for everyone. I'm not insisting on equal compensation, just fair compensation. The bands that go through lineup after lineup after lineup are the ones who are giving some of the players pennies on the dollar.

MD: That's why people quit.

LM: That's why people quit.

MD: It's like working at McDonald's.

LM: Yeah. It's worse than working at McDonald's. At least you got benefits there. I'm sure when you see the bands that split things more fairly, those are the bands that stay together and continue to do good work.

MD: Who have you had personal dealings with that do it the right way, bands and labels?

LM: Financially, I'm really happy with the Son of Sam project that came out on Nitro Records. Everything was equally split four ways. Writing, playing, etc.

MD: And the label?

LM: And the label, Nitro, is the best label that I've had any sort of dealings with. They send me statements and checks on a regular basis, and accounting, without having to go after them. The other records labels will make you go after them.

MD: Not Dischord or Touch and Go, though?

LM: Yeah. Actually, Touch and Go tracked me down to pay me, which was nice.

MD: Wow.

MD: Which band was on Touch and Go?

LM: Distorted Pony. They were on Trance, which is an offshoot of Touch and Go.

Back with Dischord you got paid in records.

MD: Regularly?

LM: Yeah, they just said, "We're going to take this amount; you guys take that amount." That was fine.

With other labels and bands, once you are out of favor you fell off the face of the earth as far as they're concerned. And when you try to go to them for support or help or promo copies or shit like that, or money that's owed to you, half of them won't take your calls. So try to establish some stuff while you're in the band. But if you're thinking of leaving, remember that you will lose all your clout, overnight.

MD: Have you been on a major label?

LM: Yeah.

MD: Which one. Which band?

LM: It was on a Capital affiliate called Bug, which was run by the hipster music publisher Bug Music. This was back in the 80s when I was in a group called Lunch Box. The label got canned, and the band got dropped. That was kind of heartbreaking 'cause we worked long and hard on that band. I was also in a band called Dead White And Blue. We did a bunch of indie records. And then the band got signed to MCA. But I was fired at the midnight hour.

MD: Before they got signed?

LM: Like two days before the contracts were signed.

MD: Why?

LM: Um...

MD: 'Cause they didn't want to pay you?

LM: No, I got a little...I put a lot of that blame on me. I pretty much fucked up...that was a situation that was an ideal three-way split. But I wanted not only my three-way financial split but also I wanted 33 percent artistic control. I wanted to be the spoiler on any sort of democracy decision that came down. If I didn't agree...

MD: Veto.

LM: Then it was vetoed. So, the singer and I had some disagreement about some artwork and I threw a fucking tantrum. And I packed up my drums and left. I left the recording studio.

MD: (Imitates bratty child voice) You took your ball and went home.

LM: I took my ball and went home. Literally. I took the carpet they were playing on. I went home, and they even asked me to come back. And I said, "No, I'm on strike." And they were like, "You're so fired. You're so fired." They signed a seven-record deal with another drummer 24 hours later and kept all the money.

MD: So, throwing a hissy fit cost you like 20 grand?

LM: Absolutely. Pick your battles. Tantrums can be expensive.

Janis Tanaka

Bass player from Pink, L7, Stone Fox, and Fireball Ministry. Seen her around for a decade. One of the coolest chicks in the San Francisco music scene. She's moving to Los Angeles soon, which is great, because we had a blast hanging. She's a wonderful human and a hell of a musician.

Web site: www.fireballministry.com

Interview with Janis Tanaka August 7, 2003, Michael Dean's front yard.

Michael Dean: Hey, Mama. What bands you been in?

Janis Tanaka: Pink—play bass, sing backups; Fireball Ministry—bass and backups; Hammers of Misfortune—sang, played bass; Our Lady of Napalm—sing, play guitar.

MD: Stone Fox!

Figure 18.3 *Janis Tanaka.* Photo by Michael Dean.

I Love Los Angeles

I was in my front yard waiting for Janis Tanaka to show up, and this guy leaned over my gate and said, "Hey, wanna buy my poems?" and held up a hand-Xeroxed chapbook. I didn't have money, but gave some water—it was hot and he was walking door-to-door selling poems! I love this guy!

I recognized him from my favorite Soundgarden video and set him up for a photo. We talked a bit. He signed a release form. I always keep a pile in my room.

Janis showed up and bought his book as he was leaving.

I love Los Angeles. Even the guys selling poems door-to-door have had their 15 minutes of fame.

Figure 18.4 *Soundgarden "Black Hole Sun" video star RC Bates in my front yard.* Photo by Michael Dean.

JT: Stone Fox

MD: Stone Fox!

JT: Auntie Christ, with Exene and DJ Bonebreak from X.

MD: Loved them.

JT: Let's see what else was I in….

MD: L7.

JT: L7. Oh my god (*laughter*).

MD: You have a fuckin' great laugh. You laugh a lot. Is that the secret to life or happiness?

JT: It's my family. The girls in my family, we laugh like crazy. We don't understand why everyone says we laugh a lot, but we all do. So, I think it was just how I was raised.

MD: Do you play a full-sized bass? You have tiny hands.

JT: I play a full-sized bass. I used to play a ³/₄, but the tone on a full-size is better. It's easier to play faster but just as easy to play a full-scale as a ³/₄, I think. And then there are dead spots on a _ that I get mad at.

MD: Would it be redundant to ask questions about being a woman in a rock band or being an Asian woman in a rock band?

JT: No.

MD: Have you heard this all a million times?

JT: Yeah, I've heard it a million times, but it's important in a way.

MD: What's your ethnic derivation?

JT: Japanese. My grandparents are from Japan.

MD: Born here?

JT: Born here. I'm a Sansei, that means third generation.

MD: Sun?

JT: Sansei.

MD: How do you spell that?

JT: S.A.N.S.E.I.—means my grandparents came over.

MD: I make everyone spell everything so I don't…

JT: You're smart.

MD: Yeah. I am. (*Both laugh.*)

JT: They came over around 1900. So, my family's been here about 100 years.

MD: Wow. I don't even know what questions to ask about that, but what's different about being a girl or an Asian girl as opposed to a guy in music?

JT: About being Asian, there are good things and bad things. It's all on stereotype, which is funny. But you just take it for what it is, I guess. You take what people give you and do what you can with it. So, being Asian in a band, the good thing is, it's not that common and people notice. It's interesting in a way.

MD: Does every review mention it?

JT: Almost every review mentions "chick" or *something* "chick," which is something about female and what that's like and if that's good or bad. In fact, I just did an interview, and she [the interviewer] said, "You're in a somewhat male-dominated music genre, playing metal. What's it like being female?"

It's not *somewhat* dominant, it's *definitely* dominated by males. And it's from generations of that. It's just slowly being okay. It's a lot easier being a female in a band than it was.

MD: Who started that? Was it Tina Weyworth?

JT: Who started what?

MD: Being the chick bass player.

JT: I don't know.

MD: Motown. There was a Motown lady.

JT: There was the Duchess.

MD: There was a white lady Motown.

JT: That was Carol Kaye. She was a jazz guitar player before she became a bass player.

MD: She wrote the books.

JT: She wrote the books. She wrote every bass line practically that you've heard. She wrote a lot of the bass lines I grew up with.

MD: But there were guitar books too, right?

JT: She wrote guitar books and bass books.

MD: Did she write them or did they just use her name?

JT: No, she wrote them because she's a theory lady.

MD: I learned guitar from one of her books.

JT: She's very theory. I actually went into one and I don't get theory so I couldn't follow it. (*Laughs.*) So, I was like, "I'll sit down with this some day." But I had another one that was just little licks you could learn from Carol Kaye.

Women play some in the smaller clubs, but the farther up you get in the money ranks of music….

MD: I've never thought of it that way, but yeah, it winnows out the women. I wonder if they just get weary of it quicker. One thing I've noticed that's weird in doing interviews for my film book—there's a lot of women filmmakers, but they don't think they have as much of a right to have something to say. Men with nothing to say who I would never interview are like, "Interview me!" And women who have a lot to say are like, "I don't know...."

JT: I think it's a combination of that and if you get into the upper echelon of money-music making, the more old-school people...the more they are into not having the chicks so much. Sometimes they say it's cool, but they're still not quite having it. Like Deanne Franklin was saying: It's the same with sound, doing sound and being female. It's almost harder for a tech than a musician.

MD: What bands did she tour doing sound for?

JT: Tom Waits, She did Pink with me. Sonic Youth; she did Gwar too. Natalie Merchant. Deanne did Kat, and Courtney Love and that's how I met her—through Kat and Courtney. Way, way, way back.

MD: Kat from Babes in Toyland?

JT: Yeah.

Deanne was doing studio work in the early 80s. So she's been doing sound forever. She says it can be kind of hard being female. I asked this woman who was playing rock music in the 1970s, and she said, "Oh yeah. The guys, not all of them but a higher percentage of them than now, would come and yell, 'Get off the stage!' and spit and throw shit."

MD: What advice do you have for people starting off in music?

JT: If you want to play music, you have to practice because the more on top of your skills you are, the more fun you'll have. You either practice with your band or by yourself. It helps me because I don't have a memory.

And make sure you keep your life intact while you play music. And just make sure you're having fun as well. I don't know. If you want to make money at it, that's a whole other ball of worms. (*Laughter.*)

MD: Are you making a living at music now?

JT: On occasion. Little spurts. Last year I paid off all my debts from the...

MD: Previous decade? (*Both laugh.*)

JT: Yeah, exactly. I paid that off and it was nice.

MD: What do you do between gigs?

JT: Silkscreen, bus tables, type letters, run errands for friends.

MD: What do you silkscreen?

JT: Textiles. Long tables on wall coverings.

MD: Didn't you work at _____?

JT: Yeah, I worked at _____. That's where I was a receptionist and executive assistant.

MD: How do I remember that?

JT: I probably gave you some shorts.

MD: Yeah, probably. Probably came by the bike messenger wall.

JT: I probably did. I still have some of those. Those were the best. That was a fun job.

MD: Okay, I'm taking that out. No product placement perks.

JT: Yeah, no worries.

MD: How did you get the gigs with Pink and L7? And tell me something about those tours.

JT: I got them both through friends.

MD: Word of mouth?

JT: The gig with Pink was through Linda, a friend of mine who knows what kind of bass player I am.

MD: Linda Perry?

JT: Linda Perry. Pink needed a rock bass player and Linda said, "I know who you need. You need Janis." And they called me. And the L7 thing I got through a friend. They needed a bass player, and he says, "I know a bass player that'll fit. Janis." And called me. They'd seen me play with Stone Fox.

MD: Stone Fox! (*Both laugh.*)

JT: They were completely different tours obviously. I went to the same cities touring with L7 and touring with Pink.

MD: Pink was stadiums?

JT: Pink was stadiums—sheds.

MD: Sheds, is that what they call them?

JT: Yeah, shed means open air, I think.

MD: How many people?

JT: 5,000.

MD: 5,000? Wow. What's the biggest crowd you even played to?

JT: 15,000.

MD: At a festival?

JT: Yeah, at a festival. It was with L7, at the LeMans motorcycle race, which was awesome. I played the Rose Bowl with Pink at the Wango Tango. And then we played this crazy place in Mexico City that was even bigger than the Rose Bowl. It was a Lenny Kravitz concert. It was huge.

MD: After you played shows like that, did you ever play shows where there weren't many people, with other bands?

JT: Yeah.

MD: Because I'm wondering how you jive that in your mind. Does it still feel okay playing for a very few people after playing for a lot?

JT: It's still fun. It's not like…I haven't played one of those shows in front of three people for decades, but I'll play for a small crowd and love it. The crowd is so fun, like at Mission Records or some place I can't even remember.

MD: Like 50 people packed in a bedroom-sized place….

JT: At the most 50. 30. Maybe 20. Oh, I know where it was. It was at Kimo's with Our Lady of Napalm. And it was so fun. You're on the ground, with the people.

MD: It doesn't take many excited people in a place like that to have the energy.

JT: Yeah, and they're my peers too. It's not like this crowd of adoring…. It's a lot different. It's more my scene really. So I had a lot of fun, and then I'd come home and play with Fireball Ministry, which is not that small. We don't play small shows. Not like 50 people, but it's not like the humongous stadiums.

MD: What size places did you tour with L7?

JT: That was 500 to 700. And I think we had some smaller places here and there. And it was incredibly hot. It was a van and Motel 6 tour, which was…having a hotel was nice.

MD: What time of year was that?

JT: Summer. It was like August.

MD: In a van? Where?

JT: Yeah, in a van. In Germany. Europe. Somehow I just dehydrated myself completely during L7.

MD: How much rehearsal did you do for those tours?

JT: With L7 I had two weeks before we actually had to play a show. And with Pink it was maybe one week, and then we had to go play a show.

MD: With Pink, did you have your own hotel room?

JT: I had my own hotel room in a nice hotel. But it took a month or so before I could actually afford room service. (*Both laugh.*)

MD: Did you take lessons?

JT: I'd take a lesson here and a lesson there. But mostly, the best guy I had was just a friend who would show me songs for like three hours for like five bucks. He'd say, "Bring the music you like," and he'd show me how to play along with the records I had. Then I could go home and play along to things that I enjoyed. If you can't figure out the parts to a song on your own, you can just ask someone to help you learn the song. Like learning how to go through different parts, like going from verse to chorus. And what a bass line does. You learn it more by playing along with a song with another bass player then any formal lesson I've taken yet.

Another thing is to start playing with other people early on.

MD: There's a lot of people who are really good in their bedroom and can't fucking play three chords with a drummer and….

JT: Yeah, well, it's different from playing in your bedroom. You play in your bedroom and you play whatever you like. But if you have to follow…if you're a bass player you follow a guitar player…I've noticed that whoever writes the songs, sometimes when you bring a song in, it's difficult for them to write parts for you cause they're used to having a song and having other people put the parts into it. I'm used to putting parts to a song that's already there, so it's hard for me to write a song and say, "Hey can you help me out with this thing?"

MD: Mike Watt has a really good take on that. He says he likes being the leader sometimes and being the side guy sometimes. He calls it being a "side mouse." He says it's really good for both aspects. Each one helps the other. Being a leader helps you to be a side mouse and being a side mouse helps you be a better leader.

JT: Yeah.

MD: It's weird 'cause bass players function as…we both know, the guy in the back that you don't really see that fills in the space. But it doesn't just have to be that, and it's hard to front a band as a bass player. It's weird. You've done that?

JT: I don't think so. I don't think I've really fronted a band as a bass player.

MD: But you sang in a band, right?

JT: I sang in Hammers, but there were two other singers too.

MD: So you shared lead vocals?

JT: Yeah, it was like split screen. There were all sorts of cookie monster vocals. There were male vocals, female vocals.

MD: Split screen?

JT: Yeah, we had this split screen thing going on.

MD: What do you mean?

JT: It was a concept thing.

MD: Wow.

JT: There was a whole story. I imagine it as…if you're watching a movie of us, our music, and there was a split screen with the two vocals. (*Laughs.*)

MD: That's funny. I like it.

JT: So, I've never really fronted a band ever….

MD: I was going to say something about your advice….

JT: From my first band to my last band…the first band we'd kick people out, we'd get really mad at each other and….I don't like kicking people out. Because a band to me is a unit, and I think one of the worst things is all the ego clashes. That's just part of growing up, in a lot of ways. The hard part of being in a band is learning how to deal with other people and not just throwing your ego around.

MD: That's something I've noticed with people who get the cool session gigs, like you do. It's musical ability, but it's also the ability to get along with people.

JT: Well, yeah. You have to know how to get along with people, but not just that. If I take a paid gig with someone, if it's not my band, and someone says, "Come and play bass," I'm not gonna say, "I think you should change this, this, and this." Whereas in Stone Fox, we did the set list together and figured everything out together.

In session work there's a definite hierarchy, and you just take your place. It's not my band, so I'll step back and I'm the bass player for this band. I'm helping do what they need to do, but it's not about me. That's an important part of taking a gig with a band that's established. But you still want to put out enough of yourself so you can add to it. So you're not just being a wet noodle. But you can't start taking over someone who has a vision and they've been doing their thing for while.

MD: 'Cause you won't last long in the band.

JT: Yeah. You need to find a balance.

MD: Do you have a manager?

JT: No, I don't personally have a manager. Fireball Ministry just recently got a manager for the band, but I haven't had a manager myself.

MD: So, when you get an offer for a paying gig, do you go into negotiation on what you're going to get?

JT: I go, "What's going on?" They say, "Oh, we're doing this." I'm like, "I need to hear the songs. Can you send me something?" and they say, "We'll send you some CDs. When can you make it down?" I'll tell them, and I get there and hope I get paid but whatever. If I don't get paid, I have to figure out how I'm going to pay my bills. That's how I feel. I'm really bad about it. Everyone gets on my case about getting what I'm worth. I don't really care.

MD: You will when you move to LA.

JT: I don't give a shit.

MD: Dog walkers have managers here. (*Both laugh.*)

JT: If I really want it, I'll go and ask. But I like to work for people who will give me a raise when they feel I need a raise. If they don't give me a raise when they feel I need a raise, then I'll quit. I like to work for people who are nice.

I really didn't negotiate, but I do know about entertainment law somewhat. I took a couple of classes on entertainment law that a friend of mine let me take pro bono. I can read a contract. I know what I'm getting into, and if I don't like it, I could talk to them if I wanted to.

I feel the most comfortable when I'm talking to someone who's honest. I can tell if they're honest…and if they're not…I've only had one person that was weird and shady. Most of the time if someone's honest and I can trust that, then I feel safe.

MD: I think more contracts should be work-for-hire and less like indentured servitude.

When you go on tour with a rock band, you probably sign a contract that says you'll play the gigs, you'll get paid, and you won't flake out. You sign contracts on tour, right?

JT: We sign them pretty late into the tour.

MD: But they weren't like....

JT: I'm probably not supposed to talk about it.

MD: Okay, that's fine. We don't have to say specific bands either.

JT: Yeah, yeah.

MD: When *one* goes on tour with a band. Not when *you* go on tour....

JT: Only...yeah, occasionally, not always. It depends. Sometimes you sign....

MD: Well, it's probably to someone's advantage *not* to have you sign. Then it's easier....

JT: Right, right.

MD: Dot, dot, dot.

JT: Yeah, exactly.

MD: But the major label contract that I signed, it was indentured servitude. It was like, if they want to own you, they own you for seven years. If they don't, they can drop you at any time.

JT: And they can charge you money!

MD: If you were a cat, what kind of cat would you be and why?

JT: *(Laughs.)* I'd be a Siamese cat because they are chatty to the point of being obnoxious and really needy and more like a dog, but they're still a cat. And they'll swipe at you if they feel like it at any moment for no apparent reason. That's unfortunate, but that's what I'm like.

MD: Thank you, thank you. You rock, Janis.

Dave Brockie

Web site: www.oderus.com

Dave Brockie is the singer in Gwar (Beavis and Butthead's favorite band). Dave and Michael Dean have been friends for over 20 years (even though when drunk he calls Michael "Mike"). Dave hit Michael in the head with a bass guitar at a show in 1983, and Michael still has the scar from the stitches. Dave is also an accomplished painter and writer. He is working on a play that he plans to present in Los Angeles in 2004.

Interview done in the parking lot of a show by a prominent Los Angeles prop rock band who remind me a lot of Gwar.

Michael Dean: So, Dave Brockie of Gwar, what do you think of "prop" rock?

Dave Brockie: Well, first of all, prop rock, in general, is bullshit. Unless you have the rock, your props are gonna suck. This might surprise people, but Gwar was never about making a visual statement. It was about using visual tools and musical tools in order to make some other kind of statement that we didn't know what we were making. If it's purely visual, it's like, it loses. It's decorative. It doesn't really have any bite to it.

I don't really see what these guys today are doing. I don't see the satire. I don't see the irony. I don't see how they're commenting on anything. I see how they're celebrating the artistic spirit by getting up there and making stuff and doing cool shit. And that, in itself, is good for people to be creative, but I just don't think anyone will do it as good as Gwar did it. Ever again.

MD: What's the future of Gwar?

DB: Sit around and wait to see if someone can do it better.

MD: So Gwar started as a one-off joke at art school like 29 years ago or something?

Figure 18.5 *Dave Brockie*. Photo by Dave Brockie.

DB: Yeah.

MD: How did it…did you think it would last this long?

DB: No, not at all. We thought it would maybe go…we never thought we'd put out a record, much less tour the fucking world. We thought, maybe it would go…I mean you were there, Mike. You saw the very beginnings of Gwar. When we were….

MD: Michael.

DB: Michael, you were there. You saw what was happening with Gwar at the beginning.

MD: Right, it was like a joke in the middle of a Death Piggy set.

DB: Exactly, and then all of a sudden 500 people were showing up. All of a sudden, people were offering us money to play. We were literally people who were working in the dining hall of our college art school to try to make ends meet. And working at Labor Pro loading chickens into trucks all day for 20 bucks.

It was like, all of a sudden, "Oh, my God, we're able to do this and actually make money off of our art." That was the biggest thing and we were able to fucking roll with it for a really long time. And as far as the future for Gwar: There's a lot of things that Gwar hasn't done that I'd like to see them do. I'd like to see a Gwar video game. A really over-the-top, fucked up computer video game. XXX. Totally crazy. I'd like to see us get into Japan and some other places in the world that we haven't. But, you know what, Gwar has already done so much more than I ever, ever, ever thought it would. The one thing that I was always afraid of when I was a little kid, when I was reading *The Agony and The Ecstasy*, was that I would go through my life and I would never really be involved with an important artistic project. And something that really seemed to make a difference to somebody out there anyway. I'm not saying that I can die happy, like all basted up like steamed oysters or whatever, but I know that I was lucky enough to work with a bunch of really talented and incredible motherfuckers. For whatever it was worth, we did Gwar, and it really did have an impact that I don't think has been measured yet.

MD: What advice do you have for musicians who are starting out?

DB: The first thing I would say (and it doesn't matter what kind of band you're in), you have to be sure about the people you're working with. If you're not really comfortable with the people you're working with, then find people you're comfortable working with because that'll like.... People who don't get along with each other in bands, it's like slow cancer. It might take three or four years of really good work for you to realize that your band sucks.

So, I would say find people that you enjoy making music with. It does not have to be a tortuous experience unless, of course, that's what your band is about. I'm sure that could work for somebody. But for me, once you've found good people, you really do have to work hard. It just can't be about partying all the time. You really do have to challenge yourself. Nowadays to try to do something new, I mean, artists, musicians who are looking at the same thing I was looking at fuckin' 20 years ago are so much more challenged because, in between now and then, there's been 20 years of development and evolution. Where everyone has been doing everything. Where everything has been re-hashed and re-invented. And we've got rap, techno, and industrial metal and everything is just all mashed up. It's like how many different ways can you write a rock n' roll song?

So, I would just say the best advice I could give anyone is just be fearless.

MD: How do you kick people out when you have to kick someone out of the band?

DB: Be cool about it. If the person's done things like steal money or is smoking crack when they should be rehearsing, it's no problem. You're gone, dude. Sorry, that's it. But if it's someone you love and it's a tough decision to make, you just have to be cool about it. But you do have to do it. That's one of the hardest things to do, and that's one of the things I had to do all the time as the leader of Gwar. It's like, "Oh, we decided we don't want this person. It's your job, Dave, to get rid of them."

MD: Did any ever sue you?

DB: No we've never been sued because we've always dealt with our members very fairly. First of all, there was no money to be forwarded anyway.

MD: How big is your nest egg? How many days can you not work before you have to get a job when Gwar calls it quits?

DB: Any money that I have saved up has absolutely nothing to do with Gwar whatsoever. We never really made any money off of it. The slave wage was $800 a month. From basically about *Scumdogs of the Universe* to *Ragnarok*, which I guess was about our ffifth or sixth album, we had a slave wage of $800 a month. And I made, as the lead singer and sometimes ad hoc manager, I made as much as the lowest slave. It got a little better on *Carnival of Chaos*; we actually got it up to a thousand a month. You know, anyone who lives in this world can tell you that a thousand dollars a month is really not going to go very far, especially if you're trying to keep you're rig (amp) in shape or whatever. So you know it was always a labor of love. And we always knew that if we lost the penises and maybe we weren't quite so shocking, and maybe we weren't such assholes about what we did onstage, and if we didn't squirt blood everywhere, and this and that, that we might have been more commercially successful. But that was not really…that was never, and was just for me, that was never the reason I got into that. Maybe some other people in the band would disagree with me, 'cause it was a true artistic democracy. But generally speaking, it was the person who argued the longest and the strongest who won and that person was usually me. I can remember fighting for the song, "Have You Seen Me?" The guys in the band were like, " Have you seen me?' How can you write such a fucked up song? It's about missing children." I'm like, well, I'm outraged about the fact that this country is so fucked up that we can't keep track of our kids and the way that we're gonna try and deal with it is by putting their faces on milk bottle cartons, you know. That outrages me and this is my way (of dealing with it). They're like, "Oh Brockie, shut the fuck up. You just think it's funny, you know you just think it's funny." Maybe. Yeah, I do. It's a big fucked up mess but…I know I don't molest children. I never kidnapped anyone.

I just feel that Gwar had a place in this world and an impact on modern society, on modern media, on modern music that people probably won't admit for another fuckin' 50 years. I mean I don't think…. If we hadn't had Gwar, we never would've had Beavis and Butthead. We never would've had South Park. We never would've had Marilyn Manson.[2] We never would've had Slipknot. We never would've gone to all those areas. When we started doing Gwar, everyone was into Nirvana. Everyone was into wearing lumberjack shirts and was total "anti."

MD: You guys started before Nirvana.

DB: Well, yeah, but it's like…there was no show. Besides Green Jelly out here, Green Jell-O, out here on the West Coast…I'm just like…I almost feel like when I look back at what we did, I almost feel like a spectator to a train wreck or something. And somehow I was able to jump out of it and not get slaughtered and destroyed by it. Some people in Gwar have been crushed, crushed by what we did. They can't really…can't really deal with it. They think we should have gotten rich, or they should have gotten a Grammy, or whatever. But I think we gave, whether you're in music or art or whatever the fuck you're doing, I think we gave everyone a good kick in the ass.

MD: You're talking about it almost like it's past tense. Is it?

DB: Yeah, it kind of is now. It's like, I think I've gone as far as I can with Gwar. I do love Gwar. There are a lot of things I haven't done with Gwar that I'd like to do…that I might now get a chance to do, like design a video game or computer game.

MD: Why don't you just find some programming nerd who wants to do a game?

DB: Well, we've spent a lot of time with people like that. We've really tried a lot to get in touch with people like this. We spent months working with people like that but, at the end

---

2. This would sound insane if it weren't absolutely true.—MD

of the day, to really make a game you have to have a development team that's backed by a lot of money. You have to have a lot of money behind that. Those people are too talented to sit around and do a Gwar game for fun. And you have to have a lot of people working on that. So....

[Some really cute young woman drags Dave away, and the interview ends.]

[Transcription of interviews with Janis Tanaka, London May, Dave Brockie and Ron Yocom by Richard Urbano. Ron Yocom interview appears on my Web site, www.30DollarMusic-School.com. Thanks Richard!]

Figure 18.9 *Richard Urbano.* Photo by Michael Dean.

Joan Jett

Web site: www.joanjet.com

Joan helped create bad-girl hard rock in her all-female band, "The Runaways." Influenced punk with her solo act, "Joan Jett and the Blackhearts." Some call her "the original riot grrrl." To me, she's just the woman I wanted to *be* when I first started playing in rock bands. My god, she has it all: loud guitars, intelligence, and sex appeal from here to heck.

How could a young boy resist?

She had huge hits with "Bad Reputation," "I Love Rock & Roll," "Crimson and Clover," "Do You Wanna Touch Me?" and "I Hate Myself for Loving You."

She's still foxy, still has a loud guitar, and still tours the world.

Figure 18.7 *Joan Jett.* Photo by Randee St. Nicholas.

Michael Dean: Hi, Joan. I was a card-carrying member of the Joan Jett Haight-Ashbury Fan Club.[3] I carried that card in my wallet (three different wallets, actually) for over 14 years. Still have it in there.

Do you remember that club?

Joan Jett: Sure do.

---

3. *Free-to-join fan club run by Kerista Commune, a freaky Frisko hippie proto-computer nurd cluster that put out* Rockhead: The Magazine for Intelligent Rockers. *They all lived in a house in a group marriage and had sexy comics of themselves in the magazine. I was not a member of their commune, nor was Joan Jett. But the magazine and the fan club were nifty.*

Joan Jett h. ight-Ashbury Fan C.
Membership ID Ca.

Name: M. hael Dou.
Address: Box 1210
S.F. CA 94101
Phone: 695-1926
Date: June 29 1989
ID #: 715

JJHAF
547 Frederick St., San Francisco, CA 94
Phone: (415) 7.

Figure 18.8 *My Joan Jett Haight-Ashbury Fan Club membership card. (This, I just realized, is probably the* only *thing I have from back then. I have some of my baby stuff, but I got it back this year. Didn't have it all that time.)*

MD: What's important to you these days?

JJ: The music is obviously important; it's what I love. But I've been immersed in that for so long that now what's important to me is to get some balance and do things other than what I do onstage—just enjoy other aspects of life. Whether that be relaxing, enjoying nature, my animals, getting to know my friends, getting to know New York, all the things I haven't done.

MD: Sounds kinda spiritual.

JJ: Yeah, absolutely.

MD: What's your spirituality?

JJ: No denomination really, just a mishmash of a lot things, Buddhist, pagan, nature, no real definitive path, just me trying to figure out what's going on.

MD: I heard an interview the other day, and someone asked Carlos Santana what religion he was, and he said, "I don't know. What religion is God?"

JJ: Well yeah, that's a good one. Exactly.

There's so much hatred with people and their religions and ranking and who's better and who's the right word. It's scary.

It's hard to define for other people. You can only speak for yourself. All these things are important, the internal things, not the external.

MD: What's it like being you?

JJ: It's hard for me to answer, I don't know what it's like to be someone else. (*All laugh.*) It's great most of the time.

MD: Any regrets in your life or career? Anything you would have done differently?

JJ: I'm sure many things, but I don't think, as far as major aspects of my life, I would have done much differently. I think you've gotta make mistakes because it's the only way you'll learn. Someone can tell you something, but that's not your experience. Until you live it, it's hard to know.

I don't know that I'd take anything back. I don't think that I would.

MD: Why do you run your own label (Blackheart Records) rather than being on a major?

JJ: Well, many years ago it was hard to get signed. Those people didn't want anything to do with our music. So to get it heard we had to do it ourselves. We had no choice. That's why we started selling records out of the trunk at gigs. And slowly it caught fire and we built a wonderful fan base in the whole United States. It started in the Northeast and spread from there. And once we had our own thing going, there was no reason to give up that control. And a lot of times people think they know what's right for me. *I* don't even always know what's right for me. (*JJ and MD both laugh.*) People have an idea for your direction, of how to spruce you up a bit and I don't like sprucing.

MD: What's different about the music industry from 20 years ago?

JJ: It's hard for me to say because I'm not super involved with the business aspect of it. Also, I don't really pay attention to what's going on with everybody else. But I'd say the biggest thing is the downloading.

MD: How do you feel about that?

JJ: I'm not one of the people who thinks it's great.

MD: Has it hurt record sales for you?

JJ: What it boils down to for me is that it's a fucked up thing to teach people that it's cool to steal. A lot of people think it's not stealing, and I just don't get that. I'd like to have someone explain to me how that's not stealing. So yeah, does that mean I get free food, any services that I get are free? That's not the way it is in this world. And that's certainly not the way it works with art either. Someone taking advantage of artists is really annoying. It happens on so many levels—not just rock and roll, but acting, etc. So I just don't appreciate people telling us what a good thing they're doing for us. Don't do me any favors, okay?

MD: How can people avoid getting ripped off in the music industry?

JJ: Get paper. Get whatever deal you're making in writing. Even if it's not a super professional thing with lawyers and all, write down your terms. Make sure that everything is discussed face to face, eye to eye. Write it down, date it, have a witness sign it. It keeps everything copacetic.

MD: Care to talk about drugs?

JJ: Wow…hmmmm…that's such a subjective thing. Some people are so destructive when it comes to getting inebriated, and other people not so much. It's hard to tell somebody not to experiment in life. But yeah, it's better if you don't get screwed up on drugs and alcohol. It's better for every aspect of you: health, mental health. In my experience it's not a positive thing.

MD: Any closing advice for young people starting out in music today?

JJ: Expect a lot of negativity. In my experience, I was so excited, I thought we were going to change the world. But pretty soon we got resistance, on a lot of different levels—people being really nasty and calling you names and being way more nasty than the situation called for. It's just so shocking; you're not sure why people don't want you to succeed. And I'm sure the reasons vary depending on who you're talking to.

I think you've got to surround yourself with some sort of support group, whether it's your band, where you're in the same headspace, or friends, or if your family's supportive. It's important having people around you who believe you can achieve your dream.

And I say, "Go for it." You've got to give it a shot. And if you don't, and you wind up doing something else with your life, you'll always look back on that time and wonder why you didn't try a little bit more.

It's difficult. There's a lot of different pitfalls beyond people trying to tear you down. It's a tough living to make. But it's fun. It's very rewarding. It's nice to connect with people. That's what it's all about for me—knowing that people are feeling good listening to what you're saying or playing. Or both.

Peter DiStefano

I interviewed Peter by phone while he was in his car. He's so busy that that was the only way to do this.

I recorded it into my computer with a 99-cent suction-cup microphone stuck on my phone. I made an MP3 and sent it to Mike Kelley in Detroit via Microsoft Instant Messenger. Mike transcribed it, I proofed it.[4]

Peter DiStefano played guitar in Porno for Pyros. I met him when I was procuring certain substances for him and Perry and Martyn a long long time ago.

He's also played on albums by Scott Weiland and Peter Murphy. He plays in Hellride with Mike Watt and Stephen Perkins. He's scored commer-

Figure 18.11 *Peter DiStefano.* Photo by Davis Factor.

4. *Mike Kelley adds: "You know I was thinking how strange it was that you recorded an interview with the suction cup thingy on your phone in Silver Lake from a guy on a cell phone in a car somewhere in LA, loaded it into your computer as an MP3, sent me a 21meg MP3 file through instant messenger, I loaded it into Sonic Foundry Vegas and transcribed it into a Microsoft Word document (34kb), and mailed it back as an e-mail attachment!*

"You might wanna add all this in the intro as a lesson in technology maneuvers."

cials for Avis and done TV work on "Larry Sanders Show," "America's Funniest Home Videos," and "ElimiDate." He played on the film scores for *Coyote Ugly*, *Private Parts*, *Spy Game*, *Jimmy Neutron*, and *Shrek*. He did music for the PlayStation 2. He's also produced countless bands.

Peter is incredibly sweet, very polite and loving, and always the consummate musician, doing anything and everything musical to keep busy and make art and support his family.

Web site: www.peterdistefano.com

Michael Dean. Any advice for people starting out in music today?

Peter DiStefano: Do it for fun and make a dollar at least.

I would say listen and learn everything you can about the bands you love. You know, study their songs, their looks, their attitude, and if you still really really love 'em and what they do, figure out a way to really be honest with your talent and with yourself.

MD: Any regrets in your life?

PD: As of today? No. But I miss my father.

MD: But you spent a lot of time with him.

PD: Yeah, I spent a lot of time with him at the very end.

MD: What's important in your life these days?

PD: My wife and my child. And trying to not let my head take advantage of me, you know, by saying, hey, there's a better wife out there for me, there's a better band, there's more sex, there's a better body out there for me. You know, to be content with the lot that I have in life. And to not get caught up in some plastic surgery or some midlife crisis.

MD: Why does everyone want to be a rock star in whatever field they're in? Why can't people be happy making good stuff but not being the top dog?

PD: I think there are a lot of people who don't like their lot in life. Everywhere, not just in California.

MD: What's different about the music industry from 10 years ago?

PD: No more diamond artists, just platinum.

MD: How do you keep sane and balanced?

PD: By having a good balance of family time with work. You know, if I don't have enough work I go nuts 'cause I'm freaking out about the bills. If I have too much work, I can't sleep at night. Then I'm not present when I'm with my wife and child. My mind's somewhere else.

So I'm excited to clean up my plate a little because I'm probably the busiest I've ever been in my life right now.

MD: What kind of soundtrack stuff do you do? And how do you get the work? Tell me about that.

PD: Harry Gregson-Williams, a top film composer in Hollywood. I'm his crony, his guitar player. So I get to play guitar in all the films he does. There's a couple here and there where he doesn't need my guitar playing; he might need a complete authentic Brazilian guitar part, not a Santa Monica, California first-generation-from-Sicily surfer dude guitar player.

But mainly by being lucky. And I think social skills are the most important thing for getting work.

Also, I do my own scores, independent films and commercials, you know, big ones with Harry and then small ones by myself.

MD: Is that what most of your living comes from now?

PD: Uh, it comes from everywhere—producing bands, record deals, advances, royalties, uh…sessions, live gigs, um, and then movies and television shows and commercials.

MD: Do you still get money from Porno for Pyros?

PD: Yeah, and then I get residuals from…. I mean Perry owns my publishing, but he pays me my share.

MD: Were you happy with the business deals in that band?

PD: Oh, yeah. Well, at first I wasn't, but then I realized what Stephen and Perry, what Perry gave me, the opportunity that he gave me and I was very very very lucky.

MD: What was it like playing Woodstock?

PD: It was surreal. 350,000 people in front of me, and then it was being simulcast live across the world so it was live to a few million people. It was like the biggest live thing ever to this date, ya know.

MD: Was it fun?

PD: Um, yeah, it was incredible. I mean the helicopter was fun and the suit and the girls.

MD: You were wearing zoot suits, right?

PD: Yeah I had this $2,000 sharkskin suit.

MD: What's it like going from playing really big shows to doing smaller stuff? How does that jive with your ego?

PD: It's a very painful experience, and I keep doing it. Like I'm gonna go play solo acoustic next week in this beach restaurant where you just go sit in a corner and play; it's miked, it's a couple of stories, you're piped into the bathroom, and no one claps after you play. They're just eating dinner, ya know? But the pay is actually really good.

MD: And you're feeding your family.

PD: And I'm feeding my family. But I embrace the pain, the ego, you know? Like the last gig I played was onstage with Jane's Addiction, "Jane Says" in front of 17,000 people. That was last Saturday. And my next gig is going to be at a place called The Red Cove which is a coffeehouse in Ventura for, like, maybe three people.

MD: That's beautiful.

PD: So I go from extreme changes; you gotta love the coffeehouse level; that's my opinion…if you can't do the coffee houses…. And I hear musicians say "Man, one day I'm gonna get out of here and I'll never have to do this again." Well, it's good to have that goal to have to have that kind of drive, but you have to never burn bridges with the small stuff because you can always end up back there.

MD: That's fucking beautiful. That's so…. So did you play one song with Jane's Addiction or the whole set?

PD: I played the second stage with my solo stuff and Perry and Stephen got up with me and the crowd was cheering; you know, it was an amazing experience. They paid me a fat amount of money to play at Lollapalooza and then they asked me to do an encore so I did…um I'm sorry, can you hold on a second?

MD: Sure.

PD: Hold on. (*Puts me on hold. Comes back after a while.*)

PD: Hi, Michael Dean?

MD: Yeah?

PD: That's the band that I'm supposed to produce and they're like, "Where are you? We're at the studio!"

They're supposed to start hitting their first note at like 10 a.m. I'm such a loser, but anyway, I'm going to finish this up with you. What were we just talking about?

MD: Um, I think we got a good close in on that. The only other thing I was gonna ask for is if you got a blurb for me. One-liner, two-liner.

PD: Okay, are you ready? "Michael Dean, definitely one of the most powerful and knowledgeable and experienced living legends still around from the heyday of, I guess you would say from the grunge post-experimental, you know Porno for Pyros and Bomb was the post-experimental era and he's, if anybody knows and if you want real punk rock it's Michael Dean."

MD: That's great. I'll probably shorten it though. I'll run it by you.

All right. I'm gonna let you go, man.

PD: Thank you. I got the band on the other line. So listen, brother, I love you, and I'll talk to you soon.

MD: I love you too, man. Thank you so much, Peter. Bye.

Jonathan Richman

Our dinner with Jonathan:

Michael Dean and his buds interview Jonathan Richman for *$30 Music School* book.

Los Angeles, 8/26/2003

Photos:
http://www.kittyfeet.com/30music/richman.htm

and

http://www.kittyfeet.com/30music/richman2.htm

Figure 18.12 *Jonathan Richman playing my guitar.* Photo by Michael Dean.

Jonathan Richman is a lovable guy from Boston, now living in San Francisco. He was the singer in The Modern Lovers[5] and still performs solo. He is an extremely influential proto-pre-punk artist. His songs have been covered by Joan Jett and The Sex Pistols, Burning Sensations (in the movie, *Repo Man*), as well as by virtually every garage and/or bar band in the history of rock.

Most people either love him immensely or have no idea who he is. Unless you say, "He's that guy in the movie *Something About Mary* who always ambles into the picture playing love songs on an acoustic guitar. Then people go, "Oh yeah!"

He wrote the songs "Roadrunner," "Ice Cream Man," "I'm Straight," "She Cracked," "I Was Dancing In The Lesbian Bar," "Something About Mary," "Girlfriend," and "Pablo Picasso" (as in "was never called an asshole").

Jonathan Richman is an amazing and wise man. Sweet as heck and very mellow. He has an innocent child-like demeanor that is the complete opposite of most "rockers." But I think that, in a lot of ways, he is the ultimate rocker.

Jonathan came over, and Lydia Lam cooked us all dinner. Me and her and my neighbor Mike De Luna hung out with him for an hour and talked about everything under the sun. He even played us some guitar.

(Thanks to Li'l Mike for helping with a few of the questions.)

Michael Dean: What advice do you have for youngsters coming up today in music?

Jonathan Richman: Do what you feel. Period. Don't do what you don't feel. That's it.

Incidentally...I had nothing to do with that commercial where that song was used. That wasn't my idea. I don't believe in my songs being used in commercials. I've since learned that

---

5. *Jerry Harrison (Talking Heads) and David Robinson (Cars) were also in the band.*

we have something called "voice protection." They can't use your voice. So you won't hear my voice in any more commercials. You might hear some of my songs once in a while, but you won't hear my voice in any more commercials. I apologize for that last one; I couldn't control that.

MD: How can they do that?

JR: You sell your rights when you're a kid and they can do it.

MD: How do you avoid losing control and getting ripped off?

JR: At the time I had a word-of-mouth agreement. I always assumed that I would be consulted before they used anything.

MD: Seems like they take advantage of people when they're hungry, give them a little bit of money now to sign it all away later.

JR: No, I wasn't starving. I was happily hungry, and they seemed like honest people. I liked their company, they seemed to have high moral principles. We had an agreement in writing.

MD: So, the moral is, get all the details in writing?

JR: No, the moral is use your instincts but don't try to "help" people. (*MD laughs.*) My mistake was, I won't say which company this was....

MD: Can *I* say which company this was?

JR: No. But let me say this: The individual involved told me that he was planning to not take so many drugs any more and I believed him. That's what I get for trying to be a little savior. It's my own fault. So take everyone at what they are now. Like, if little companies have high moral principles, fine, but they've gotta be acting them all right now. Not later.

Little is my favorite kind of company, but it's not necessarily better. There are companies that play up their small size. And sometimes they're small for a reason. (*Both laugh.*) But all things considered, I don't like to work with big corporations: I like to work with much smaller companies.

MD: The one record I did on Warner Brothers, they did pay the little they said they'd pay. The only time I got ripped off was from a small company going out of business owing me (and a lot of other people) money.

JR: Yeah. It's often like that. When I was with Warners in the 70s, they had a woman there named Mary Martin who was the head of A&R. That was one of the biggest record companies in the world, but either she or her assistant listened to *every* tape and personally wrote a response to everybody. So sometimes a big company can be good. You've just gotta go by your gut feeling.

Nowadays, big is so much bigger than it used to be.

MD: Do you know what's happening now with radio where a couple of companies are buying up all the stations and it's all homogenized and there's no local DJs picking the songs anymore; it's a national corporate monopoly?

JR: Yes, I do.

MD: Do you have an opinion on that?

JR: Yes. I think it could be very good. Because then the smaller community stations will be appreciated. They are very valuable, and they will be seen as such in the near future.

MD: Did you play gigs with the Velvet Underground?

JR: I opened a show once as a solo guy at one of their shows in Springfield, Massachusetts. They let me borrow one of their guitars and I played a few songs, but I never played with the band.

MD: What was it like seeing the Velvet Underground in action?

JR: Great. I saw them probably 80 times. Hypnotizing on a good night.

MD: Didn't you work with Kim Fowley? (Kim Fowley is the guy who discovered/assembled Joan Jett's old band, The Runaways, and molded their career in an almost puppet master fashion.)

JR: Yeah, but not when he says I worked with him (*laughs*). Not anything like his liner notes. But he's an adorable guy. I like him. Nothing he said was true, but I like him.

We did a few demos together that got released without my permission.

MD: Have you had a lot of that happen? You've mentioned two instances in about five minutes.

JR: Yeah. Yeah, I have. A lot of people never paid me in any way that I can think of. But I'm not bitter. They can have all that old crap if they want it. I don't really worry about the past. But, yeah, it's happening right now. People are releasing things that they didn't ask me about—compilations, loads of compilations in England for some reason. There've been all these bootlegs, half the records of mine that are out I've had nothing to do with.

MD: How do you feel about downloading on the Internet?

JR: Well, I don't know…I don't do it, so I don't know what it would feel like. I let others worry about those things. Sounds boring to me though. (*MD, Lydia, and Mike De Luna all crack up laughing, hard.*)

MD: Your drummer lives in Tucson, right? How do you get away with working with someone who lives in a different city?

JR: No problem. I pick him up and off we go…then we do the first show in Austin, then New Orleans….

MD: What are you driving?

JR: Oh! (Jonathan gets really excited). I bought an old diesel car; we're going biodiesel. I'm selling the van. Biodiesel has vegetable oil and 20 percent alcohol to give it some kick. Biodiesel is the way to go.

Lydia: They're starting to tax it in Ireland, because they're losing money from oil revenue.

JR: Isn't that nice of them? But Ireland has done some nice things. They put a tax on plastic bags.

MD: Are you Irish?

JR: No. I'm a Heeb. Russian Jewish on both sides.

MD: Do you have a spirituality?

JR: Yeah. I love life.

And I love playing music. And when I play, the idea is to feel what I'm really feeling. And if you're really feeling it, then you're not bothered by your mind rambling around, and you get to the truth.

MD: How different is it getting things done in the music biz and getting things done in film biz?

JR: They're both fun. Doing the movie *Something About Mary* was really fun. And doing the score music was as much fun as doing the acting. It was really fun being on the set for about three months. But there's a lot of waiting, so bring a book.

Soundtrack work is a very hard thing to crack. But small independent films are easier.

I thought of another thing to recommend to young bands: Be a good live act.

I make my money touring. I'm my own manager. I record for a nice record label that I like, Vapor Records in Santa Monica. I like them a lot. But I make my money on the road. And it happens that I like it a lot. And live is just you and the audience.

Don't depend on records.

MD: I think one of your biggest contributions to rock is taking the third chord out of three-chord rock. Tell us about the song "Roadrunner."

I avoided the third chord in "Pablo Picasso" too. I can't claim it, I think others were there before me (*laughs*). But I simplified it for beginning guitarists. I eliminated that third chord (*all laugh*). We just sticked with A and D and you get pretty good results without too many other fancy chords.

MD: The Velvet Underground did that a lot too, with the song "Heroin" and....

JR: Yeah, they did a lot of things that I copied. (*All laugh.*)

MD: What's different in the music business now from 30 years ago?

JR: There's this new coffee house scene now, which I think people might wanna check out. If you're not getting booked in a bar, try little coffee houses. Just walk in and talk to them.

(*He leans in to the tape recorder*) This is gonna be the hard part, kids: You play soft, you'll get hired. And the neighbors won't complain. You will think that I'm taking away your teenage angst and your God-given right to blast everyone's ear drums (*all laugh*). (*Leans in closer, almost whispering.*) You will think that I'm taking away your God-given right to express teenage rebellion in its most pure form. But I have this to say: Eddie Cochran and Gene Vincent had amplifiers that would fit in your wallet. Elvis Presley shows for 5,000 people were less loud than you are playing in your bathroom. So, you don't need to really do that if you've really got "the thing." You can swagger without all that stuff.

MD: I heard somewhere that you gave up playing electric music because it hurts little kids' ears. Is that true?

JR: In fact, I was living in Los Angeles in 1973, and my band was breaking up. I just looked up hospitals in the phone book. I only brought an acoustic guitar the first time. And there were 110 people of all ages, learning disabled, and they could dance. They were *with* the beat. I didn't use a microphone or amp. Now I realize how 1890s dances could have happened, because 110 people *can* dance with just an acoustic guitar; they just have to feel the beat. These people were making a lot of noise, but they were feeling the beat so it worked.

MD: Did you have a drummer?

JR: No, just an acoustic guitar. And a cheap guitar at that.

So I brought my electric guitar next time thinking it would make it better. I just brought a small little Ampeg B15 amp and a Fender Jazzmaster guitar, and I was thinking, "They'll love this."

Well, the kids in front put their hands over their ears, and I realized, "This stuff gets out of hand really easily." It *can* be done. But it's really hard to keep it down to a volume where it doesn't tax the natural hearing of people. And these people weren't inhibited by society yet, and their ears were what they were and they put their hands over their ears. There was no....

MD: No needing to be polite.

JR: Exactly. There we go. So...I learned a lot from playing in places like that. And I learned from playing in hospitals that there's things you can do with an acoustic that you can't do loud. There's a certain calm you can bring to these places. If you listen to a really good Flamenco record, you'll see that a really good player can take an acoustic instrument and make it as exciting as anything you want to hear.

I still like the sound of electric guitars. I think Buddy Holly was fabulous, and Ritchie Valens. I think there's a lot of good electric players. I still pick an electric up once in a while. But I think if you can do it with an acoustic....damn! Then do it.

MD: What's important to you in life now?

JR: It's important to me to not use petroleum products because they cause death. People really are being forced off their land all over the world by big oil companies. And it's because we, Americans especially, use so much oil.

Biodiesel is good. And when you can't find biodiesel, you can still use diesel in those cars, and it's still better than gas. Look at the figures. It's better for the world and the air. And you need to use less of it than with gasoline.

> **NOTE**
>
> Michael Dean Note: Check out www.biodiesel.org.

It's also important to me to communicate with people, talk to my family, and become a better listener.

Mike De Luna: When you're touring and you're on the road, do you do merchandising? Are you selling CDs and T-Shirts?

JR: No, we just play a live show. We keep it really simple. We just play. The club rents us a drum kit; we bring a bag of chords. We have a little mixer that I bring, so we control the sound from the stage. We plug into the house speaker system. I mike my voice, I put a mike in front of my guitar, I don't have one that plugs in any more. I just mike an acoustic guitar with no amp. We bring a teeny little monitor speaker with us in our chord bag for Tommy (the drummer—the only other musician onstage with Jonathan).

Oh…I've got another piece of advice for young bands. They're gonna hate this one at least as much as the other one (*laughter all around*). Get used to hearing yourself without monitors in your rehearsal hall and live. Monitors usually don't work, as you know. You're always saying, "Turn up this, turn up that," and the reason you're always saying it is because the more you turn up this, the more you have to turn up that. And it's a war which ends in feedback and rings. So what do they do? They take a graphic equalizer and take out all the ringing stuff. Great. But you lose all your sound. So you get this horrible squeal that somehow does cut through everything but to what avail? Sounds like shit. And that's what most sound sounds like now. And you sound like everybody else. There's no color to the sound. You can't hear what your voice sounds like, and the audience sure can't; it's just a big war. But, hey, if all you're about is violence, don't listen to this advice at all (*laughter*). But if you want the audience to hear you, consider using less monitors, and practice in your rehearsal thing using no monitors. Yes, you can do it!

Mike De Luna: Any advice with regards to a musician's diet?

JR: What we've been doing is eating more and more out of bags on tour. We go to a health food restaurant and get some oats and beans…less and less restaurants can be trusted. GMOs[6] are everywhere. You don't want them. And if you're eating meat, you don't want the hormones. So, if you like veggie stuff you *can* do it on the road. Take a bowl with you, get some oats, some nice water out of a glass bottle and make yourself some mush…a little salt and brown sugar.

Lydia: Rice?

JR: Rice is good, but you gotta cook that. Rice cakes are good. But there's a lot of stuff you can eat on the road: Cashew nuts. Sunflower seeds. All kinds of boring stuff you'll hate.

---

6. *Genetically modified organisms—a.k.a. Frankenfood.*

(*Laughter.*) I'm not trying to say, "Don't eat what you like," but I'm saying if you wanna eat healthy or even vegan on the road, you can do it. Walnuts, almonds, cans of beans, grape leave rolls if you wanna get fancy. Take a bottle of olive oil with you as long as it's not too hot where it'll spoil; put that in your van and buy powdered hummus and add water. Maybe a little hot sauce if you're down in New Orleans or Texas....

Lydia: Chick pea powder.

JR: That's what I'm saying...you can do all kinds of fun stuff...the Baja egg plant dip. Another cool thing about this is, you get there too late, you're late for sound check. You gotta go on at nine, but you get to sound check at seven. That means you're not out of sound check until eight, if you're lucky. All right, so now you gotta play in an hour, now what do you do? If you've got stuff in your van, you just go out to the back of the club, grab a few bowls and eat something, instead of traipsing around asking people, "You know a good restaurant?" You end up waiting for the waiter and you glare at him and he glares at you. And you get back just before show time and you're sweating? No! Just go out to your van and eat your crap out there.

(Lydia makes a doo-doo joke and Jonathan gets goofy and flustered. It's cute).

Mike De Luna: Do you do some kind of cardio?

JR: Me and Tommy walk all over the place. We get to a town and we just walk.

MD: I saw you walk like a crab one time, on all fours in San Francisco. That's how I met you. (*Laughs.*)

JR: That's good too. And it amuses your friends. And makes strangers stop and think. I still like to do that. It's fun. Walking up hills is good too. All those things...you can do them and tour at the same time. You gotta get your exercise.

MD: Any closing advice?

JR: I didn't care about money. I'm not sorry I signed that contract I did. I didn't make much money, but I had a good time all the way through. I never wished I hadn't done something.

If someone doesn't pay you for a song, don't get mad. Don't worry. You're going to make up more songs. Don't worry about taking people to court. If someone doesn't live up to their contact, that's their problem, not yours. If you're honorable, don't throw the paper down when you learn they've stolen $40,000, you will get $40,000 more. Relax. It's their problem because they've done something that isn't good karma. What goes around really does come around. Relax and enjoy.

MD: Thank you very much.

JR: Thank *you.*

JR: Oh yeah. I've got some more advice for young bands. When the choice is between someone who's got more "muscle" in the music business, and someone you like better, choose the guy you like better.

NOTE

Look on my Web site www.30DollarMusicSchool.com for more interviews as well as Recommended Reading, Surfing, Viewing, and Listening, all cut from the book for length to satisfy the bean counters. I did an excellent interview with producer Warren Huart, and we had to cut it for length. However, it is on the CD in MP3 format in the Goodies folder (Warren1,Warren2, Warren3 and Warren4). It is also on the Web site in text format.

$30 MUSIC SCHOOL

Appendix A

What's on the CD-ROM?

Songwriting tutorial by Michael Woody. "Songwriting as a Lyric-Delivery System"

Flash-based animation that shows how to write a great song. Plays in your browser. This thing is so cool it's probably worth the $30 price of this book alone. It's all centered around one of the coolest songs I've ever heard. Sometimes I listen to it on Repeat for hours.

Movies

Keep in mind, you can play these full-screen in most players. They'll look pretty good. You don't have to watch them in the tiny size they first open up in.

I Left My Band in San Francisco

A movie I shot on Mini-DV and edited on my computer, illustrating how to tune guitars and drums, do vocal warmups, and more. It features *London May's 99-Cent Drum Clinic*. (Lydia sez his thing about, "Be ready for anything on your drums; be prepared to sound great even if things suck," which is a great analogy for life, not just drums.)

The trailer from one of the author's films, *D.I.Y. or Die: How to Survive as an Independent Artist*.

Michael Dean Talks about Art from a Jail Cell

A movie of me being interviewed in my garage by Blaine Graboyes. It's me talking about promoting film, but almost all of it applies to music, too. Was made by Blaine for a government DVD authoring convention he spoke at in D.C. Was shown to 400 government scientists and media creators on a big screen. Scary.

Music Videos of Me

By JP Kelly: (Happy_all_the_time: a Bomb video), Lapin (a Michael Dean solo video of my one-off project, Lapin Mort with my girlfriend at the time, Marie.

webmv: Slish song "The Web." Video by Paul Della Pelle.

Whore_love_song: Michael Dean solo song. Video by Michael Woody.

Also in movies folder, OmittedAudioLondonDrumSectionPart1 and part 2. Stuff that we took out of London May's 99-Cent Drum Clinic for length so it would fit on the CD and still look good, but left the audio for edification. The video was just a still shot of the stuff he's describing.

PC Software Demos

Sound Production

      Acid

      Sound Forge

      Sound Forge Noise-Reduction Plug-In

      Vegas video

      FL Studio (Fruity Loops)

CD and DVD BURNING

      RecordNowMAX (*working* 30-day version)

Miscellaneous

      emailstripper. For reformatting forwarded e-mails for press stuff.

      EasyTagger. For adding meta information to MP3 files.

EPK (Electronic Press Kits)

Examples of good ones.

Sample Loops: Very cool royalty-free loops to use in Acid or other programs. Made by Skip Frederiksen and Joel Legros from Beauty's Confusion. Get more at www.monochromevision.net.

Some noises, for Acid demo and more.

Printable diploma for completing *$30 Music School.*

Printable I.D. card for attending *$30 Music School.*

Songs

Lots of MP3s by me and my friends, demonstrating various things mentioned in the songwriting, equipment, and recording chapters, including:

> *Roach girl.* Re-recorded for this book with Sarah Amstutz on back-up vocals showing in action the harmony notation thing I came up with. Works in conjunction with Word document called "Roach Gurl words and chords.doc" in the Goodies folder.

Goodies

Contracts. (Note: Inclusion is for informational purposes only and does not constitute legal advice.) Examples. CD templates. Excel booking sheet templates. Track sheets for recording. Much more, including:

> MouseCount—a small P.C. utility that I designed and a friend programmed for counting and displaying mouse clicks. Counts clicks by session, day, week, month, year, and total. See just how insane you are about computers. I also use it for promo. It has a little ad and link for my book. Feel free to e-mail it to others or post on your Web site. (I also do custom versions for a fee.)

> Wallpaper. High-rez photos used in this book, in color and with the name of the book. Make good computer desktop themes. Feel free to pass on to friends. Also included is a text layer and other photos so you can have fun making your own in Photoshop.

> And a whole bunch more stuff. Just poke around and check it all out!

Thanks

London May. Lydia Lam. Blaine Graboyes. Skip and Beauty's Confusion. Joe Folladori. P. Kimé Lê. Reuben Chandler. Miles Montalbano. Lee Jones in the UK. John Abella. Mike Stan. Doug Hilsinger. Jay Crawford. Tony Fag. Paul Kirk. Pete Steele. Aaron Nemoyten. Richard Urbano. Tiffany Couser. Michael Woody. JP Kelly. Tracy Hatfield. And as always, I wish to thank and praise Todd McNeill, my genius Web provider.

Figure A.1 *Special thanks to Mike Kelley.*

Book Cover Photo Credits

Front cover: photo, Michael W. Dean. Model: Sarah Lynn Amstutz.

Back cover photo of Michael W. Dean: Nick Plotquin. He also took the photo on the back of *$30 Film School* and didn't get credit. So here ya go, Nick. Love ya.

Contact

Book Web site: www.30DollarMusicSchool.com

Michael W. Dean's e-mail: RockBook@kittyfeet.com

Join Michael W. Dean's list. Send an e-mail to: kittyfeet69-subscribe@topica.com

Index

License Agreement/Notice of Limited Warranty

By opening the sealed disc container in this book, you agree to the following terms and conditions. If, upon reading the following license agreement and notice of limited warranty, you cannot agree to the terms and conditions set forth, return the unused book with unopened disc to the place where you purchased it for a refund.

License:

The enclosed software is copyrighted by the copyright holder(s) indicated on the software disc. You are licensed to copy the software onto a single computer for use by a single user and to a backup disc. You may not reproduce, make copies, or distribute copies or rent or lease the software in whole or in part, except with written permission of the copyright holder(s). You may transfer the enclosed disc only together with this license, and only if you destroy all other copies of the software and the transferee agrees to the terms of the license. You may not decompile, reverse assemble, or reverse engineer the software.

Notice of Limited Warranty:

The enclosed disc is warranted by Premier Press to be free of physical defects in materials and workmanship for a period of sixty (60) days from end user's purchase of the book/disc combination. During the sixty-day term of the limited warranty, Premier Press will provide a replacement disc upon the return of a defective disc.

Limited Liability:

THE SOLE REMEDY FOR BREACH OF THIS LIMITED WARRANTY SHALL CONSIST ENTIRELY OF REPLACEMENT OF THE DEFECTIVE DISC. IN NO EVENT SHALL PREMIER PRESS OR THE AUTHORS BE LIABLE FOR ANY OTHER DAMAGES, INCLUDING LOSS OR CORRUPTION OF DATA, CHANGES IN THE FUNCTIONAL CHARACTERISTICS OF THE HARDWARE OR OPERATING SYSTEM, DELETERIOUS INTERACTION WITH OTHER SOFTWARE, OR ANY OTHER SPECIAL, INCIDENTAL, OR CONSEQUENTIAL DAMAGES THAT MAY ARISE, EVEN IF PREMIER AND/OR THE AUTHORS HAVE PREVIOUSLY BEEN NOTIFIED THAT THE POSSIBILITY OF SUCH DAMAGES EXISTS.

Disclaimer of Warranties:

PREMIER AND THE AUTHORS SPECIFICALLY DISCLAIM ANY AND ALL OTHER WARRANTIES, EITHER EXPRESS OR IMPLIED, INCLUDING WARRANTIES OF MERCHANTABILITY, SUITABILITY TO A PARTICULAR TASK OR PURPOSE, OR FREEDOM FROM ERRORS. SOME STATES DO NOT ALLOW FOR EXCLUSION OF IMPLIED WARRANTIES OR LIMITATION OF INCIDENTAL OR CONSEQUENTIAL DAMAGES, SO THESE LIMITATIONS MIGHT NOT APPLY TO YOU.

Other:

This Agreement is governed by the laws of the State of Indiana without regard to choice of law principles. The United Convention of Contracts for the International Sale of Goods is specifically disclaimed. This Agreement constitutes the entire agreement between you and Premier Press regarding use of the software.